CHILD CARE RESEARCH POLICY AND PRACTICE

CHILD CARE RESEARCH, POLICY AND PRACTICE

edited by

Barbara Kahan

for the Open University

Hodder & Stoughton

LONDON SYDNEY AUCKLAND TORONTO

in association with the Open University

Every effort has been made to trace and acknowledge ownership of copyright of the poem on page 165. The publishers will be glad to make suitable arrangements with any copyright holder.

ISBN 0 340 51331 4

First published in Great Britain 1989

Typeset by Wearside Tradespools, Fulwell, Sunderland
Printed in Great Britain for the educational publishing division of Hodder and Stoughton Ltd, Mill Road, Dunton Green, Sevenoaks, Kent by Richard Clay Ltd, Bungay, Suffolk

Contents

Foreword

Bill Utting

Research may be a buzz-word or a turn-off. Both reactions are unhelpful. Being professional imposes, among other requirements, the responsibility of keeping up to date with professional developments, extending knowledge and improving skills in one's chosen craft. Conscientious application to the lessons of relevant research is an essential part of this process.

People are remarkably and endlessly interesting. Knowing why we behave and function as we do – as children and adults, employees, members of families, social groups, communities and whole cultures – is part of the necessary context of knowledge for social workers, who need to identify and evaluate information and impressions about their clients. Discovering how people lived in the South Seas may illuminate understanding of how young people are socialized into our own society. Finding out what motivated men working in an American industry 60 years ago can tell us something about group behaviour now. Contemporary research into fostering, adoption, residential care, family therapy and child abuse helps us to understand the factors that may be particularly important in diagnosis and treatment, and the methods and techniques which are most likely to be effective in particular circumstances.

Research discovers information, selects, orders and interprets facts, and comments on or draws conclusions from them. Methods of inquiry in the human sciences are necessarily more flexible and may be less precise than those of the physical sciences. The factors determining human behaviour are so many and variable, and so difficult to measure, that 'answers' are rarely certain and at best probable. There is no need for embarrassment about this. Knowledge drawn from 'soft' observation can be as useful as the findings of 'hard' research, and for a social worker the insights that research offers into the human condition may be of more immediate and relevant application than the laws of gravity.

To get the best out of research you need an inquiring mind, the desire to improve performance and a critical and sceptical intelligence. Research does not provide complete and ready-made answers to all the problems of life, social work and child care. Its product needs to be worked at in order to interpret and understand it in relation both to your own experience and to the situations in which you wish to apply it. Research is a means, not an end in itself – a tool with which to improve and perfect one's business, whether this be making policy, managing services or working face to face with people: it is not a machine which dispenses neat answers on cardboard squares.

A critical intelligence is needed in applying our minds to what research 'tells us'. Nothing should be taken on trust, however attractive. Ask what the assumptions and perspectives of the researcher were, whether the questions addressed were the right questions, whether the method or system of inquiry was sensible, whether the findings can be translated into practice. Research, like the product of other forms of human activity, may itself be good, bad or indifferent. One's own experience – correctly interpreted – is a modest but valuable touchstone. Text-books, reviews and articles in professional journals provide valuable reference points or guides to the value of research. Caution is needed, however, before swallowing cellophane-wrapped morsels designed for mass consumption. They may bear little resemblance to the large and nutritious product from which they have been hacked.

Presenting the findings of research in such a way that they can be picked up and used throughout its potential market, by policy makers as well as by practitioners, is a perennial problem. At one extreme is the long, jargon-laden report, the conclusions of which have little bearing on the real issues of the day; at the other is the popularized account which in simplifying messages so distorts them that it directs the readership along mistaken and possibly harmful paths. In this, as in policy and practice issues themselves, there is a necessary point of balance: at which important messages are accurately summarized and presented in an attractive, stimulating and challenging way.

To get the very best out of reasearch you must, above all *need*, to know more; be able to add the product of research to your own experience; and reinterpret that experience in the light of additional information and intellectual knowledge. The personal quest for ways of doing the job better is a hallmark of professionalism and an obligation of professional activity.

Preface

This book and a second volume of readings entitled *Child Care: Concerns and Conflicts*, edited by Sonia Morgan and Peter Righton and also published by Hodder and Stoughton, are integrated components of *Working with Children and Young People* (K254) an Open University multi-media pack.

The decision to produce the course resulted from concern about the lack of adequate training available to those working with children and young people in a range of services and settings. Proposals made by the Gatsby Project that the Open University should provide increased opportunities led to a major grant from the Department of Health and Social Security. The course has been developed jointly by the Open University's Department of Health and Social Welfare, the Gatsby Project (also known as the Child Care Open Learning Project) and four Certificate in Social Service Schemes, West of Scotland, South and West Wales, Greater Manchester, and Cleveland and North Yorkshire. The Central Council for Education and Training in Social Work has approved the course as a contribution to qualifying training in social work.

The core of the course consists of a series of workbooks focused on key issues in human development and major problems which affect children and young people and give rise to need for child care services. Three hours of video and six hours of audio materials are designed to stimulate thinking about good and bad practice and an additional workbook offers practical guidance on child care law. The course is anti-racist and anti-sexist in its approach and challenges social class bias.

Course materials may be purchased in pack form and further information is available from:
The Department of Health and Social Welfare, The Open University, Walton Hall, Milton Keynes MK7 6AA.

1 Introduction

Barbara Kahan

The propositions that this book addresses are that research is an important ingredient in the formation and implementation of effective policies and good practice in child care; and that those who work in the child care services can not only incorporate research into their general experience, knowledge and skill but also contribute to it through their own careful observation and recording. The writers include in their definition of research academically based studies, operational research, careful analysis of regular and accurate working records, and the process of evaluation which reviews practical day-to-day transactions in order to sharpen individual and collective knowledge and skills, and raise standards of service relevance and sensitivity to need. Put more succinctly, this book is an attempt to make child care research 'user friendly' to those who work with children and young people, and those who plan and resource services for them. It is hoped that a wide range of other readers in allied services and occupations may also find something of interest in it.

Although 'the growing relevance of social work research to daily practice' may be one of the 'most significant of the changes to face social workers and agencies in recent years' (David Jones, General Secretary, British Association of Social Workers) it is still regrettably true that knowledge and use of research findings in policy and practice are relatively uncommon, and rarely a regular part of routine thinking and planning.

The Seebohm Committee, responsible for the broad shape of modern social services departments, declared in 1968 that they attached great importance to research:

> The personal social services are large-scale experiments in ways of helping those in need. It is both wasteful and irresponsible to set experiments in motion and omit to record and analyse what happens. It makes no sense in terms of administrative efficiency and, however little intended, it indicates a careless attitude towards human welfare. (para. 455)

The report also says:

> Research depends upon basic data being readily available, but at the moment there is inadequate provision for the systematic collection and sharing of information. Although central government departments bear a considerable responsibility for this failure, the ability of local authorities to perform this vital function depends in part upon how they are organized. It is important therefore that any reorganization should better facilitate this task. (para. 97)

When social services departments were first established a number, perhaps a majority, incorporated some research capacity into their structure and in some departments this capacity has survived the many reorganizations, changes of policy and fluctuations of resources which have taken place since 1970. Yet by 1984, when the House of Commons Social Services Committee reported its investigation on *Children in Care* they commented:

> There is a lack of systematic research into children in care, and an even more noticeable absence of a co-ordinated approach to dissemination of research once completed. Some aspects have been profoundly and even repetitively studied; others apparently neglected. (para. 258)

Since their report was published more attention has been paid to dissemination, particularly by the Department of Health (formerly DHSS) but, as some of the writers of this book will show, there is considerable unevenness in knowledge about children in care, and in the research which is carried out to provide more knowledge. The Committee identified some of the gaps in research as related to inadequate statistical information, particularly in central government. They urged that there was a 'need for accurate and complete information in an area of social policy all too liable to be affected by partial research, individual cases and anecdotal evidence' (para. 255).

Some chapters in this book will support the strength of the Committee's criticism and their recommendation that the Department of Health (then DHSS) should, in consultation with outside interests, re-establish fuller collection of relevant statistical information (Recommendation 73).

In spite of the Department's 'determination to ensure that new research projects should include suggestions as to the best means of dissemination' (para. 261) the Commitee believed, from their evidence, that 'many social workers go about their complex tasks unaware of research findings which might influence and assist their decisions'. As Roy Parker had said in 1980:

> Theory and practice are often treated as exclusive categories. Despite pleas for a better blend, the penetration of practice by well-grounded theory still seems to be a painfully slow process. The time lag is substantial and conventional wisdom is hard to dislodge . . . Yet we actually know a good deal about the characteristics of good care . . . It is unnecessary to feel our way forward in ignorance on all fronts . . . There is a broad knowledge base from which a high quality service can be created.

This book is a contribution to the dissemination process and in attempting to make research 'user friendly' the style and language used are directed to non-academic readers primarily, it being well established that the language and presentation of academic research reports do not encourage wide readership. The book is also an attempt to link together and blend theory, policy and practice in the belief that well-informed policy and practice are likely not only to be more sensitive to the realities of clients' lives and needs, but also more cost effective in the long term.

> In times of severe economic stringency, it is more than ever essential that painful strategic choices should be based on sound information about the need for and effectiveness of services. (DHSS, 1977)

The plan of the book is related to its overall purpose of demystifying research, making it more accessible and more a part of everyday work and decision making. It begins with a discussion by *Roger Bullock* of what research is, what its uses can be, some of the essential ingredients of research methods of investigation and some of the pitfalls which must be avoided if reliable results are to be achieved. He also demonstrates that research need not be remote, academic and unrelated to everyday work, but can be very close to the recording and analysis which practitioners are carrying out in case after case throughout their jobs. It can even help them with their jobs, in the difficult choices and decisions which have to be made, in thinking more clearly about the task as a whole, and in achieving a higher quality of life for their clients.

The next writer, *Erica De'Ath*, begins to open up the field in which child care needs arise, families and children, and the many changing patterns of family life which characterize the latter half of the twentieth century. She discusses marriage trends and how these have affected where the children live and who cares for them, the ethnic diversity of British life, and different cultural attitudes towards bringing up children. She also asks the questions what is a good parent? And what supports do some families need in carrying out their parental roles?

The writer then explores what research can tell us about the impact of national policies on families, the impact of community attitudes, children's experiences of divorce and step-families and some of the traumas children suffer in the course of family life, sometimes so great that they are driven to run away and then incur other serious problems for which inadequate provision is made in the community as a whole.

Traditional views of family life are seen to be unsupported by research findings, but research can assist the identification and development of policies and good practice which can help children at risk and in need to become good parents in their turn.

From examination of family life and some of the needs of children at home, the next writer, *Nigel Parton*, moves to the tragic issue of child abuse, a form of adult behaviour which makes some children's home life a nightmare and which social workers find is one of the most difficult problems they have to address. This chapter continues the discussion of the relationships between research, policy and practice, demonstrating that political interests and values may pervade these relationships and that approaches to and uses of research in this field may need to be rethought. The stance taken is that child protection work must be relocated within the heart of good practice with children and families. Nigel Parton concludes a carefully argued and wide-ranging chapter by drawing attention to the importance of prevention and treatment. Further discussion is shown to be necessary in recognizing that 'child abuse is centrally concerned with debates about the way we bring up children and is hence centrally concerned with child care'.

It is logical then to proceed with *Jean Packman*'s research into the way decisions are made when children and young people, home life being temporarily or long term unable or unsuitable to sustain them, for whatever reason, are received into care – or, in spite of referrals and requests, not received. What are the differences, if any, between those received into care and those left at home? She describes the context of the child care service, the preventive services and what happens when they are not enough to maintain children at home. Parents' views are explored – and this will be of value in the implementation of the new Children Act 1989 which will require greater attention to parents' views.

The dilemmas of decision making for families and social workers are then related to the legal routes into care, some of which are shown to be misused in practice. The importance of parents' participation in decision making is supported by the research, and the distinctions between those who go into social services, health or education resources, are revealed as having little to do with the children's own needs. Jean Packman concludes by showing that new policy embodied in future legislation owes something to child care research studies in recent years.

Having looked at research and related policy and practice of child care in the community and what happens before a child is received into care, the next chapters then deal with a range of issues which are related to what happens when children and young people are in care.

When a child or young person is received into care a placement with a carer or carers has to be made. *Peter Marsh* looks at research links with policy and practice in substitute care and the difficult relationship which can, and often does, exist between researcher and practitioner. Although recognizing the problems each has with the other, he discusses, like Roger Bullock, how research can help with the task of enquiry, 'a central task in social work and social care'. The careful thinking, the logic and the process of the thinking which are necessary for research, he suggests, have similarities with the work required for good practice; and research itself should be seen, not just as a product but also a process. Both process and product can contribute to policy and practice.

Like other writers he points to the way in which political direction colours practice, and recognizes too that there may be conflicts within research itself, as there are amongst practitioners. Yet an alliance between research and practice is essential to the development of good services.

Using particularly Roy Parker's early study (1966) of foster home breakdowns, Peter Marsh examines the way in which practice can be assisted by the 'new view' taken in this study (still a classic example of the alliance 'between research and practice' at its best). He demonstrates the kind of questions which practitioners might usefully ask if they use a 'research-minded' approach and supports his argument with more recent research. Taking Jane Rowe's *Children Who Wait* study (1973) he then compares it with another American study (Goldstein *et al.*, 1973) in the same year. Both these studies highlight issues that needed urgent attention from policy and practice.

The latter part of his chapter he devotes to ways of 'reducing the distinction between researcher and practitioner/manager' showing how refinement of questions and greater care in examining data in everyday work can lead to more careful and thoughtful consideration of practice and policy. An example of practitioner as researcher, in the field of adoption, demonstrates how a practitioner can enrich her practice and make a contribution to knowledge at the same time.

He concludes with a brief discussion of the 'alliance for the future' between research and practice and the need for a constructive dialogue (this book being one example) from which each will benefit.

Substitute care while a child or young person is away from home, must continue to provide for the child's overall development. In this the child's health and education are of major importance.

The health of children in care was found by the House of Commons Social Services Committee under the chairmanship of Renée Short, MP, to be receiving minimal attention. The evidence they read and heard made them strongly critical of the way in which local authorities and health services failed to carry out their important responsibilities in this respect. In the research following the Committee's Report (House of Commons, 1984) were two papers produced by Dr Frank Bamford and Dr Stephen Wolkind at the request of the Economic and Social Research Council. It had been hoped that Dr Bamford and Dr Wolkind would contribute a chapter for this book but time constraints made this impossible. They gave permission, however, for *Barbara Kahan* to make extensive use of their material, in the chapter on 'The physical and mental health of children in care'. The chapter indicates how, in spite of the fact that medical reports are a statutory requirement for children entering care, no systematic collation of information takes place, and little is known about the children's physical health. In addition medical examinations and records are often grossly inadequate.

More is known, by comparison, about the mental health of children in care – but it is still too little and too fragmented. Both doctors make a plea for more systematic data collection, and pose many important questions which are vital to the general development and wellbeing of many children in care. They believe that the routine records and investigations of doctors, social workers and others concerned with the children could contribute significantly to greater knowledge and therefore to better services.

There is reason to believe that young children admitted to care have greater medical needs than their peers who are not in care; and that a greater proportion are handicapped. These differences require definition. More careful examination and recording might also help to define the incidence of child abuse. More needs to be known about what becomes of the babies of very young mothers in care themselves. Parents need to be more involved in medical history-taking and information about their own illnesses leading to their children's admission to care might provide valuable material for improved policy and practice.

The health of children and young people is too important to neglect and adequate research, assisted by standardization of records, could contribute to significant improvements.

The education of children in care was also severely criticized by the House of Commons Social Services Committee and, recommending further research into this area of practice, they said:

> We consider that a child in care has a right to at least as good an education as any other child. In view of the disadvantage which being in care all too often represents, that may sometimes mean making a special effort to ensure the quality of education given to children in care.

Sonia Jackson, who contributes this chapter, was one of those who gave written evidence to the Committee. In this book she reviews, first the paucity of research or literature on the subject, and then the various ways in which their education, or lack of it, affects the lives of children in care, not only in their childhood, but influencing their life chances as adults. The expectations and priorities of social workers are seen to be very low in relation to the children's education; changes of placement lead to changes of school and this is seldom taken into account in placement decisions. Little is known about the effect of different care settings on the children's education though the fact that many foster parents and residential staff have had limited educational opportunities themselves may influence them in the importance they attach to the children's success in school.

A number of children are admitted to care each year for education-related problems, but again little is known about what happens to them afterwards. Consumers' experiences suggest, as do government inspection reports, that much remains to be done in providing adequately, or even suitably, for these children.

The chapter concludes with a discussion of whether educational failure for children in care is inevitable or whether their prospects could be improved. Available research suggests that changes in attitudes and practice could significantly improve their prospects. It demonstrates that there is a case for arguing that the child care system should no longer reinforce inequities but become a means of redressing them, and like improved health should see education as a proper means of laying foundations for the children's futures.

The chapters on substitute care, health and education relate to all children and young people in care. The next three chapters address special issues which affect only a proportion. These are the care of children from ethnic minorities, children with disabilities and young offenders.

Bandana Ahmad, in her chapter, concentrates on the need to demythologize research on black children, young people and their families. She argues that, in Britain, most research has been carried out so far by white researchers whose approaches have been eurocentric. She also postulates that there is a tendency to group ethnic minority children in studies of 'problem' topics, such as emotional disturbance, educational retardation, runaway girls and one-parent families. The majority of the black population, she points out, are 'ordinary citizens'.

Further problems highlighted by the chapter are the failure to recognize ethnic diversity and differences (Asian is used to describe people from India, Pakistan, Bangladesh, Sri Lanka, for example); over-simplification of correlations and exclusion of environmental and societal influences (e.g. attributing a black child's intellectual and emotional impairment to parenting rather than to school and/or other family and community). Distinctions are not made between poor working class, middle class and rich as they are in research on white people.

She suggests that the faulty research approach tends to lead to similarly faulty interventionist initiatives.

Against this background she discusses the emergence of alternative theorization of research initiated by black sociologists, academics and professionals in the USA. She suggests that as yet the British social work field has neither wholeheartedly accepted the credibility of the black perspective nor realized the benefits of alternative black expertise which would enhance black child care research.

Social services tend to be perceived as 'enforcement agencies', cultural myths and distortions are sustained, and both clients and services suffer. Having looked briefly at a number of issues – under-fives, black children in care, adoption and fostering, and young offenders – and highlighted problems such as the disproportionate custody decisions concerning young black people, she challenges the current position on policy and practice. 'Too often both policy makers and practitioners get trapped in a vicious circle' which involves research as well.

As with children and young people from ethnic minorities it is not known with any certainty how many children in care have disabilities. *Philippa Russell* draws attention, however, to the higher-than-average need for supportive services which families with a handicapped child have. This may be, in many instances, because the stress engendered by handicap is additional to many other social stresses such as restrictions on social and family life, poor physical health and marital or economic difficulties. In addition many parents find current educational procedures difficult to understand and are uncertain how to express their views. If the family of a disabled child is one of an ethnic group, research has shown that parents are likely to feel even more unhappy about the education of their child than other parents of disabled children. They are seen to suffer from some of the myths and lack of understanding which Bandana Ahmad's chapter explores.

Philippa Russell explores the range of respite services needed and some of the practical problems described in studies of service provision. Research is still patchy in this field, and particularly research into the lives of disabled children living in residential accommodation. She links the growing concern about lack of residential accommodation due to social services policies of closure with the growing number of disabled children attending residential schools, primarily for residential care rather than for education. Provision of 52-week accommodation but not necessarily the additional focus on care, or a series of different short-term holiday placements, can lead to fragmentation of the children's lives and inadequate preparation for the adult world.

As yet research is not available, nor has substantive work been done on the relative merits of different approaches to providing residential care for children with disabilities. Fostering for disabled children can be a satisfactory alternative, but studies in Britain and the USA demonstrate the need for very careful and supportive work if it is to succeed. As might be expected young disabled people entering the adult world of employment, housing and social life face even greater problems than their peer group.

Philippa Russell's chapter reviews a wide spectrum of ideas and work, but it is clear that disability is an area in which much more research is needed and that policy and practice should both be reviewed in the light of such research as it becomes available. The Children Act 1989 bringing disabled children into the same system as children in care, will provide an opportunity for a much needed impetus to research and to development in policies and practice concerning disabled children.

The chapter by *Henri Giller* moves into the politically sensitive field of juvenile offending in which research is only one of a large number of influences on policy, many of them conflicting. In this field politicians, central government departments, special advisers, academics, royal commissions, local government, lobby and pressure groups, the media and public opinion are all involved. Public order is an election rallying cry and fear of crime can influence practice as well as policy.

In the sphere of juvenile justice, policy making is further complicated by more than one government department being involved and a wide range of statutory and voluntary services as well as the police and the penal system. Delinquency can be seen, depending on perceptions of society and its organization, as the result of poverty, deprivation and inequity, or as a personal iniquity to be identified, punished and discouraged as firmly as possible.

Henri Giller traces changes in the relationships between researchers and policy makers in England and Wales over 25 years, and examines some of the main threads of research in this field. He then discusses briefly some recent interactions between them, including diversion from courts, adversarial proceedings in juvenile courts, determinate sentencing, and sentences proportionate to offences in juvenile courts.

He concludes by suggesting that the relationship between research, policy and practice concerning offenders is often not either an equal nor an easy one and that it is not characterized by consistency. He believes that of the three, research, policy and practice, it is practice which has the greatest potential to achieve change, both positively and negatively, and that the researcher is dependent upon the practitioner, even where the policy maker defines the research brief. The joint participation of all three parties in the triangular relationship has, in the past, been rare. Ideally each should be able to offer something to the others, but for this to happen an agenda has to be clarified and values made explicit. In the arena of juvenile offending there is too often a lack of a shared agenda and a myriad of value systems.

Some of the most vulnerable young people in care are those who are still away from home during their later adolescence. The fact that they are still in care at 16, 17 and 18 years old is likely to be evidence of no viable alternatives. How do they fare at the hands of those who provide the services both in these later years and in the years after going out of care? *Mike Stein*'s chapter reviews what his research revealed and the policies and practice currently focused on this vulnerable group of young people.

It is a disturbing picture. He quotes how, once again, the House of Commons Social Services Committee was concerned at the lack of services available and the lack of care shown by agencies. Whether the full extent of their concern, i.e. that local authorities should have a legal obligation to assist these young people, will become part of the Children Act 1989 is, at the time of writing, not known.

What is known is that nearly 8000 young people leave care each year at 18 and many others at 16 and 17, and are not provided with any semblance of the help and support which a good parent would give not only to these age groups but often to many young people of 19, 20 or even older.

Mike Stein demonstrates that this is another area of child care in which there has been no large-scale research, but the numbers of small studies available show that the 'crude stereotype' of care leavers being 18-year-olds without families, who have spent their lives in large institutions, must be abandoned. They are a cross-section from all types of care, and very far from being a homogeneous group amenable to standard service responses. They have experienced considerable movement and disruption in care, and have inadequate knowledge of their past, too little suitable preparation for leaving care, and little or no reliable help and support once they have left. Loneliness, depression, unemployment, lack of any contacts with the immediate past, homelessness, poverty and social isolation feature significantly in their lives.

Implications of the research for policy and practice are discussed and comparisons made with our nearest continental neighbours, France, and with what could be expected in normal families.

Some of the findings of this research are based on evidence from the young people themselves. The next chapter by *Ruth Gardner* is devoted to consumers' views and their involvement in decision making about services, policy and practice.

The concept of clients' involvement and taking their views into account in service provision is still relatively recent. The Children Act 1989 is likely to require much more account to be taken of the children's views and those of their parents and other interested parties, but it is a process which is still seen as difficult, and is less frequently carried out than is desirable.

Ruth Gardner reviews the arguments for inclusion of service users' views, and then surveys some national and local research studies which reflect consumer views. Subsequently legal changes and current policy developments are examined and finally some examples of successful involvement of children and parents in key decision making are presented.

DHSS (now Department of Health) funded research studies, National Children's Bureau, Children's Society and the National Association of Young People in Care, Black and in Care, Voice for the Child in Care, all feature in this context. Some of the other writers in this book, and a number of other researchers are also seen to contribute to knowledge in this area. Famous legal cases, Gillick vs. W. Norfolk, Graham Gaskin at the European Commission of Human Rights and the work of Guardians *ad litem*, in addition, enlarge the perception of the importance of clients' views and involvement in decision making.

The chapter concludes by discussing policy in social work agencies in the light of research findings, legal requirements and developing opinion. Ruth Gardner suggests that the crux of a relationship between child and responsible adult is centred on decision making, control, letting go, risk taking and ensuring that advice and support are reliably available. Most important of all is the message, confirmed by the Cleveland inquiry into child abuse, that the child or young person is 'entitled to be taken seriously'.

The pattern of the book, therefore, moves from examining the research process, through the areas of family life, child abuse, how decisions to remove children from families are made, substitute parenting after they leave home, their health and education in care, special issues affecting children in ethnic minorities, handicapped children and young offenders, what happens to those leaving care, and the consumers' perceptions and involvement. The services involved, whether for children at home or in care, have to be resourced by public funding, from central and local government or from voluntary sources.

The University of Kent Personal Social Services Research Unit has been carrying out research on outcomes and costs for a number of years. *Martin Knapp*, the deputy director, and *Eileen Robertson*, in the penultimate chapter of this book, examine the costs of child care services and their implications for research and policy. They demonstrate how the integration of cost and effectiveness insights within 'value for money' and 'efficiency' reviews has revealed how poor are the costs data 'lovingly tended by local authority accountants over many years' and how limiting are the so-called effectiveness data. Linking together a series of public initiatives involving the District Audit Service, the government's Financial Management Initiative, the work of the Select Committee on Social Services, the Audit Commission and the Social Services Inspectorate, they examine the impact of the three Es, 'economy, efficiency and effectiveness' in the provision of public services. Suggesting the need for a fourth E, equity or distributive justice, as a policy criterion they proceed to discuss current child care policies with their tendency to polarize choices, e.g.

residential versus foster care, based on the belief that preferred child welfare grounds coincide 'by happy coincidence' with cheapness of fostering. In the 'new cost awareness' in child care organizations, Martin Knapp suggests that fundamental flaws in the costs data, obvious to anyone who cares to take more than a 'cursory glance' are too often overlooked, 'presumably on the assumption either that they do not matter, or that nobody else, including elected members and auditors will notice'.

He shows that the cost information which underpins today's policy and practice decisions is of poor quality, and employed in ways which can easily produce the wrong conclusions and encourage inappropriate action.

Some of the warnings in Roger Bullock's chapter about faulty use of information are demonstrated in the points made by Martin Knapp about the use of cost information to come to flawed conclusions. He then discusses the flaws under the headings of completeness, disaggregation, like with like comparisons and outcomes. Presentations of costs of residential and fostering care and intermediate treatment which ignore these important considerations can result in unjustified conclusions about cost effectiveness. Demonstrating from a wide range of examples how appropriate costing presentations should be made, he argues that because of the complexity of child care needs and services, costs information is needed, but that because this information can have a significant influence on policy and practice it must be 'sensibly defined and appropriately measured'. It can then be a useful instead of a 'dangerously misleading tool'.

The concluding chapter by *Roy Parker* takes an overview of child care research, identifying and developing a number of themes which have echoes elsewhere in the book. His own seminal research work is referred to by other writers, and his experience in studies of the history of child care, policy trends, practice and organizational issues enables him to take both a broad and a detailed view of this complex field of human need and the research carried out within it.

He points out that we need to distinguish between the contribution that research can make to policy and that which it can make to social work practice. He argues that we need more practice-orientated research, but indicates some of the obstacles that need to be surmounted if that is to happen. He also considers the problems that are created as a result of the fragmented nature of much research and the rather narrowly defined categories and classifications which research in child care is in danger of having to use; categories that are essentially administrative and legal constructions. Then there are the difficulties that both practitioners and policy makers face in utilizing research which is often focused on one particular field or issue when in reality, they have to make choices between different options. When one of these is better researched than the other such judgements may be distorted. Those who could use the results of research also face the problem of deciding how much confidence they can place in a study. Professor Parker shows that this is not always a matter of dispassionate assessment but may turn on whether the research is seen to be delivering 'good' news or 'bad' news. Finally, he looks at the availability of the basic data which are accessible to researchers in child care; to the kind of housekeeping information that should be kept by organizations and which if it is, makes it unnecessary for researchers to start from scratch every time. In examining the sources of information that researchers can exploit he also emphasizes the importance of treating, in a serious fashion, what children and the adults around them have to tell us.

Roy Parker closes the book by reiterating the case for research: stressing that its ultimate purpose must be to help us to improve the quality of life of children generally and of some of the most disadvantaged in particular.

The importance of the relationships between research and practice was the focus of a joint CCETSW and Personal Social Services Council working party in 1980. One of its conclusions was that:

> An essential attribute of any profession is that its members are active in creating and extending its knowledge, the theoretical bases for its practice and the means by which it is evaluated. (CCETSW and PSSC, 1980)

Whilst this chapter was in preparation, a further CCETSW publication, *Research by Social Workers – Capitalizing on Experience* (1989) was published. Discussing how practitioners can not only be involved in research, but may conduct research studies themselves, with many potential pay-offs for workers, managers, agencies and the field, the writers suggest:

> Many skills already in the social worker's repertoire can be drawn upon and applied to the design and conduct of research on practice issues. Parallels exist between both research and practice as activities. Both are problem-solving activities. In each case one begins with a problem, seeks to understand it as fully as possible, works out purposes, devises a plan of action, carries it out, and reviews what has happened in order to judge its implications for future action.

The importance of the integral relationship between research and practice was also the subject of discussion by Lord Rothschild, head of the Central Policy Review Staff whose paper 'The organisation and management of Government research and development' (1971) did much to lay the foundations of the structure of research in the public sector. Suggesting that 'the end product of basic research is an increase in knowledge' in applied research he suggested it was first a product, e.g. an antibiotic, an artificial hand, a drought-resistant variety of wheat; then a process, e.g. for the manufacture of an antibiotic, or for removing nitrogen oxides from exhaust gas; then a method of operation, e.g. to prevent collisions in the English Channel, to speed up the delivery of letters, *or to give advice, sometimes in the discharge of a statutory obligation* (the emphasis is mine). Although much of the research Lord Rothschild was discussing was in more material areas than human behaviour, he recognized the inadequacy of science and technology without much closer integration with the social sciences, so that new knowledge can be used 'in harmony with the economic and human needs of the situation'.

Social workers, teachers who work with children and young people in schools, staff in courts, community centres, housing, social security and health services, are amongst those whose tasks can help to use new knowledge 'in harmony with economic and human needs'. They are people whose lives are full of activity and demands for immediate responses; they often have little time for reflection and study. This book has been written with the objective both of making knowledge gained by research more easily accessible, and of demonstrating how in the course of providing services practitioners can use the knowledge and add to it by their own skill and commitment. If this book assists those who read it to become more 'research minded' it will have achieved its objective.

> We need a more active approach to the promotion of new knowledge provided by research . . . to carry out large numbers of research projects and then put them on shelves and in pigeon holes is appallingly wasteful, as is also the vast amount of information available in hundreds of central and local government reports published each year and then forgotten, and never collated or analysed within an overall framework of reference. Even negative research results can be valuable and at the very least they could help us to ask some of the right questions. (Barbara Kahan 'The implications for the personal social services', unpublished seminar given at the National Institute for Social Work, 1975)

References

CCETSW and PSSC (1980) *Research and Practice*, Report of a working party on a research strategy for the personal social services.

House of Commons Second Report from the Social Services Committee Session 1983–84, *Children in Care*, Vol. 1, together with proceedings of the committee, 28 March 1984, pp. 360–1, HMSO.

Jones, D. N. (1986) 'Research', supplement to *Social Work Today*, 27 October 1986.

Lord Rothschild (1971) 'The organisation and management of Government research and development' in Civil Service Department, *A Framework for Government Research and Development*, Cmnd 4814, HMSO.

Ministry of Housing and Local Government (1968) Report of the Committee on Local Authority and Allied Personal Social Services (Seebohm Report), Cmnd 3703, HMSO.

Parker, R. A. (ed) (1980) *Caring for Separated Children – Plans, Procedures and Priorities*, National Children's Bureau.

Report of the Records Project-Development Group, Social Work Service, DHSS (1977) HMSO.

Secretary of State for Social Services (1988) *Report of the Inquiry into Child Abuse in Cleveland 1987*, HMSO.

Stock-Whitaker, D. and Archer, Lesley J. (1989) *Research by Social Workers – Capitalizing on Experience*, CCETSW Study 9.

2 Social research

Roger Bullock

Introduction

What is research? Is it any use? What are people supposed to do with it? These are the most common questions I get asked as a social researcher. As discussions ensue, I am frequently surprised by the rigidity of my enquirers' attitudes. Research is viewed as something abstract and intellectual, distanced from day-to-day work and of interest only to clever people, with little to offer to those who plan, manage and deliver personal social services. Neither does it inform complex and stressful child care decisions.

Such a dismissive attitude, which fails to see research as part of a professional task, seems to me unhelpful because whenever we make a decision, it is based on assumptions and values. Sometimes these are clearly stated but more often than not they are implicit in attitudes and actions. It seems self-evident that decisions involving the lives of children should be well informed. So in this chapter I hope to show how research *can* contribute to social work policy and practice and how all who seek high professional standards can benefit from research, whether their own or that of others.

If we think of the ways in which the term *research* is used, a variety of activities spring to mind. People 'do research' into their ancestors, perhaps plotting family trees and collating information from register offices and parish records. We also talk of 'doing research' when we investigate the history of a place we intend to visit, looking up information in travel guides and brochures, finding out how best to get there, what to avoid and how to get value for money. Gathering and assessing information is an integral part of any research. Indeed, we would take it as a compliment if our presentation of an argument were described as 'well researched'. But research implies something fresh about the material we obtain. Those studying for a PhD degree are expected to generate new knowledge. More is expected than a scrutiny of existing evidence. Original information has to be gathered and the links between various factors explored in a novel way. We hear, for example, of someone 'doing research' into child abuse or, on a grander scale, of a three-year research project into the causes and effects of deprivation or addiction. But even then we can still be confused about research, as other terms suggest similar activities. For example, how does research differ from monitoring and evaluation? To clarify matters, let us go back a step and ask some basic questions.

What is research?

A straightforward answer to this question is that the function of research is to explain how and why things happen. This may seem simple but, as I shall try to show, it involves a series of steps, each of which poses difficult problems. For example, we may try to explain an observed phenomenon well known to social workers, such as why children enter care. At a general level the answer is easy; it is because their families are unable to look after them, control them or because they cause them to be 'at risk'. But this conclusion is not particularly illuminating as it merely says that children come into local authority care when no one else can care for them, a repetitive statement we call a *tautology*. Also, since some children in care are placed at home on trial, this explanation is blatantly false.

To answer the question fully, we need a more considered discussion. This would need to look at why we have a welfare service of 'being in care', how this has developed historically, what routes are taken by children coming into care and the circumstances surrounding their entry. We may eventually need to relate these factors to one another or to other events in a child's life, such as educational progress, length of stay in care or destination on exit. To do this effectively we may need to construct typologies and identify patterns that improve our understanding of the problem. For example, we might find that the experiences of children in care differ according to the circumstances surrounding their entry, so that grossly abused children may stay longer and occasionally be adopted, while offenders might return to their parents after a relatively short spell in a residential establishment. Good research, therefore, should consider not only the cause of the events that concern us but also their *nature* and *consequences*. Let us look at this problem of the nature of phenomena in more detail as it explains some of the difficulties faced by social researchers.

We have just argued that an important feature of research is its concern with the nature of the event under scrutiny. Often, this is more complex than it first appears. For example, let us consider how we would set about studying levels of violence in residential establishments for children. Our inquiry would have to begin by defining violence, an exercise which may appear straightforward. If we were asked to offer a definition, we would probably suggest something along the lines of 'the use of physical force against an unwilling party'. But if we think more carefully about this definition, it becomes clouded by ambiguity. Obviously, an unexpected and unprovoked physical attack, such as a street mugging, presents no problems; it is clearly an act of violence. But what about self-defence or the shaking and pushing that accompanies the control of an unruly mob? What of heroic exploits during armed service or the caning of school children? Violence can also be verbal and emotional and, some would argue, is intrinsic to the wider power and economic structures of society and world economics. We have, therefore to consider these other aspects of violent acts. These include the *context* of the events and people's perceptions and interpretations of violent behaviour, as the same behaviour in different situations will be perceived very differently. The exploits of football hooligans would probably be praised if they were part of resistance to an invading army.

Given the complications, we have to strive for a definition of violence which incorporates all these aspects. We may conclude that violence is such a wide term that we need a typology, each item of which may have its own consequences and causes and so be best dealt with by different interventions. For instance, we may need to negotiate with political agitators but offer treatment to the dangerous psychopath. Thus violence, like many other social phenomena, is seen in different ways by different people and is therefore to some extent socially constructed. Researchers themselves are bound to adopt one social construction of the phenomena they are investigating rather than another and however objective their methodology, the chosen perspective cannot be completely neutral, nor can social research be entirely value free.

Questioning the nature of the issue under study is an important part of research as it clarifies initial concepts and examines the definitions employed. It is a feature that distinguishes research from monitoring, where we take categories and definitions as 'given' and do not worry too much about the nature of the phenomena being recorded. For example, the Home Office monitors violent crime by looking at numbers and trends in patterns over time and produces annual figures for offences and convictions, but in so doing avoids the problems of definition that bedevil the researcher. When modifications are made to the categories employed in the monitoring, large statistical changes can follow. For instance, much violence in the family now involves the police and so gets recorded as violent crime. However, we cannot be certain whether the subsequent rise in recorded incidents stems from the way the public refers domestic violence to the police or from a real increase in domestic strife.

Simple comparisons of statistical trends, while useful in some instances, can be misleading if the categories are ambiguous or if the contexts in which they occur differ. For example, local authority child care statistics state the number of children in care placed 'home on trial'. We can look at these and easily see not only an increase nationally over time but also big differences between local authorities. However, research by Farmer and Parker (1988) has shown that this placement is used for two quite distinct groups of children in care. These are abused young children going back to a parent and troubled adolescents returning home from residential care. These two groups of children have quite different characteristics, care histories, prognoses and needs for social work support. A change in policy for either group, whether tightening up criteria for returning abused children home or by developing community alternatives to residential care for difficult adolescents will affect the 'home on trial' figures. Thus, when we see an increase in the numbers, it is difficult to know what it means, other than the obvious fact that more children live at home while legally in care.

Let me emphasize that there is nothing wrong in comparing local authority figures for numbers of children placed 'home on trial'. This may be an interesting and illuminating exercise. Similarly, there is nothing intrinsically right about Farmer and Parker's typology of children affected; it merely seems to be a revealing distinction. What we need to remember is that a crude comparison of local authority figures is of limited value and our understanding of trends and contrasts would be improved if we took account of Farmer and Parker's findings.

A study of the *nature* of the phenomena under investigation is, therefore, an important first step in any research study. The development of definitions and typologies helps clarify the issue under investigation and indicates its component parts, some of which, as we have seen, may be in contrast to each other. It is important to remember that the definitions and typologies we employ can only be judged by their usefulness. To say that they are right or wrong is virtually meaningless.

The special features of social phenomena and human behaviour

For many phenomena in the natural world, definitions and typologies are relatively simple. For example, the moon is and will continue to be the earth's satellite. Its boundaries are easily defined. Similarly, a metre equals 39.38 inches and can actually be seen in a Paris museum. We could devise alternative definitions of these phenomena but they are not likely to be any more helpful those those we have.

When we deal with *social* phenomena, however, things are more complicated as they have an additional dimension not found among inanimate objects, namely the *meaning* of behaviour. Human beings experience emotions, control their actions and, as we saw with violence, define social situations. So, for example, the behaviour of people who fall in love, such as kissing in public, is tolerated rather than drawing censure as it might in other circumstances. Any definition of behaviour has to incorporate the context of behaviour and its meaning for the participants. Returning to the problem of violence in residential care, we have seen that violence has to be defined by someone and that each person, whether instigator, recipient or third party, may have a different perspective. Similarly, a sexual proposition in a bus queue is likely to be seen as a degrading assault while at a party it may be viewed as less violating. Yet as an observer we may be alarmed or jealous if the recipient is the object of our own affection.

The definition eventually agreed for The Dartington Social Research

Unit's study of violence in residential care was 'the use of force in a social situation in a way that those in power define as illegitimate', a perspective which sought to incorporate all the dimensions we have discussed. It was certainly much wider than the definition required by the local authority for an official notification of a violent incident or by the police for pressing charges of actual bodily harm.

This discussion illustrates the limitations of a static model of human behaviour in social research. Disciplines that use such models, such as demography and statistics, can provide great depth of argument but their scope is inevitably limited. The need to understand the meaning of behaviour also makes it difficult to predict how individuals will behave. For example, the relative positions of the moon and earth result from gravity and we can calculate exactly where each will be in 50 years time. Human beings, in contrast, interact with one another not only because of gravity but because of dependence, love, envy, hate, etc. They can also choose to behave differently at any time. Thus, we cannot predict social events with absolute certainty and have to couch our forecasts in terms of probabilities, provided other factors do not change, which of course they can. We can, however, take action to prevent or avoid a predicted catastrophe and much of social skills training and health education are designed to do precisely this. If I am warned that my weight makes it highly likely that I will suffer health problems in hot climates, the probability of my being ill is reduced if I do either one of two things – lose weight and/or avoid the tropics, Thus, I have some choice about my life.

The complexities of factors affecting social behaviour

But how much choice do I actually have? I am male which means I cannot have children, I am somewhat reserved by nature so I am unlikely to be the life and soul of anyone's party, and my chances of becoming King are very slim. So, although we have an element of choice over our actions, these are circumscribed by virtue of biology, features of our personality and by the social and cultural context into which we are born. Historical and economic factors also limit our options.

This balance between an individual's freedom of choice, or 'free will' as it is often described, and the influences of forces external to each individual, called determinism, has been the basis of much philosophical and theological debate. Although the details of these arguments need not concern us, the issue *is* relevant to understanding social research. We have to incorporate elements of individual choice in our theories but recognize that much is determined by a range of other factors, biological, psychological and social. What is more, these factors interact with one another and different combinations and sequences will determine what eventually happens.

Let us again consider as an example children coming into local authority care. Such children are affected by all the factors described. There is a gender factor associated with certain reasons for admission, such as delinquency or moral danger, and the likelihood of certain outcomes, such as adoption. The children, like all others, grow up and pass through childhood into adolescence. Certain life experiences may also influence their personality, for example, children in care often have poor self-esteem and difficulties in making relationships. Their family backgrounds are also usually socially disadvantaged and being in care can be stigmatizing and isolating. Thus, a young person who has stayed long in care is affected by a multitude of factors. But, even if we are able to measure them, we then have the further problem of how we can distinguish their significance from the effects of normal maturation. After all, it is said that children grow out of crime and naturally move to independence from their families.

A problem in social research is that we cannot easily isolate factors. Thus, the main research methods of natural science, the laboratory experiment and the controlled trial, cannot be used except in very special circumstances and even then serious ethical issues may arise. For example, we could, as an experiment, allocate similar child care cases randomly to different interventions to see whether one is more effective than the other. But is this fair on clients who are vulnerable and in need? Similarly, we could follow up people 20 years on to assess the results of our child care work, but even if we could successfully trace them, is it right to contact them after all that time when their spouses and children may not know of their earlier histories?

I hope from this discussion that you can see that social research is a complicated and difficult exercise because:

- social phenomena have meaning for the participants and may be perceived differently depending on their context
- we are the product of historical, biological, psychological, economic and social factors which interact, cluster and impinge on our lives sequentially
- it is hard to distinguish the effects of much of what we do from other processes, such as the natural maturation of children
- it is difficult to measure precisely the influence of factors by isolating them in experiments and, even if we could, there may be ethical problems which prevent us from doing so
- we cannot predict outcomes with absolute certainty since individuals can take remedial action in the light of our forecasts. We talk, therefore, of probabilities or outcomes provided circumstances do not change.

All these issues influence the nature of social research. It has to incorporate a wide range of factors and develop methods of investigation other than laboratory experiments. These problems have been tackled in different ways and with different degrees of success, as I shall later try to explain. But first, bearing all these matters in mind, let us return to consider the activities that come under the heading of social research.

Types of social research

Social research covers a range of activities each of which is different in its time and resource implications as well as in its functions. They can be divided into three groups:

1 Theoretical research which fashions concepts and perspectives – this is usually part of an academic discipline or sub-discipline.
2 Large-scale empirical work which is intended to provide new information based on reliable data. This reviews situations, provides evidence on hypotheses and surveys client and other groups. Usually it requires external funding to meet costs of staff and data processing.
3 Evaluations of particular situations, client needs or professional practice. These studies are short term and can be extremely useful if they are placed in the context of wider knowledge. On their own, however, they are difficult to interpret. They rely on an enormous amount of research capital; that is, the expertise and knowledge built up by research workers or teams and on the body of knowledge generated by others who have undertaken previous studies.

This distinction between these three types of research is somewhat artificial because all are closely interlinked. In order to be good, type two (the large-scale empirical approach) has to be guided by theoretical perspectives produced by type one, otherwise it can become 'mindless fact gathering' with little structure, purpose or links between the parts. On the other hand, the first type relies on the information provided by the second which polishes, refines and leads to a redefinition of the problem. Type three, the short-term survey, can only be interpreted if we are aware of developments in types one and two. One of the problems is that this last type of research tends to be attractive to local authorities and central government departments who face pressing problems, and there is a danger that such studies can become too influential on policy when little else is available. Conclusions are often drawn from small samples and single case studies and findings can rapidly cross boundaries. A good example concerns the assumption that residential care is ineffective. Conclusions about the lack of success with young offenders have been transferred to quite different groups such as the elderly or mentally handicapped as well as to children and young people in care generally.

If research is a varied activity, so are the methods we use to undertake such studies, as I shall now explain.

Types of research methods

I have explained why it is difficult to use laboratory experiments and controlled trials in social research except in the cases of narrowly focused psychological studies. We have, therefore, to use other methods, the following four of which are the most frequently employed.

First, it is possible to gather information relevant to the issues under study from *records and documents*. This may consist of files on clients, historical papers, minutes, prospectuses, handbooks, codes of practice, etc. These provide a ready source of material on areas such as clients' backgrounds, professional standards and good practices. However, such documents have usually been compiled for purposes other than research and the investigators have to glean from them what appears relevant to their study. Thus there is the problem of selectivity and inconsistency in the data. For example, if the deprivation experienced by the mother of a child in care is not mentioned in a case file, can we assume that it is absent? Such an assumption is dubious; several research studies have found that, when interviewed, parents of children in care often reveal their own experiences of abuse, although this was not known previously.

Secondly, there is the method of *participant observation* by the researcher. This may involve sharing in the experience of those under study and trying to put oneself in their position. This is an excellent method of understanding the contexts of situations and its meaning for those involved, even though one can never truly be a *participant* observer. There is also the problem that the researcher's observations can be subjective and are difficult to record in a systematic way.

Thirdly, we can seek information from participants by means of *questionnaires*, that is a printed form completed by respondents and returned to the researcher, or by an *interview*. The advantage of the former is that standardized information can be gathered from a large population, although there is always the problem of those who do not respond and how far the characteristics and opinions of such people match the general population. Interviews, in contrast, are labour intensive but allow for elaboration on issues, so charting people's perceptions, evaluations and responses. Naturally, there are numerous possible designs for these, such as the use of open or closed questions, whether interviews are done singly or in groups, in the respondent's home or work environment, or in some other setting.

Lastly, we can employ *standardized tests*, *scales* and *measures*, such as those that assess intelligence, commitment or stress. Often, these have been successfully used in other research and this allows us to compare our own work with that of others. *Indicators* based on available information may also be used, such as attendance registers, punishment logs and so on. It may be possible to apply all of these to groups who contrast in some way, so facilitating a comparative analysis. Thus, the matching of cases and the use of 'control' groups are common procedures.

Each of these methods has its own strengths and weaknesses and no single approach is perfect. The choice of methods for a particular study will depend on the nature of the task and the resources available. For a study of clients' perspectives with fairly limited time and money, group interviews can be very productive, as in the National Children's Bureau's '*Who Cares?*' study (Page and Clark, 1977) in which young people in care spoke at length about their experiences. On the other hand, a study of how well deprived children fare as parents 20 or 30 years later would require not only individual interviews but careful measures of parental competence. This combination has been employed by Quinton and Rutter (1988) in their studies of the inter-generational transmission of deprivation. In contrast, Roy Parker (1988) has successfully gathered information about the assisted emigration of children in care to the colonies in the nineteenth and early twentieth centuries from records held in the offices of governments, shipping companies and voluntary agencies.

It is clear, therefore, that no single research method suits all kinds of study and a combination will probably be necessary. It also adds to the objectivity of research if information gathered from several independent sources points to the same conclusion. If in a residential school staff tell me in interveiws that the children are happy and well behaved but records show high levels of absconding and excessive punishment, I would be suspicious about the validity of the interview material. It may be that children can be happy and well behaved but also abscond and be frequently punished, but I would need to resolve this apparent contradiction. It is useful, therefore, to incorporate as many cross-checks as possible into the methods adopted for a study and to be aware of the limitations of material gleaned from a single source.

Research models

Once we have considered the nature of the phenomena under investigation, worked out definitions and devised appropriate research methods, we have to select a research model which answers the questions investigated by the research. Several approaches can be employed. First we can examine outcomes in comparison with some baseline and ask, 'What was the situation then and what is it now? Is the client better for our actions?' This is a relatively straightforward procedure, provided suitable research instruments can be fashioned. Similarly, we may contrast the 'before and after' situations of alternative interventions to see whether one is more effective than the other. The effects of an intervention can be clarified if we compare the experiences of different groups, such as recipients and non-recipients of services. Contrasts are sharpened further when the latter group is selected to act as a 'control' for the former. To do this, members of the two groups are 'matched' for potentially influential factors such as age, social class or gender.

The exploration of clients' adaptations provides a good example of this 'before and after' approach. Despite the problems of understanding the meaning of actions from our observations, this perspective is particularly relevant when behavioural change is sought and discussions of this kind abound in the literature of treatment and therapy. As before, the problems of interpreting outcomes outweigh the difficulties of assessment and some of the criteria used in research have been criticized for their cultural and class bias. Indeed, adaptation often seems to be compared with some assumed saintly lifestyle and, as social services clients are often closely scrutinized, their short-comings are manifest. While some behaviour, such as violence against the defenceless or excessive exploitation of the weak is generally regarded as unacceptable, there are many grey areas. We may need to look, therefore, at adaptation in various ways, not only adjustment to general social norms but also to deviant and unorthodox sub-cultures as well as to self-aspirations and family wishes.

A quite different method of evaluation is to construct a *process model* which seeks to relate input to output. This is useful in understanding the working of social and other service systems and is particularly helpful in understanding the place of services within a child's care career. But again there is the problem of knowing to what extent inputs are associated with outcomes and how relevant are any statistical associations found. For example, we know that for those leaving care, a stable home contributes to their viability in the community, yet the factors contributing to survival skills are quite different from those which determine where a client goes to live, even though either can produce the same outcome of homelessness.

A third perspective is to consider *consumer views* on services and here the achievements of our approaches *vis-à-vis* expectations and agreements can be charted and gaps in perceptions highlighted. We can never be sure how far clients' perspectives are related to other behaviours or how far they are overwhelmed by the structural constraints which they may face. Nevertheless, such studies help us fashion a better service and there may be many other benefits, such as better relationships between professionals and clients.

A fourth and less myopic perspective is one which deals with the *functions* of a service for the wider welfare system or for society as a whole. While we know that putting young offenders in penal settings is likely to lead to poor results in terms of behaviour modification, it has the function of being a punitive symbol and keeping awkward clients out of circulation. However, we should always ask whether the functions identified could be better served by alternative methods, as has happened with the development of intermediate treatment for adolescent offenders. Similarly, we may find that a service is important symbolically or bolsters the social work profession. Functional justifications for a social service are always attractive but it must be remembered that they are only provisional.

Lastly, we can also consider services in terms of their *continuity*. This is rarely done but consistency in outcome is important for dealing with social casualties who may need services at any time. When a longitudinal view is taken, however, we often find great discontinuities amongst children in care as they experience a series of unrelated interventions and moves which can often be isolating and stigmatizing. For example, we may do great things while they are in care, achieving personal growth and forming relationships, but this is vitiated as adolescents face, at the age of 18, the constraints of joblessness, social isolation and poor accommodation.

Thus, we see that several research models can be employed, depending on the nature of the questions to be answered.

How can we judge a piece of research?

One of the problems facing practitioners is judging the quality of a piece of research. Sometimes, dubious studies achieve publicity or may be attractive for other, perhaps political or novelty, reasons. To help judge the quality of research, I would suggest the following questions are asked:

- Does the study group or written material on which the research is based represent those for whom the findings are said to apply? Particular attention should be paid to any bias in the selected samples, levels of response and limiting characteristics, such as age groups, length of time involved with services, etc. It is particularly important to check that findings are not generalized beyond the group studied. For example, Fanshel and Shinn's large study (1978) of children in care in New York State excluded those entering care over the age of 11, offenders and those whose stay in care was less than 90 days. Thus, although their findings are often applied by others to *all* children in care, only one in eight of children entering care in England and Wales meet the criteria for inclusion in their study.

- Are the methods appropriate to the study? Is there bias in the questions asked, or not asked? Is the wording of questionnaires ambiguous or likely to encourage particular replies? Are findings achieved by one research method checked by results obtained using others? Naturally, in a research report, the author cannot provide all the data; on the other hand, the reader must be satisfied that all material has been considered and that the conclusions represent a comprehensive analysis of all the evidence.

- Does the evidence say what the conclusions claim? Social researchers wish to establish clear findings from their work but it is natural for them to want to stretch or overplay the evidence. Tests of statistical significance control the validity of some conclusions from numerative evidence but I still remember reading a draft report which said, 'A huge majority of 51%'!
- Even if the evidence appears satisfactory, are there explanations other than those offered by the researcher? This is a particularly important part of a research exercise, for results often take the form of associations, that is, establishing factors that go together. But, unless we look deeper into the causal links, these can be misleading. For example, the amount of damage done in a fire correlates with the number of fire engines that attend. However, two possible explanations fit this evidence: one that the size of the fire determines both factors or, more absurdly, that it is the fire engines that do the damage. Needless to say, the research literature is full of argument and counter-argument about the explanations of agreed associations between factors.

By asking these questions, practitioners can judge the validity and applicability of research and incorporate the findings into that part of their professional knowledge which is informed.

How practitioners can improve their use and understanding of research

I have tried to explain why social research takes the form it does and the difficulties faced by those undertaking it. I have also suggested that although research is a key component of professional practice, it takes many forms, and the various types of research I have described feed professional knowledge in many ways. The relationship between research, policy and practice is not smooth and its past history with regard to social services for children has not always been happy. I have also stressed that research is a powerful tool but like all sharp instruments can do harm as well as good if not properly used.

What, then, can practitioners do to improve the situation? One response is to turn away and say that research is difficult and irrelevant and so rely on practical experience and rules of thumb. Clients may be fortunate that practitioners' preferences match those suggested by research, but often this is palpably not the case. It seems irresponsible and morally indefensible to intervene in clients' lives if you are uncertain about what can be achieved and the best methods of doing so. It also makes professionals vulnerable. Yet, it is only by research that answers will be provided. So an avoidance strategy is dangerous all round.

Secondly, it would help if practitioners could understand the different contributions of various types of research. No one expects a practitioner to have time for much theoretical musing or for large empirical studies. Yet the third type of research I described, the quick investigation, is possible as part of a regular monitoring of clients' situations and the quality of services. A careful analysis of clients' backgrounds, their experiences when involved with social services and longer-term situations would sharpen the focus of practice and can be easily undertaken. Much relevant information has to be collected for administrative reasons and the same forms used for record-keeping could be adapted to provide regular research results. For example, if a local authority finds that most of its children in residential care are over the age of 14, this has enormous implications for provision, for the style of residence and for issues of control and staffing. Similarly, if it is found that 45 per cent of boys admitted to a regional observation and assessment centre have already been in prison or custody, there is little point in promoting the value of a punitive stance to their behaviour. If it is shown that young people who leave care and have been trained to live independently move quickly into group living situations, what does this tell us about provision for older adolescents? A careful monitoring of clients' background characteristics, experiences and longer-term situations is possible and should be part of every professional's brief.

There could also be more dialogue between practitioners, their managers and their professional associations about issues that might benefit from research. Because there is little tradition of using research, social workers find it difficult to suggest areas for investigation and most of the running is, therefore, made by central government. Because social workers face considerable stress and often feel depressed and beleaguered, such suggestions for research as they make often reflect current problems rather than long-term issues. I well remember asking a conference of 150 heads of residential schools for children with emotional and behavioural difficulties (EBD) for research suggestions. There was silence until one proposed 'absconding'. Despite all the responsibilities and experience of these delegates, it is sad that they could only view research as relative to one problem, admittedly an important one, rather than to key issues of the service. After a while the chairman added, 'Surely we do more than deal with absconding?' Then a wider range of ideas emerged and all kinds of fruitful areas for study, such as admission procedures, leaving arrangements, staff needs, links between home and school, etc., were proposed. There is a need to create a positive view of research and to get tired and defensive staff to look beyond their immediate responsibilities and worries.

How researchers can improve liaison with practitioners

Researchers also have an important role to play in this process. They should strive to present findings in a way that can be understood by practitioners without sacrificing the truth of their assertions, and should pay attention to the dissemination and development of findings. Inbuilt grant resources for dissemination need to be sought, time must be allowed for lay versions of research to be written as well as academically respectable reports, and there should be greater opportunities for co-operation with policy makers and practitioners in discussions concerning implications of research. Unfortunately, there are problems within the research community with regard to the commissioning of projects, the academic status of applied research and the training and support of staff, so researchers have to get their own house in order. In the child care field, however, there have been recent initiatives which have improved the situation. The DHSS publication, *Social Work Decisions in Child Care* (1985), summarizes nine research projects and offers exercises for practitioners to test their work against research knowledge. In 1987, the Social Services Inspectorate ran a series of regional seminars to disseminate this information. Another important development is the Child Care Open Learning Project, part of the Gatsby Project, which has led to the availability of the Open University Courses 'Caring for Children and Young People' (P653) and 'Working with Children and Young People' (K254) both of which are making a wide range of knowledge and research available to many practitioners and others.

What is in it for practitioners?

When all is said and done, we are left with the question, what use is research to practitioners? Is not social work the application of skills picked up in the 'University of Life' and do we not all know what deprived infants and troublesome adolescents need? Would that life were that simple!

It is true that as human beings we may be able to empathize with social work clients who are short of money or bereaved as we probably have been in these situations ourselves. But common understandings are not sufficient for effective remedial action. The identification of clients' presenting problems and the selection of suitable remedies require greater knowledge than this, the foundation of which must be research.

Research links with practice in several ways. First, it can clarify concepts and issues and so help with the assessment and understanding of clients' problems. For example, anti-social behaviour which is opportunistic and situational, as is much juvenile delinquency, may require quite different strategies from that which suggests an individual pathology, such as the arson or sex attack committed by a 'loner'.

Secondly, research can link present and future states in a way that may be difficult to comprehend when we are deeply involved at a particular time. Just as a doctor links smoking at 20 with chest disease at 50, research can indicate to social workers the long-term outcomes of current actions. Some of these may seem common sense when pointed out but this is not always the case. For example, when selecting a foster home, it often seems a good idea to social workers to choose parents with children of similar age to those being placed, but several research projects have shown that this greatly increases the risk of placement breakdown. With abused children the immediate and undisputed need is for protection but, in achieving this, we may cut them off from cherished family and community links, an isolation that may prove damaging. The five-year-old we sought to protect may become the lonely 18-year-old hanging himself in prison. On the other hand, he may *not*; and only research can tell us, particularly if we want to know about outcomes for numbers of people. If these contributions of research are correct, research should help practitioners to target ends, fashion approaches and link ends and means more effectively. This may sound somewhat grand but it has very down-to-earth aspects, such as indicating what is possible and realistic and what tasks are long and short term. For instance, if children are not out of care within six weeks after reception into care, research tells us that they have a 60 per cent chance of still being in care after two years, a finding that has clear implications for the resources and inter-agency co-operation needed for many social work clients. When research goes further and links ends and means, it can help us gauge the significance of factors that seem relevant to a situation. Indeed, one important function of research is to indicate what is *not* relevant, a particularly important contribution in view of commonly held views on matters such as the causes of delinquency – is it 'latch-key' children or television violence? – and prevailing stereotypes about single parents and ethnic minorities.

When the research knowledge is sufficiently conclusive, we can use findings to construct checklists, scales and indicators which can ensure that practitioners consider all factors pertinent to a situation and alert us to danger signs. For example, as educational research has found, the child who cannot read at eight is unlikely ever to learn, and that eight is the latest age at which a child can function in school as an illiterate. Social workers responsible for eight-year-olds should see non-reading at this age as a danger sign and a precursor of learning and behaviour problems. Many other examples could be given on such issues as the placements of children in care, behaviour problems and the family links experienced by children. There is little excuse for allowing these situations to drift; and it is in preventing such situations that professional practice based on research parts company from common sense and rules of thumb or the use of 'hunches'.

All of this should also help social workers to distinguish the important from the trivial. This is not always easy when dealing with so many aspects of a client's life. I recently read an assessment report which stated, 'Her mother seems to have disappeared and hasn't been heard of for six months.' This point was thrown away in almost cavalier fashion within a long description of the girl's mercurial behaviour. Although her reluctance to wear a tooth brace and her dislike of school are important at one level, they pale into insignificance compared with the long-term consequences of losing contact with her sole relative. Child care research should help practitioners distinguish what is grave and enduring from the less serious and transient.

Finally, it must be emphasized that social workers need confidence in handling research as evaluative studies will reveal disappointments as well as achievements. Some established approaches may prove less effective than hoped and this can damage morale. But, as I said earlier, to shy away from research on these grounds seems unwise. It opens the door to those who seek to attack or curtail social work activity and, after all, knowledge is 'power' as much for one's enemy as for oneself. It is also an irresponsible stance, for our obligations are to clients, in this case children, and I have tried to show why research must be an integral part in generating excellence in the services we seek.

References

Bulmer, M. (ed) (1982) *The Uses of Social Research*, Allen and Unwin.

Dartington Social Research Unit (1983) *The Dissemination of Research Findings in Social Work*, Dartington Social Research Unit.

Department of Health and Social Security (1985) *Social Work Decisions in Child Care: Recent Research Findings and their Implications*, HMSO.

Fanshel, D. and Shinn, E. (1978) *Children in Foster Care*, Columbia University Press.

Farmer, E. and Parker, R. (1988) *Children Placed Home on Trial*, Research Report, School of Applied Social Studies, University of Bristol.

Millham, S., Bullock, R. and Hosie, K. (1976) 'On violence in community schools', in Tutt, N. (ed), *Violence*, HMSO, pp. 126–65.

Page, R. and Clark, G. (eds) (1977) *Who Cares?*, National Children's Bureau.

Parker, R. A. (1988) 'An historical background', in Sinclair, I. (ed), *Residential Care: The Research Reviewed* (The Wagner Report), pp. 1–38, National Institute for Social Work and HMSO.

Quinton, D. and Rutter, M. (1988) *Parenting Breakdown*, Avebury.

3 Families and Children

Erica De'Ath

Marriage and family life in the 1980s

It is still widely held that the traditional or conventional nuclear family is the only suitable environment in which children can grow up and that any deviation from this norm puts children at a considerable disadvantage. Yet research into contemporary demography and statistics soon demonstrates that in recent years there have been dramatic changes in trends and patterns of marriage, divorce and cohabitation. Not only are expectations of family life changing, but since families also operate as groups or systems within a wider environment some families are more vulnerable to social change than others. Families are influenced by many factors besides how well individual members get on with each other. Education, social welfare and health systems; legal, political and economic systems; and, particularly, communications systems all influence our actions and choices, our values, attitudes and beliefs. These are some of the issues to be explored in this chapter.

First a quick look at current marriage trends. Compared with 100 years ago marriage is now an almost universal experience i.e. 92 per cent of women and 86 per cent of men marry (Rimmer, 1981). But there are other more recent changes. Compared with 25 years ago people marry later. In 1961 28 per cent of first-time marriages involved teenage brides (women under 20 years) whereas there were only 14 per cent in 1986. The average age at marriage in 1986 was 26.3 years for bachelors and 24.1 for spinsters (Central Statistical Office, 1988). This trend is partly accounted for by the steady increase in cohabitation. The annual General Household Survey has only included questions on cohabitation since 1979 and estimates suggest that the proportion of women aged 18 to 49 years cohabiting has doubled from 3 per cent in 1979 to 6 per cent in 1987. Figures for 1987 indicate that 27 per cent of divorced women, 17 per cent of single women, 15 per cent of separated women and 11 per cent of widowed women were cohabiting (OPCS, 1988). For those who have already been married, there had been pre-marital cohabitation by 62 per cent of women remarrying aged under 25 years, and 74 per cent remarrying between 25 and 34 years. A sample by OPCS of over 1000 couples divorced in 1979 showed that about one-third of both divorced husbands and divorced wives had remarried within two and a half years (Central Statistical Office, 1988). Other research has indicated that five years after divorce half of all custodial parents have remarried (Leete and Anthony, 1979).

Not only are more people marrying but they are marrying more often. One in three marriages in 1986 was a remarriage for one or both partners.

Divorce has increased by almost 600 per cent in 20 years. One in three marriages is now likely to end in divorce and 60 per cent will involve children under 16. Each year approximately 160 000 children see their parents separate, and lone-parent families have increased, from 8 per cent in 1971 to 14 per cent in 1987 (OPCS, 1988).

Where are the children?

Four out of five of the 11.6 million children aged under 16 in Britain in 1986 were living with both their natural parents (OPCS, 1988). This figure declined slightly for older children, a growing proportion of whom lived with a natural parent and a step-parent. The Child Health and Education Study (CHES) (Osborne *et al.*, 1984) of 13 135 children born in 1970, found that one in ten five-year-olds were not living with both natural parents. Half were in lone-parent families, a quarter in step-families and a quarter had been adopted or were living with grandparents or foster parents. These figures are higher than in previous studies. The National Child Development Study of 17 000 children born in 1958 found only just over 5 per cent of 16-year-olds living with a natural parent and an adoptive step-parent or parent's cohabitee (Ferri, 1984); the Family Formation Survey in 1976 found 7 per cent of all children under 16 (928 000) were living with a step-parent (Dunnell, 1979).

These findings suggest an increasing trend towards family disruption during childhood. In 1984 custody of approximately 170 000 children was considered by courts (Law Commission, 1986) and in 1985 the parents of 50 265 under-fives were seeking divorce, an increase of 14 per cent (OPCS, 1986a). It has been estimated that if present rates of divorce and fertility continue, one in 22 under-fives will have divorced parents, and one in five 16-year-olds. A minority of children will be involved in two or more divorces and therefore have a growing number of step-relatives and half-siblings.

We know that in any one year approximately 160 000 children experience the divorce of their parents (Central Statistical Office, 1988). We also know that at any one time there are approximately one million lone-parent households caring for 1.5 million children. A quarter of these parents will be widowed mothers or lone fathers. The vast majority will be separated and divorced mothers. Some will be single mothers. Some will remain lone parents, some may have one or more cohabitees over a period of years; many will remarry after a period of cohabitation and become a step-family. We have no statistics to tell us how many children are involved, how long they spend in any one of these stages of transition, nor do we know what effect these experiences have on them or on their relationships with natural or step-parents.

There is also an increasing trend towards greater variety in family formations. In 1986 21 per cent (158 000) of 755 000 live births in the

United Kingdom were registered outside of marriage; 66 per cent of these were jointly registered by cohabiting parents who had chosen not to marry (Central Statistical Office, 1988).

Adoption has decreased dramatically during 20 years as a reflection of changes in legislation and public attitudes. However, even among adopters, family patterns vary according to the status of child or parent. Examples are an orphaned marital child adopted by a couple neither of whom were its natural parents; a marital child adopted by a couple one of whom was the natural parent; a non-marital child adopted by a couple one of whom was the natural parent; or adopted by a couple neither of whom was the natural parent. More efficient contraception, easier access to abortion and more unmarried women choosing to keep their babies has reduced the numbers available for adoption. At the same time step-parent adoptions have been discouraged and have almost halved since the Children Act 1975. In 1986 just under 9000 adoptions were registered in Great Britain compared with a peak of 25 000 in 1968. The proportion of children aged 10 or over at adoption, however, has increased considerably since 1976 (from 20 per cent to 28 per cent) while the proportion of infants adopted under two years of age has decreased slightly (from 26 to 25 per cent) (Central Statistical Office, 1988).

Ethnic diversity of families

The total population of Britain in 1986 was 54.25 million, 51.1 million white and 2.4 million ethnic minorities (0·7 million not stated). About 4 per cent of the UK population were born outside the UK. But country of birth does not equate with ethnic origin and a significant proportion of all minority groups (43 per cent) are now born in the United Kingdom. Ethnic minority groups account for 5 per cent of the population, Indians, Pakistani, Bangladeshi and West Indians accounting for just 1 per cent each of the population overall (Central Statistical Office, 1988). Many families do not identify with the global ethnic terms sometimes used. For example, it is inaccurate to refer to Punjabis, Tamils, Pakistanis and Bangladeshis simply as Asians since their cultural differences are as great as their similarities (Sillitoe, 1979).

In looking at ethnic minority families and children in Britain one factor which is immediately obvious is the difference in age structures between some ethnic minority groups and the white population. Thus about 48 per cent of the Pakistani/Bangladeshi group are aged 0–15 compared to 20 per cent in the white population, and at the other end of the age spectrum only 2 per cent are aged over 60 compared to 21 per cent among the white population (Central Statistical Office, 1988). These differences also imply differences in family size, with a higher percentage of some minority groups having four or more births. In some ethnic minority families as a result, women are likely to have more children to look after than white families and less older relatives around them to help.

It is now acknowledged that the educational, health and social welfare systems are often not adequate or appropriate for the needs of most ethnic families. Attempts have been made to try and address this problem in relation to the needs of all children and families. Thus the Committee of Inquiry into the Education of Children from Ethnic Minority Groups (DES, 1985) states that existing provision for under-fives 'is generally inadequate to meet the needs of the population as a whole, and may be particularly ill-suited to the needs of West Indian families'.

The Health Education Council project on providing effective health care in a multi-racial society provides a useful checklist for assessing local services. It emphasizes that black and ethnic minority children and their families may need particular support from the health service as they are likely to share childrearing problems such as lack of play space, damp and over-crowded housing with other socially disadvantaged groups. In addition it affirms 'most developmental tests and assessments are culture-specific . . . many parents may have approaches, practices and priorities in childrearing which are different from those of the child health practitioner, but which are nonetheless equally valid' (HEC and National Extension College, 1984).

Ethnic diversity is multi-racial, multi-cultural and multi-dimensional. Many children are brought up in two cultures: the culture of their parents and that of the host community. There are differences in family size and family structure, in numbers of children and extended kinship systems. In many areas there are relative concentrations of ethnic groups, Irish, Orthodox Jews, East Europeans, West Indians, Italians, Greeks, Indians, or Pakistanis/Bangladeshis. The challenge for adults arriving in this country and establishing a new life and family is different from that of the children born and brought up here.

Research cannot tell us how to work with people whose cultural norms and traditions are different from our own. It can, however, help to identify aspects of family life where clashes of values or attitudes may raise difficulties – whether in child care practices or gender issues, arranged marriages or disagreements between parents and adolescents. It can also identify where personal, institutional or structural racism exists and recommend ways in which such issues can be tackled and monitored, for example, through positive discrimination policies and anti-racist child care practice.

Bringing up a family

Britain does not have an explicit family policy. Many arguments have been put forward for a family perspective or policy statements to counter the apparently poor 'fit' between much existing social policy and significant social change (Henwood and Wicks, 1988). Three areas in particular are relevant to the relationship between family life and the wider society: the changing role of women, patterns of work and unemployment, and the role of the welfare state. Space only allows brief reference to these issues here.

We have mixed expectations in Britain about the responsibilities of family life and parenting. On the one hand, bringing up children is seen as a purely private matter. The Review of Child Care Law stated an acceptance that the state should not intervene between parent and child simply because it could provide something better than the parents but only if parents were falling so far below an acceptable standard that their children were suffering harm as a result (DHSS, 1985). However, there is a danger that parents who cannot raise their children appropriately, or find a job, or provide sufficient income to support their family, or whose children engage in delinquent activities, are seen as having some form of personal failing or character weakness. They may be seen as lacking basic training which can be rectified by the intervention of psychiatrists, psychologists, social workers, probation workers or other similar welfare professionals. A national survey of parent education and support found that all too often parents were seen as falling into one of two camps: either they were coping adequately and were considered to need no assistance, or they fell below an accepted level of 'good parenting' and became the focus of immediate state intervention (Pugh and De'Ath, 1984).

On the other hand, there is clear evidence that social and economic conditions are critical to the well being of children (Graham, 1988). Indeed research from the National Child Development Study clearly identifies public matters where the state could intervene to prevent harm to children:

> The combination of poor housing, low incomes, uncertain health, insecure employment (coupled often, no doubt, with limited knowledge of parenting skills) offers a prescription for low-achieving, poorly behaved, disenchanted or alienated young people. It represents a 'prescription for anti-welfare' for children. (Wedge, 1984)

In the 1970s there was concern about the 'cycle of deprivation' (Joseph, 1972) and the war against poverty (Jordan, 1974). The promotion of preparation for parenthood provided the focus for two DHSS seminars at which Sir Keith Joseph stated that 'there is little argument that the way families function is vital to the health of our society' (DHSS, 1974).

The concept of the 'good parent' is an extension of the 'good-enough mothering' first identified by Winnicott (1960). Although early writers such as Bowlby (1951, 1972) and Winnicott emphasized the mother–child relationship rather than parent–child, both called for support to ordinary families as a starting point to improved standards of child raising. In the aftermath of the Maria Colwell tragedy a report by the Central Council for Education and Training in Social Work took this concept as its title and stated that 'good enough parenting involves, among other things, a capacity to provide continuity of love and care which is realistic in its expectations of both parent and child and deals with 'real' conflicts of interests and not those whose origins lie only in the parents' past' (CCETSW, 1978). More recently Bettelheim has stated that 'to be a good enough parent one must be able to feel secure in one's parenthood, and one's relation to one's child' (Bettelheim, 1988).

Support for families

So what do parents require if they are to function effectively as a family? How should they set about their task? What can be offered to help them provide the expected level of care and to feel more secure in their parenting role? Most parents manage to raise their children successfully with a little help and advice from friends and family and occasionally relevant professionals. What is becoming increasingly clear is that parents need practical support (adequate housing, income, employment, educational, health and social welfare services), psychological and emotional support (interpersonal within the family and the community) and a network of supportive services.

Eminent speakers at the 1974 DHSS seminars identified the need for skills in interpersonal relationships, communication, coping with stress, shaping behaviour and for certain 'permitting circumstances' or necessary life opportunities and facilities (Rutter, 1974). They made recommendations on how to provide support systems for families in relation to work, school, the neighbourhood and the home (Bronfenbrenner, 1974). More recently Rutter *et al.* (1983) have suggested that parenting and parenting resources need to be considered in terms of other variables: time available for parenting, parent's own emotional state, presence of life stresses and problems, existence of satisfactions and achievements apart from parenting, and the availability of adequate social supports and housing conditions. These other variables are particularly relevant in the light of the estimated 60 per cent of working women with dependent children in 1987 (OPCS, 1988).

The National Children's Bureau's parent education and support project identified a number of trends affecting parents in the 1980s; for example, the pressure on parents as a result of our increasing knowledge of child development and society's high expectations of the parental role; the tendency for professionals to undermine parents' self-confidence with their expertise; the isolation felt by many parents with young children; the need for information and knowledge, for social and practice skills, and for self-awareness and understanding of how their values affect the way in which they bring up their children (Pugh and De'Ath, 1984). Differing values and influences over generations of childrearing in the English speaking world have included concepts of religious morality, medical morality, natural development and natural needs, individualism and the 'fun' morality, added to which there is now the parental dilemma of whether to be friend or authority (Newson and Newson, 1974).

Over the last 20 years there has been a move away from looking at children and adults in isolation towards looking at the needs of both, in terms of the family. However, most of the research on families is based on clinical samples of families with problems rather than research on 'normal' families. In Britain two examples of cohort studies provide descriptive accounts of patterns of infant care in urban communities. For the 1000 families in Newcastle (Spence *et al.*, 1954) it was the overcrowded or inadequate buildings that caused the greatest strain on family life. For the 709 Nottingham mothers also it was the differences in living conditions that affected the attitudes and methods of infant care and particular aspects of child rearing (Newson and Newson, 1963). Close proximity of neighbours and thin council-house walls affected the general irritability of mothers and how long the baby was left to cry, while the lack of washing machines inhibited toleration of toilet training and wet bed clothes.

In Britain support for families has focused less on parent education and teaching parenting skills and more on a range of informal support services (De'Ath, 1982, 1983). Under this general umbrella of family support is a wealth of informal groups, intervention schemes, home visiting, crisis telephone lines, and individual befriending in the context of family, neighbourhood or community centres, playgroups and drop-in centres (Pugh and De'Ath, 1984; De'Ath, 1985). Such self-help and community support, a 'family centred' approach, is not new. Early examples include university settlements in 1913, the Peckham Health Centre with its family club which opened in London in 1926, Parents and Child Centre in Birmingham in 1934, Pacifist Service Units in 1940 which became Family Service Units in 1948 and Family Advice Centres in 1965. Such community-based approaches, and family centres in particular, have developed rapidly during the 1970s and 1980s (Henderson, 1988; De'Ath, 1988a).

Perhaps, the greatest shift in offering support to families has come through awareness of the need to work in partnership with parents and for specialist and intervention services to work more within community and across agency settings.

Learning from research

Does research have any effective impact on everyday family life in Britain? As already noted there have been calls for national statements to encourage central and local government to develop sensitive and appropriate family and child care policies, and good child care service and practice. Research, particularly in the context of family and children, demonstrates seven key factors which inhibit or discourage effective links between research, policy and practice.

1 Separation of private troubles and public issues

There has been a tendency generally, but particularly in the years since 1979, to disregard what are seen as private troubles (family poverty, poor marital relationships, isolation) and to consider primarily public issues, e.g. dependency of lone parents on welfare benefits, reception of children into care because of homelessness or family breakdown and juvenile crime. The impact of poverty and disadvantage on children and families has been amply recorded in reports such as *Born to Fail?* (Wedge and Prosser, 1973) and *Children in Adversity* (Wedge and Essen, 1982), but it has not been matched in current social security, housing, day care, education or other welfare policies.

2 Unwillingness to accept collective responsibility

Research has also clearly demonstrated that some children and families are more vulnerable than others but that such disadvantage can be alleviated if society's policies are designed to do so. American Head-Start programmes have demonstrated the value of early educational activities with parents and children (Berrueta-Clement *et al.*, 1984), the National Child Development Study follow-up of truants shows they are more likely to marry early, have larger families and to experience separation or divorce (Hibbett and Fogelman, 1988; Hibbett *et al.*, in press). Studies of take-up of welfare benefits indicate that universal child benefit is more successful in reaching impoverished families than targeted means-tested benefits (Brown, 1988), yet policies frequently do not reflect such knowledge.

3 Delay between identification of issue and changing practice

We are slow to analyse research in terms of the impact any particular findings may have for a wider field of social analysis, education, training and delivery of services. For example, in 1960 a survey of women at home with young children noted, 'Clearly the nature of women's roles is changing, and the situation at present is one of conflict and stress' (Gavron, 1966). Three key issues were identified: a reanalysis of education for girls; a reanalysis of women's roles and capacities as workers; and the reintegration of the mother with young children into society. It was over a decade later that the link between 'personal troubles' and 'public issues of social structure' of clinical depression and women's daily experience was demonstrated (Brown and Harris, 1978).

A decade later we are only just beginning to find ways of alleviating some experiences related to such stress (Pound and Mills, 1985) and seriously addressing the role of social support as a protection from depression (Koziarski *et al.*, 1986; Hodgson *et al.*, 1987). Childcare for working mothers remains a personal issue and Britain is the only member of the EEC which has not endorsed the directive on parental leave.

4 Failure to appreciate the extent of social change

Sometimes research itself takes too narrow a view of social changes, and their impact on family relationships. Eekelaar (1971), for example, concentrating primarily on the needs of one-parent families and viewing step-families as just another form of nuclear family, confidently asserts that 'whether a marriage has been terminated by death or divorce, the social and personal disruption is best healed by successful remarriage'. Such a view ignores the combined impact of adversarial divorce courts, lack of support for separating couples going through loss and change, lack of awareness of different roles and responsibilities of step-parents, lack of recognition of step-families in legal or welfare systems, and the negative image of step-families, all of which have contributed to the difficulties of remarriage and a rising re-divorce rate.

5 Lack of co-ordinated analysis of issues and impact

Research tends to focus on discrete areas of work, agency settings or a particular age range or group of children. Services also tend to take this segmented approach rather than offering an integrated package of support services to families. Parents often complain that they can only get help or support when they have identified themselves as having a specific problem, and it is not unusual for some families to have several different workers trying to offer support and advice on specific problems which, in reality, are part of a whole situation.

Equally, we often fail to take a life-cycle approach in recognizing the importance of key areas of research to the development of family services. There is now a considerable body of knowledge on developmental stages of childhood, the family life cycle, on crisis events such as a new baby, onset of adolescence, loss and separation, marriage, moving house and the effects of divorce on children. As increasing numbers of families experience several of these events at the same time, and out of sequence of the normal family life cycle, we should be reviewing practice, services, support networks and training to accommodate such changes. For example, what are the support needs of a step-family where the step-mother has recently given up work, had a new baby, where there are two sets of step-children in pre-puberty and puberty who have just changed house and schools, where one set of children have a good relationship with the non-custodial parent and the others do not?

6 Inability to adapt services to meet consumer needs

Several studies demonstrate that the kind of help people want, or the priority they attach to particular needs, does not coincide with what they are offered (Mayer and Timms, 1970; Lerner, 1972; Merrington and Corden, 1981). This can also result in investment of considerable social work resources and therapeutic effort with inconclusive outcomes (Mattinson and Sinclair, 1979; Sainsbury *et al.*, 1982). Families in poverty, families who have a disabled child, lone parents or step-families, families whose children have been taken into care, all are particularly vulnerable to the mismatch between needs and services. As one mother described it, 'Nobody had neglected or ignored her. Unfortunately, however, they had offered counselling when practical advice was what was needed' (Russell, 1978).

7 Impact of prevailing values and beliefs

Whatever research might indicate, the power of existing values and beliefs about current issues is often stronger than the empirical evidence. Notable examples are custodial sentences for young offenders (Juvenile Crime Advisory Committee, 1987), attitudes towards day care for babies and young children (Lindon and Lindon, 1988) and perceptions of the greater risks of health and social problems in teenage motherhood (Melhuish and Phoenix, 1987).

Working with individual children and individual families

Children in the same family

Family life is never static and no two children in a family are the same. In addition to their genetic differences they will each have a different nurturing experience within their family, for example being the first born and only child is different from being the second or third child of parents already used to dealing with small babies and the noise, bustle and demands of older siblings.

The richness and complexity of research in this area of family life and child development has been well illustrated by the longitudinal television series 'Citizen 2000'. Each year the 20 selected children born in 1982 were captured on film as their families developed, chronicling the arrival of brothers and sisters, moving home, starting at playgroup, being cared for by granny, a nanny, an au pair or childminder. The families represent a cross-section of cultures, religions, classes, incomes, working parents, occupations and locations, from the wealthy manor house to the high-rise tower block, the inner-city to the isolated farm.

The fact that the majority of families now only have two children may add additional value and intensity to the sibling relationship. The impact of family disruption may also have significant effects. As many as one in five motherless children in the NCDS sample of lone-parent families had brothers or sisters living away from home (Ferri, 1976). Not only had the children suffered the loss of a parent but the family was further fragmented by the absence of one or more children as a direct or indirect result of the marital breakdown. In her research into the effects of divorce on children, Mitchell (1985) found that some siblings had been divided between the two parents, though some were reunited after the divorce. Wallerstein and Kelly (1980) found that 'only' children had greater exposure to parental conflicts and pressure during the divorcing period than children with brothers and sisters although many children did not consider their siblings helpful.

In the absence of much research on ordinary families awareness of the role and importance of siblings inevitably comes from situations where families are brought to clinical or public scrutiny. Berridge (1985) found that the separation of siblings when children come into care was strongly linked with unsettled care experience. There is now a growing body of information (but little research) on the effects of step-family formation on the role and status of a child, which can change from special roles of oldest or youngest, of only boy or only girl, through integration with step-siblings and half-siblings.

Children in a lone-parent family

The proportion of lone-parent families has remained fairly steady at 14 per cent for the last five years (OPCS, 1988). Some people dispute the use of the phrase 'one-parent' on the grounds that children have two parents but are being raised by a 'lone' parent. Lone-parent families are not a homogeneous group and it is difficult to obtain reliable estimates of the numbers of families and children involved. Although the GHS asks about cohabitation, it classifies information on legal marital status without including information about cohabitation or remarriage. Parents are classified as either married or lone. It is reported that most cohabiting lone parents describe themselves as married and are therefore classified as such (OPCS, 1985).

At any one time there are approximately 1.5 million children in lone-parent households but this is only a single snapshot count and the number of children currently estimated to be in step-families (between 1 and 1.5 million) indicates that a far higher proportion of children spend part of their childhood in a lone-parent family than such a figure indicates, and that some children may spend repeated periods of time in a lone-parent family, or in a newly constituted family.

There are differences in lone-parent families. Lone fathers tend to be older than lone mothers; there are more West Indian and less Asian families headed by a lone parent; they are more likely to have lower incomes and to live in local authority housing than two-parent families.

There are also strong geographical variations with a particularly heavy concentration in certain inner-city areas, for example Inner London and Newcastle. This has obvious implications for services at a local level and provision needs to be related to regional trends and census figures.

The term 'schoolgirl mother' strictly refers to those under the age of 16 at the time of conception. However, many 16-year-olds who give birth or have a termination are still of compulsory school age for up to six months after their birthday and their pregnancy occurs while they are still schoolgirls. In 1982 there were 5585 live births to mothers aged 16 and under; for those under 16 the figure was 1281. For individual schools a pregnant teenager is still a relatively rare occurrence and one in which it is difficult to cater for all the physical, medical, social, residential and educational needs of the prospective mother and baby. Local education authorities vary enormously in their policies towards the education of pregnant girls and schoolgirl mothers. Home tuition may be requested, and some areas have established special education units, for example Bristol, Sheffield and Liverpool. Mothers under the age of 16, and their families, often experience considerable financial hardship as they are not eligible for most state benefits.

Teenage pregnancy is not a new phenomenon but it remains controversial and attracts disproportionate and misleading media attention. For example, statements that young girls deliberately or increasingly conceive in order to secure local authority accommodation have yet to be substantiated. In fact, teenagers in the UK are less likely to become pregnant and less likely to become mothers than they were 15 years ago and far less likely to do so than teenagers in the United States. But teenage pregnancy is still associated with a variety of physical problems for the mother, low birth weight of the child and high rates of foetal, perinatal and maternal mortality, as well as psycho-social risks such as non-accidental injury (Bury, 1984). Many of these ill effects, however, are related to low socio-economic status, unemployment, poor housing and social environment, low educational achievements, lack of support and stable relationships, inexperience, isolation, depression and poor levels of attendance at antenatal and other clinics, rather than to age *per se* (Wells, 1983). Early mothering is associated not only with poor housing but also with frequent moves and insecure tenure (Butler *et al.*, 1981).

Unmarried teenage mothers are more likely nowadays to keep their children than to place them for adoption. In a national sample of 533, only four teenage mothers had their babies adopted in 1979 (Simms and Smith, 1982). Many professional and voluntary workers in the health, education, social and youth services express concern that young girls are choosing parenthood as an alternative to unemployment or tedious unskilled jobs (Johnson, 1980). A study of 79 London mothers aged 16–19 in late pregnancy confirmed that they are still usually of working class status with few or no qualifications and little chance of career-type employment. However, this did not suggest that they became pregnant by default or because they had nothing else to do, rather motherhood was a central focus of their lives (Phoenix, 1987).

Single mothers and teenage pregnancies have often been presented as a pressing social problem. In 1985 in England and Wales there were 797 000 conceptions of which 15 per cent were to women under 20 years old. A quarter of these conceptions or pregnancies were inside marriage but the others should not necessarily be regarded as an indication of increasing single parenthood since 59 per cent of these 'illegitimate births' were jointly registered indicating the child was part of a stable, though non-marital, relationship (Central Statistical Office, 1988).

The majority of lone parents become so as the result of separation, divorce or death. There are various factors which may affect the emotional and intellectual development of their children. First, there is the actual death or separation leading to the formation of the majority of such families. For most children this is, inevitably, a stressful period in their life; for some it will be sudden and unexpected, for others a sad and sometimes long drawn-out experience. Children will react differently according to their age, their personality, the relationship they have (or had) with both their parents, the presence or absence of brothers and sisters, aunts and uncles, grandparents or other significant people in their life (Mitchell, 1985; Wallerstein and Kelly, 1980). Reactions to stress to some extent depend on a child's age. Pre-school children are likely to show management problems in feeding and sleeping, temper tantrums, irritability and misery; middle school children may exhibit aggressive behaviour, truancy, lying, stealing or overtly emotional problems such as depression, anxiety, fearfulness or withdrawal. Adolescents may show a combination of middle school age and more adult type behaviour with depressive reactions and anxiety states (Graham *et al.*, 1985).

Recent figures indicate that 20 per cent of the 100 000 households accepted as homeless by local authorities in 1986 had recently experienced the breakdown of the relationship between the partners (FPSC, 1988).

The National Child Development Study report on disadvantaged children identified children from one-parent families with low incomes and poor housing as less likely to be successful at school than other children (Wedge and Prosser, 1973). The problems of poverty are further exacerbated by many parents having to work full time and needing substitute or day care, holiday and after-school provision, all of which are in short supply and costly. The CHES report confirmed that at age five there were differences in behaviour, in cognitive abilities and vocabulary between children of lone parents compared with those who had two parents. Much of this (though not all) could be attributed to the poorer socio-economic circumstances, loss of a parent, family isolation and curtailed parent–child interaction (Osborn *et al.*, 1984).

The impact of divorce upon children

Divorce is now a fact of life and needs to be seen as a process, not a single event, dissolving a marriage. Bohannen (1971) describes six stations of divorce which may be happening simultaneously or in succession and which continue until some resolution is found. This process includes:

- the emotional divorce: the phase when the marriage is deteriorating
- the legal divorce: when the divorce is granted
- the economic divorce: dealing with money and property
- the co-parental divorce: arrangements for child care, custody and access
- the community divorce: relationships with friends, neighbours and colleagues
- the psychic divorce: coming to terms with the marital breakup and regaining individual autonomy.

For many thousands of children experiencing actual separation and the consequences of divorce of their parents, it is likely to be a continuous process of change and adjustment and of considerable anxiety as their parents try to resolve the different stages identified above. It has been argued by some that children suffer when their parents' marriage ends, and by others that a child removed from embittered parental conflict will be happier. Family conflict and family tension certainly affect children's mental health (Rutter, 1981) and in assessing the impact of the loss of a parent through death and divorce it was the distortion of family relationships not the disruption of the bond with the parent in divorce that was critical (Rutter, 1981). This appears to hold true both before and after divorce. Lund (1984) looked at three groups of six- to nine-year-old children post-divorce: those with no contact with the non-custodial parent, those with access but whose parents were in conflict, and those whose parents worked harmoniously together. The last group were reported by teachers and mothers to have the fewest emotional problems and highest self-esteem of the three groups.

Research seems to indicate that how parents manage the divorce process is the critical factor for children rather than the divorce *per se*. However, children rarely seem to be informed about the possibility of separation or divorce. Parents seem to believe either that the less said the better or that the reasons are obvious and do not need explaining. Research studies with children clearly contradict both these points of view (Mitchell, 1985; McCredie and Horrox, 1985; Walczak and Burns, 1984; Wallerstein and Kelly, 1980). Children want and need information in order to make some sense of their parents' behaviour, to avoid distorted and unnecessary fears and fantasies, and to come to terms with the change in circumstances. It should be expected that children will be upset by such dramatic changes in their lives and this needs to be acknowledged and supported.

It is rare for children to welcome their parents' separation even though they welcome an end to any violence, arguments, shouting or unpleasantness. Many children, particularly younger ones, develop anxieties about the possible loss or disappearance of their remaining parent and may show clinging behaviour or fear of being left alone. The majority of children feel great sadness and, for some, this is expressed as anger, bitterness and resentment towards the remaining parent. In others it may lead to depression. Parents have reported problems which might have been caused by the separation or earlier conflict: truancy, clinging, withdrawn behaviour, bed-wetting, aggressiveness, nightmares and poor work at school (Mitchell, 1985).

The majority of children whose parents separate and divorce are of school age and a significant amount of their time will therefore be spent at school. Teachers can play an important role in helping them to adjust, but since practical and financial arrangements often cause difficulties for parents, teachers need to be sensitive in offering help so that it does not seem intrusive. The proposed post-divorce reform of a jointly agreed statement of parenting arrangements for children is welcome in principle, but many parents will require access to conciliation to enable them to concentrate on their children's needs. Wallerstein and Kelly (1980) have described a 'diminished capacity to parent' during the divorce period, when parents who feel humiliated, depressed or angry are unable to cope with the distress, anxieties or needs of their children. Clulow and Vincent (1987) describe the role of the Divorce Court Welfare Service as a 'no-man's land between the interests of parents and children, between the conflicting parents themselves, and ultimately between the interests of the State and the individual; the meshing of private complaint and public response'.

Marriage breakdown and divorce is still portrayed as a private matter, the result of personal inadequacy or moral failure, yet the Finer Report (1974) emphasized that children were often helpless victims of marital strife and envisaged conciliation services being developed in the context of a major reform of family law and creation of family courts. The report made 230 recommendations for action which would radically improve or reduce legal, financial, housing, employment and other problems facing Britain's one-parent families.

Research indicates that support for families, especially those identified as vulnerable, should have high priority in social policy and public spending. Matrimonial legal aid cost £61 million in 1983–84 but little money was available for independent conciliation services or to help couples to consider the options available to them and to separate, if necessary, without severe conflict and distress. In 1982–83 nearly 800 children in England and Wales were made the subject of care orders as a result of divorce or other family proceedings and the cumulative number of children in care as a result of such orders was more than 7000, costing approximately £400 million a year (Family Courts Campaign, 1986).

The links between research, policy and practice are very clear and could be cost-effective(!) but to date most of the resources for dealing with the aftermath of marital breakdown have been allocated to the judicial system. More financial support for family life and access to preventive services would help to reduce marital distress. The creation of family courts and a unified system of family law, ending the adversarial system, with its inconsistencies and confusion, conciliation services to help clarify arrangements in the best interests of children and encourage joint parental responsibilities, would all reduce the distress inherent in the divorce process. Interdisciplinary training for all those working with families – lawyers, conciliators, probation and court welfare services, as well as health, education and social services, would create a network of support for children, parents and families. Such changes would also encourage a more positive and better negotiated start for many step-families which often fail as a result of unresolved divorce issues.

Children in step-families

Step-families have always existed but the increasing rate of divorce and remarriage mean that there are now more of them and that more are formed following parental divorce than parental death. A step-family is created when two adults form a new household in which one or both brings a child or children from a previous relationship. Such families may be preceded by single parenthood, separation, divorce or bereavement, and may arise through cohabitation, marriage or remarriage. It has been estimated that there are 26 possible permutations of step-family formation. Step-children may be full-time or part-time members of the household. Step-family relationships cut across all generations and many adults who are step-parents may also become step-children as many of the older generation remarry. This may lead to an increasingly varied and complex network of 'family' relationships.

There is little research or information on remarriage in Britain. A longitudinal sample of 1084 couples who divorced in 1979 found that one-third of both husbands (34 per cent) and wives (33 per cent) had remarried within two and a half years, and that those with children were just as likely to remarry as those with no children (Haskey, 1987; Bhrolcain, 1988). Although basic information on those remarrying can be obtained from marriage records there are no details of the children involved or duration of the previous marriage (Haskey, 1987). Exact numbers of step-families are unknown, but it is estimated that there are between 1 and 1.5 million. In 1982, 7 per cent of all children (809 000) were living with their natural mother and a step-father (OPCS, 1982). Over one-third of single mothers with dependent children were cohabiting in 1985, and many divorced and separated women, some of whom will have children, constitute a significant number of additional step-families, in fact, if not in law (Central Statistical Office, 1988). Within five years, half of all non-custodial parents (usually fathers) have remarried, creating some full-time and some part-time step-families where children visit or stay overnight for short periods (Leete and Anthony, 1979).

Little research exists on the difficult task of raising another person's child in this situation or on the distinctive features and potential problems of step-parenting as opposed to adoption or fostering. The first investigation of a large representative sample of step-children confirmed that the documented economic and social problems created by divorce were considerably alleviated by remarriage, especially where this provided a step-mother (Ferri, 1984). The development of children, including educational attainment, social and emotional behaviour, and aspirations for the future, differed little from those of two-parent families. However, in a minority of cases involving boys with step-fathers, there were developmental difficulties. This study suggested that such problems may lie in the confusion surrounding roles and relationships of step-parents and children and the lack of clear and realistic expectations for step-families.

While society continues to idealize the two-parent family and regard it as the norm, there is a danger that remarriage will be seen as the solution to the individual and social problems associated with widowhood, marital separation and single parenthood. Not only is there a lack of research evidence to support this view, but it has been argued that many children do better remaining in a single-parent family than in having to make further adjustments to a third form of family life – the step-family (Richards and Dyson, 1982).

Step-parent adoptions of marital children increased from approximately 3000 in 1965 to over 9000 in 1975, almost all accounted for by post-divorce applications. The Children Act 1975 sought to discourage such step-parent adoptions and a research project was established to monitor the changes. Adoption was intended to create new family relationships not change those which already existed and joint custody was introduced as an alternative and to give some legal recognition to step-parents. The research (Masson *et al.*, 1983) looked at 1255 step-families applying to adopt from the step-family population of 6150 in 1980, and identified a major problem of variable treatment by courts of step-families seeking adoption. In some courts applications were successful in 96 per cent of cases; in other courts only 9 per cent were successful.

Information on step-families has come primarily from researchers following up the impact of divorce, practitioners working with divorced parents and step-families, and most recently from step-parents themselves. Mitchell (1985) found that five years after divorce in four-fifths of the 71 families in the study the children had one parent with a new partner and at least one-third had two parents with new partners. Of the 30 per cent of custodial parents who had remarried, one-third of the remarriages had already broken down. Ferri (1984) concluded that difficult parent–child relationships and sibling conflict were more common in step-families. McCredie and Horrox (1985) illustrated how children, who had lost one parent through divorce and adjusted to a lone-parent family, expressed anxiety and often outright resistance to any further changes, particularly remarriage of their parent/s.

Practitioners working with step-children and step-families emphasize the importance of understanding the particular needs of step-families and not treating them as if they were two-parent families. An early guide from America (Visher and Visher, 1979) outlined the myths and realities of step-family life, while in Britain, Brown (1982) looked at the implications for social work, and Roys (1984) focused on working with adolescents where there are problems. Essentially such guidelines highlight the need to enhance communication, to accept ambiguity and differences in step-families and the value of history taking. It is important for practitioners to remain flexible, sometimes widening the focus to include extended current or previous family members, to avoid triangulation or colluding with any one family member, and to avoid judging which includes the assumption that problems are all related to being a step-family. An American clinical study (Anderson and White, 1986) also suggests that problems in step-families are more likely to relate to parenting issues between adults and children than to the parents' marital relationship. Burgoyne and Clark (1984) describe the 'conscious parenthood' of step-parents as a rational rather than an emotional effort to be a 'good parent' compared with child rearing as a central and spontaneous activity for natural parents.

Parents and step-parents are increasingly writing about step-family life in an attempt both to warn parents and inform practitioners. Maddox (1980) describes how love and anger, ghosts and grandparents, home and food, jealousy and authority can make it difficult to live with other people's children. Hodder (1985) provides an extremely practical guide to all you need to know before and after becoming a step-family! Inglis (1986) explores myths, ghosts, roles, priorities and feelings, and De'Ath (1988c) identifies the differences, difficulties and divided loyalties in step-families. Step-family life is multi-dimensional and multi-faceted, making it a complex arena for parents and children to live in, or practitioners to work in.

Children who run away

Leaving home should be a normal part of young adult development, but running away or leaving prematurely is an indication that life at home is no longer acceptable or bearable. Children usually exhibit symptoms or signals long before they run away: they may lie, steal, truant, experiment with drugs or alcohol, create conflict, throw tantrums, be angry or depressed; finally they run away. Based on a national postal survey to chief constables in 1986, it is estimated that 75–80 000 young people are reported as missing each year in Britain (De'Ath, 1987).

Various terms are used to describe children and young people who are no longer at home, frequently incorrectly and often as though they were interchangeable (De'Ath, 1986). The most common are:

- missing children – those who disappear; some may have been kidnapped or abducted, some will have run away
- runaways – those who leave their normal residence without permission
- absconders – absent from an address where they should be residing under various legal provisions (foster/children's home, hospital)
- homeless – no fixed abode or permanent accommodation
- rootless drifters – seeking jobs in cities or coastal towns, moving from place to place, in squats, on beaches or the streets.

Running away from home is not a new phenomenon. In 1975 a television documentary 'Johnny Go Home' about runaway children, estimated 2000 per night on the streets of London, and caused an uproar in the press, public and parliament (Deakin and Willis, 1976). Another study looked at the consequences of family conflict and a 'new wave of teenage girls breaking away' (Willans, 1976). A DHSS report highlighted the dangers facing runaways and homeless youngsters (DHSS, 1976). Despite all this, very little attention has been given to the issue in Great Britain as compared with other countries. In America, the 1974 Runaway Youth Act and the 1977 Runaway and Homeless Youth Program provided funds for community-based short-term shelters, food and clothing, and a national runaway switchboard. In this country, a debate on runaway children in the House of Commons records 'There is no comprehensive policy or practice covering runaway children' (*Hansard*, 1986).

Interest in runaways, street children and child prostitution has heightened during the 1980s. An International Commission on unprotected children on city streets called it a growing urban tragedy needing concrete action not just concern (Agnelli, 1986). A study of child prostitution in Britain, America and West Germany reports that 'every runaway child who goes into full-time child prostitution has a history of continual and profound family conflict' (Sereny, 1984).

Three key dimensions are recognized as specific to runaways: age; absence of permission to leave or covert or forcible ejection; length of time since leaving. In the United Kingdom there are no clear definitions, discrete criteria, national statistics, nor comprehensive policy or practice by central or local government for runaway children. The Children's Society, a national voluntary child care organization providing the only safe houses for runaways and the only comprehensive research on this issue in England (De'Ath and Newman, 1987; Newman, forthcoming), has suggested the following as a basic operational definition for further work in this area:

> A runaway is a young person, aged under 17 years or in local authority care, who has either left home (or residential care) of their own accord but without agreement or is forced to leave, and is missing for one or more nights.

Such a definition would combine two currently separate categories of young people (runaways and absconders) and could provide the basis for the collection of national statistics to estimate the prevalence of runaway behaviour. An interim report from the safe house research, based on 532 young people (737 admissions) for the period June 1985 to May 1987, shows that the majority of young people ran from home (347, 65 per cent), a third from local authority care (179, 34 per cent) and a few from boarding schools (6, 1 per cent). Eighteen per cent of these young people had been sexually abused at some time and 4 per cent of the females cited this as the main reason for running (Newman, forthcoming).

Children and young people run away for many and varied reasons. Some are seeking independence and freedom from family or institutional repression; some are escaping from problems or abuse whether at home, within the family, or at school; some are running back to the family and away from care authorities. The image of the runaway as adventurer or 'fun seeker' heading for the bright lights of the city for a couple of days or weeks is not realistic. Rather, the reasons given by the young people followed a consistent pattern of circumstances.

- running from home: most frequently given reasons were – lack of understanding within the family, problems arising from separation, divorce or remarriage of parents, breakdown in communication, trying to trace absent natural parent, rows and arguments often ending with the youngster being thrown out, violence at home often accompanied by drunkenness, other physical or sexual abuse, and bullying at school.
- running from care: over half the 179 youngsters who had run from care were persistent absconders and had already run away at least five times before going to the safe house. They said they were unhappy in their placement, had been in care for too long, nothing appeared to be getting sorted out, they were being bullied, they wanted more independence, problems with foster or adoptive families, feeling stigmatized in care, feeling unable to cope with independent or semi-independent living (De'Ath and Newman, 1987).

Working with youngsters who have run away is not easy. Many have survived days, weeks or even months lacking regular food or safe accommodation, often by begging or shoplifting and sleeping in squats, derelict buildings, on the streets or under bridges in cardboard boxes. Loneliness and the absence of advice, guidance and support often lead to them striking up friendships with others in the same situation which can offer peer-group support or may increase risks of involvement in prostitution, drugs or solvent abuse. Gaining the trust of such youngsters is one of the most important elements of the work, listening to them, exploring the circumstances leading to running away, giving them time to disclose painful incidents from their past, involving them openly in all aspects of planning and negotiating a mutually agreeable solution for their future with parents or guardians (De'Ath and Newman, 1987; Adams and Adams, 1987; De'Ath, 1987).

On the basis of current trends, the impact of divorce and remarriage on young people will no doubt not only continue but is likely to increase. The changes in social security legislation will make it more difficult for young people estranged from their parents or who have suffered physical or sexual abuse to receive financial or practical help. As a recent Barnardo's report on the plight of the young homeless states 'those young people who run away have been failed both by their families and by the society in which they live' (O'Mahony, 1988).

From this examination of some of the many patterns of family life which exist in Britain in the 1980s it can be seen that traditional views of the family are unsupported by research findings. It also demonstrates that the findings of research support a coherent policy to identify family needs at times of stress and develop services and good practice to match them as far as possible. Children are deeply affected by their family life and to help parents provide them with a satisfactory experience and model is likely to be an investment in the future when they will become parents in their turn.

References

Adams, P. R. and Adams, G. R. (1987) 'Intervention with runaway youth and their families: theory and practice', in Coleman, J. C. (ed) *Working with Troubled Adolescents*, Academic Press.

Agnelli, S. (1986) *Street Children, A Growing Urban Tragedy, Report for the Independent Commission on International Humanitarian Issues*, Weidenfeld and Nicolson.

Anderson, J. Z. and White, G. D. (1986) 'An empirical investigation of interaction and relationship patterns in functional and dysfunctional nuclear families and step-families', *Family Process*, Vol. 25, pp. 407–22.

Barrow, J. (1982) 'West Indian families: an insider's perspective', in Rapoport, R. N., Fogarty, M. P. and Rapoport, R. (eds) *Families in Britain*, Routledge and Kegan Paul.

Berridge, D. (1985) *Children's Homes*, Basil Blackwell.

Bettelheim, B. (1988) *A Good Enough Parent: The Guide to Bringing Up Your Child*, Pan Books.

Berrueta-Clement, J. R. B., Schweinhart, L. J., Barrett, W. S., Epstein, A. S. and Weikart, D. P. (1984) *Changed Lives: The Effects of the Perry Pre-School Program on Youths Through Age 19*. Monograph 8, Ypsilanti, Michigan, High Scope.

Bhrolcain, M. N. (1988) 'Changing partners; a longitudinal study of remarriage', *Population Trends*, Vol. 53, pp. 27–34.

Bohannen, P. (1981) *Divorce and After*, Doubleday.

Bowlby, J. (1951) *Maternal Care and Mental Health*, World Health Organisation.

Bowlby, J. (1972) *Child Care and the Growth of Love*, Penguin.

Bronfenbrenner, U. (1974) 'Children, families and social policy: an American perspective', in *The Family in Society: Dimensions of Parenthood*, DHSS.

Brown, D. (1982) *The Step-family: A Growing Challenge for Social Work*, University of East Anglia, Social Work Monograph.

Brown, G. and Harris, T. (1978) *Social Origins of Depression, A Study of Psychiatric Disorder in Women*, Tavistock.

Brown, J. (1988) *Child Benefit: Investing in the Future*, Child Poverty Action Group.

Burgoyne, J. and Clark, D. (1984) *Making a go of it*, Routledge and Kegan Paul.

Bury, J. (1984) *Teenage Pregnancy in Britain*, Birth Control Trust.

Butler, N. R., Ineichen, B., Taylor, B. and Wadsworth, J. (1981) *Teenage Mothering*, Report to the UK Department of Health and Social Security.

Cant, D. (1980) 'Can there ever be enough for me? Reparenting the young single parent', *Journal of Adolescence*, Vol. 3, No. 1, pp. 51–64.

Central Council for Education and Training in Social Work (1978) *Good Enough Parenting: Report of a Group on Work with Children and Young People and the Implications for Social Work Education*, Study No. 1, CCETSW.

Central Statistical Office (1986) *Social Trends*, No. 18, HMSO.

Clulow, C. and Vincent, C. (1987) *In the Child's Best Interests? Divorce Court Welfare and the Search for a Settlement*, Tavistock.

Deakin, M. and Willis, J. (1976) *Johnny Go Home*, Futura and Yorkshire TV.

De'Ath, E. (1982) 'Interventions with families: preparing the way for teaching parenting skills', *Journal of Family Therapy*, Vol. 4, pp. 229–45.

De'Ath, E. (1983) 'Teaching parenting skills', *Journal of Family Therapy*, Vol. 5, pp. 321–35.

De'Ath, E. (1985) *Self-help and Family Centres. A Current Initiative in Helping the Community*, National Children's Bureau.

De'Ath, E. (1986) *Young People Under Pressure: Runaways and Others*, The Children's Society.

De'Ath, E. (1987) 'The world of runaways', *Community Care*, Inside Supplement, No. 5.

De'Ath, E. (1988a) *The Family Centre Approach, Focus on Families No. 2*, The Children's Society.

De'Ath, E. (1988b) *Divorce and its Effects on Children, Focus on Families No. 1*, The Children's Society.

De'Ath, E. (1988c) *Step-parenting*, Family Doctor Publications, BMA.

De'Ath, E. and Newman, C. (1987) 'Children who run', *Children and Society*, Vol. 1, pp. 13–18, National Children's Bureau.

Department of Health and Social Security (1974) *The Family in Society: Dimensions of Parenthood*, HMSO.

Department of Health and Social Security (1976) Report from the Working Group on Homeless Young People (unpublished).

Department of Health and Social Security (1985) *Review of Child Care Law: Report to Ministers of an Interdepartmental Working Group*, HMSO.

Dunnell, K. (1979) *Family Formation 1976*, Office of Population Censuses and Surveys Report SS 1080, HMSO.

Eekelaar, J. (1971) *Family Law and Social Policy*, Weidenfeld and Nicolson.

Family Courts Campaign (1986) *A Court Fit for Families. Response to Interdepartmental Review of Family and Domestic Jurisdiction*, c/o National Children's Bureau, London.

Family Policy Studies Centre (1988) *Family Policy Bulletin No. 4*, FPSC.

Ferri, E. (1984) *Stepchildren: A National Study*, NFER-Nelson.

Finer Report (1974) *Report of the Committee on One Parent Families*, 2 vols, HMSO.

Gavron, H. (1966) *The Captive Wife, Conflicts of Housebound Mothers*, Pelican.

Graham, P. (1988) 'Social class, social disadvantage and child health', in *Children and Society*, Vol. 2, No. 1, National Children's Bureau.

Graham, P., Pearson, L. and Sheldon, B. (1985) 'National case study (England and Wales) child mental health and psychosocial development', *ACPP Newsletter*, Vol. 7, pp. 2–18.

Hansard (1986) Runaway children (London), Col. 1137–1142, 27 March.

Haskey, J. (1987) 'Social class differentials in remarriage after divorce: results from a forward linkage study', in *Population Trends*, No. 47, pp. 34–42, HMSO.

Health Education Council and National Extension College (1984) *Providing Effective Health Care in a Multiracial Society, A Checklist for Looking at Local Issues*, National Extension College.

Henderson, P. (ed) (1988) *Working with Communities*, The Children's Society.

Henwood, M. and Wicks, M. (1988) *Family Policy Studies Centre: Family Policy Position Statement*, Association of County Councils.

Hibbett, A. and Fogelman, K. (1988) *Early Adult Outcomes of Truancy*, NCDS Users' Support Group Working Paper, available from Social Statistical Research Unit, City University.

Hibbett, A., Fogelman, K. and Manor, O. (in press) 'Occupational outcomes of truancy', *British Journal of Educational Psychology*.

Hodder, E. (1985) *The Step-parents' Handbook*, Sphere.

Hodgson, S., Brown, G., Koziarski, M., Rickleton, M., Fundudis, T. and Nicol, A. R. (1987) 'Mother and toddler groups', *ACPP Newsletter*, Vol. 9, pp. 10–14.

Home Office (1979) *Marriage Matters; A Consultative Document by the Working Party on Marriage Guidance*, HMSO.

Inglis, R. (1986) *The Good Step-parent's Guide*, Grafton.

Johnson, D. (ed) (1980) *Disaffected Pupils*, Brunel University, Educational Studies Unit.

Jordan, B. (1974) *Poor Parents, Social Policy and the 'Cycle of Deprivation'*, Routledge and Kegan Paul.

Joseph, K. (1972) 'The parental role', in *Concern*, No. 11, National Children's Bureau.

Juvenile Crime Advisory Committee (1987) *Time for Change: A New Framework for Dealing with Juvenile Crime and Offenders*, NACRO.

Koziarski, M., Hodgson, S. and Nicol, A. R. (1986) 'Family therapy in a community mother and toddler project', *Journal of Family Therapy*, Vol. 8, pp. 207–24.

Law Commission (1986) *Family Law Review of Child Law: Custody*, Working Paper No. 96, HMSO.

Leete, A. and Anthony, S. (1979) 'Divorce and remarriage: a record linkage study', in *Population Trends*, No. 16, HMSO.

Lerner, B. (1972) *Therapy in the Ghetto*, Johns Hopkins University Press.

Lindon, J. and Lindon, L. (1988) 'Achieving quality in day care for young children', *Children in Society*, Vol. 2, pp. 102–16.

Lund, M. (1984) 'Research on divorce and children', *Family Law*, Vol. 14, No. 7, pp. 198–201.

Maddox, B. (1980) *Step-parenting, How to Live with Other People's Children*, Unwin.

Masson, J., Norbury, D. and Chatterton, S. (1983) *Mine, Yours or Ours? A Study of Step-parent Adoption*, HMSO.

Mattinson, J. and Sinclair, I. (1979) *Mate and Stalemate*, Basil Blackwell.

Mayer, J. and Timms, N. (1970) *The Client Speaks; Working-class Impressions of Casework*, Routledge and Kegan Paul.

McCredie, G. and Horrox, A. (1985) *Voices in the Dark, Children and Divorce*, Unwin.

Melhuish, E. and Phoenix, A. (1987) 'Motherhood under twenty: prevailing ideologies and research', *Children and Society*, Vol. 4, pp. 288–98, National Children's Bureau.

Merrington, D. and Corden, J. (1981) 'Families' impressions of family therapy', *Journal of Family Therapy*, Vol. 3, pp. 243–61.

Miller, J. and Cook, T. (eds) (1981) *Direct Work With Families*, Bedford Square Press.

Mitchell, A. (1985) *Children in the Middle: Living Through Divorce*, Tavistock.

Newman, C. (forthcoming) *Young Runaways*, The Children's Society.

Newson, J. and Newson, E. (1963) *Patterns of Infant Care in an Urban Community*, Pelican.

Newson, J. and Newson, E. (1974) 'Cultural aspects of childrearing in the English-speaking world', in Richards, M. (ed) *The Integration of a Child into a Social World*, Cambridge University Press.

Office of Population Censuses and Surveys (1986a) OPCS Monitor FM2 86/2, *Divorces in England and Wales during 1985*, Tables 1, 2, 8, OPCS.

Office of Population Censuses and Surveys (1986b) OPCS Monitor FM3 86/1, *Adoptions in England and Wales, 1984*, OPCS.

Office of Population Censuses and Surveys (1988) *General Household Survey 1987*, OPCS.

O'Mahony, B. (1988) *A Capital Offence, The Plight of the Young Single Homeless in London*, Dr Barnardo's.

Osborn, A. F., Butler, N. R. and Morris, A. C. (1984) *The Social Life of Britain's Five Year Olds, A Report of the Child Health and Education Study*, Routledge and Kegan Paul.

Phoenix, A. (1987) 'Early motherhood and employment', *Youthaid Bulletin*, No. 34.

Pound, A. and Mills, M. (1985) 'A pilot evaluation of NEWPIN – home-visiting and befriending scheme in South London', *ACPP Newsletter*, Vol. 7, pp. 13–15.

Pugh, G. and De'Ath, E. (1984) *The Needs of Parents: Practice and Policy in Parent Education*, Macmillan.

Richards, M. and Dyson, M. (1982) *Separation, Divorce and the Development of Children: A Review*, HMSO.

Rimmer, L. (1981) *Families in Focus: Marriage, Divorce and Family Patterns*, Study Commission on the Family.

Roys, C. (1984) *Working with Step-families with Adolescents where there are Problems*, Bristol University, Personal Social Services.

Russell, P. (1978) 'Help starts here', *Concern*, No. 28, National Children's Bureau.

Rutter, M. (1974) 'Dimensions of parenthood: some myths and some suggestions', in *The Family in Society: Dimensions of Parenthood*, HMSO.

Rutter, M. (1981) 'Stress, coping and developing: some issues and some questions', *Journal of Child Psychology and Psychiatry*, Vol. 22, pp. 323–56.

Sainsbury, E., Nixon, S. and Phillips, D. (1982) *Social Work in Focus: Clients' and Social Workers' Perceptions of Long-term Social Work*, Routledge and Kegan Paul.

Sereny, G. (1984) *The Invisible Children, The Shattering Tragedy of the Runaways on our Streets*, Pan.

Sillitoe, K. (1979) *Ethnic Origins, 1, 2, and 3*, OPCS Occasional Papers 8, 9 and 10, HMSO.

Simms, M. and Smith, C. (1982) 'Teenage mothers and adoption', *Adoption and Fostering*, Vol. 6, No. 4, pp. 43–8.

Spence, J., Walton, W. S., Miller, F. J. W. and Court, S. D. M. (1954) *A Thousand Families in Newcastle-upon-Tyne*, Oxford University Press.

Visher, E. and Visher, J. (1979) *Step-families, Myths and Realities*, Citadel Press.

Walczak, Y. and Burns, S. (1984) *Divorce: The Child's Point of View*, Harper and Row.

Wallerstein, J. S. and Kelly, J. (1980) *Surviving the Break-up: How Children and Parents Cope with Divorce*, Grant McIntyre.

Wedge, P. (1984) 'Disadvantaged children: the scale of the problem and the scope of the solutions', in De'Ath, E. and Hill, M. (eds) *Towards a Coherent Policy for Disadvantaged Children*, University of Dundee, Extra Mural Department.

Wedge, P. and Essen, J. (1982) *Children in Adversity*, Pan.

Wedge, P. and Prosser, H. (1973) *Born to Fail?*, Arrow.

Wells, N. (1983) *Teenage Mothers*, European Collaborative Committee for Child Health, Children's Research Fund.

Willans, A. (1976) *Break-away, Family Conflict and the Teenage Girl*, Maurice Temple Smith.

Winnicott, D. W. (1960) 'The theory of the parent–infant relationship', in *The Maturational Process and the Facilitating Environment* (1979), Hogarth Press.

4 Child abuse

Nigel Parton

This chapter has three central aims in its discussion of child abuse research. The first is simply to provide a framework for analysing, together with some criteria for assessing, what we currently 'know' about child abuse. However, rather than attempt a comprehensive summary or distillation of 'research findings' it will concentrate its efforts on identifying the main issues and questions that research has addressed, together with some of its main conclusions. It will then attempt to analyse critically the current state of knowledge about child abuse or – more to the point – what we don't 'know'.

Secondly, I will try to demonstrate that the relationship between research, policy and practice is far from straightforward. For rather than research coming up with unequivocal findings which can then influence and be integrated in a professional and neutral way into policy and practice I will try to demonstrate how political interests and values, in all their guises, influence and pervade the relationship in a variety of ways. Nor is this influence obvious or straightforward, for a major reason why different research comes up with different findings and has different implications for policy and practice is that those findings are subject to different underlying assumptions and have different ideological agendas.

Thirdly, I will conclude that the way we approach and use research perhaps needs to be rethought. What will become apparent is that practitioners are unlikely to find answers to the tensions and problems of child abuse and child protection work in any clear-cut way in the research. In fact the nature and direction of child abuse research may itself be a not insignificant part of the problem of deciding what to do. I will argue that in seeing child abuse and child abuse research as distinct from child care and child care research more generally, practitioners and policy makers are, at best, forgetting and, at worst, refusing to recognize what we already 'know' about good practice with children and families. A central part of my argument, then, is that a major step can be made simply by relocating the issue of child abuse into the mainstream of child care research, policy and practice. In recognizing that child abuse and child care are not discrete areas we should start from the premise that the understanding and skills developed in relation to child care should inform our approach to child abuse.

Research, public inquiries and practice

The issue of child abuse, or child protection as it is often now described (Parton and Parton, 1989), perhaps more than any other area of child care policy and practice has brought the activities of a variety of health and welfare professionals into considerable public, political and media focus in recent years. During the last 20 years well over 30 public inquiries have put the practice and decision making of social workers in particular under the microscope (DHSS, 1982; Hallett, 1989). In many respects the issue has provided the main vehicle for articulating a series of debates about how the state, via its social workers, responds to the needs of children more generally and intervenes in the private sphere of the family in particular (Parton, 1985; Frost, 1989). In the late 1980s it has seemed that social workers and their agencies have been caught in a political crossfire between being criticized on the one hand for allowing some children to suffer unnecessarily, sometimes to the point of death, at the hands of their parent(s) or guardian(s), and on the other hand of intervening unwarrantably into other families and removing their children inappropriately. Put another way, it has seemed that the primary concern addressed in the Beckford (London Borough of Brent, 1985), Carlile (London Borough of Greenwich, 1987) and Henry (London Borough of Lambeth, 1987) reports was that social workers did too little too late, while the primary concern addressed in the Cleveland report (Secretary of State for Social Services, 1988) was that social workers did too much too soon.

Much of this public criticism directed at practitioners, often reinforced and fuelled by the reports themselves, is that these tragedies and scandals have arisen because practitioners 'failed', in part, because they lacked the knowledge about child abuse which a thorough grounding in the research and its findings would have given them. It is assumed that research has established what the nature of child abuse is, who the actual and potential perpetrators and victims are and hence what are the associated factors which put children at 'high risk'. It is assumed that child abuse is preventable and predictable via a judicious reading of the research findings. If only social workers and other professionals familiarized themselves with these research findings and integrated them into their everyday practice both tragedies and unwarrantable interventions could be avoided or kept to an absolute minimum. This lack of knowledge is seen to reflect both unprofessionalism in practice and poor training prior to practice.

Such an assumption is perhaps made most explicit in the Beckford Report when it comments on the apparent failure of the area officer in the case to recognize the apparently obvious indications that he was dealing with a 'high risk' child abuse case when chairing the initial case conference:

> He now appreciates that the combination of a physically abused child's abnormally low weight, understimulation and the general lack of competent parenting are the indicia of predictive child abuse. *His failure to appreciate that at the time is no more than a commentary on the absence of knowledge*

> *about child abuse generally among social workers*. The yawning gap in that knowledge should now be filled by the publicity given to this case during the public hearings and, we trust, by the publication of our report, (London Borough of Brent, 1985, p. 83) (My emphasis.)

Clearly it is of concern if health and welfare professionals are unfamiliar with the relevant research and it is one of the aims of this chapter to contribute to that understanding. However, the report fails to convey any sense of the complexity and lacunae of research findings and of the difficulties that await those who avail themselves uncritically of them. Apart from the difficulty of distilling research findings without distortion for the benefit of practitioners, there are critical methodological loopholes and inconsistencies in the research itself. As I hope to demonstrate, while a familiarity with research findings may provide important new insights they cannot substitute for sound professional judgement nor can they solve some of the inherent tensions and ethical dilemmas inherent in this area of work. To assume that the messages from research for the practitioner are clear and straightforward is naive. If practitioners can become aware of and able to understand and transcend these complicated messages from research, however, not only may they become more confident in reflecting on their knowledge when making such judgements, they may also become more confident in discussing these complexities and difficulties with both other professionals and the wider public, thus enhancing social understanding of the day-to-day realities of work in this area.

Similarly the role of research needs to be rethought. Up until now researchers have taken on the guise of distant experts who hand down their findings, leaving practitioners with the task of making sense of and using them. I will argue that a major readjustment needs to be made whereby the researcher takes on a more participative role working with and alongside practitioners and clients. I will argue that the best way of seeing research is as an aid to increasing enlightenment and not as providing the answers. Practitioners and clients are the best experts on their problems so researchers need to make a greater effort to learn from and listen to practice. The primary role for researchers should be to work alongside practitioners and help them understand not only what clients are saying but help them think through the nature and impact of their interventions. It is crucial that researchers aim to be more participative in the way they frame research questions and their methodologies and at the same time be more sympathetic to the subject(s) they are researching.

Underlying models and central conceptual frameworks

Since the early 1970s a variety of child abuse inquiries and DHSS circulars have emphasized that the establishment of child abuse registers, case conferences and increased inter-professional co-ordination will enhance the central aims of attempting to predict, prevent and identify the children who may be in actual or potential danger of child abuse. The emphasis on the need for medical and social assessment (DHSS, 1988) is an attempt to improve our abilities to identify the 'high risk' case or family (Parton and Parton, 1989).

Such an approach is based on what I have called elsewhere (Parton, 1985) a disease model of child abuse, but which may be more appropriately conceptualized as a public health model (Giovannoni, 1982; Greenland, 1987). Such a model has been influential in the way we think about and respond to a variety of social problems but has been particularly significant in framing research, policy and practice in child abuse. As the Beckford Report commented, quoting the work of the late Henry Kempe, it is assumed that 'child abuse is a disease whose carrier is the parent and whose victim is the child' (London Borough of Brent, 1985, p. 88). Elsewhere reports have referred to the 'pathogenesis of the disorder' (London Borough of Brent, 1985, p. 87) or 'the psychopathology of the Carlile family' (London Borough of Greenwich, 1987, p. 106) and have made frequent reference to the seminal article by the late Henry Kempe and his colleagues (Kempe *et al.*, 1962) that child abuse is a 'syndrome'. What are the basic elements of this model which are embedded in its essential concepts and ideas?

As Giovannoni (1982) has demonstrated, the model was developed in the late nineteenth century when public health developed a methodology and a terminology for mounting programmes and interventions to control and eliminate acute infectious diseases (Armstrong, 1983). Such an approach assumes that the disease is attributable to a particular virus or bacteria which can be clearly demonstrated and which hence constitutes the essential cause of the disease. Not only can its causal links be shown but its habits, strengths and weaknesses can be determined so that ultimately disease may be tackled. Other facts about the disease can be established with regard to its point of onset, duration, symptoms, impact on other parts of the body and ultimate outcomes, ranging from minor discomforts to death.

Having established this knowledge a system of ideas has been formulated for intervening and hence preventing the disease or problem. Most crucially it means identifying the population which is at 'risk' of being exposed to the noxious or infectious agent via proximity or because of certain characteristics which make them more vulnerable. When applied to child abuse, then, it is assumed that if we can identify the characteristics associated with actual or potential abuse we will be able to identify and hence predict and prevent the problem. The crucial role for the researcher thus becomes one of establishing the factors or characteristics associated with actual or potential cases of child abuse.

Ideally the model suggests three stages whereby the disease can be prevented. Primary prevention refers to attempts to eliminate the noxious or infectious agent at its source, either through changes to its habitat or immunization which makes the body invulnerable to it. In effect it aims to stop the disease from ever occurring. Secondary prevention attempts to curtail the spread of the disease and interrupt its course. It aims to detect problems, perhaps by screening, as early as possible and then to treat or cure them. Finally, tertiary prevention aims to reduce the duration and severity of the disease which is established. It aims to minimize its impact and subsequently treat and cure it.

When it then comes to assessing the efficacy of preventive interventions, the goals of the model are not only clear but open to evaluation. There are two key measures: (1) the incidence rate (the number of *new* cases over a given period, usually a year) and (2) the prevalence rate (the number of *cases/persons affected* in the population *at a particular moment in time*). The effectiveness of prevention can thus be assessed by measuring the incidence or the prevalence. If primary prevention is successful the number of new cases (the incidence) should reduce, while if secondary or tertiary prevention is successful then the prevalence rate should reduce.

How far does the phenomenon of child abuse approximate to this model? Is there agreement amongst researchers about the nature of child abuse and how it can be defined? What are the characteristics or factors that have been associated with child abuse whereby it can be identified? How far can it be predicted, prevented and treated?

Definitional clarity, incidence and prevalence

Clearly an unambiguous definition of what constitutes child abuse is fundamental for the efficacy and utility of the model described above. However, the definition of what constitutes abuse varies amongst professional groups; across cultural, ethnic and religious groups; and by geographical location (Giovannoni and Beccera, 1979; Gelles, 1982; Starr, 1982; Valentine *et al.*, 1984).

There is no standardized definition of child abuse that has been developed by researchers and accepted by welfare professionals. More particularly, the definitional boundaries of the problem have broadened. The 'battered child syndrome' first discovered by Henry Kempe in 1962 referred to a clinical condition in young children, invariably under three, who had received serious physical abuse, usually from a parent, and was identified by the association of subdural haematoma (a pooling of blood around the skull) together with evidence of broken or healing long bones (Kempe *et al.*, 1962). By 1976, however, Henry Kempe and his colleagues had abandoned the concept of the 'battered child syndrome' in favour of a more all-inclusive term, 'child abuse and neglect', which referred to 'the permanent adverse effects on the developmental process and the child's emotional well-being' (Helfer and Kempe, 1976, Introduction).

As Robert Dingwall (1989) has argued, the definition of the problem has undergone considerable 'diagnostic inflation' and the growth of research 'reflects the transformation of the original concerns to embrace virtually any problem which may have an adverse impact on a child and can possibly be attributed to some act of commission or omission by an adult'.

He quotes a number of examples in illustration, which include the administration of cannabis by teenage babysitters (Schwartz *et al.*, 1986), the keeping of household pets where a child has asthma (Franklin and Kahn, 1987) child labour in Nigeria (Asogwa, 1986) and the mistaken diagnoses of abuse seen in themselves as a form of abuse (Kirschner and Stein, 1985). What this broadening and wide variation demonstrates is that over the past 30 years the issue of child abuse has become symbolically and politically very powerful (Parton, 1985; Nelson, 1986) in arguments about the welfare state and the family. As a consequence, 'Scientific research is not a neutral activity: child abuse was launched as a public issue out of a variety of private interests and its subsequent development has continued to reflect those and other interests' (Dingwall, 1989).

This lack of definition is the most telling indicator that research in the area of child abuse is at a very rudimentary level. Clearly without a standardized definition research findings can be misleading and invariably confusing because they are referring to very different phenomena. Nowhere is this more in evidence than in the area of sexual abuse.

The Cleveland Inquiry (Secretary of State for Social Services, 1988) noted that: 'It has been impossible from the evidence provided to the Inquiry to arrive at any consensus or to obtain any reliable figures of the general prevalence of sexual abuse of children in the country or in Clevelend' (p. 4) and later comments that: 'We are strongly of the opinion that great caution should be exercised at the present time in accepting percentages as to the prevalence and incidence of sexual abuse. We received from published articles and oral evidence figures of 5%, 10% and upwards. Such figures depend on what is meant by sexual abuse' (p. 5).

These comments were in part reflecting a recent review of eight research studies on the frequency of childhood sexual abuse in the UK, published in *Health Trends* (Markowe, 1988). The prevalence of sexual abuse in the studies varies from 3 per cent (BBC, 1986) to 90 per cent (BBC, 1987). A major reason why there was such variation was that the studies used quite different case definitions of sexual abuse, many of which included a number of elements. For example, the often quoted MORI survey (Baker and Duncan, 1985) considered:

> A child (anyone under 16 years) is sexually abused when another person, who is sexually mature, involves the child in any activity which the other person expects to lead to their sexual arousal. This might involve intercourse, touching, exposure of the sexual organs, showing pornographic material or talking about sexual things in an erotic way. (p. 458)

The interviews with a nationally representative sample of adults about their childhood yielded a figure of 10 per cent who reported being sexually abused. Of these, 51 per cent of the experiences reported as abusive involved no physical contact, 44 per cent involved physical contact but not sexual intercourse and 5 per cent reported full sexual intercourse. What we should note from this is that the 10 per cent prevalence figure, which received considerable publicity during the Cleveland scandal and subsequently, includes a wide range of abuse apart from sexual intercourse. A number of commentators have argued that these and other abuses are just as significant in terms of the experience of and damage perpetrated upon the victim (Macleod and Saraga, 1988). What is important, however, is that when statistics on incidence and prevalence enter the public and professional domains we should be clear exactly what behaviour is being referred to and what is included in the operational definition of abuse.

The primary point I am demonstrating here, however, is that the wide variation reported in research concerning the incidence and prevalence of childhood sexual abuse in part reflects the very different definitions of the problem used (Wyatt and Peters, 1986). No definition is inherently and necessarily 'correct', it depends on the reasons and purposes for which it is being used. The *Health Trends* review also noted that:

> Figures for the frequency of CSA [child sexual abuse] are often quoted out of the context of the study from which they are derived. This can be very misleading, either because the study was inherently faulty – in design, performance or analysis – or because, though a valid study, the results were not suitable for generalization. (Markowe, 1988, p. 2)

La Fontaine (1988, p. 3) has also shown that while the British surveys she reviewed all used sample designs of the whole population 'they suffered from serious limitations [and] . . . there is evidence that the methods of obtaining information influence the reporting rate'. She feels they might underestimate the prevalence and notes that in the American study by Russell (1986), which was particularly careful in choosing and training interviewers, the prevalence rate uncovered, for intrafamilial and extrafamilial sexual abuse was 58 per cent when non-contact abuse was included and 38 per cent when it was excluded.

While these issues of definition, incidence and prevalence are sharply demonstrated in relation to recent research and debate about sexual abuse, they pervade the whole area of child abuse. As a consequence they pose real problems to the policy maker, practitioner and manager, who are expected to respond to a problem the magnitude and significance of which are open to wide and sometimes conflicting interpretations.

Brian Roycroft, President of the Association of Directors of Social Services in 1988, in answer to the question 'What is the incidence of child abuse and child sexual abuse?' in his evidence to the Cleveland Inquiry, reported that:

> We don't know! There are no firm statistics available at either national or local level to determine the incidence of child abuse. Such statistics as are kept by some national organizations are suspect and local agencies keep

> statistics only to satisfy their own particular needs. (Association of Directors of Social Services, 1987, p. 5)

He went on to say, however, that his association undertook a survey in July 1987 of 100 local authorities and found an increase in child abuse registrations of 22 per cent for the country over the previous year, with the most significant increases in child sexual abuse. He also demonstrated an increase in the number of related referrals and investigations. Similar changes have been noted by the NSPCC (Creighton, 1987). However, both organizations consider these increases are more likely to reflect growing public awareness and improved detection rather than 'an actual increase in the incidence of abuse' (Association of Directors of Social Services, 1987, p. 6). They are of most use in monitoring the investigative and administrative workloads of the different agencies together with giving some insight into the agencies' changing priorities and interventions with children and families.

Factors associated with child abuse

However, this issue of the way the definition of abuse is operationalized for research is not simply of significance for debates about incidence and prevalence, it also crucially impinges on the characteristics and factors associated with abuse. These in turn have implications for attempts to predict and prevent the problem and particularly which families and sections of the population are seen as 'high risk'.

Central to the concept of prevention in the public health model is the idea of cause. In the case of acute infectious diseases, attempts are made to isolate a single identifiable organism. How has such an approach been operationalized in child abuse research and how appropriate is it? Essentially the approach has been to try and identify the factors or characteristics that are associated with cases or situations of abuse, to assume that these are qualitatively different from the rest of the population and finally to hypothesize that these factors or characteristics in some way relate to the basic cause(s) of the problem. As a consequence these factors or characteristics should direct attempts to identify and predict, and hence prevent.

The first difficulty is, as we have seen, that the term 'child abuse' covers a range of behaviours and problems, so that a search for a single or even a cluster of 'causes' is likely to be in vain.

The vast majority of research in the 1960s in America and the 1970s in Britain was based on relatively small-scale, retrospective clinical studies of cases that had come to the attention of health and welfare professionals. Essentially, the cases and their history were studied to establish what factors or characteristics they had in common. They suffered from two fundamental problems. First, they used variable and often vague definitions of abuse, so that in many cases it was not clear that they were dealing with established cases of abuse. Invariably the cases studied had been referred for a variety of concerns and worries about the children but there was no unequivocal evidence that the children were abused – according to any definition. Secondly, such studies rarely used any matched control groups. As a consequence we have no evidence to suggest that the factors identified as associated with abuse were in any way specific to this group (Spinetta and Rigler, 1972). They may simply have reflected the population from which they were drawn. In 1978 Allan concluded her survey of such research by writing:

> The quality of research in the area of child abuse still leaves much to be desired. There has been little attempt to review previous research with a view to formulating and testing specific hypotheses . . . frequently studies seem to start and finish with relatively untested common sense assumptions. Much of our existing knowledge has been gathered from descriptive studies which lack controls and proper sampling procedures. This has enabled authors to make claims and counter claims about the importance of different variables in the absence of any sustained efforts to discover which are directly and which are artefactually related to abuse. (Allan, 1978, p. 59)

As a result different research came up with different findings so that the policy maker and practitioner ended up with long lists of poorly defined and sometimes contradictory characteristics.

More recently studies have attempted to refine their research methodologies so that reviews of this research are much clearer about what we can claim to know and not know about abuse and in particular that it is a much more complex problem than was first thought. However, much of this literature and research is American. Recent British exceptions are Birchall (1989) and Dingwall (1989).

It is now suggested that it is much more appropriate to see child abuse as a result of multiple interacting factors, including the parents' and children's psychological traits, the family's place in the larger social and economic structure, and the balance of external supports and stresses, both interpersonal and material. The role of the different health and welfare professionals is also now seen as crucial in this process. Not only will the balance of factors vary depending on the severity and type of abuse being analysed, but there appears to be no uniformity in the associations found between sets of factors/characteristics and different types of abuse. It is also now recognized that even where there may be some correlation between certain factors and certain forms of abuse, it is inappropriate to assume that the one causes the other; both may be linked to a third but underlying set of structures and mechanisms.

For example, early marriage has been noted as being associated with particular forms of abuse and neglect. Yet early marriage itself reflects particular class and gender divisions in society which in themselves limit people's, particularly women's, life chances. As a result both abuse and early marriage may be associated with factors which are not readily observable. Similarly, the fact that mothers may be associated with certain types of abuse may reflect the position of women within the family and the wider society more generally (Parton, C., 1989).

So while we may now know something about who is more likely to abuse and who is more likely to be a victim, we do not know why, when, how often and with what degree of certainty, abuse will take place, nor what the consequences will be for the child.

When looking at the factors associated with abuse it is, however, important to differentiate 'what we know' about physical abuse and neglect from sexual abuse. In some respects all families are at risk since being a child and being a parent is never easy.

As far as physical abuse and neglect is concerned, a variety of factors may put a family at risk. Cohn summarizes these factors as follows:

> Larger families, families with closely spaced children, families with young children, and single-parent families are at greater risk. Also vulnerable are families under great stress, which may result from financial difficulties, marital discord, social isolation, or poor health. Parents' child management and social skills, as well as their self-esteem, help to define who is at risk. Certain characteristics or traits of the child, including low birth-weight, prematurity, illness in infancy, and impediments to attachment and bonding may also be factors. (Cohn, 1983a, p. 171)

However, parallel research specifically concerned with sexual abuse has identified risk factors which, while similar in some respects, also include important differences. David Finkelhor (Finkelhor, 1986; Finkelhor and Baron, 1986) has reviewed a variety of American surveys of adults in order to assess the information provided about the relative risk of people from different backgrounds experiencing sexual abuse during childhood. Significantly the surveys were consistent in failing to find differences in rates according to social class or race. This is an important difference as physical abuse and neglect do seem to be associated with social, material and environmental stress and hence seem to be related to social class.

However, in Finkelhor's review, several factors emerged as being consistently associated with higher risk of sexual abuse: when a child lives without one of the biological parents; when the mother is unavailable to the child either as a result of employment outside the home or disability and illness; when a child reports that the parents' marriage is unhappy or conflictual; when the child reports having a poor relationship with the parents or being subject to extremely punitive discipline or child abuse; when the child reports having a step-father. While girls are at higher risk than boys, increasingly research is suggesting more boys experience sexual abuse than was at first thought. Pre-adolescents appear to be more at risk than either younger or older children. Girls with few friends in childhood report more abuse, though this may be an effect of abuse and not a risk factor. Perpetrators are almost exclusively male, though a few women are reported, particularly in retrospective studies. La Fontaine (1988) has identified similar factors in the pattern of sexual abuse in British surveys.

An important element that emerges is that discussions and explanations of physical abuse and neglect may be seen most productively as a problem relating to parenting, which in turn needs to be located in an understanding of social class and the gendered divisions of child care, while sexual abuse, to a much greater extent, needs to be understood in relation to male power and masculine socialization.

Identification and prediction: in search of the holy grail

In the light of this current state of knowledge of the various factors associated with abuse, how far is it, in fact, possible to predict abuse? As I will suggest, there are certain fundamental problems. For while the associated risk factors may help in informing the more general preventive strategies and decisions about resource allocation, because child abuse is such a complex problem we have not developed sufficient understanding for successful prediction. At the moment we are unable to predict with accuracy who will or will not abuse. In particular such attempts at prediction are bedevilled by what Dingwall (1989) calls firstly the 'definitional fallacy' and secondly 'the statistical fallacy'.

First, the definitional fallacy. Essentially this relates to the previous discussion on the failure by researchers, and for that matter policy makers and practitioners, to operationalize a clear and widely agreed definition of what constitutes abuse. As suggested this arises in major part because the term has proved symbolically powerful in drawing attention to a series of adult–child issues and phenomena and legitimating them as a social problem. However, the way the problem has been constructed and made the subject of public, political and research concern is influenced by a whole variety of different values and political interests (Parton, N., 1985, 1989). Essentially child abuse is a moral category which is open to wide and differing interpretations. Research has invariably failed to recognize this and as a consequence failed to approach its task in an explicitly neutral and scientific way, i.e. to account for the nature and incidence of particular forms of adult/child interactions and their consequences. It is a subsequent and primarily political/moral question as to which of these should then constitute child abuse.

Perhaps ironically, more general social scientific studies of children, child care and family life have rarely been drawn upon to inform and clarify what we know as a basis for discussions of child abuse. For example, during the 1970s the Department of Health and Social Security and the Social Science Research Council funded a number of studies concerned with the nature, causes and outcomes of deprivation and disadvantage in families. This initiative arose out of the then Secretary of State Sir Keith Joseph's interest in the 'cycle of deprivation' (for a comprehensive review see

Brown and Madge, 1982). From these studies an attempt was then made to identify 'families in difficulty'. What is apparent is that the risk factors identified run parallel to and are in many respects very similar to those already noted in relation to child abuse.

> Whether problems stem from personal shortcomings, from the structure of society or from some combination of these two broad influences, the focus must be on the family and on signs that something is likely to be 'wrong'. Certain areas of family functioning are particularly useful for predictions of this kind. These features of family life – which it should be re-emphasized are indicators of, rather than the reasons for, problems – include the age and maturity of the parents, burdens carried by a family, consistency and change in the lives of children, dynamics and support within the family, and the experiences and characteristics of individual family members. (Madge, 1983, p. 201)

While Madge does not claim this guide is infallible nor that the list is complete, she does argue that these items in 'an alphabet of risk' both singly and cumulatively help to establish the probability that individual families will be under stress. It is claimed as a major contribution to identifying and predicting 'families in difficulty'. Clearly, however, the moral, legal, policy and practice connotations of 'families in difficulty' are qualitatively different from those of child abuse. The question that this begs is simply then, what are predictive studies claiming to predict? It clearly has crucial implications for the way research studies are understood, perceived and used.

The statistical fallacy, while related, draws attention to another problem. In recent years there has been considerable interest in assessing the general feasibility of predicting future violence and dangerousness in individuals and families (see Parton and Parton, 1989; Parton and Small, 1989). However, it is now recognized that research on such prediction falls down in terms of both its reliability and its validity. Whatever method of screening is used, prediction rates rise no higher than two wrong judgements for every right judgement. Empirical support for the prediction of future violence is very small.

This arises from the statistical problems of 'false negatives' and 'false positives'. If the rate of violence amongst families in the population is relatively low, and we have noted that the incidence of sexual abuse may be around 10 per cent while the incidence of serious physical abuse may be 3–4 per cent (Straus *et al.*, 1980) (see note 1 on page 75), and the accuracy of the prediction technique is relatively weak, there is considerable potential for wrongly identifying some who will never abuse (false positive) and missing others who will abuse (false negative). If the criterion to predict abuse is 80 per cent accurate (and no device available has such a high level of accuracy) and if the rate of abuse in the population is 10 in a 100, then if 1000 people/families are screened, 80 out of the 100 will be correctly identified while 20 will be missed (false negative). However, we will also incorrectly identify 20 per cent, or 200 of the original 1000 screened. Thus for every 80 correctly predicted we will have 20 false negatives and 200 false positives.

Research carried out in Bradford during 1979 provides a useful illustration (Lealman *et al.*, 1983). A checklist of predictors was applied to the maternity notes of all non-Asian women who had delivered a child under consultant care when they were discharged from the maternity unit. Of the 2802 maternity case-notes screened, 511 families (18 per cent) were predicted as being 'at risk'. Subsequently two-thirds of all the recognized abuse in their population was found to occur in the 18 per cent predicted high risk group – 19 out of the total of 28 recognized cases. The net result is that while only nine cases were missed (false negative), 492 were included in the original high risk group but did not subsequently abuse (false positive).

These problems of prediction related to the definitional fallacy and the statistical fallacy are very evident in the Beckford Report, which was so critical of social workers' lack of knowledge and use of predictive research. While the report argues that it is crucial that social workers identify 'high risk', the report comments that 'We do not define "high risk", mainly because we think that it is not susceptible of definition' (London Borough of Brent, 1985, p. 288). The report also draws upon research presented to it by Professor Cyril Greenland (reported in full in Greenland, 1987) and comments as follows:

> The proportion of 'high risk' cases out of all proved cases of persistent child abuse will be small, and the task of identifying may not be easy. But the attempt to isolate such cases from the majority of child abuse cases must always be made. To the question, can 'high risk' situations be identified in advance, Professor Greenland told us that he could give an answer, 'a cautious yes – in some cases'. He went on to say that it seemed prudent to classify all non-accidental injuries to young children as 'high risk' cases, since 80% of all children unlawfully killed by their parents had been previously abused. (p. 288)

Thus not only are we not given a definition but we are not given any clue as to which of all the cases that come to social worker's notice are *not* high risk. By definition they are all high risk and there is thus no significance to the issue of false positives. The Beckford Report completely fails to address the problems arising from both the definitional and the statistical fallacies.

In contrast, however, the Cleveland Report is particularly sensitive to such issues in relation to sexual abuse and spends considerable time trying to weigh the often conflicting evidence it received on identification and assessment, particularly in terms of the reflex anal dilatation test. It is particularly concerned that assessments should not falsely accuse parents and families on the basis of unproven diagnostic and predictive techniques. For example: 'We are satisfied from the evidence that the consensus is that the sign of anal dilatation is abnormal and suspicious and requires further investigation. *It is not in itself evidence of anal abuse.*' (p. 193, my emphasis.)

And more generally:

> It was accepted that anal abuse may cause a range of signs, from surface skin damage, fissures, defects of anal verge, to severe lacerations, but that *in our present state of knowledge, none of these in themselves, or in various clusters, establish with reasonable certainty that anal abuse has occurred.* We are, or may be, open to alternative explanations. (p. 189, my emphasis.)

Finally, in commenting on the nature of the social work procedures and practice adopted following the medical diagnosis of sexual abuse, the report explicitly comments that: 'it requires cautious measured intervention which will allow *the risks of a false positive finding to be balanced against those of a false negative*' (p. 85, my emphasis).

The report here identifies a crucial issue. We do not have the predictive tools to identify correctly all actual and potential cases of abuse – nor are we likely to have them. What, therefore, is the balance to be struck between missing some (false negative) and falsely accusing others (false positive)? For efforts to keep false negatives to a minimum will increase the likelihood of false positives, while attempts to reduce false positives will increase the likelihood of tragedies in false negatives. While research can clarify such issues, how they are resolved is essentially a political and ethical question – in the same way as how child abuse is itself defined is essentially a political and ethical question.

What do we know about prevention?

Being at risk of abuse, then, does not lead to a simple intervention strategy. While it is now widely accepted that an effective solution should rely in major part on a co-ordinated interagency and interprofessional effort (DHSS, 1988), the possibilities range from those that provide immediate relief (tertiary prevention) to long-term strategies designed to change attitudes, values, behaviour and circumstances (primary prevention). The relative merits of different preventive measures depend both on political considerations about what is acceptable to society and on technical considerations about the effectiveness of different approaches. Gough, Taylor and Boddy (1987), Boddy (1986) and Cohn (1983a) have reviewed available research on this technical question of the efficacy of different preventive programmes. Such prevention includes: educational approaches concerned mainly with child sexual abuse; programmes targeted at adults and the community which focus on developing appropriate child care and thus lessening the possibility of neglect, emotional abuse, and potential loss of parental control resulting in over-chastisement; services using volunteers and parent aides rather than professionally trained staff; antenatal and postnatal services; and finally other programmes aimed at children older than infants.

The studies reviewed by Gough, Taylor and Boddy (1987) varied from demonstration projects to narrow experimental designs, with many studies falling in between and containing aspects of both models. They conclude:

> However, the various limitations of both models results in there being few clear conclusions from the research. It is not that the interventions were no good. The studies did provide evidence that the services could have useful effects on families that might be expected to reduce the risk of child abuse. The problem is that the research does not allow us to distinguish the relative usefulness of the different interventions or their component parts. (p. 134)

They also suggest, following Gelles and Cornell (1985), that child abuse is not a manifestation of something qualitatively different, or resulting from the fundamentally abnormal, but that parents and families are simply experiencing the same problems as others but to a greater *degree*. They thus suggest that the services offered to non-routine families with problems in child care generally may be highly pertinent to child abuse prevention.

Such a conclusion is very similar to that outlined by Cohn (1983a). She argues that while the research provides clues about the types of preventive programmes that may be of help we also know what a complex problem child abuse is:

> Families have many needs and those needs change at different stages of the family life cycle. It is doubtful that any one of the described prevention programs – in isolation – will effectively prevent abuse. And, it is doubtful that any of the described prevention programs, unless well-integrated into the fabric, the values, and the mores of a given community, and indeed neighbourhood, will effectively prevent abuse. In order for most families to benefit from the types of prevention activities described, they probably need to be made available to all families on a voluntary basis, and they probably need to be relatively non-obtrusive and in essence, common. (Cohn, 1983a, p. 181)

The implication seems clear. To have the best chance of preventing the more serious family and child care problems, what we might call child abuse, the best chance of success is to improve and develop universal, non-stigmatizing services which are integrated into the mainstream of social provision for all children.

What do we know about treatment?

Perhaps the final element of the public health model which we need to consider is what evidence there is available concerning tertiary prevention or treatment, i.e. the efficacy of interventions specifically designed to reduce the likelihood of further abuse once child abuse has occurred. What do we know about the relative effectiveness of different treatment strategies to improve the functioning of individuals and families once abuse has been perpetrated? Soon after the discovery of the 'battered baby syndrome' in the 1960s there seemed considerable optimism amongst health and welfare professionals that such efforts would be effective. What has the evidence of the last 25 years to tell us?

Since 1974 the US federal government has funded four major multi-year evaluation studies to determine the relative effectiveness of different approaches to the treatment of child abuse and neglect (Cohn, 1983b; Cohn and Daro, 1987). A total of 89 different demonstration treatment programmes were studied, and data on 3253 families experiencing difficulties with abuse and neglect were gathered. In addition to descriptive data, which provides greater clarity on how to differentiate among families experiencing a variety of types of abuse when providing the treatment, the studies also provide a better understanding of how to deliver such services to both the adults and the children who have suffered. The studies document treatments which improve clients' functioning, notably lay counselling and group services, including Parents Anonymous, group therapy and parent education classes, and suggest greater success with clients experiencing difficulty with sexual abuse than other forms of abuse. On balance the findings suggest that successful treatment requires a comprehensive package of services which address both the interpersonal and concrete needs of all family members. However, the studies also indicate a note of caution:

> Treatment efforts in general are not very successful. Child abuse and neglect continue despite early, thoughtful, and often costly intervention. Treatment programs have been relatively ineffective in initially halting abusive and neglectful behaviour or in reducing the future likelihood of maltreatment in the most severe cases of physical abuse, chronic neglect and emotional maltreatment. One-third or more of the parents served by these intensive demonstration efforts maltreated their children while in treatment, and over one-half of the families served continued to be judged by staff as likely to mistreat their children following termination. Whether one views this level of success as notable or disappointing is largely a function of personal perspective and professional choice. (Cohn and Daro, 1987, p. 440)

Cohn and Daro conclude by suggesting that perhaps putting all resources into intervention after the fact does not make sense and that intervention should take place at a much earlier preventive stage. Having said this, however, we have noted earlier the difficulties inherent in trying to mount preventive strategies.

More specifically, certain studies have attempted to evaluate treatment strategies that are concerned with sexual abuse. Again, however, both the development of such services and evaluations of their effectiveness are far more advanced in America. Such studies have recommended the development of multi-model interventions that incorporate individual, dyadic or group, and family components (Dixen and Jenkins, 1981; Summit, 1985). Where applicable, the incorporation of offender treatment and court intervention services has also been encouraged (Forseth and Brown, 1981; Woodcraft, 1988).

However, the absence of empirical evidence regarding the outcome and effectiveness of treatment (Mrazek, 1983) together with various methodological limitations in the design and analysis of selected programmes should again not be overlooked (Conte, 1984; Finkelhor, 1986). Kolko (1987) notes that: 'Many programs do not incorporate standardized instruments to assess those variables purported to change following treatment, and only rarely include needed control or comparison groups and statistical analyses to evaluate program impact' (p. 313).

With the exception of a few large-scale programmes (Giaretto, 1982; Sgroi, 1982) and a single case study (Kolko, 1986), little is known about the suggested success of specific approaches. At present no controlled group study has been reported with child victims and their families and, even when attempts have been made to evaluate interventions, findings suggest that the treatment of abusive parents has only been marginally effective. However, it has also been suggested (Kolko, 1987) that such programmes are severely limited by the lack of funding and the restricted availability of therapeutic services. Such a situation is even more evident in Britain.

Conclusions: the relationship between child abuse and child care in research, policy and practice

From what I have suggested so far we should not be surprised that a recent authoritative and comprehensive review of child abuse research commented that:

> Despite the considerable volumes of research conducted in the field of child abuse in the last 20 years, there are still large gaps in our knowledge concerning the phenomenon. In particular, disagreement exists as to how child abuse is best defined, and practitioners are confused concerning the best ways of preventing non-accidental injury and dealing with it once it is identified. (Graham *et al.*, 1985, p. 1216)

As we have seen, research itself, like policy and practice, has increasingly become surrounded by controversy over questions of definition and the most appropriate form that approaches and interventions should take. As a consequence the research review identifies as a central issue for investigation: 'the variety of human interactions in which children are harmed in some way (physical, emotional, sexual), the manner in which these investigations are perceived, and the behaviour which such interactions elicit in both professional and lay people' (Graham *et al.*, 1985, p. 1218).

Increasingly it has been recognized that there is a need to focus explicitly on the nature and form that child abuse or child protection interventions take in everyday practice, and in the process to try and identify models of good practice which can then be developed in the future.

At present, however, there is only limited British research available on such issues and much looks at only parts of the process. Parker, Casburn and Turnbull (1981) have looked at court decision making and Lawson (1980) at social services departments. The most comprehensive research has been that carried out by Dingwall, Eekelaar and Murray (1983), based on participant observation in social services departments, NHS child health services and casualty departments, and juvenile courts. They concluded that while different professionals and agencies use quite different definitions of the problem, on the whole the system operates according to a 'rule of optimism' whereby, wherever possible, the most favourable interpretation of family, particularly parental, circumstances is made and hence situations of actual and potential abuse are kept to a minimum. The location of the fieldwork meant that little comment could be made in relation to differences which might arise from work in an inner-city area with a significant ethnic minority population. Perhaps most crucially, particularly in the light of the Cleveland Inquiry (Secretary of State for Social Services, 1988), the research was only concerned with analysing and understanding the experiences of the professionals – it was not concerned with the parallel issues related to the parents and children.

Recently, however, two small-scale studies have been completed which take on board the perceptions and experiences of parents who have been on the receiving end of child protection interventions. Celia Brown's (1986) study was carried out in two districts of Avon County; 23 parents were interviewed and a further two completed questionnaires. The interviews were carried out some time after the abuse had been established, so that while all had been on the child abuse register only half were still on the register when interviewed. The cases had either been closed or the closure was in sight when the interviews took place. The research was therefore concerned with parents' retrospective impressions and reflections, and not put alongside similar commentaries from social workers or children. Even so, some important findings were forthcoming. For example, the major criticism which parents made of social workers concerned their poor communications, lack of openness and honesty, failure to value parents' strengths and to treat them as equals, and a failure to involve parents in decisions. Some parents found social work visits made them fearful and anxious and their self-esteem was reduced.

Some related findings are evident in Corby's work (1987a; also 1987b and Corby and Mills, 1986). This study took place between 1981 and 1985 in a large northern, metropolitan social services department. Most of the data came from observing 55 case conferences, interviews with the social workers in 25 of the cases together with an analysis of case records. Interviews also took place with parents in 10 of the 25 cases selected for follow-up. The study looked at cases during the first six months after the initial case conference.

Not surprisingly, all the parents found the experience of being investigated traumatic and distressing. While a few felt that the social workers were helpful and supportive an equal number considered them to be patronizing and authoritarian. Nearly all felt their experience at the hospitals, to which they were initially referred, to be stigmatizing and degrading. The small number who had contact with the police experienced considerable distress. The most worrying aspect of all, for Corby, however, was that many parents felt they were kept in the dark about what was happening, so that while there were exceptions, and in some cases social workers had gone to great lengths to explain the system and the likely outcomes, in two cases the parents were not aware until later in the process that they and their children were the subjects of child abuse investigations.

An interesting finding in the light of my previous discussion about the efficacy of the identification and diagnosis of abuse was that in only two of the 25 families selected for follow-up was abuse admitted. Four were thought not to have abused their children, but still to be in need of social work intervention, while 16 were considered to have abused their children but there was no unequivocal evidence that they had done so. Issues concerning denial and/or the differential interpretations of events and their implications were evident throughout the study.

The social workers experienced the child abuse system in a variety of ways. Some accepted it without comment and others were positive about the support provided by case conferences, procedures and registers in dealing with complex and difficult cases. Others were critical. Many commented that the concentration on child abuse skewed their professional response to the needs of children and families more generally:

> Implicit in these views was the fact that child abuse was considered to be only one of a range of problems that many families who come under the system's microscope were experiencing, and that there was a need to respond to all the problems including child abuse, rather than of necessity giving it priority. (Corby, 1987a, p. 129)

Finally, one study (McGloin and Turnbull, 1986; 1987a; 1987b) has focused on the much more restricted issue of the effects of parental participation at child abuse review case conferences. Its overall conclusion was that such a policy increased the mutual respect and understanding of social workers and parents and contributed to improving the thinking, discussion and decision making. However, such a policy could not be seen in isolation as it had implications for practice more generally, including procedures and training.

None of these studies explicitly attempted to identify and evaluate, from the perspective of social workers or parents, when, why and how some types of intervention had beneficial outcomes and others did not.

It is perhaps particularly ironic that as yet we have no studies which have attempted to evaluate interventions from the point of view of the children themselves. It is to be hoped that in the light of the Cleveland Report's comment that 'the child is a person and not an object of concern'

(Secretary of State for Social Services, 1988, p. 245) that urgent efforts will be made to ensure that the child's views and perceptions of practice are articulated via sensitively designed research.

What is important is that the studies outlined in this section have attempted to gain an insight into day-to-day practice. In some respects their concerns run parallel to the much more extensive studies recently carried out on social work decisions in child care more generally and which have been extensively referred to elsewhere in this volume (summarized in DHSS, 1986). A number of these latter studies explicitly included data derived from the experience of parents as well as social workers (Packman *et al.*, 1986; Millham *et al.*, 1986) and one study also included interviews with children (Fisher *et al.*, 1986). In many respects the issues identified seem similar to those identified by Brown and Corby in that: the differing perspectives of parents and social workers may go unrecognized; parents of children may feel pushed aside and disillusioned; and when parents felt that their problems and wishes were understood they valued this highly. The implication seems quite clear – the models of good practice developed in more general child care are equally applicable to child abuse and child protection work.

If, as I have tried to demonstrate, the problem of child abuse is itself one dimension or label given to the way problems between children and adults manifest themselves then this should be recognized in practice. Rather than seeing child abuse as an exceptional problem requiring an exceptional response, and hence a qualitatively different practice, we should see it as part of child care and hence child care practice.

At many points in this chapter we have noted the problems of trying to define child abuse, identifying the characteristics which separate the high risk from the rest and hence aid prediction, together with the problems of constructing preventive and treatment interventions which concentrate exclusively on child abuse. I am not arguing that children do not suffer at the hands of adults; clearly they do and again we have looked at the evidence concerning incidence and prevalence. What I am suggesting, however, is that we could gain considerably by recognizing in research, policy and practice that child abuse is centrally concerned with debates about the way we bring up children and is hence centrally concerned about child care. In the process the message for practitioners seems to be that child abuse and child protection practice should be located in child care practice. Thus the values, principles and skills which inform the latter should also inform the former. In doing so the 'enlightenment' that can be gained from research in helping us develop good child care policy and practice should be just that which should inform good policy and practice for child abuse. In the process we should critically re-evaluate how we understand the relationship between research, policy and practice in child care and research, policy and practice in what we refer to as child abuse and child protection work. Such a re-evaluation requires a debate on issues of central importance for both the professionals and researchers involved.

Note

1 While their methodology has been subject to considerable criticism, the only serious attempt to measure the exposure of children to acts of *physical* violence causing serious injury in the home was that carried out in a survey by Straus, Gelles and Steinmetz (1980) in America. They concluded that 3.6 per cent of children, aged 3–17, living with two parents, suffered severe violence in 1975. Severe violence included: kicking, biting, hitting with a fist; beating up the other; threatening with a knife or gun; using a knife or gun. Using a slightly modifed methodology Gelles and Straus (1987) replicated the study in 1985. They concluded that, while there was essentially no change in the overall use of violence against children, the rate of severe violence had decreased by 47 per cent over the decade (see also Schene, 1987).

References

Allan, L. J. (1978) 'Child abuse: a critical review of the research and theory', in Martin, J. P. (ed) *Violence in the Family*, John Wiley.

Armstrong, D. (1983) *Political Anatomy of the Body: Medical Knowledge in Britain in the Twentieth Century*, Cambridge University Press.

Asogwa, S. E. (1986) 'Sociomedical aspects of child labor in Nigeria', *Journal of Occupational Medicine*, Vol. 28, pp. 46–8.

Association of Directors of Social Services (1987) 'Statement of Brian Roycroft, CBE, President of the Cleveland Inquiry', ADSS (unpublished).

Baker, A. W. and Duncan, S. P. (1985) 'Child sexual abuse: a study of prevalence in Great Britain', *Child Abuse and Neglect*, Vol. 9, pp. 457–67.

BBC (1986) 'Childwatch – overview results from 2,530 self-completion questionnaires', BBC Broadcasting Research (unpublished).

BBC (1987) 'Childwatch – national survey on child abuse', BBC press briefing, 9 July (unpublished).

Birchall, E. M. (1989) 'The frequency of child abuse – what do we really know?', in Stevenson, O. (ed) *Child Abuse: Public Policy and Professional Practice*, Wheatsheaf.

Boddy, A. (1986) 'Is child abuse preventable?', *Child Abuse Review*, Vol. 1, No. 3, Summer, pp. 17–21.

Brown, C. (1986) *Child Abuse Parents Speaking: Parents' Impressions of Social Workers and the Social Work Process*, Bristol, SAUS, Working Paper 63.

Brown, M. and Madge, N. (1982) *Despite the Welfare State: A Report on the SSRC/DHSS Programme of Research into Transmitted Deprivation*, Heinemann.

Cohn, A. H. (1983a) 'The prevention of child abuse: what do we know about what works?', in Leavitt, J. E. (ed) *Child Abuse and Neglect: Research and Innovation*, Martinus Nijhoff.

Cohn, A. H. (1983b) 'The treatment of child abuse: what do we know about what works?', in Leavitt, J. E. (ed) *Child Abuse and Neglect: Research and Innovation*, Martinus Nijhoff.

Cohn, A. H. and Daro, D. (1987) 'Is treatment too late? What ten years of evaluative research tell us', *Child Abuse and Neglect*, Vol. 11, pp. 433–42.

Conte, J. R. (1984) 'Progress in treating the sexual abuse of children', *Social Work*, Vol. 29, pp. 258–63.

Corby, B. and Mills, C. (1986) 'Child abuse: risks and resources', *British Journal of Social Work*, Vol. 16, No. 5, pp. 531–42.

Corby, B. (1987a) *Working with Child Abuse: Social Work Practice and the Child Abuse System*, Open University Press.

Corby, B. (1987b) 'Why ignoring the rights of parents in child abuse cases should be avoided', *Social Work Today*, Vol. 19, No. 13, 23 November, pp. 8–9.

Creighton, S. J. (1987) 'Child abuse in 1986', *Social Services Research*, Vol. 16, No. 3, pp. 1–7, Department of Social Administration, University of Birmingham.

Department of Health and Social Security (1982) *Child Abuse: A Study of Inquiry Reports*, HMSO.

Department of Health and Social Security (1986) *Social Work Decisions in Child Care: Recent Research Findings and their Implications*, HMSO.

Department of Health and Social Security (1988) *Working Together: A Guide for Inter-agency Co-operation for the Protection of Children*, HMSO.

Dingwall, R., Eekelaar, J. M. and Murray, T. (1983) *The Protection of Children: State Intervention and Family Life*, Basil Blackwell.

Dingwall, R. (1989) 'Some problems about predicting child abuse and neglect', in Stevenson, O. (ed) *Child Abuse: Public Policy and Professional Practice*, Wheatsheaf.

Dixen, J. and Jenkins, J. O. (1981) 'Incestuous child sexual abuse: a review of treatment strategies', *Clinical Psychological Review*, Vol. 1, pp. 211–22.

Finkelhor, D. (1986) *A Sourcebook on Child Sexual Abuse*, Sage.

Finkelhor, D. and Barron, L. (1986) 'Risk factors for child sexual abuse', *Journal of Interpersonal Violence*, Vol. 1, No. 1, pp. 43–71.

Fisher, M., Marsh, P. and Phillips, D. with Sainsbury, E. (1986) *In and Out of Care: The Experiences of Children, Parents and Social Workers*, Batsford.

Forseth, L. B. and Brown, A. (1981) 'A survey of intrafamilial sexual abuse treatment centers: implications of intervention', *Child Abuse and Neglect*, Vol. 5, pp. 177–86.

Franklin, W. and Kahn, R. E. (1987) 'Severe asthma due to household pets: a form of child abuse and neglect', *New England and Regional Allergy Proceedings*, Vol. 8, No. 4, pp. 259–61.

Frost, N. (1989) 'Official intervention and child protection: the relationship between state and family in contemporary Britain', in The Violence Against Children Study Group, *Taking Child Abuse Seriously: Contemporary Issues in Child Protection, Theory and Practice*, Unwin Hyman.

Gelles, R. J. (1982) 'Problems in defining and labelling child abuse', in Starr, R. H. (ed) *Child Abuse Prediction: Policy Implications*, Ballinger.

Gelles, R. J. and Cornell, C. P. (1985) *Intimate Violence in Families*, Sage.

Gelles, R. J. and Strauss, M. (1987) 'Is violence toward children increasing? A comparison of 1975 and 1985 national survey rates', *Journal of Interpersonal Violence*, Vol. 2, No. 2, pp. 212–22.

Giaretto, H. (1982) *Integrated Treatment of Child Sexual Abuse: A Treatment and Training Manual*, Science and Behaviour Books.

Giovannoni, J. M. (1982) 'Prevention of child abuse and neglect: research and policy issues', *Social Work Research and Abstracts*, Vol. 18, No. 3, pp. 23–31.

Giovannoni, J. M. and Becerra, R. M. (1979) *Defining Child Abuse*, Free Press.

Gough, D. A., Taylor, J. P. and Boddy, F. A. (1987) 'Child abuse interventions: a review of the research literature. Part B, Intervention studies: preventing abuse',

Report to DHSS, Social Paediatric and Obstetric Research Unit, University of Glasgow (unpublished).

Graham, P., Dingwall, R. and Wolkind, S. (1985) 'Research issues in child abuse', *Social Science and Medicine*, Vol. 21, No. 11, pp. 1216–28.

Greenland, C. (1987) *Preventing CAN Deaths: An International Study of Deaths due to Child Abuse and Neglect*, Tavistock.

Hallet, C. (1989) 'Child abuse inquiries', in Stevenson, O. (ed) *Child Abuse: Public Policy and Professional Practice*, Wheatsheaf.

Helfer, R. E. and Kempe, C. H. (eds) (1976) *Child Abuse and Neglect: The Family and the Community*, Ballinger.

Kempe, C. H., Silverman, F. N., Steele, B. F., Droegemueller, W. and Silver, H. K. (1962) 'The battered child syndrome', *Journal of the American Medical Association*, No. 181, pp. 17–24.

Kirschner, R. H. and Stein, R. J. (1985) 'The mistaken diagnosis of child abuse: a form of medical abuse', *American Journal of Diseases of Children*, Vol. 139, No. 9, pp. 873–5.

Kolko, D. J. (1986) 'Social-cognitive skills training with a sexually abused and abusive child psychiatric patient: training generalization and follow-up', *Journal of Family Violence*, Vol. 1, No. 2, pp. 149–66.

Kolko, D. J. (1987) 'Treatment of child sexual abuse: programs, progress and prospects', *Journal of Family Violence*, Vol. 2, No. 4, pp. 303–18.

La Fontaine, J. (1988) *Child Sexual Abuse: An ESRC Research Briefing*, ESRC.

Lawson, A. (1980) 'Taking the decision to remove the child from the family', *Journal of Social Welfare Law*, No. 3, pp. 141–63.

Lealman, G. T., Haigh, D., Phillips, J. M., Sloan, J. and Ord-Smith, C. (1983) 'Prediction and prevention of child abuse – an empty hope', *The Lancet*, No. 8339, 25 June, pp. 1423–4.

London Borough of Brent (1985) *A Child in Trust: The Report of the Panel of Inquiry into the Circumstances Surrounding the Death of Jasmine Beckford*, London Borough of Brent.

London Borough of Greenwich, (1987) *A Child in Mind: Protection of Children in a Responsible Society. Report of the Commission of Inquiry into the Circumstances Surrounding the Death of Kimberley Carlile*, London Borough of Greenwich.

London Borough of Lambeth (1987) *Whose Child? The Report of the Panel Appointed to Inquire into the Death of Tyra Henry*, London Borough of Lambeth.

Macleod, M. and Saranga, E. (1988) 'Challenging the orthodoxy: towards a feminist theory and practice', *Femininst Review*, No. 28, pp. 16–55.

Madge, N. (1983) 'Identifying families at risk', in Madge, N. (ed) *Families at Risk*, Heinemann.

Markowe, H. L. J. (1988) 'The frequency of childhood sexual abuse in the UK', *Health Trends*, Vol. 20, No. 1, pp. 2–6.

McGloin, P. and Turnbull, A. (1986) *Parent Participation in Child Abuse Review Conferences*, Directorate of Social Services, London Borough of Greenwich.

McGloin, P. and Turnbull, A. (1987a) 'Strengthening good practice by bringing in the parents', *Social Work Today*, Vol. 18, No. 46, 20 July, pp. 14–15.

McGloin, P. and Turnbull, A. (1987b) 'Child abuse reviews – the impact of the parents', *Social Work Today*, Vol. 19, No. 6, 5 October, pp. 16–17.

Millham, S., Bullock, R., Hosie, K. and Haak, M. (1986) *Children Lost in Care: The Family Contacts of Children in Care*, Gower.

Mrazek, P. B. (1983) 'Special problems in the treatment of child sexual abuse', in Mrazek P. B. and Kempe, C. H. (eds) *Sexually Abused Children and their Families*, Pergamon Press.

Nelson, B. J. (1986) *Making an Issue of Child Abuse: Political Agenda Setting for Social Problems*, University of Chicago Press.

Packman, J. with Randall, J. and Jacques, N. (1986) *Who Needs Care? Social Work Decisions About Children*, Basil Blackwell.

Parker, H., Casburn, M. and Turnbull, D. (1981) *Receiving Juvenile Justice*, Basil Blackwell.

Parton, C. (1989) 'Women, gender oppression and child abuse', in The Violence Against Children Study Group, *Taking Child Abuse Seriously: Contemporary Issues in Child Protection Theory and Practice*, Unwin Hyman.

Parton, N. (1985) *The Politics of Child Abuse*, Macmillan.

Parton, N. (1989) 'Taking child abuse seriously', in The Violence Against Children Study Group, *Taking Child Abuse Seriously: Contemporary Issues in Child Protection Theory and Practice*, Unwin Hyman.

Parton, N. and Parton, C. (1989) 'Child protection, the law and dangerousness', in Stevenson, O. (ed) *Child Abuse: Public Policy and Professional Practice*, Wheatsheaf.

Parton, N. and Small, N. (1989) 'Violence, social work and the emergence of dangerousness', in Langan, M. and Lee, P. (eds) *Social Work in Recession – a Radical Contribution*, Unwin Hyman.

Russell, D. E. H. (1986) *The Secret Trauma: Incest in the Lives of Girls and Women*, Basic Books.

Schene, P. (1987) 'Is child abuse decreasing?', *Journal of Interpersonal Violence*, Vol. 2, No. 2, pp. 225–7.

Schwartz, R. H., Pearcy, P. and Mistretta, D. (1986) 'Intoxication of young children with marijuana: a form of amusement for "pot-smoking" teenage girls', *American Journal of the Disease of Children*, Vol. 40, p. 326.

Secretary of State for Social Services (1988) *Report of the Inquiry into Child Abuse in Cleveland 1987*, HMSO.

Sgroi, S. M. (1982) 'Family treatment', in Sgroi, S. M. (ed) *Handbook of Clinical Intervention in Child Sexual Abuse*, Lexington Books.

Spinetta, J. J. and Rigler, D. (1972) 'The child abusing parent: a psychological review', *Psychological Bulletin*, Vol. 77, No. 4, pp. 296–304.

Starr, R. (ed) (1982) *Child Abuse Prediction: Policy Implications*, Ballinger.

Straus, M. A., Gelles, R. J. and Steinmetz, S. K. (1980) *Behind Closed Doors: Violence in the American Family*, Anchor/Doubleday.

Summit, R. (1985) 'Causes, consequences, treatment and prevention of sexual assault against children', in Meier, J. H. (ed) *Assault Against Children: Why it Happens, How to Stop it*, College Hill Press.

Valentine, D. P., Acuff, D. S., Freeman, M. L. and Andreas, T. (1984) 'Defining child maltreatment: a multidisciplinary overview', *Social Work Information Bulletin*, Vol. 62, No. 6, pp. 497–509.

Woodcraft, E. (1988) 'Child sexual abuse and the law', *Feminist Review*, No. 28, pp. 122–30.

Wyatt, G. E. and Peters, S. D. (1986) 'Issues in the definition of child sexual abuse in prevalence research', *Child Abuse and Neglect*, Vol. 10, pp. 231–40.

5 Decisions in child care

Jean Packman

Deciding whether, when and how to provide public care for children away from their own families is one of the most sensitive and onerous duties undertaken by social services departments and it is with this area of decision making that this chapter is concerned. Legislation obviously provides the framework for these decisions, spelling out the circumstances in which families may be unable to provide children with 'proper accommodation, maintenance and upbringing' (Child Care Act 1980, Section 2), the kind of harms from which they must be protected and, if necessary, rescued, and the sorts of behaviour that cannot be tolerated and may lead to their removal.

Over the years a large body of legislation developed which has now been revised, simplified and co-ordinated in the Children's Bill 1989. Part, at least, of the impetus for this came from research findings which highlighted deficiencies and suggested the need for certain legal changes. Although the law appears to be relatively specific, there is often wide scope for interpretation and the exercise of judgement on the part of decision makers and practitioners. What action, for instance, should be taken 'in the interests of the welfare of the child' (Child Care Act 1980, Section 2) and how were the authorities' duties of 'diminishing the need to receive children [into care] . . .' (Child Care Act 1980, Section 1) to be balanced against their duties to receive or remove them in each particular case? A thorough knowledge of child care law, though vital, is not therefore sufficient to guide the planners of services, or the practitioners who work within them, and much more information is required.

Local authorities' own records translated into annual statistics collated and published by the DHSS add some quantitative flesh to the bare bones of the legislation. They show something of the size and character of the child care task which the law outlines. By charting changing numbers of children in care, their age and sex, reasons for entering and leaving, their legal status and where they are placed whilst in care, the statistics reveal how much the picture changes over time and from authority to authority. Thus, numbers of children in care in England and Wales rose throughout the 1970s, to peaks of over 100 000 – higher than at any time since the Second World War and the equivalent of nearly eight children out of every 1000 in the population as a whole. Since 1980, in contrast, they have steadily declined to below 70 000 and a rate of less than six out of every 1000 under 18 years old, a figure lower than at any time since 1971, when social services departments were created. But there are also some consistencies. Boys have always outnumbered girls in the child care system – even in the days of the Victorian Poor Law – and currently there are about four boys in care for every three girls. Teenagers massively outnumber pre-school children in the annual count, though the picture is different taken over a whole year. Similarly a quarter of those in care on any one day are over 15 years old, compared with 10 per cent of under-fives.

The legal routes by which children come into care show shifting patterns. Those who are in care, 'voluntarily', with the consent or at the request of their parents, have diminished compared with those whose legal parent is the local authority – those, that is, who have been committed through the courts and those over whom local authorities hold parental rights, who represent on any one day about three-quarters of all the children in care. Placements in foster homes have expanded at the expense of those in residential homes and hostels and half of all children in care are now fostered. Meanwhile, against this national backcloth local patterns differ enormously, and have always done so. Some social services departments support five times as many children in care per 1000 than others and fostering rates vary too though not as dramatically.

So statistics are one source of information but they raise as many questions as they answer. Why do numbers of children in care rise and fall? Why are local patterns so different? What effects do policies have upon the figures and what, on the other hand, do the figures suggest the policies ought to be?

Care in context

Before we see if research can offer any answers to some of these questions, it is important to set the children who come into local authority care into the wider context of all children who spend some time away from home, to discover whether and how they are different, and where any overlaps occur. For example, in any year in England around one million children under 18 years of age are admitted to health service hospitals, of which about 18 000 are admissions to hospitals for people with a mental handicap (DHSS, 1986, Table 4.1). Research shows that child health problems do sometimes contribute to admission to care, but which sick children leave home in this way rather than spending time in hospital wards? Conversely, how many abused children spend time in hospital, rather than being admitted to care? Similarly, a proportion of mentally handicapped children come into care, but what differentiates these from the much larger number admitted to mental handicap hospitals and units? Statistics show that a very high proportion of these hospital admissions (two-thirds) are short-stay patients, and for 'social' rather than medical reasons (DHSS, 1985, Tables 9.7 and 9.8). Why is this form of care used, and is it preferred by professionals or by parents?

There are no reliable statistics of the number of children in the population being cared for at any one time by relatives other than parents, but we can assume that it is high. Research suggests that the parents of children in care have often quarrelled with their own relatives, especially their parents, so they may well lack the possibility of this alternative.

Next, in the United Kingdom, approaching half a million children are in boarding schools. These comprise state schools, fee-paying 'public' schools and special schools, including schools for children with handicaps, and those whose behaviour at home or in school is difficult or disruptive. So some parents with sufficient means make a positive choice to send their children away from home, and for other children (around 16 000 in England alone), education departments decide that their needs would be better met in this way (DHSS, 1986, Table 7.12).

Finally, in England and Wales in 1985 over 4000 children under 17 were sent by the courts to detention centres, and another 2000 to youth custody as punishment for offences (Central Statistical Office, 1987). Since the courts still have the option of making a care order for offenders of this age, this is clearly an official decision in favour of putting children and young people in the custodial rather than the care system. Only 1200 care orders were made in the same year for children or young people who had committed offences.

Once we recognize that local authority care is only one, relatively unusual, way in which a child may leave home, we can also see that there are many ways in which a child may be helped to stay at home, and hence for a family to cope with a bad patch, either in the parents' own lives, or in a child's health or behaviour. Indeed parents who can afford it often regard a nanny or an au pair as being a normal requirement of family life with children. Many families get help from relatives, friends and neighbours, and more expert advice from doctors, child guidance clinics and school psychologists. When children are young, they may attend playgroups or nursery schools, and when they are older, parents share the responsibility with teachers for large parts of the day.

Social services departments also offer parents a range of assistance with bringing up their children, including home helps and family aides, places in nurseries and family centres, advice and support from social workers, and group activities for older children. So, just as boarding schools are part of a support system for better-off parents, which includes nannies and holiday camps, so care is part of a support system for parents who have no access to these privileged resources, and usually little or insufficient access to help from relatives and friends.

Various research studies have identified the particular characteristics of families whose children come into local authority care, or who are prevented from doing so by social services support. The picture which these studies, old and new, convey of the family circumstances of children who enter local authority care is one which social workers will recognize instantly, so the value of the research in this instance is not that it 'discovers' hitherto unknown facts, but that it highlights and measures them. Two features stand out: poverty and family disruption. Each interacts with the other, material deprivation adding to the stress on family relationships and fractured relationships increasing the likelihood of poverty, as breadwinners depart and try to set up new families. Usually, but not invariably, the families are amongst the poorest in the community, living on state benefits or low wages, often in poor housing in run-down neighbourhoods, or actually 'homeless' and existing in temporary accommodation. Disproportionate numbers are likely to be unemployed. A study in the south of England in the early 1980s (Packman *et al.*, 1986) looked for a year at the families of children who were considered for admission to care. One-third of the fathers were unemployed – three times the local unemployment rate at that time – and most had been out of work for over a year. Employment rates amongst mothers were low (only one in five had a job) and nearly half the children concerned lived in households where there was no breadwinner. Even when parents (usually fathers) were in employment, a disproportionate number – three times the national average – were in low-paid and often unstable manual occupations and were likely to be little better off than those on benefits.

To many of these families the struggle to make ends meet had become a chronic fact of life. This is a pattern repeated over and over again in research studies and in the records of any social services department. But levels of poverty and deprivation obviously vary throughout the country and where they are at their most severe the familiar picture is even more vividly drawn. Strathclyde social work department, for example, conducted its own survey of the circumstances of all children who entered the council's care between 1978 and 1979. This showed that no less than 70 per cent came from households with an unemployed person at its head and, most importantly, the poorest and most deprived areas of the city produced the highest rates of children entering care. Other studies have also highlighted a strong relationship between deprivation and numbers of children in care, which goes some way to account for the great differences between one authority and another, although other factors like resource levels and variable child care policies also play a significant part.

Family disruption in a variety of guises is equally striking. Only a minority of families whose children enter public care resemble the 'normal', perhaps idealized family unit of a married mother and father, and their own jointly produced children. In more than one research study for example, only just over a quarter of the children were living with both their natural parents prior to admission to care, and only one in three lived with their fathers (Fisher *et al.*, 1986; Packman *et al.*, 1986). One-parent families seem especially vulnerable. Forty per cent of children in the south of England study lived in one-parent households – exactly the same proportion as in a nationwide study conducted 20 years earlier (Packman, 1968). In Strathclyde the equivalent figure was 70 per cent. Divorce and illegitimacy rates have been rising steadily for at least 20 years, but these are nevertheless disproportionate figures since national statistics suggest that roughly one child in 10 lived in a one-parent household in the early 1980s – a figure that has now risen to about one in eight (Family Policy Studies Centre, 1986).

Most of the remaining children are to be found in 'reconstituted' families, more especially in those where a step-father has entered the scene. Step-parents can also bring step and half brothers and sisters to complicate family dynamics further, and many families of children in care are characterized by their complexity.

Behind these 'here and now' snapshots of fragmented and tangled family structures of many of the children who come into care lie the unhappy and sometimes violent relationships that have led to breakdown. For some, their whole childhood has been lived in an atmosphere of uncertainty. There is also no guarantee that new relationships will be any more successful than the old; in fact second marriages carry a somewhat higher risk of breakdown than first-time alliances. So studies which have followed up the families of children who have entered care show that, in a substantial number, the instability of relationships and the coming and going of key family members persists, and the family that the child left may be nothing like the family to which he or she hopes to return.

Preventive services

Families suffering such multiple disadvantages require considerable support and a wide range of child care services but only a proportion will actually receive them. Take the example of day care. It is well known that many more women (working mothers, single parents, mothers of large families) ask for day care for their pre-school children than there are places available. Statutory provision of this kind has, in fact, been shrinking steadily since the Second World War and by 1984 there were places for only three per cent of children under five in local authority day nurseries. This means that rationing is applied to those in 'greatest need'. In most areas this amounts to restricting provision to children who are regarded as being otherwise 'at risk' of coming into care. In other words, day care is seen as a means of preventing admissions to care (and research suggests that it can, in fact, have this effect) rather than as a service to parents who want help in bringing up their children.

This perspective on local authority support services has led them to be seen as 'preventive' and there has been a considerable policy debate, and some theoretical dispute, about the best way to understand prevention, and the most effective strategy in carrying it out. In everyday life, people who help parents – either because they are friends or because they are paid to do so – do not regard themselves as preventing anything. But the origins of local authority support services meant that from their beginnings a major reason for providing them was preventing unnecessary or damaging admissions of children to care.

The original 1948 legislation gave local authorities a duty to admit children to care in certain circumstances, and to care for them in certain ways, but it did not specify any duties to support parents. In the 1950s several authorities started offering a range of support services, including visits from social workers and some practical assistance to hard-pressed families who seemed likely, if they did not receive such support, to break up under stress. The Children and Young Persons Act 1963 placed on all local authorities the duty to give such assistance and, in exceptional circumstances, financial aid (Section 1), as an alternative to admitting children to care or bringing them before a juvenile court. Thus the legal justification for visiting 'at risk' families, and the money spent on assistance with immediate needs and debts was largely preventing admissions to care.

In the 1970s, research cast doubt on this original strategy. First, studies done in the United States suggested that long-term, unfocused work with families made them worse rather than better, and that planned, short-term, goal-orientated work was more effective (Reid and Shyne, 1969). In Britain NSPCC research showed (in rather similar terms) that anxious, unfocused 'monitoring' of families in which child abuse was suspected seemed to increase the risk of abuse, and that clearer, more purposeful work was required in this important field (Skinner and Castle, 1969). This message was strongly reinforced in the mid-1970s by a series of child abuse scandals, in which social workers seemed to have been more concerned with supporting parents in a general way, and avoiding admission of their children to care, than with recognizing specific risks and protecting the children from them.

Second, criticism of the use of powers to give financial assistance grew. In the early 1970s, social workers believed they were able to relieve poverty in the poorest families by giving emergency aid and occasional lump sums, hoping to lift them out of the greatest disadvantage and provide better for their children. But research showed that there were unintended consequences of these practices, and the local authority policies which supported them. In the first place, most payments were very small, and for immediate needs such as food or rent (Heywood and Allen, 1971). Next, they were almost always for items of entitlement from supplementary benefits, under urgent or exceptional needs payments (Jackson and Valencia, 1979). So the supplementary benefits system was being encouraged to run down its provision for these needs, and shuffle off its responsibilities, especially for out-of-hours problems. In this way claimants who were not clients were being encouraged to turn to social workers for help. Finally, far from being more generous and less judgemental than social security staff, research suggested that social workers were more likely to discriminate against the neediest applicants (Heywood and Allen, 1971), and more likely to make payments conditional on changes in behaviour (such as 'better' parenting) (Handler, 1973).

It is difficult to tell whether this research was the main cause of a change which took place in the mid to late 1970s in policy and practice in the field of prevention. Perhaps the child care scandals which followed the Maria Colwell case were more influential, along with resource constraints which began to affect departments after 1975. However, two major changes became apparent. First, and with much greater attention being paid to child abuse, social workers began to plan and focus their work with families more carefully. Instead of seeing what was to be prevented as family breakup or admission to care, they began to identify specific risks to children, and devise programmes aimed at reducing these risks. At the same time, rather than giving money themselves, social workers became more concerned with advocacy for clients in supplementary benefits claims, and welfare rights advisers were appointed in many areas.

The effects of this change can be seen most dramatically in the falling numbers of children under five coming into care who now represent only 30 per cent of admissions, compared with over 50 per cent 20 years ago. Numbers have fallen as policy has shifted towards providing planned 'packages' of support and therapeutic/educational programmes for parents with problems. For example, more day nurseries have been transformed into 'family centres', where children are carefully assessed, and parents receive detailed advice and assistance on how to deal with difficult behaviour, or to improve their own skills. One interesting recent research finding was that children identified as 'at risk' of physical, sexual or emotional abuse were less likely to be admitted to care than other candidates for care who were not on the 'at risk' register (Packman *et al.*, 1986, p. 52). One explanation for this apparent paradox was that identification of risk triggered a focused and often elaborate programme of preventive work which was much less likely to be on offer to families where such risks were not perceived (Packman and Randall, 1989).

In addition to changes in local authority preventive services there have also been dramatic developments in the voluntary and self-help sphere. Most of the major child care charities now concentrate on support services for families rather than on residential care of children, which used to be their specialism, and pioneering schemes of domiciliary help, parent-to-parent befriending, day care and short-term relief have flourished, to fill some of the gaps in statutory services. Not all of these schemes are confined to the most 'needy' families, as most local authority services are; indeed, some deliberately have an 'open door' policy, which is designed to encourage all families and to remove the stigma of being in 'special' need. Comparative studies of their role in 'prevention' are still awaited, but there is no doubt that they have played an important part in widening the choice for families in need.

Admission to care

'Preventive' strategies by social services departments and by a host of voluntary agencies and self-help groups have clearly proliferated and become sharper in their focus. But what happens when these supports are not thought sufficient and full-time care away from the family is seriously considered? How are the decisions made, who is involved and with what results? Research in the 1980s offers some insights from the viewpoint of both the professionals and the families themselves.

First, it is clear that field social workers play a crucial role in making these decisions, even when children are the subjects of multi-disciplinary case conferences, or are removed compulsorily from their homes by order of a magistrate, or the court. It is social workers who meet the families face to face and whose prime task is to evaluate the referrals that have brought them to the attention of their department and to assess the needs of the children in question. Their decisions will be based, not on the poverty or disruption of the families' lives, as such, but on the risks and difficulties in relationships and behaviours which stem from those circumstances. More especially, they will be concerned with the quality of parenting and the behaviour of the children.

Of course the social workers are not free agents, but are bound by legislation and constrained by available resources. Where will they place a child? Are foster homes or beds in residential care available, or are there accessible alternative facilities – day care for example – which might tip the decision in a different direction? They may also be guided by specific departmental policies on admissions to care, although the research studies found that this kind of guidance was often unhelpfully negative and general – 'Our first priority is to prevent children from having to be admitted to care' – or it was patchy and fragmented and poorly disseminated throughout the departments – 'You tell me what the policy is, and I'll tell you whether my decision fits in' (Packman *et al.*, 1986, p. 101). Exercising professional discretion within a policy vacuum is stressful for staff and can lead to idiosyncratic and even damaging decisions for families. This is a gap that many social services departments are now endeavouring to fill with more carefully constructed goals and guidelines.

In broad terms at least three sorts of *reasons* for admission emerge from social workers' assessments, and these relate quite closely to the legal framework. First are those concerning family difficulties which make caring for the children impossible for the time being. One thinks of parental illness or incapacity, but many other stresses may be involved. The children are likely to be young and to come from some of the poorest and most fragmented families, and they will probably enter the care system through the 'voluntary' route, with the agreement or at the request of their parents. The purpose of such admissions will be the provision of a full-time child care service for the families.

Second, there are children who are the victims of inadequate or harmful parenting – the 'abused' children in all the many senses of that term. They, too, are likely to be young and to come from amongst the most deprived families – often marked by chronic unemployment. However, as the relevant research studies were conducted before the great increase in referrals of sexual abuse (which spreads throughout the age range and seems to be must less closely tied in with poverty) the picture might look rather different now. For these children the purpose of admission is clearly protection and rescue and they are more likely to be admitted via the courts or on Place of Safety Orders.

Third, there are the children whose behaviour has become intolerable to families, schools or the community at large. These will generally be older – frequently in their teens – and their families are more likely to be 'intact' – albeit frequently 'reconstituted'. Their homes will probably be less marked by material deprivation. For them the purpose of admission will be to hold, 'control' and, hopefully, modify their behaviour. Like the victims of abuse, they are more likely to enter care compulsorily than by the voluntary route, though both gateways are open to them.

However, although these different reasons for and purposes of admission are identifiably distinct, they also overlap. 'Victims' of abuse will often have behaviour problems; family difficulties can beget poor parenting and so on, and it is the emphasis of the families' complex problems which differs. Exactly how the children become categorized, and the way in which they are admitted is therefore, itself, a matter of judgement and this in turn contributes to variations in practice within and between local authorities. Not surprisingly, it has also been shown that children who are referred to social services departments but not admitted to care are very similar to those who are admitted. So the task for the decision makers is not the easy one of identifying obvious candidates for care who stand out from the rest, but a matter of judging where to draw the line amongst a mass of needy families and children. But social workers and their own agencies are only some of the parties to the decision-making process which determines whether or not a child is received into local authority care. Referral agents like the police, education and health services can all exert a powerful influence by pressing hard for (or against) admission – as the findings of the Cleveland Inquiry clearly demonstrate (Secretary of State for Social Services, 1988).

The parents' view

What part do the parents themselves play in the decision-making processes which are of such critical significance to them and their children? Research, by giving them a voice, helps to throw light on the other side of the social services fence. It shows that, to some degree, they share the social workers' perceptions of their problems, confirming the facts of poverty and family disruption and the unruly child behaviour that the professionals describe. In other ways the parental perspective reveals some large gaps in the information upon which some social workers base their decisions. The workers tend to concentrate on the 'here and now' and are often unaware of much of the child's developmental history or of the parents' own childhood experiences. Yet both are seen as highly significant by the parents themselves, and could contribute to a much better grasp by the social workers of the nature and severity of current problems. Indeed, in one study, the social workers' narrow concentration upon the 'last straw' of the children's most recent bad behaviour, baffled and frustrated parents, making them feel unheard, misunderstood and inadequate – their difficulties minimized by being seen out of their historical context (Fisher *et al.*, 1986, Chapter 3).

Social workers' knowledge, or acknowledgement of, the strengths of families is also sometimes tenuous. Their understandable concern with 'problems' means that their assessments can neglect the potential helpfulness of wider family and neighbourhood networks, which are often only superficially explored. Sometimes, too, they appear blind to the 'good side' of family relationships which parents are more ready to identify.

Most crucially, social workers and parents frequently hold very different views about the appropriateness of admission to care as an answer to family problems. In all the most recent studies of child care decision making, the pervasiveness of very negative views of care on the part of social workers and their departments is striking. It is often enshrined in departmental policy statements and paraphrased by the workers themselves; 'you should keep children out of care at any cost'. Such views are reinforced, on the one hand by understanding about the importance to the child of his or her natural family and the potential damage that can be done by separation, and on the other hand by the care system's obvious deficiencies. Social workers are well aware of their failure to guarantee stability of placements, or continuity of links with home and the poor record of safeguarding and nurturing the children's health and education – if not from their own experience then because research has demonstrated it all too clearly! To them, it is a 'last resort'.

To parents, however, and even to some of the older children who enter care, admission is seen more positively. It can provide respite and a breathing space or a chance to head off problems before they become disastrously acute. Certainly, some parents who fear they may harm their children quite clearly ask for separation before they do them damage. 'They should be put away from here. I'm frightened of what I might do to them. My mind goes blank when I hit them' (Packman *et al.*, 1986, p. 129). In the same way, parents who are desperate about their children's behaviour can also see admission to care as an answer to their problems of discipline and control. Lone mothers, in particular, often face real difficulties with rebellious youngsters whose anti-social and delinquent exploits seem beyond their power to check. 'He needs that male influence.' 'As he gets older, its harder for a woman to discipline a boy' (Fisher *et al.*, 1986, pp. 36 and 37). Nor does the problem necessarily go away when a new father figure joins the family: indeed, it may make it worse, as rivalries and resentments between children and step-fathers have to be handled. It is no coincidence that, as we have seen, children who enter care on account of their behaviour come disproportionately often from reconstituted families, with a step-father in residence. Research shows how demoralized and powerless parents and particularly mothers can feel in such situations and how removal to the care of 'experts' is, in their view, a responsible and logical step to take. (It is only later, if the youngster is admitted to care, that disillusionment sometimes sets in, as the 'experts' prove unable or even unwilling to exercise the controls that parents believe are necessary.) Interviews with parents also show that the long and vain struggle to try to control and discipline their children leaves many of them exhausted and fatalistic in their attitudes, convinced that there is nothing they can do to improve the situation. To social workers this flatness and apathy is often interpreted as lack of feeling or concern, and their request for care as a sign of rejection.

Thus, the stage is set for considerable misunderstanding and frustration. Parents and social workers, because of their very different attitudes to the care system, will often be working at cross-purposes. Studies have shown that, when parents have requested care, whether for fear of their own destructive behaviour or through concern about the behaviour of their children, social workers have repeatedly tried to convince them that alternative, 'preventive' solutions were preferable. Even in the face of persistent parental pressure 'the social workers usually responded with hesitation and reluctance' (Vernon and Fruin, 1985). Most worryingly, when parents were asking for help to avoid abusing their children, 'the child's admission was generally preceded by several requests for "something" to be done . . .' and when admission finally took place it 'occurred at a point where the parent abandoned the child or reported or threatened non-accidental injury' (Vernon and Fruin, 1985). Thus, the 'last resort' attitudes of social workers can sometimes precipitate the very kinds of crises they are hoping to prevent.

Parental views on 'prevention' are also instructive. As we have seen there have been encouraging developments in the range of facilities that are available to help families with their children and there is also evidence that they are targeted at the most vulnerable groups. Children whose names are on child abuse registers, for example, are particularly likely to receive whole packages of assistance, including day care, family aides in the home and frequent attention from health visitors and social workers. But not all families experience these alternatives to care as helpful, and for some no real alternative appears to be offered. In one research study, which interviewed the parents of children who had not been admitted to care, as well as those who had, some of the most despairing and disillusioned responses came from those where admission had been 'prevented'. No less than one-third of these parents felt that the social workers and their departments had been no help at all, or had actually made things worse. They often felt neglected and abandoned, unvisited or unsupported, even when visits were still being made.

> She comes about once a fortnight usually. She asks 'How's Pat' and 'How are you feeling' and that's it. When I say I'm depressed she just says 'OK'. She doesn't do anything at all. (Packman *et al.*, 1986, p. 185)

Dilemmas of decision making

Thus all the evidence points to the fact that the task of deciding whether or not children should be admitted to care is fraught with difficulties, for families and social workers alike. First, and fundamentally, there is the very complicated nature of the problems with which the families are struggling, in which often gross material deprivation is a backcloth to unhappy family relationships and inappropriate or damaging behaviour on the part of parents, or children, or both. As one research document puts it, 'The depth, complexity and long-standing nature of child care problems makes them fiendishly difficult to deal with, whatever one's level of knowledge, experience and competence' (DHSS, 1985).

Furthermore, most social services departments are faced with very large numbers of families sharing similar characteristics and difficulties and, given their limited resources, they have to make choices about whose needs are best met by admission and whose can be eased in some other way. In the face of this, families are caught in an uncomfortable dilemma, needing to press their case hard, but not so hard as to appear inadequate or rejecting.

> I laid it on thick about the problems, in case the social services department took no notice. (Packman *et al.*, 1986, p. 127)

There are no published figures to show exactly how many children are referred to social services departments each year, but in one research study more than twice as many children were seriously considered for admission to care in a year as actually entered the care system (Packman *et al.*, 1986).

For the social workers there are other dilemmas. In reaching their decisions they are not much helped by research which, so far, has had little to contribute about the outcomes of decisions of this kind. Follow-up studies, comparing the wellbeing of children who have been admitted to care, with that of similar children who have remained at home are very rare. One recent study made some simple comparisons after a brief six-month period and found few differences between them, in terms of improved relationships, behaviour or family circumstances, itself an unhelpful finding for decision makers! (Packman *et al.*, 1986.) But much more precise and sophisticated studies are needed if practitioners are to be guided by more than their own beliefs and experience. So far, much more is known about what happens to children in the care system than about what happens to them at home, so decisions rest on a lopsided knowledge base.

Finally, to these difficulties, as we have seen, are added the very different perceptions that parents and social workers sometimes have, both of the cause and intensity of child care problems and the value and helpfulness of admission to care or of the various alternatives. It is scarcely surprising that a substantial proportion (though by no means all) of parents feel that they have little say in the actual decision making and that what eventually happens, whether admission to care or not, is taken out of their hands.

This feeling is reinforced in situations where case conferences are held but parents are excluded, and in court, where procedural rituals often mystify and intimidate the families concerned. It is no coincidence that parents of children admitted to care compulsorily appear more likely to feel shut out of the decision-making process than those whose children enter under a voluntary arrangement. In one study, over half of the parents of children compelled into care claimed they had had little or no influence on the decision compared with less than one in five parents whose children had taken the voluntary route (Packman *et al.*, 1986). It is nevertheless disturbing that even a sizeable minority of 'voluntary' parents felt they had played no part in what should have been a joint decision. It is therefore to the choice of legal route into care that we will now turn.

Legal routes into care

At the beginning of this chapter it was noted that compulsory admissions to care, under court orders, had for a long time been increasing in proportion to voluntary admissions. Some of the causes are obvious. The 1969 Children and Young Persons Act opened the doors of the child care system to young offenders, and they usually make their entrance via a court appearance. This certainly accounts for part of the upward trend in compulsion throughout the 1970s. Now, however, policy has changed, to a considerable extent because of the influence of research concerning the juvenile justice system (see Chapter 11). Delinquents are more often diverted from court altogether, or given non-custodial sentences like Intermediate Treatment. If they are removed from home they are more likely to be sent to penal establishments like detention or youth custody centres than into the child care system.

A more powerful cause of compulsory admissions lies in the upsurge in care orders as a result of divorce proceedings and the ever-increasing number of children referred for abuse. The growth in referrals of physical and emotional abuse and neglect since Maria Colwell's death in 1973 has been reinforced by the 'discovery' of sexual abuse in the 1980s. Wide-spread publicity and a generally heightened awareness of the extent of the problem has increased pressures on social services departments and the ADSS reported a 22 per cent increase in numbers of children on child abuse registers in only one year (1986–1987) (Association of Directors of Social Services, 1987). Enquiries into child abuse scandals have added to the pressure to 'use' the law and the use of compulsory measures to protect and rescue vulnerable children has grown in consequence.

The relationship between these changes and social work attitudes can be seen in a number of research studies. A preference for the protection and control that compulsory measures are thought to guarantee is expressed, both by individual social workers and in policy documents. 'Policy is to err on the side of caution. If in doubt put it before the court to safeguard the child. It's not a persecution but a protection thing' (Packman *et al.*, 1986, p. 102). Control is thought, by many, to be a prerequisite for good planning: if the department holds parental rights then plans can be made in the child's best interests, without the disturbing influence of 'parental whim'. The other side of the argument is the frequently expressed view that voluntary arrangements are ineffectual and inappropriate in many cases, especially those concerning abuse or difficult child behaviour. 'Although over half the admissions of older children were to voluntary care, the notion that the voluntary admission of adolescents was inappropriate was very powerful . . . [social workers] waited for the opportunity of compulsory admission' (Vernon and Fruin, 1985).

What, in practical terms, are the consequences of the two dominant social work attitudes to admission that have been described? The perception of care as a regrettable last resort and the preference for compulsory rather than voluntary admissions obviously overlap and reinforce each other. Compulsory admissions generally take place in a crisis or when problems have become acute. There must be explicit grounds for taking care proceedings or for removing a child on a Place of Safety Order, grounds which are not necessary for a voluntary admission. In other words, compulsory procedures are 'last resort' procedures and we have already seen how requests for care in less extreme circumstances are sometimes repeatedly refused, until a crisis occurs to force the issue. That, in itself, is unlikely to be in the child's best interests.

This, in turn, obviously has serious effects on the way the child enters the care system. Rather than being planned carefully in advance, the admission is often a last-minute, ill-prepared event, causing maximum distress to the child and family. In one study, half of the decisions to admit a child were made within a week of first consideration and one-third were reached within only 24 hours (Packman *et al.*, 1986, p. 77). In such circumstances, placements have to be found in a hurry and children can rarely be introduced to them in advance. In the same study only 13 per cent of all admissions, voluntary and compulsory, were preceded by a pre-placement visit by the child. Being accompanied on that first journey into care by a parent or familiar adult was also something of a luxury; only one-third of all children were helped in this way.

Place of Safety Orders are the extreme example of precipitate compulsory removals, when social workers or the police, armed with a magistrate's order, remove children usually without warning and sometimes in the absence of their parents and in the middle of the night. Official records of growth in the number of orders are unreliable and unsatisfactory, but research has revealed that, during the 1980s, they became a major route into care. One study found that Place of Safety Orders were applied to one in five of children admitted to care (Millham *et al.*, 1986) and in another the figure was as high as one in three (Packman *et al.*, 1986). What is more, by no means all were concerned with abused children, for as many or more were taken in order to deal with older youngsters whose behaviour was 'beyond control'.

So the combined effects of a 'last resort' and 'compulsory' orientation mean that admissions are likely to be traumatic and their rushed and last-minute style must certainly contribute to the subsequent instability of placements which has been one of the worst features of the child care system. Again, research has shown that half the children who have been in care for two years have had at least three different placements and one in seven is likely to have had four or more (Millham *et al.*, 1986). Children who enter care by compulsory routes are also likely to remain in care for longer than children whose admission was arranged on a voluntary basis and the longer children remain in care the more the prospect of rehabilitation with their families diminishes. One research study also found little evidence that the controls that accompany compulsion led to more purposeful or successful planning for the children's future, yet this is one of the justifications that is often used in its support (Packman *et al.*, 1986).

To summarize, the emphasis on 'prevention' in the negative sense of keeping children out of care 'at all costs' and the tendency to prefer compulsion if they have to be admitted combines to emphasize some of the most unsatisfactory features of the care system, helping to turn it into the 'last resort' that professionals and parents fear and distrust. In the words of one mother 'My only regret is that the placement didn't come earlier. It's wrong to have it as a last resort' (Packman *et al.*, 1986, p. 187).

So far, all the research evidence that has been discussed has tended to be critical, pointing to faults and failures in the system. But lessons can be learned from successes as well as mistakes and although most research studies tend to dwell on the latter they also carry some heartening messages. Many of these come from the parents of the children concerned. It is clear, for instance, that much of the help they receive, whether in terms of support at home or admission to care, is valued. It is worth remembering that there are, in fact, as many 'satisfied' customers of local authority child care services as there are disillusioned and angry ones, and researchers are sometimes to blame for not emphasizing this enough. Follow-up studies, for example, show that a substantial minority of families saw a definite improvement in their problems following social service intervention (Packman *et al.*, 1986).

What appears to be valued most is the style of that intervention. Social workers are experienced as helpful if they really listen and take pains to understand the difficulties from the family's point of view. They are also valued if they are practical as well as sympathetic and supportive, and do more than just listen! Honesty and directness are important qualities that parents are well able to appreciate – even if some messages are hard and unpalatable. As one mother of a sexually abused child said, 'She's given me full information and has been very honest and has answered me very fully, everything I've asked; very much moral and emotional support' (Packman *et al.*, 1986, p. 130). Workers who 'act natural' and present a human rather than an official face are also much appreciated. 'She's almost part of the family. She came to the baby's funeral and I told her off for crying, because she was trained not to' (Packman *et al.*, 1986, p. 130). Above all most parents wish to participate in decisions about their children and to be included as important partners in negotiations before, during and after an admission decision has been reached. Where this happens their sense of responsibility and worth is less shaken and undermined by having to relinquish the care of their children to others and there are indications that their children's welfare is better safeguarded as well. There are thus a number of lessons for practitioners in recent research findings, not least that some of the basic values and skills of social work are valued and valuable in child care, as much as in other branches of the work.

Research and policy

As we have seen, a considerable amount of critical research concerning the state of local authority child care services has been published in recent years and it remains to be seen what effects this is likely to have on policy and practice. It has to be said that research does not always have influence and much will depend upon whether its messages are clear, consistent and politically palatable, whether it is well publicized and whether greatly increased resources are implicit in its recommendations. To date, the impact of the most recent studies appears to have been unusually strong. This seems, in part, to be because so many different studies conducted in different places and each with a slightly different focus, have nevertheless reached similar conclusions. It may also be because care has been taken to disseminate the findings as widely as possible to local authority councillors, social service managers and practitioners, as well as to central government itself. There have been several stages in this process and it is interesting to follow them through.

Between 1983 and 1984 the all-party parliamentary Social Services Committee chose as its special topic of concern for that session 'Children in care' and evidence was collected from many sources, including researchers who were currently engaged in child care studies. Many of their particular concerns were picked up in the committee's report. For instance, they criticized the low priority given by many authorities to 'prevention', and the lack of organizational supports within and between agencies for this important aspect of the work. They also deplored the pessimistic view of local authority care that seemed to lie behind so much decision making. 'The idea of "preventing" care . . . gives an unduly negative picture of local authority care. Care is not something like a disease or a road accident: nor is it something to be regarded as a last-ditch solution such as imprisonment' (House of Commons, 1984).

The committee were also concerned at the use and possible abuse of the law, particularly as demonstrated by the massive growth in the use of Place of Safety Orders. Here was a trend that appeared to have happened without any explicit policy decision having been made to move in this direction. In effect, practice had become policy, and the committee thought it should be investigated further. The whole tangled web of child care law, that had accumulated over the decades, was also of considerable concern, and the committee recommended there should be a working party on child care law 'as soon as possible'.

A year later, in 1985, two influential documents were published. The promised review of child care law had taken place and produced its recipe for reform (DHSS, 1985b): and the DHSS published a summary of some of the major findings of nine research reports on social work decisions in child care (DHSS, 1985a). This was used as the basis for a whole series of seminars throughout the country, designed to share and discuss the research messages with social services personnel, and to explore their implications for policy and practice.

Finally, in January 1987, the government published a White Paper on 'The Law on Child Care and Family Services', and fresh legislation has resulted. It is interesting to see how some of the research that has been discussed in this chapter appears to have influenced the shape of things to come. Four points in particular stand out. One is the proposal to break down the perceived barrier between 'prevention' and 'care' fusing the present Sections 1 and 2 of the Child Care Act 1980, and including voluntary admission to care as one of a wide range of supports that local authorities offer to families. Rather than being seen as an alternative to day care, family aides and the like, it is seen as an additional way in which families can be helped to maintain responsibility for their children. Thus, it is hoped that 'prevention' will cease to mean the rather narrow and negative prevention of admission to care, but will instead mean prevention of 'the breakdown of family relationships which might eventually lead to a court order committing the child to the local authority's care' (DHSS *et al.*, 1987). In other words, the prevention of 'last resort' crises and compulsion.

A second feature of the White Paper was its insistence that, wherever possible, decisions about children who leave home must be taken in partnership with parents. Thus, voluntary admissions to care are favoured and the necessity to involve parents in all negotiations over admission, access, placements, schooling and, of course, rehabilitation is stressed. 'An essential characteristic of this service should be its voluntary character, that is it should be based clearly on continuing parental agreement and operate as far as possible on a basis of partnership and co-operation between the local authority and parents' (DHSS *et al.*, 1987).

A third theme concerned the use of compulsory powers and the need to balance improving the protection of vulnerable children with respect and safeguarding of their parents' rights to a fair hearing and a continuing place in their children's lives. In this respect, the influence of child abuse scandals and, in particular, the Cleveland Inquiry has probably been greater than any piece of research, but the proposed reform of Place of Safety Orders owes something to the findings that have been outlined. Their new title of 'Emergency Protection Order' emphasizes that they should only be used in extreme circumstances and not for the wide spectrum of troublesome child care crises that were revealed in the research reports. Even in extremis the principle of keeping parents informed of what is happening and allowing them access to their children is spelled out. The 'partnership' ideal is not to be easily extinguished.

Finally, children who live away from home for substantial periods, in health or education authority establishments, are drawn under the same umbrella of child care legislation as children in local authority care. Some of the artificial distinctions between children in care and others, that have been touched on in this chapter, will therefore be broken down.

The intended direction of future child care policy, therefore, owes something to the researches of recent years. But real changes will depend on resource policies that are realistic and generous enough to enable local authorities, and the practitioners within them, to translate intentions into a more positive, supportive and 'shared' stance towards families in need. Future research will doubtless tell us whether this has been achieved.

References

Association of Directors of Social Services (1987), Press Release, July.

Central Statistical Office (1987) *Social Trends*, No. 17, 1987 Edition, HMSO.

Child Care Act 1980, HMSO.

Department of Health and Social Security (1985a) *Social Work Decisions in Child Care*, HMSO.

Department of Health and Social Security (1985b) *Review of Child Care Law*, HMSO.

Department of Health and Social Security, Personal Social Services Local Authority Statistics: *Children in Care of Local Authorities*.

Department of Health and Social Security (1985) *Health and Personal Social Services Statistics*, 1985 Edition, HMSO.

Department of Health and Social Security (1986) *Health and Personal Social Services Statistics*, 1986 Edition, HMSO.

Department of Health and Social Security, Home Office, Lord Chancellor's Department, DES, Welsh Office, Scottish Office (1987) *The Law on Child Care and Family Services*, Cmnd 62, HMSO.

Family Policy Studies Centre (1986) 'One-parent families', Fact Sheet No. 3, December.

Fisher, M., Marsh, P., Phillips, D. and Sainsbury, E. (1986) *In and Out of Care*, Batsford/BAAF.

Handler, J. (1973) *The Coercive Social Worker: British Lessons for American Social Services*, Rand McNally.

Heywood, J. and Allen, B. (1971) *Financial Help in Social Work*, Manchester University Press.

House of Commons (1984) *Children in Care*, Second Report from the Social Services Committee, Session 1983–1984.

Jackson, M. P. and Valencia, B. M. (1979) *Financial Aid through Social Work*, Routledge and Kegan Paul, pp. 41–3.

Millham, S., Bullock, R., Hosie, K. and Haak, M. (1986) *Lost in Care*, Gower.

Packman, J. (1968) *Child Care: Needs and Numbers*, Allen and Unwin.

Packman, J. and Randall, J. (1989) 'Decisions about children at risk', in Philpot, T. and Stills, P. (eds) *Current Challenges for Child Care and the Management of Child Abuse*, London Boroughs Training Committee and Community Care.

Packman, J., Randall, J. and Jacques, N. (1986) *Who Needs Care?*, Basil Blackwell.

Reid, W. J. and Shyne, A. W. (1969) *Brief and Extended Casework*, Columbia University Press.

Secretary of State for Social Services (1988) *Report of the Inquiry into Child Abuse in Cleveland 1987*, HMSO.

Skinner, A. and Castle, R. (1969) *78 Battered Children: A Retrospective Study*, NSPCC.

Strathclyde Social Work Department (undated), *Who Are They?*, SSWD.

Vernon, J. and Fruin, D. (1985) 'In care', National Children's Bureau, quoted in DHSS (1985) *Social Work Decisions in Child Care*, HMSO.

6 Substitute care

Peter Marsh

How well do researchers, practitioners and managers get on? Let us imagine a child's eye view of the current situation:

> *A children's story:*
> Once upon a time there was a researcher, a practitioner and a manager – they all worked together to look after the children whose mummies and daddies weren't with them any more. The researcher lived in the Ivory Tower on the hill, the practitioner had a small hut in an area called the patch, and a part of an old house that was filled full of children. The manager lived far away, in a place that was difficult to find known as the HQ. Every now and again the researcher would be asked to visit the practitioner and the manager. During these visits there was often a great wailing and gnashing heard in the land, as the researcher asked questions that no one understood and sometimes, even worse, the researcher told the others that they were naughty and no good at their jobs. When this happened everyone ended up angry – the researcher felt unloved, the practitioner felt misunderstood and the manager didn't know who to listen to. They all put their hands over their ears to avoid listening to the gnashing and wailing. They rarely seemed to be friends, and they often retreated to their tower, hut, house and HQ and flung little bits of paper over the walls at each other.

The tense relationship between researchers and practitioners, and between research and practice, is not new. It has been a long and tortuous relationship and it is not surprising that there should be difficulties in it.

Researchers will always feel in a double bind regarding their research findings; if they tell others what they already know then it is just an expensive way of confirming common sense. If they tell something else then it is clearly wrong – as anyone with common sense could have told the researcher in the first place!

On the other hand, practitioners and managers often have to struggle with impenetrable language in research reports, and put up with suggested actions that are clearly impractical.

This chapter explores the connections between research and practice/policy. It will argue that research has a valuable role to play in helping us to understand the world of substitute care for children, and that its findings can be and should be practical and useful. We shall examine some of the things that researchers do, and how these actions may be related to a particular concept of research. We shall look at the range of activities that can be encompassed by the idea of research and we shall think about some of the ways that a research-minded approach could be further developed in practice and in policy. The examples used will be from the field of substitute care for children, but this is not a research review and there will of course be many important issues that we are not able to mention here.

Understanding your own world

Enquiry is a central task in social work and social care; the enquiries of practitioners assessing the complexities of family situations; the enquiries of managers planning for the provision of child care services. These are careful investigations into facts and opinions. Following most enquiries, whether large or small, there will be a need to justify actions to a number of different audiences. Clients, politicians and others may all ask for accounts of practice and policy. Conducting enquiries and describing what you are doing – research can help with both these tasks.

Research can provide an insight into the quantities and the patterns of the work in substitute care. Research is itself a form of structured enquiry. It should be able to describe events and make links between them to show patterns and problems. It should conduct these descriptions and analyses in ways that can be examined and repeated by others. Good quality research will outline in a clear and concise form the process as well as the product of enquiry. It is the product, rather than the process, that is usually seen by practitioners and managers.

The patterns, the quantities, the viewpoints that research can show form the material that most practitioners and managers see as the valuable part of research. The careful thinking that has gone into the generation of this material is often skipped over. But this thinking, especially the logic and the process of the thinking, is also important. Much of that logic and process has similarities with the work required for good practice and management. Seeing the many ways that a question could be tackled and choosing between them, deciding how reliable some evidence is, deciding how important a particular finding is – all these things are part of the researcher's work. They are often part of practice and management as well. We shall be looking at a number of examples of these links later in the chapter, emphasizing that research is not just a product, it is also a process, and that both parts of the research endeavour have a contribution to make to practice/policy. Understanding the nature of the research process, as well as paying attention to its product, is vital to the development of sound practice and policy. Research and practice should be allies – they are partners in enquiry.

We shall be exploring the nature of the alliance between research and practice and seeing how close it can be in the field of substitute care. However no alliances occur in a vacuum, and a number of different factors will impinge on this alliance. We must recognize that neither practice nor policy will be based solely upon a dispassionate assessment of the facts. The provision of substitute care is subject to political direction, and it responds to public and professional fashions. These factors will inevitably colour, and will sometimes direct the actions of practitioners and managers irrespective of all research findings. Equally the time scales for practice and policy decisions are usually short and the period of investigation of relevant issues, including relevant research, is necessarily brief. Actions will always be taken on the basis of imperfect knowledge and it is a skilled professional judgement to decide when the level of knowledge is satisfactory enough for the job in hand. Increasing the level of knowledge may be too costly and may not be possible because of other deadlines. There are likely to be many factors crowding in and all clamouring for attention when decisions are taken about policy and practice in substitute child care. Research must be one of those factors, but it would be foolish to suggest that it should be, or could be, the dominant one on all occasions.

Having sounded a note of warning about the place of research let us also recognize that research is often not up to the job of playing a dominant role. Research findings may conflict one with another. Even if the findings do not conflict the conclusions may not be self-evident. Occasionally a research study will show this in a direct manner. For example, the work of Johnson and her colleagues (1987) on transracial adoption. This research team have been examining the progress of black children adopted into white families. They have been able to follow a number of children through from the early 1970s. The 1987 report describes their findings about the development of black identity at the age of eight. The findings are common to all members of the research team, but two members of the team interpret them in quite different ways. Both researchers agree that the children are doing as well as black children adopted into black families, but each one offers a very different view as to whether or not this is likely to continue. These differences are occurring within a research team; practitioners and managers, who are one step removed from the researchers, are equally likely to develop different views regarding the conclusions of research.

Furthermore many areas are comparatively unresearched. This is particularly common for recent developments. Research takes time to conduct its enquiries and time to respond to current concerns. For example, in 1988 the issue of child sexual abuse was a dominant one within social services departments, but literature on the substitute care of sexually abused children hardly existed at all.

Research and practice are allied in their concern for careful and thoughtful enquiry. The alliance is crucial to the development of good services but it must be recognized that it is conditional on a range of factors that relate to the nature of practice, of policy and of research.

Linking research and policy

Exactly how can research help the development of substitute care? We shall examine this issue through two examples concerning the stability of placements for children in substitute care. The stability of placements has been a major concern over the past years and it provides a good guide to the interconnection of practice and research.

Disruption of placement

One of the earliest pieces of UK child care research considered the question of breakdown of foster placement (Parker, 1966). The study is small in scale but contains many of the elements that make the alliance between research and practice such an important one. The study's starting point was the emphasis given to foster care as the most desirable substitute care placement for children. Parker notes that the 15 years preceding publication of the study had seen central and local government firmly suggesting that foster care should be the first choice for the substitute care of children in the public care system. The author comments that 'the foster home has come to be regarded as the best way, other than adoption, of providing for the needs of the child who for one reason or another cannot remain in his own home' and he then goes on to say:

> Notwithstanding the apparent desirability and humanity of such a policy it ought, like any other, to be regarded as an experiment which needs to be observed and tested. Neither the policy nor the practice of child placement can develop intelligently without reference to what is happening and has happened in a variety of foster homes throughout the country. The modification of existing policies, the formulation of new ones, and the improvement of social work techniques all depend upon the accessibility of past experience. (Parker, 1966, p. 13)

This is a fine formulation of the need for research-minded practice. As Parker says, the 'accessibility' of past experience is a vital ingredient in the decisions that we need to take about future policies and practices. Research has an important role in improving that accessibility.

The Parker study provides a snapshot of the experience of a number of foster placements. It gives a carefully argued analysis of what may be said to constitute success in a foster placement and the factors that appear most likely to contribute to this success. The researcher analysed the concept of success in a foster placement as a precondition of examining the experiences. As a researcher he needed criteria of success and failure that met three conditions. The criteria had to be clear cut enough to distinguish reliably between success and failure, simple enough to avoid excessive expense of data collection, and relevant to the welfare of the child.

These three elements, being clear in distinguishing 'a' from 'b', being as simple as can realistically be achieved, and being relevant to the practice and policy concerns of substitute care, will be needed for all criteria that are used as research tools. Clarity of demarcation between events, elegant simplicity and relevance are major issues to the researcher. They are of relevance to the practitioner and manager but the time that can and should be allotted to them is markedly different. If all criteria used in practice and policy decisions had to be considered as carefully as those used in research then the backlog of work would grow very quickly! There is simply not time to think in this research manner for the vast majority of analyses that have to be undertaken in the world of practice. But the researcher must have the time to do this thinking; it is an inescapable part of the research task. It is one of research's most important contributions to the policy–practice–research alliance.

Parker provides some clear thinking on the topic of placement success which still makes valuable reading. The lesson for us, in the context of the discussion here, is that the very nature of the research task makes it inevitable that researchers will consider with care and precision (but of course with variable skill!) the criteria that will help to make sense of the data. The practitioner is offered a new view of the construction of the practice world; it may be rejected, accepted or improved, but it contributes to the understanding of the practice and policy issues by its 'outsideness'. As Parker says, it is a contribution to making the past accessible.

Research in its very nature must attempt to clarify the boundaries of its discussions, and the limits of its assessments. It can therefore highlight issues that practitioners and managers had not seen before, or ask them to view their work in new ways. But there are other contributions that research has to make to the policy–practice–research alliance. Let us return to the Parker example. Having defined success and failure (in a way of course that we may or may not agree with) Parker then goes on to examine 209 placements to see how they related to his classification. In terms of his definition, 52 per cent were successful. Parker went on from finding this overall rate to seeing if some types of placement or child or experience of care, led to variations in the rate, i.e. to see if particular factors seemed to make success more likely.

He suggests that the placements can be divided into five bands, each of the bands having a different success rate. Success in the bottom band is 94% and in the top band is just 16%. The bands are derived from a point system which itself gives points for different factors in the child or the placement. The top band has scores of 80 and over and the bottom band has scores of 15 or less. So the more points that are scored the less likely it is that the placement will be successful. His allocation of the points, derived from a statistical multivariate analysis, is as follows:

There is a child of the foster parents under five	add 33 points
The child's own mother is dead	add 28 points
The child is more than four years old	add 23 points
The child has exhibited behaviour problems	add 17 points
The child has not been previously fostered	add 15 points
There is a child of the foster parents whose age is within five years of that of the child to be placed	add 14 points

(Parker, 1966, pp. 76–7)

He is careful to point out limitations on the use of the table, for example that the factors need to be taken as a whole rather than thought of as separate causes, and that the table needs validation on other samples before it can be used with full confidence. Bearing in mind these caveats, what is being offered here is an invitation to think carefully about six different factors that appear to contribute to the stability of foster placements. The factors range from those concerned with the foster family themselves to those relating to the child to be placed.

The researcher is asking us to review the world of practice and policy; in fact to 're-view' it through the analyses of the research. The new view offers practitioners the chance to consider the placements that they are involved in and think how far the Parker categories for points accord with their professional view of the factors that make for more difficult placements. It suggests that managers might try and apply Parker's points system to the past work of a team and see if it does predict the actual outcome. We are all encouraged to consider what is important (and what is not important) to the outcomes of our work.

Parker's study is now over 20 years old but the ways in which it provides new views for the practitioner and manager is a classic example of the alliance at its best. The research on the stability of substitute care placements has grown and we can now call upon a wide variety of studies to provide additional views on the issues. If we are interested in the total breakdown rate within foster care (now usually referred to as 'disruption' of care) then Berridge's (1985) study of children's homes, Aldgate and Hawley's (1986) and Berridge and Cleaver's (1987) studies of foster disruptions all confirm a view that around one-third of placements do not end in a planned way. Although there are different factors at work, residential care also involves children in movement between placements. Berridge (1985) found that 43 per cent of the (234) children in his study were in their third residential unit.

But let us come back to the essence of research-minded practice. We need to ask alongside these general rates of disruption the more detailed questions, like Parker's 'what factors lead to a stable placement?', and beyond that to more detail still. The range of factors that lead to stability may in themselves have costs that are not acceptable. For example it may not be possible to recruit or have permanently available foster parents for children of the right ages. This consideration will lead us to ask further research-minded questions such as, 'in what circumstances might an unstable placement be considered satisfactory?'. This in turn might lead us to ask, 'are some forms of instability more harmful to children than others?', or 'what techniques appear to help the best if placements do disrupt?', and so on. This process of the progressive refinement of questions is a major contribution of research to the practice–research alliance.

Let's take these discussions a little further and note how some of the views of placement success have altered in the light of the research material. For example, it is now clear that some children have almost no stability in their substitute care experience – one child in Berridge's (1985) study had been to more children's homes than the researcher (who had been to 20)! In our own *In and Out of Care* study (Fisher *et al.*, 1986), 4 per cent of the 340 children had experienced seven or more placements. There are other challenging findings. For example, the most stable placement in substitute care is probably one that has been viewed with much suspicion by the professionals – that of the long-term foster placement made with a relative. Jane Rowe and her colleagues in their study (1984) found these placements to be very long lasting (a much smaller sample of this type of placement in Fisher *et al.* (1986) found the same). These findings put stability in its context as there may be, or there may not be, other more important factors which mean that foster placements with relatives are not to be encouraged.

We have shown the scope for a dynamic dialogue between research and policy/practice. It is a dialogue that aids our thinking about the professional world of substitute child care, and makes the experience of that world more accessible so that we may learn from it. If the dialogue is productive, then it will highlight issues and views that may not accord with individual experience or professional wisdom. That form of challenge shows the practice–research alliance working at its best.

Finding a placement

One of the most influential pieces of research that has been conducted in the UK was the study by Rowe and Lambert (1973) called *Children Who Wait*. The study showed that social workers identified large numbers of children under nine years old in long-term care who had little chance of returning home and who were, in the social worker's view, wrongly placed. They were waiting for suitable family placements and there seemed little positive evidence that there was active planning for their care and upbringing. These children were languishing in care and they faced an uncertain and impermanent future. This phenomenon was entitled 'drift' and it became an important part of the considerations of child care professionals over the years following the Rowe and Lambert study.

It is worth noting that Rowe and Lambert's study was small in scale and did not use complex research tools. It was also relatively inexpensive and quick. Research does not necessarily need large budgets and long time scales to make an important contribution to practice.

The way that the *Children Who Wait* study was taken up raises some interesting questions about the use of research in policy and practice development. As we have seen, the study showed that large numbers of children in care needed more permanent long-term placements. At about the same time as this was highlighted by Rowe and Lambert, a publication by Goldstein *et al.* (1973) in America raised similar-sounding issues. This was a polemical piece that argued for the primacy of the 'psychological' parent and the need for the comprehensive transfer to that parent of all the legal rights and responsibilities for a child. The logic of Goldstein's position was that children who enter care, and who therefore receive 'psychological' parenting away from their natural parents, should rapidly be permanently placed with the new parents in order to avoid psychological damage. In this view of child care the problem of drift should be dealt with quickly by the removal of the link with the birth parents, and the assumption of full parental roles in a new, probably adoptive, family.

Here we have two, very different pieces of research which highlighted issues that needed urgent attention from policy and practice. The large numbers of children who were in temporary placement but permanent care had not featured prominently on the agenda of practitioners and managers. The Rowe and Lambert study made the issue visible and encouraged debate and the consideration of alternatives. Equally the Goldstein monograph raised an issue to prominence – that of a child's need for a sense of certainty regarding day-to-day and longer-term care and parenting. The research put before practitioners some uncomfortable facts and issues that could so easily be ignored in the urgent daily business of practice and management.

The Rowe and Lambert research showed, over and above any individual experience, that poor placements were relatively common. It demonstrated that there was a real need for better and more active planning for placement of children in long-term care. The Goldstein work challenged social workers to consider the nature of parenting, and the ways that care might or might not provide good parenting.

The double challenge provoked a range of other studies, and a number of policy and practice responses which have themselves been researched. We can now see that some of the responses to the issue of drift and the question of permanency have led to solutions which encourage agencies to ignore the wishes of parents and children by a planning process which itself ignores the multiple links which children can maintain. At its worst it suggests that once they enter care the complex world of caring which they left (from grannies to step-fathers) should be replaced by a simpler one of 'psychological' parenting needs. This has often led to adoption being seen as the only truly permanent placement. The complexity of the real world has been ignored.

The problem was that the reception of the studies on 'drift' had not, in the initial years, been 'research-minded' in the sense which we are developing here. Careful thought in the reception and use of research is just as important as it is in carrying out that research. We need to promote a practice–research alliance with each partner analysing the work of the other and not just responding uncritically to it.

Research has now come full circle, and recent studies highlight the many links that children can maintain, and suggest ideas of 'shared parenting' in care (Fisher *et al.*, 1986). They link the need for permanency of placement into the idea of prevention of permanent care, such that natural families are the first and main aim for establishing the permanent placement (Maluccio *et al.*, 1986). The alliance continues to develop.

Research and practice links – doing it yourself

One of the ways to promote the constructive use of research is by reducing the distinction between researcher and practitioner/manager. We have already noted some similarities in the task of structured enquiry which is undertaken by researchers, practitioners and managers. Doing research as a practitioner or manager might have many important benefits. We shall look at a number of these benefits by using examples from substitute care.

Exploring research thinking – an example: the scale of substitute care

If this chapter had been a research review then it might have begun by defining substitute care and discussing the scale of such care in the UK. In order to do this a small piece of research would be needed – thinking through the definition of substitute care, analysing the available figures on it and finding ways to present them. We shall do some of that research. We shall not present it solely as a finished product, but try to show how it needs to be conducted and therefore how a research-minded approach can help to clarify our thinking. In laying the process of research more open the value of process as well as product should become clearer.

Substitute care, that is care outside the immediate family, is provided for children in many different settings. Children who enter the public care system, for example, are placed with foster parents or in various types of residential units. For some children these placements will be for all of their childhood, but the majority will move back to their family at some time. A few of these children in care, and others who are outside the care system, may be adopted and thus provided with permanent care outside their family of origin. The numbers involved in each of these different processes vary greatly. In round terms, in England and Wales on the most recent figures, there are 70 000 children in care of whom about 35 000 are fostered, 15 000 are in residential units and 20 000 are placed back with parents or relatives (DHSS, 1988). In Scotland there are around 13 000 children in care with a larger percentage living at home. So in total there are about 50 000 children in England and Wales (and about 7000 in Scotland) who are in substitute care via the public care system. This is an approximate picture which ignores specialized placements, but it does give an idea of the numbers of children involved. Adoption, on the other hand, involves much smaller numbers with around 8000 children adopted in England and Wales in 1985 (DHSS, 1987). Around half of these 8000 children were being adopted by one of their natural parents. So approximately 4000 children entered the full substitute care of adoption outside their family of origin in 1985 in England and Wales. In comparison with this group of 54 000 children who were part of the statutory substitute care system there is a much larger group whose parents arrange the substitute care largely on their own for day-time periods only. In 1985 there were approximately 130 000 placed with childminders in England and Wales, and a further 7500 in Scotland (Pugh, 1988).

Obtaining these figures is not very difficult but, as you will probably recognize by now, presenting them to the reader is rather more tricky. It is likely that you feel a little confused by the jumble of numbers and it is very likely that you are not clear as to the relative scale of different forms of substitute care. Is it, for example, clear to you that within the care system there are large numbers of children who are not in substitute care?

Sorting, dividing, regrouping and then presenting these figures on care requires some detailed thought. We noted with Parker's 1986 study that research involved separating 'a' from 'b', providing elegantly simple measures and making sure that such measures were relevant to policy and practice. It is just the same in the piece of work that we are undertaking here. Separating children in substitute care within the larger group in the care system is our starting point.

Let us assume that we decide to use the simple categories of 'fostered', 'residential', 'adopted (non-parent)' and 'relatives and other'. These categories are clearly distinguished, reasonably simple (they are used in the published data, and the 'other' group is very small) and they provide information that relates to practice and policy concerns. Some more detailed thought has already gone into our use of these categories as we have had to be careful to distinguish within the adopted group between adoptions by own parents (which are not substitute care cases) and adoptions by non-parents. We will work out the percentages and then produce a simple chart to show them so that the numbers become clearer when they are presented as the segments of a pie (see Figure 1).

It is now clear that we should be careful not to confuse 'a child in care' with 'a child in substitute care' – they do not necessarily mean the same thing.

What about the forms of substitute care that are used? Do we know from the analysis so far the relative numbers of children in residential as compared with foster care? It is there in the figures and in the diagram but it is not at all easy to find. Making it clear is the work of the research, to do it we need to remove the placement with relatives from our diagram and just look at substitute care for care system and adopted children.

As we can see from Figure 2, around two-thirds of children in substitute care (as distinct from children in the care system) are in fact placed with foster parents.

We can now have a clear, numerical and visual representation of the types of substitute care. We may be satisfied with this, or we may want to include those children who use day care, such as childminding. We will add this in, and obtain the picture of the main substitute care numbers outside the nurseries and the health system (see Figure 3).

We could continue to alter our view point in many different ways. We have been laying bare a little bit of research and providing some useful general data on the scale of substitute care. Let us end this analysis by

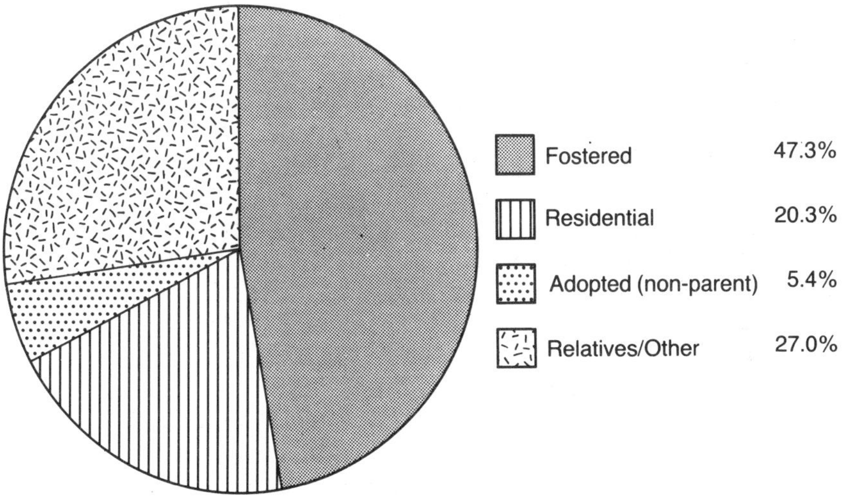

Figure 1. *Types of care in the care system*

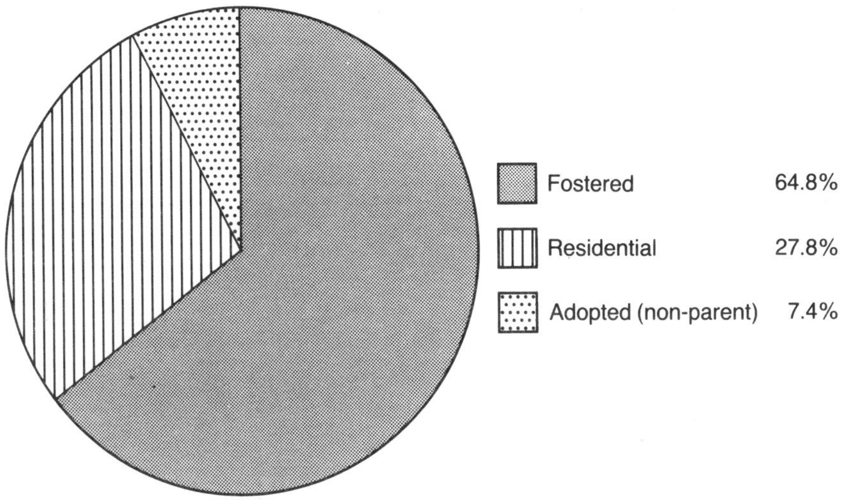

Figure 2. *Substitute care: care system and adoption*

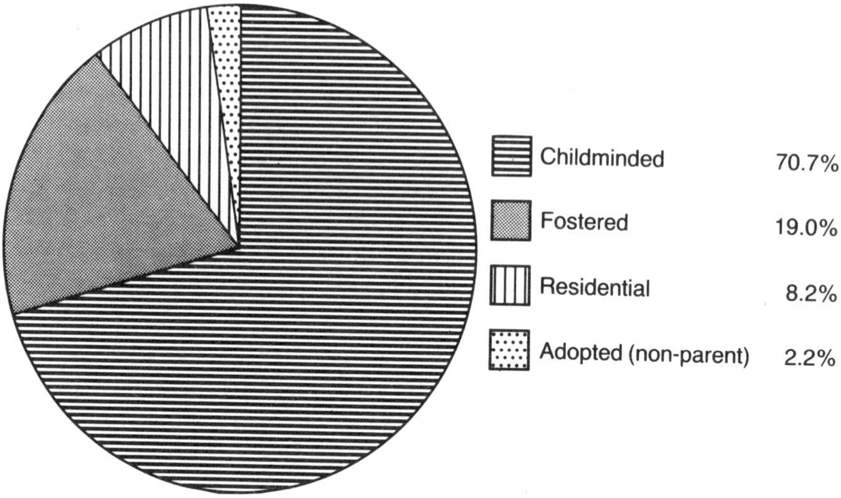

Figure 3. Substitute care

noting that the very different pictures presented are all valid – their value simply depends on what you want to know. Thinking carefully about what it is that you want to know is the hallmark of the research-minded practitioner. It is not, of course, a requirement for others. Consider for a moment the possible headlines that could be invented for a newspaper coverage of substitute care. On the basis of the totals in care and with childminders there could be a front page lead: '180 000 children not cared for by parents'. On the other hand if the numbers of children adopted were being used there would probably be a paragraph buried deep on an insidc page: 'Families cope: only 4000 children have little prospect of links'. Both appear to be discussing substitute care but in fact are discussing quite different things.

Research can therefore give us a picture of the scale of the problem or issue that we are dealing with and can help us to focus our concern. But to use it well demands that we think very carefully about the categories that have been used in the research. Do they include all the groups that we want to consider; do they (perhaps inadvertently) include some that we do not want to consider; do they exclude some that we are specifically interested in? It is not a task beyond the intelligent non-researcher to assess this (assuming clear and explicit research work and some knowledge of the general field under consideration). It demands careful thought. You must analyse just what it is that you are really interested in, and then read the research noting all the small print and all the detail.

Process and product

In examining the scale of substitute caring we have been forced to consider the detailed definition of the term substitute care and the material that will best indicate the range of such caring. In doing this we have been doing secondary research. The process of refinement of the question and the care taken to examine the type of data to be used would be a very important part of any research work. Research is both process and product. Refining the question and thinking through the data that are needed are key elements of research work. The thoughtful care needed to do this may pay as many dividends as the product itself, but it is often invisible to the practitioner or policy maker using the research report. Research is not just a technical question to be left to the researcher.

An example from a different area may help to emphasize the distinction between process and product. Perhaps a residential unit is considering computerizing its records to aid practice and research. The technical questions of the software and hardware development seem to be the difficult ones and the initial response may be to call in the expert in computing. He or she will ask you what you want to record and why you want to record it. These decisions are the ones that are likely to be the most important – do you want all the children of a family to be listed; does this mean all children at home or all children in total; and yet again would this mean all children by all marriages/relationships, etc., etc.? Thinking about the kind of record that you need will be an important part of the apparently technical problem of the computerization of records. It might be the most important part. The decisions taken at this stage may be useful in their own right irrespective of the final computer enactment as they will provide a careful analysis of the purpose of records and hence the nature of the record needed. You may decide that you can improve on what you've got without computers. You have not become an expert in computerization but you have been forced into a careful and thoughtful consideration of your practice and policy.

So research is not just a technical business. We should not think, 'we have a problem with this area – we need to call in the researcher'. Careful analysis of the nature of the problem, and careful thought as to what information might aid in resolving it are vital elements of the research process. They can be carried out by research-minded practice and policy staff. Remember the data on substitute care that we used earlier – ask the wrong question and you will get an answer that is misleading – one person's 180 000 substitute care places is another person's 4000 places. Think about what you need to know, why it would be valuable to you, how it might be presented, and then consider the need for technical help.

Practitioner as researcher – an example: the withdrawal of requests for adoption

A growing number of practitioners are now going further into research and conducting their own projects. Again an example might help. A social work practitioner (in an adoption unit) came to see me recently. She was interested in the fate of children who had initially been put forward by their mothers for adoption, but whose mothers had withdrawn from the process and kept the child. She had come across a number of cases of children in care where there had been an earlier request for adoption. She wondered if the adoption request, despite its subsequent withdrawal, had meant that the parents were not happy parenting the child and that this unhappiness had resulted in the later request for care.

This is the research-minded approach in action. The social worker is sensitive to the connections that might exist between different events in a family's life. She is research-minded in that she first of all recognizes the possible connection. The initial focus of this is that she is trying to see patterns in the work she conducts. If these patterns exist and regularly repeat then there may be important lessons for policy and practice from them. In the case of the adoption withdrawals, for example, it may be that more support should be offered when parents withdraw from requests to place their child for adoption.

So the social worker took the names of all the parents who had withdrawn from adoption in one year and checked to see if the children had subsequently entered care. This task also demanded a research-minded approach. Decisions had to be made regarding the number of years to examine and the number of years that would be followed up after the adoption request was withdrawn to see if the child entered care. It was decided that three years of adoption records would be examined and that three years after withdrawal of request would be checked for entry to care. These decisions are based upon sensible views of what might constitute a pattern. It would be easy to resort to the technical view of research and ask what numbers you might need for statistical proof. Statistical analysis could help in various ways. For example, to confirm whether or not the numbers entering care after adoption withdrawal were greater than would occur by chance. This might well be needed at a later stage but at this point it would be over-complex. The social worker thought that three years would give her a good idea of the existence of a pattern – if it was not prominent over that time scale then it was probably too difficult for her to research.

She looked at the figures and found that in the year which had initially interested her a number of withdrawals from adoption had been followed by the child entering care. This appeared to confirm her concern that the withdrawal of the adoption request did not mean that parenting problems were resolved. But when the other years were examined there were no entries to care after withdrawal. One particular year seemed to be quite abnormal. It appeared that the withdrawal did not link in a straightforward way to a subsequent request for care.

She was research-minded enough to see a possible link and, equally importantly, she was research-minded enough to examine it and find that it appeared to be more chance than pattern. By now, however, she had become interested in the topic of withdrawal from adoption. She wondered what the experience of asking for your child to be adopted did to your subsequent parenting of that child and what the circumstances were that led parents to withdraw. Being research-minded she looked at the literature and found that very little was known about this process, so she decided to mount her own small-scale enquiry.

The enquiry involved an approach to 23 adoption applicants who had withdrawn in the two years from April 1983 to April 1985. The social worker decided to interview as many of the applicants as possible to see how they viewed the withdrawal of the application. She considered her practice experience and she reviewed some of the literature on adoption. She drew up a number of questions which addressed relevant themes. Contacting the parents proved difficult and some refused to be interviewed; nine were eventually seen by her. She was now conducting a research study which had been prompted by a pattern that did not turn out to be there but which had started her puzzling about the overall experience of the withdrawal of adoption requests.

The study (Odams, unpublished) found the parents managing quite well and proud to 'show off' their children. All the children appeared well loved, all the parents with partners seemed settled and those who were on their own were coping and proud of their independence. It was clear that they had made and maintained their own decision in spite of some opposition, that there had been major difficulties at the time of the adoption application but that those difficulties had now been resolved. In the early days of deciding about the application it appeared to be family support rather than official support that had been their mainstay and they had retained close contact with particular family members. The majority were planning to tell their children of the adoption enquiry.

The initial concern of the social worker was that parents who withdrew from the adoption process may be unable to cope with the child at a later stage. This appears to be quite wrong (although the sample of the parents who were researched may have emphasized the success stories). In the course of exploring this concern the social worker became a researcher, initially doing some relatively simple work on the agency child care figures and then undertaking a quite complicated study of the experience of adoption withdrawal. She devoted a reasonable amount of time to the initial enquiries and a great deal of time to the interview-based study, and the result is an addition to our knowledge in an area that has hardly been touched on at all by other researchers. The process of research has been very important to this social worker: it led to a careful review of the support that parents do or do not obtain at the time of application to place their child for adoption, and how the decision and its aftermath are handled. She had to think through a number of explanations for adoption decisions, she met past agency clients and heard their views on adoption social work, and she was able to consider the ways in which people may handle child care and all of its demands. Her practice is richer for this process and her contribution to our knowledge is an important one.

Research-minded development – an example: foster care agreements

There has been a trend towards the use of written agreements for the placement of children in substitute care. Although the majority of adolescent foster placements probably use written agreements, it seems unlikely that anything more than a small minority of other placements do so. Given their success in these adolescent foster schemes (Hazel, 1981; Show and Hipgrave, 1983; Smith, 1986) could they be introduced into all types of foster placement? What might a research-minded practitioner or manager do about this?

In 1986 the National Foster Care Association applied for some charitable funds to develop the use of written agreements in foster placements. They set up a small working party to look at the available research and produce a pro forma agreement and accompanying training notes. The working party discussed the wide gap between the practice indications that written agreements were an important element of good practice and the fact that most placements still occurred without such an agreement. Why was this gap so large? Research seemed unlikely to reduce the gap in the short term. A publication extolling their virtues could have been prepared but there was no reason to think that these exhortations would meet with much success. The working party therefore agreed that it should be concerned with adding to our knowledge about this area. If the existing arguments did not result in the widespread use of written agreements, then what other arguments were needed?

Perhaps there was not enough material covering what should actually be done and so the main issue was to develop guidelines as to the contents of written agreements? Maybe it was impractical to use written agreements in some circumstances – if so what were those circumstances and could they be minimized? These questions, prompted by practice experience within the working party, led to an interest in the development of material to support the use of written agreements in the practices and policies of agencies.

This developmental research required a broad base in the experience of different agencies and practitioners in order to make sure that it would be relevant in different settings, authorities and teams. The collected wisdom of parents, children, social workers and foster parents was needed to work on the contents and the context of written agreements. The first step was to provide a reasonable model agreement to follow, the second step was to try that out in a number of different settings and the third step was to refine that experience and disseminate it. We decided to involve as many clients and workers as we could in discussion and in role play at a day conference, and then follow this with a pilot of the agreement. The pilot would provide feedback from practitioners, clients and foster parents.

So the model agreement was made the subject of a day conference. Parents, children in care, social workers and foster parents all worked in role play sessions to test out the viability of the design. The professionals were challenged by the clients, who said, 'we need to have the outline of the agreement in advance of the meeting; what normally happens is that social workers know the agenda in advance and then we have to struggle to learn what it is as we go along'. The working party agreed to put in its guidelines that clients should have the pro forma of the agreement in advance. The clients were challenged by the professionals, who said 'we need to have a section for the child's views as sometimes the parents and the child disagree – despite your personal experience that this has not happened, it can do so'. The separate sections were put in the pro forma.

The next stage was to see if the ideas hammered out in the calm conditions of the day conference would still stand up in the rougher world of practice. We invited social services departments to participate in a pilot run of the agreement model. We would supply the format and a very brief questionnaire for feedback from parents, children, social workers and foster parents. The questionnaires were simple, on one side of coloured paper and could be returned FREEPOST. They asked if it was the first agreement that the individual had made, if they found it helpful and if so why, and if anything important was left out or was particularly difficult. Eight departments agreed to pilot the form. The responses were positive but we found a wide variation in the number of written agreements used in different departments. This appeared to be due to internal problems (primarily the reorganization of the departments, which created uncertainty and dislocation) but it was clear that we needed to double-check that the agreement was practical. We arranged another day conference and asked one of the most active departments to present their experience, and we used this as a starting point for the debate. It was clear from the responses at this conference that the pro forma covered the right ground, that it was practical to use and that it was welcomed by the parties to the agreement (although social workers were slightly less enthusiastic as compared with foster parents or families! – a finding which supports the evidence that the introduction of these agreements is an uphill task).

We had assembled evidence that we used to refine and improve the model agreement, we had checked that it was practical, we had further arguments (from professionals and clients) supporting the value of such an agreement. We had started from research and practice experience, and analysed this to see what guidelines it could give us for written agreements.

In effect we had conducted a small-scale research study with a hypothesis, data gathering and data analysis. The hypothesis which we wanted to explore was 'if there was suitable guidance then a written agreement could be used in the initial placement of all children entering foster care'. We gathered data from role play and from practice experience, via discussion and questionnaire, to see if our development and our hypothesis was supported. This kind of work takes time (the final publication had still not appeared in 1988) but the principles of research-minded development enabled us to produce a better model for practice and to improve our knowledge of this area.

Research and practice – an alliance for the future

The examples that we have given so far have noted the contribution that research can and should make to practice and policy in substitute care. Research is both a process and a product. It is a way of careful thinking that shades into the kind of careful thinking that the best practitioners will be doing as part of their practice. It can provide an 'outsideness' of thinking and a re-viewing of practice that is crucial to the development of substitute care. The cumulative progress that can be made by research-initiated and research-informed development could be seen in the development of the agreement for foster placements that has just been discussed. On a much wider scale we can see how this kind of process is and is not occurring in other areas of substitute care.

The different partners in the alliance could point to gaps in research and in policy/practice in substitute care that should be addressed urgently. Practitioners, for example, are faced with continuing problems regarding the placement of siblings. Seventy per cent of the children in Fisher *et al.*'s (1986) study had siblings currently in care or they had had siblings in care; Berridge (1985) reports a similarly high figure. A number of practitioners have commented in the literature that decisions may have to be made to split a family and that judgements in this situation are very difficult (see, for example, Jones and Niblett, 1985; Bellwood, 1985). It may be that this is a common issue – we don't really know. It may be that splitting a family has particular effects that practitioners do not recognize. For example, there was some anecdotal evidence in our *In and Out of Care* study (Fisher *et al.*, 1986) that splitting was perceived by the children as punishment whereas it was actually done because of lack of placements. It may be that different foster placements or residential policies are needed to deal with this – we don't really know.

It is reasonable that practitioners and managers should call on their research colleagues to provide some further assistance in a number of different areas of practice and policy concern. Research in substitute care has a number of surprising gaps. We have a research literature that devotes a great deal of attention to adoption, which, you will recall, is a rather small part of substitute care. It gives a reasonable amount to fostering, not much to residential care and almost nothing to day care. A literature review of material on family placement by Shaw (1988) runs to 27 pages on adoption and 25 pages on foster care – the practice needs would not support this bias. It is also surprising, given a great deal of practice and policy concern, that the twin issues of gender and ethnicity in substitute care have only recently started to feature in research studies. There will always be gaps in the research literature, but surely a better dialogue between researchers and practitioners as joint members of an alliance would help to avoid some of the worst gaps?

Researchers could assist their practice colleagues in another important manner by establishing more reviews of past research, and by attempting to build cumulative research progress. A literature exercise to summarize work is particularly valuable – it avoids work getting lost, it provides a periodic assessment of the areas of clear research agreement and those that are subject to dispute. A recent example of this has been notably successful. *Social Work Decisions in Child Care* (DHSS, 1985) was a review of a number of studies that covered in all about 2000 children and 49 social service/social work departments. Sometimes a major study is needed to attempt to clear up a particular area. Adoption research, for example, seemed to be stuck with a permanent interest in the question of how 'successful' adoptions are. With the publication of material from a national long-term study of all children born on a particular date (the National Child Development Study, see Seglow *et al.*, 1972; Bagley, 1980, and Lambert, 1981) interest has now expanded to include other areas of adoption work. The national study showed that in most respects adopted children do as well as other groups. Research has moved on to look at the issues of adoption of older children, at issues of ethnicity and other factors involved with the changing practices and policies in adoption. Researchers have helped to move the work on in a way that will help and strengthen the alliance.

On the other side of the alliance researchers could of course point to gaps in the implementation of research. Parker's (1966) study that was discussed earlier and George's (1970) study of foster parents illustrate the point – their careful thinking concerning successful foster care has not been used in the way that it merited.

Researchers and practitioners need to engage in a constructive dialogue – they need to ensure that the fairy story that we began with remains firmly in the land of stories and does not become the true picture. If practitioners can recognize that research is a matter of careful thinking as well as technical skills, and if researchers can see that the real practice and policy concerns of social work merit their full attention, then the alliance will grow in strength. Each party to the alliance will benefit.

There are numerous pointers that this is now occurring. The book you are reading could be seen as one of them. The research summaries, the new journals, the practitioners registered for higher degrees could be seen as others. In the future it seems likely that we will see more blurring of the boundaries of research and policy and practice. This can only be to the benefit of the clients whom child care programmes are trying to serve.

References

Aldgate, J. and Hawley, D. (1986) *Recollections of Disruptions: A Study of Foster Care Breakdowns*, National Foster Care Association.

Bagley, C. (1980) 'Adjustment, achievement and social circumstances of adopted children in a national survey', *Adoption and Fostering*, Vol. 4, No. 4, pp. 47–9.

Bellwood, P. (1985) 'Assessing siblings for family placement', *Adoption and Fostering*, Vol. 9, No. 3, pp. 33–4.

Berridge, D. (1985) *Children's Homes*, Basil Blackwell.

Berridge, D. and Cleaver, H. (1987) *Foster Home Breakdowns*, Basil Blackwell.

Department of Health and Social Security (1985) *Social Work Decisions in Child Care*, HMSO.

Department of Health and Social Security (1987) *Adoptions in England and Wales*. HMSO.

Department of Health and Social Security (1988) *Children in Care in England and Wales*, HMSO.

Fisher, M., Marsh, P. and Phillips, D. (1986) *In and Out of Care*, Batsford/BAAF.

George, V. (1970) *Foster Care: Theory and Practice*, Routledge and Kegan Paul.

Goldstein, J., Freud, A. and Solnit, A. J. (1973) *Beyond the Best Interests of the Child*, Free Press.

Hazel, N. (1981) *A Bridge to Independence*, Basil Blackwell.

Johnson, P. R., Shireman, J. F. and Watson, K. W. (1987) 'Transracial adoption and the development of black identity at the age of eight', *Child Welfare*, Vol. 66, No. 1, pp. 45–55.

Jones, M. and Niblett, R. (1985) 'To split or not to split; the placement of siblings', *Adoption and Fostering*, Vol. 9, No. 2, pp. 26–9.

Lambert, L. (1981) 'Adopted from care by the age of seven', *Adoption and Fostering*, Vol. 5, No. 3, pp. 28–36.

Maluccio, A. N., Fein, E. and Olmstead, K. A. (1986) *Permanency Planning for Children: Concepts and Methods*, Tavistock.

Odams, M. 'A decision reversed? A study of mothers who withdrew from seeking adoption', unpublished study completed for Joint Unit of Social Services Research at Sheffield University.

Parker, R. A. (1966) *Decisions in Child Care*, George Allen and Unwin.

Pugh, G. (1988) *Services for Under Fives – Developing a Co-ordinated Approach*, National Children's Bureau.

Rowe, J. and Lambert, L. (1973) *Children Who Wait*, Association of British Adoption Agencies.

Rowe, J., Cain, H., Hundelby, M. and Keane, A. (1984) *Long-term Foster Care*, Batsford.

Seglow, J., Pringle, M. K. and Wedge, P. (1972) *Growing Up Adopted: A Long-term National Study of Adopted Children and their Families*, National Foundation for Educational Research.

Shaw, M. (1988) *Family Placement for Children in Care – A Guide to the Literature*, British Agencies for Adoption and Fostering.

Shaw, M. and Hipgrave, T. (1983) *Specialist Fostering*, Batsford.

Smith, P. M. (1986) 'Evaluation of Kent placements', *Adoption and Fostering*, Vol. 10, No. 1, pp. 29–33.

7 The physical and mental health of children in care

Barbara Kahan

It is now recognized that parents know more about their own children than professionals. In an average good and caring home their expertise is matched with concern, both of which are developed from the day the child is born. The times when a first tooth appears, the first words are babbled and the hundred and one other small indicators of development take place are of great importance to loving parents. Eyes, ears, teeth, height, weight, growth, energy, sleep, appetite are all watched and checked as a matter of routine; acute anxiety is readily engendered by illness or mishap and continues until the child is restored to normal health. Relationships between health and schooling, general wellbeing and happiness are clearly identified and the future safeguarded as far as possible by looking after any problems in the present.

When disruption of family life is great enough to lead to reception into care, however, parents are obliged to hand over responsibility, temporarily or long term, for their children's health as well as other aspects of their lives, to the local authority or voluntary agency whose task it is to provide substitute parenting for the time being. Do the local authorities and other agencies act as careful and anxious parents would in these circumstances?

The health of children in care was one of the subjects on which the House of Commons Social Services Committee, under the chairmanship of Renée Short MP, took evidence when it was conducting its inquiry into Children in Care in 1983–84. Amongst the individuals and groups of health professionals offering evidence were health visitors, the Royal College of Nursing, the Royal College of Physicians (Faculty of Community Medicine), the British Medical Association, the Tavistock Clinic, the Society of Area Nurses, members of the Royal College of Psychiatrists, the British Paediatric Association and local health authorities. The picture painted by their evidence was disturbing. There were a number of reasons for this, only some of which related to: 'failures in liaison between social services departments and the various parts of the NHS' or to 'organizational weaknesses within social services departments' (HMSO, para. 330).

The problem was seen by the Committee as sufficiently serious to devote a complete session of oral evidence to representatives of the medical profession.

The picture they saw, as expressed in the report, contrasts sharply with the approach of the average good family suggested above.

> Because a child in care often lacks one single person intimately familiar with his medical history, symptoms which normal caring parents would be in a position to observe and interpret may go unnoticed, so that they may suffer

> from non-acute but serious problems such as hearing or sight defects or other long-standing conditions such as asthma or diabetes. Younger children in particular may miss out on the proper series of inoculations, and dental treatment may be unduly intermittent. (HMSO, para. 331)

The committee was told by Dr Wolkind of the Royal College of Psychiatrists that 'it is very easy for a child to go through care with no one knowing whether they are left handed or right handed'.

An individual child or young person in care is in no position to ensure that his or her health is safeguarded and properly cared for without the kind of help and concern which good parents provide. When a public authority takes on parental responsibility the expectation at the end of the twentieth century is that this responsibility should not be carried out in the minimal way typical of the earlier part of the century, but should be modelled on the lines of good parenting. Even in the mid-1940s, when the Welfare State had yet to be born, the inquiry carried out by Sir Walter Monckton, KC, into the death of the foster child, Dennis O'Neill, who died of ill-treatment, starvation and pneumonia at the hands of his foster parents, stated, 'the . . . local authority . . . must care for the children as its own: the relation is a personal one. The duty must neither be evaded nor scamped.'

Careful examination by the doctor responsible for his medical attention had not been ensured for Dennis O'Neill and Sir Walter Monckton noted, 'I was informed that many local authorities do not comply with this . . . requirement'.

Compared with 1945, how much do we know about the health of children and young people in care in the late 1980s?

This chapter rests heavily on the work of two doctors, Frank Bamford, Reader and Honorary Consultant in Development Paediatrics (St Mary's Hospital for Women and Children, Whitworth Park, Manchester), and Stephen Wolkind, Consultant Child Psychiatrist (Maudsley Hospital, Denmark Hill, London), quoted above. They were commissioned by the Economic and Social Research Council's Children in Care Panel in 1988 to look at the research needs in the field of physical and mental health of children in care.

Their papers were considered by the ESRC to be of significant interest and importance to agencies, public and voluntary, in their policy and practice (the papers are available from the Economic and Social Research Council, see Bamford and Wolkind, 1988, for details).*

Following the Children Act 1948, an extensive child care service was established based on detailed legislative powers and intended to be carried out in the caring spirit referred to by the Monckton Inquiry and the Curtis

* In what follows there are many quotations or near quotations from their papers. Quotation marks have not been used in general as this would have been confusing and tedious. The author of the chapter accepts responsibility for selection with the permission of the writers of the two papers.

Report. The service developed and grew and many major improvements in child care services were made. Yet in spite of this little information is available about the physical health of children in care. Many thousands of children and young people are received into or committed to care by the courts each year (approximately 30 000 in 1984 – perhaps between 1.25 and 1.5 million since 1948) and a medical examination is part of that procedure, yet 'we have neither a clear knowledge of their physical state on reception nor any idea about changes in health that may occur while they are in care' (Bamford and Wolkind, 1988).

There is some overlap between what is already known about children admitted to care and those who suffer Sudden Infant Death and child abuse (Lynch and Roberts, 1977; Protestos *et al.*, 1973). For example, a greater than normal proportion of children in all three groups are born to young mothers and are premature at birth. Also those subsequently admitted to care, in common with children who are abused, are less likely to have attended infant welfare clinics and are more likely to be shorter in height and lighter in weight than other children. Dr Bamford suggests, however, that looking at health by categorization of children in terms of reasons for admissions to care and the health factors related to each group, would have limited usefulness because numbers would be too small in each group for adequate samples. Longitudinal studies of specific groups of children at risk of admission to care could provide better information than cross-sectional studies. These have, however, an intrinsic problem in that such studies may alter the health of the children concerned. In addition random allocation of children into experimental and control groups is likely to be impractical and community-based intervention programmes are preferable (Farquar, 1978).

As already noted, a legal requirement concerning admission of children to care is that they should be medically examined, whether they enter foster or residential care, and each year many thousands of medical examinations are carried out at considerable cost and often at some inconvenience to carers, children and doctors. Yet no published evaluation of their worth is available. Their purpose has been defined (see Bamford, 1979) and it is necessarily limited in scope, but if the findings were properly recorded a vast amount of information concerning the health of children at this critical point in their lives would be available. If good basic data were available a number of important points could then fairly easily be resolved. Perhaps the most important would be the extent of untreated remediable illness – no assessment has ever been made of its duration.

There is reason to believe that young children admitted to care have greater medical needs than their peers who are not in care, not only because of the effect of adverse socio-economic factors on health but also because a greater population of those admitted are handicapped compared with those who are not. The differences between the two groups require definition. At the time of admission to care a small proportion of the children show evidence of recent or past abuse, and careful examination in this respect might assist in assessing the incidence of undetected abuse in the community.

What effect does being in care have on the health of children? The National Child Development Study showed greater prevalence of developmental and health difficulties in children in care than in those who had never been in care. Those still in care at 16 were in good physical health but were more likely to be clumsy and have speech problems than peers never in care. Physical health appeared to improve during the care experience, but the nature and extent of improvement were uncertain. More knowledge of circumstances in which it may occur could affect child care practice and possibly policy also.

Medical examinations of children on admission to care and annual medical examinations while placed in foster homes are shown in practice to be undervalued and often fail to provide relevant information for the care of the children (DHSS, 1982). Not surprisingly they are seldom used in considering the children's total welfare. In some local authorities those required by the Boarding Out of Children Regulations still go by default (as was the case in 1945 when the Monckton Inquiry took place). In all this not only is the practical situation unsatisfactory but academically an opportunity for systematic data collection is being lost.

Dr Bamford suggests two fundamental problems exist: first the acquisition of a full medical history and second the education of doctors about the scope and requirements of the examinations. Normally paediatric diagnosis is based on a very full medical history and provisional opinions arising from it are confirmed or otherwise by examination.

The medical history of children in care, however, is usually not only grossly inadequate but parents are rarely interviewed, as recommended, by a medical officer prior to children's admission to care (British Paediatric Association, 1982). If children are to remain in care for long or indefinite periods of time the extent of examination and assessment could with benefit be similar to that undertaken on children placed for adoption (Forfar, 1979).

Stress is likely to be an inevitable factor in reception into care, and stress is known to influence susceptibility to infections, such as common infections of the throat. Children in care appear to suffer an excess of such infections. Furthermore children with recurrent physical illnesses such as infections of the ears and chest have been stated to be more likely than average to have developmental and behavioural disorders as well (Bax *et al.*, 1983). On the other hand diseases commonly thought to have a psychosomatic element in their aetiology are not uniformly more prevalent among children in care. In the National Child Development Study a greater proportion of children in care at 11 years old were enuretic as compared with those who had never been in care, but asthma seemed to be less common among those still in care at 16, and there was no increased prevalence of migraine.

The effect of emotional wellbeing on somatic growth has been known for many years but its significance has received increasing recognition many years but its significance has received increasing recognition during the 1980s. Standard growth charts have enabled deviations from normal speed of growth to be detected with a high degree of confidence provided that accurate measurement of height and weight are recorded. The importance of these in child care practice can hardly be over-emphasized.

An association between feeding problems and failure to thrive in infancy is now known to be also associated with subsequent physical abuse. It is often presumed that parents do not give their children sufficient food to maintain normal growth but it is also possible that sad and rejected children do not have the appetite to eat the food provided for them. When children are relieved from parental maltreatment by admission to care the growth of many of them accelerates and we need to know the conditions under which optimum growth can take place, and over what periods of time. There are many factors which can affect attained growth but speed of growth mirrors the overall wellbeing of children to a remarkable extent. This has considerable implications for child care practice which have not yet been explored or exploited.

Many receptions into care happen because of illness or disability in parents or children. Acute illnesses of childhood rarely lead to child care problems but short-term illness of parents is the most common reason for reception of children into care. There is, however, no information about the illnesses concerned, nor whether parents are admitted to hospital, and if so whether their admissions were necessary. It is not known, for example, whether the illnesses could have been dealt with at home if sufficient and appropriate domiciliary services were available and whether the doctors concerned were aware of the implications for the care of the children of parents admitted to hospital.

The general physical health of children in care has so far gone unrecorded and therefore unanalysed as has been seen; but the same is even true of children and young people with special problems. For example, there is little if any information regarding the physical consequences of delinquent behaviour, e.g. damage sustained from accidents or self-injurious behaviour. Nor is any published work readily available about possible links between offending and certain behaviour-influencing conditions such as acute viral infections, diabetes, epilepsy and its treatment. Neither has any attention been paid to the potential importance of physical health in the prevention of socially unacceptable behaviour.

About a quarter of all children in care are girls betwen 10 and 17. Some are sexually promiscuous due to a variety of reasons, but a group at special risk of sexually transmitted diseases are those who abscond from care. One small study of 44 girls who returned to children's homes and hostels after running away showed that 15 had gonorrhoea, 21 had trichomonas vaginalis infection, 10 had candida albicans and two had pubic lice (Bamford, 1980). Yet there are no published studies on preventive aspects of this problem.

Deprived girls who become pregnant are generally less likely than others to request a termination of pregnancy. Sometimes they and their babies are brought up in care together, but the long-term effects on the health and development of the children of these young mothers are not known, except that they are thought to be at high risk of non-accidental injury. There is also little known about what happens to them later in their lives.

Children with congenital handicaps may also be in care at the request of their parents because they are unable to accept them; in addition they have a greater than average chance of being committed to care because of child abuse and neglect. The National Child Development Study showed that 24 per cent of children in care at 16 years old were receiving special education compared with two per cent of those who had never been in care. It is probable, however, that only a small part of this difference is accounted for by differing proportions of children with physical defects in care and that most of it is due to the effect on learning capacity of long-standing deprivation. The extent of the problem of severe handicap is confused by the fact that a proportion of children are abandoned in hospital and their care provided by the National Health Service rather than by local authorities. About one-fifth of children in long-stay hospitals are abandoned (defined as not visited by parents or having not gone home within the preceding six months) and about one-third are abandoned early in their lives (Hood, 1976).

It is clear from this brief view of what is known about the physical health of children and young people in care, that little importance has so far been attached to either routine information gathering, medical examinations, or analysis of what could be known. The implications of this for policy and practice are inevitably significant.

The mental health of children in care, by comparison, has received more attention than their physical health, and studies of children in both residential and foster care have played a key role in various theoretical models advanced in an attempt to explain the origins of childhood psychopathology. Basic to these studies has been the theory of the negative and irreversible impact of separation from mothers. This theory was highly influential in the 1950s and has been re-evaluated since, particularly in the 1970s and later. Newer evidence points to reversibility (under certain circumstances) of some effects of adverse early experiences and balances the significance of separation caused by admission to care against the total context in which it occurred and the care given to a child following it (Rutter, 1980).

Whatever the reasons for behavioural and emotional disturbance amongst children in care, there is agreement that the rates of disturbance are high though the evidence may not be as firm for some care situations as it is for others.

'In care' is an administrative term which comprehends short- and long-term arrangements, all ages from early infancy to 18 years and older, and a wide range of human situations from relatively benign to highly traumatic and deeply damaging. In these circumstances, Dr Wolkind asks, is it possible to talk of the mental health of children in care?

Studies examining rates of disturbance have tended to be of specific groups, for example children in large, long-stay institutions or in foster care. High rates of disorder found, particularly in large, long-stay institutions, may, however, be atypical and a very different picture would be seen in children admitted to short-stay homes or living in small family group homes (Berridge, 1985).

Data on the mental health of children who have at some time been in local authority care are available from the National Child Development Study, e.g. Mapstone (1969) reported on 314 children out of a total sample of 15 000 who by the age of seven years nine months had spent some time in the care of a local authority or voluntary organization.

One important finding was that some individual children were doing very well. As a group, however, they did badly. On the Bristol School Adjustment Guide, a third were 'badly adjusted', a figure three times higher than in the general population. Behavioural difficulties were paralleled in poorer school attendance and attainment. They had been seriously disadvantaged both biologically and socially at birth, born into large overcrowded families and to younger mothers, having lower birth weights and being less likely to be full-term babies. This study and another by Wolkind and Rutter in 1973 with children from an inner London borough and the Isle of Wight both demonstrate that children who at some time in their lives have been in care, and in most cases have then returned home, are amongst the most vulnerable in the community in terms of psychological disturbance.

During the 1980s work has been carried out looking at the adjustment and mental health of adults who, as children, had spent some time in local authority care. The majority of a group of young adults in care in Glasgow in the 1940s and 1950s, despite their relatively high rate of problems, did not appear to be in any major difficulty and were maintaining themselves independently in the community (Ferguson, 1966).

More recently studies by Wolkind (1977a), Wolkind and Kruk (1983) and Rutter *et al.* (1983) found that compared with a random sample of the general population women who had been in care were more likely to be in their teens and unmarried at first pregnancy, scored higher on the Malaise Inventory (a screening device for detecting neurotic ill-health), had a significantly higher rate of psychiatric disorder during the early years of parenthood and interacted less with their very young babies. Their children, in one study, had higher rates of behavioural problems at school at the age of six.

The women also had poorer relationships in their marriages, and poorer housing. But in both studies some of the women were doing very well. There have been no studies of the psychiatric state of men who have been in care.

There has been little research comparing the psychiatric status of children in residential facilities provided by social services, education and health services. Many children go through formal observation and assessment processes, as a result of which some go to children's homes or CHEs, boarding schools for maladjusted children, or hospital adolescent units. There is, however, little information available to show if the recommendations made after assessment are carried out, and if they are whether they meet the needs of the children and young people. We do not even know to what extent the child's psychological functioning contributes to the final placement decision.

Early studies of children in institutional care included pictures of gross psychological dysfunction, accompanied by a poor level of cognitive skills and attainment. It has now become clear that much of the picture was due to the particular institutional regimes and that such gross results were rare. It has also become apparent that there is no one global syndrome associated with being in care, but that different types of outcome in behaviour relate to different experiences (Wolkind, 1974). Some of the characteristics popularly associated with children in care, and often with residential care in particular, are also seen in children brought up in neglecting, disorganized families.

From studies carried out so far it has become increasingly clear that, in the main, age at entry, and thus separation from the mother, explains little, if any, of the variation in mental health amongst children in care. Similarly, the pattern of admissions and length of time in care relate only marginally or paradoxically to disturbance. Studies of children not in care have produced consistent findings linking sex differences and psychiatric disorder. Boys are heavily over-represented in virtually all conditions, except neurotic disorders where there is equal sex distribution. Studies of the effects of stress in the family or the community show boys to be far more vulnerable than girls (Maccoby and Jacklin, 1980).

Amongst children in care, however, rates of disorder are about equal in the two sexes (Yule and Raynes, 1972). Amongst children who have been in care, and have then left, a very different picture is found. Extremely high rates of disturbance, predominantly of the anti-social variety, are found amongst boys, while in girls disturbance is virtually confined to the very few who spent most of their early years in residential care (Wolkind and Rutter, 1973). The work on adults referred to earlier suggests, though, that it may not be that girls are unaffected, but that the in-care and related experiences leave them vulnerable, through quite a different mechanism, to later problems. There are, as yet, no real explanations for these differences (Wolkind and Kruk, 1983a; Rutter *et al.*, 1983).

There can be little doubt that a child's temperament must be considered in relation to origins of psychopathology. If assessed prior to the birth of a second sibling, for example, temperament can predict response to that event (Dunn and Kendrick, 1982). We do not, however, have information on how a child's temperament relates to his or her adjustment to different types of care. Temperament might be a crucial factor in how a child relates to a move from residential to foster care, and might be important in which kind of care should be given priority. Children with physical handicaps who have been in residential care show very high rates of behavioural disturbance in placement for adoption (Wolkind, 1983). No such effect was found with similar children placed from foster care.

The most neglected area of all is that concerned with the nature of the life and relationships of children actually in care. A few studies, for example, on how changing the staffing structure of a residential home can make a dramatic improvement in the behaviour and social development of its children (Flint, 1966), on language development of young children (Tizard *et al.*, 1972), and on the nature of peer relationships in children's homes (Schaffer and Emerson, 1964) are available but there need to be many more. The work of Flint, cited above, and of others (see Wolins, 1974) show that both foster and residential care can have the potential to heal and allow growth.

The impact of available attachment figures for children was originally seen in terms of infants' relationships with main caretakers, particularly mothers. It is now apparent that relationships showing many of the features of attachment are of significance throughout an individual's life span (Parkes and Stevenson-Hinde, 1982), and the absence of figures fulfilling an attachment role has been described as a contributory factor to the genesis of neurotic disorders in adults (Henderson, 1982). For children in care the availability of a continuing relationship with an external adult may be a key variable which could prevent severe maladjustment. Of even more importance may be the quality of the relationship being offered (Wolkind, 1977b).

Of equal, if not greater, importance is the availability of attachment figures after a child has left care. The mental health problems and difficulties in parenting of the women studied by Rutter (see above) could be better explained by the absence of attachment figures in the years following discharge than by early damage caused by reception into care and associated problems. If correct, this hypothesis has major policy and practice implications, since what research there is suggests that at discharge from care, this very vulnerable group of children and young people are very likely to be left in a highly unsupported state (Mulvey, 1976).

The material drawn from Dr Bamford's and Dr Wolkind's papers demonstrates how little is known about the physical and mental health of the army of children who, in the last 40 years, have spent some part of their life in care, some for short but significant periods, some for many years during which the major responsibilities of their parents have been held by public agencies. Policy and practice formulated and carried out in the face of ignorance must lack the awareness needed to care for these children and young people as sensitively and positively as both they deserve and the public agencies are required to do. If some of them do well in spite of the knowledge gaps, it speaks more for their resilience than for the appropriate level of concern on the part of public services.

What is to be done about this serious lack of knowledge? First there is a need for recognition of the very large number of people in the community who, at some time in their lives, have been in care. Dr Wolkind suggests it may be as many as between four and six per cent of the population. Amongst the great diversity of their circumstances and experiences they share in common the fact that at some time in their lives they have been cared for by people who are expected to be experts on the emotional needs of children. As a group they also have a higher risk of psychiatric ill health and social deviance than any other easily identified group in our society. As adults they are far more likely than others to look back on their childhood as having been an unpleasant and sad experience (Wolkind and Kruk, 1985). Taken together, these three facts, Dr Wolkind suggests, should be a totally unacceptable statement for a society that claims to care for its children. In physical terms, Dr Bamford suggests that what is needed initially is good basic data collection. There is no doubt that this group of children is gravely disadvantaged and the emphasis of research should be on the preventive aspects of child care.

Some of the practical measures, among many, which might be taken, would include

- design of medical examination forms which would facilitate mechanical data storage and retrieval
- evaluation of medical examinations at the time children are received into care
- involvement of parents in medical examinations and efforts to obtain full medical histories
- studies of growth in relation to various child care situations
- investigation of illnesses in parents contributing to the need for reception of their children into care
- investigation of the long-term outcome for babies born to adolescent girls in care
- studies of factors contributing to the abandonment of handicapped children
- long-term evaluation of the effect of family placement of handicapped children.

Questions need to be asked, like what is the best staffing structure to meet the emotional needs of children in a children's home? What is the prognosis of a certain disorder or condition seen in children in care? The answers to apparently very practical questions could have important theoretical implications. With the deep concern frequently expressed about children in care, these questions are urgent.

Progress might be made through better integration and dissemination of existing knowledge, more systematic collection and use of data routinely collected, and the commissioning of new research.

Existing knowledge dealing with mental and physical health needs is predominantly in scientific journals and medical publications. These are unlikely to come to the attention of field or residential social workers. Nor is there much evidence that the body of available knowledge is used systematically in social work training. The research carried out by local authorities themselves (Clearing House for Local Authority Social Services Research, 1981) has also made little or no impression on workers in, for example, university research groups. The National Children's Bureau provided a unique service in the 1960s in bringing together work on residential and foster care, giving sources of original work, and attempting to integrate and draw conclusions for policy and practice (Dimage *et al.*, 1967a and b). Prosser's updating in 1978 was valuable and could beneficially become a regular exercise (Prosser, 1978a and b).

Of even greater importance is practitioners' need for existing knowledge and particularly combining data on the special circumstances of children in care with that from other fields.

It has already been suggested there is a need to standardize, and use for research, the large body of data which is being routinely collected by child care agencies, particularly local authorities. One of the best examples is seen in observation and assessment procedures. Several thousands of children each year are likely to have included in their assessment folder, school and social work reports, together with the results of medical, psychological and psychiatric examinations. Some standardization of the records collection would provide a large amount of usable data on children entering the system. Some joint work between, for example, the Economic and Social Research Council and the local authorities might explore the feasibility of such a process and the possible benefits.

This chapter owes much to the work of Dr Bamford and Dr Wolkind, who in their papers for the ESRC not only demonstrated the gaps in knowledge of the health of children in care, but also provided pointers for new research, better data collection and more thorough dissemination of existing knowledge.

The Children Bill, 1989, through its requirements for greater involvement of parents and children in decision making, reviews and choices of placements, will provide opportunities to improve the knowledge that both social workers and doctors have of the children's health. By bringing within the same legislation handicapped children and children in care another artificial boundary will be demolished. The greater emphasis in the Act on preventive work before care and the positive potential of being in care will together provide good reasons for changes of perceptions and attitudes which will be necessary before the health of children in care is adequately safeguarded and promoted.

Childhood is a period of foundation laying. Another chapter in this book concerns the importance of education in laying the foundations. Health and education together are seen by most parents as the vital constituents of their children's future lives. If the education and health of children in care

are appropriately valued by public agencies, even short episodes in care could make a valuable contribution to strong foundations for adult life.

References

Bamford, F. N. (1980) 'Sexual development of children in care', in Elstein, M. (ed) *Clinics in Obstetrics and Gynaecology*, Vol. 7, No. 2, p. 211.

Bamford, F. N. (1979) 'Medical examination of children admitted into care', in Wolkind, S. N. (ed) *Medical Aspects of Adoptions and Foster Care*, Spastics International Medical Publications.

Bamford, F. N. and Wolkind, S. N. (1988) *The Physical and Mental Health of Children in Care: Research Needs* (two papers), ESRC.

Bax, M., Hart, H. and Jenkins, S. (1983) 'The behaviour, development and health of the young child: implications for care', *British Medical Journal*, Vol. 286, pp. 1793–6.

Berridge, D. (1985) *Children's Homes*, Basil Blackwell.

British Paediatric Association (1982) *Report of Working Party on Children in Care*.

Clearing House for Local Authority Social Services Research (1981) *Report Number 1*, Department of Social Administration, University of Buckingham.

Department of Health and Social Security Social Work Service (1982) *A Study of the Boarding out of Children*, DHSS.

Dinnage, R. and Kellmer-Pringle, M. L. (1967a) *Residential Facts and Fallacies*, Longman.

Dinnage, R. and Kellmer-Pringle, M. L. (1967b) *Foster Home Care: Facts and Fallacies*, Longman.

Dunn, J. and Kendrick, C. (1982) 'Temperamental differences, family relationships and young children's responses to change within the family', in *Temperamental Differences in Infants and Young Children*, Ciba Foundation Symposium, 89, Pitman.

Farquar, J. W. (1978) 'The community-based model of lifestyle intervention trials', *American Journal of Epidemiology*, Vol. 108, pp. 103–11.

Ferguson, T. (1966) *Children in Care and After*, Oxford University Press.

Flint, B. M. (1966) *The Child and the Institution. A Study of Deprivation and Recovery*, University of London Press.

Forfar, J. O. (1979) 'Paediatrics, adoption, fostering', in Wolkind, S. N. (ed) *Medical Aspects of Adoption and Foster Care*, Spastics International Medical Publications.

Henderson, S. (1982) 'The significance of social relationships in the etiology of neuroses', in Parkes, C. M. and Stevenson-Hinde, J. (eds) *The Place of Attachment in Human Behaviour*', Basic Books.

Hood, C. (1976) 'Children abandoned in long-stay hospitals', *Child Care, Health and Development*, Vol. 2, pp. 239–50.

House of Commons Second Report from the Social Services Committee 1983–84, *Children in Care*, HC 360–1, HMSO.

Lynch, M. A. and Roberts, J. (1977) 'Predicting child abuse: signs of bonding failure in the maternity hospital', *British Medical Journal*, i, pp. 624–6.

Maccoby, E. E. and Jacklin, C. N. (1980) 'Psychological sex differences', in Rutter, M. (ed) *Scientific Foundations of Developmental Psychiatry*, Heinemann.

Mapstone, E. (1969) 'Children in care', *Concern*, Vol. 3, pp. 23–8.

Monckton, Sir Walter, KC (1945) *Report on the Circumstances which led to the Boarding Out of Dennis and Terence O'Neill at Bank Farm, Minsterley, and the Steps Taken to Supervise their Welfare*, HMSO.

Mulvey, T. (1976) *After Care – Who Cares?*, MA dissertation, Essex University.

Parkes, C. M. and Stevenson-Hinde, J. (eds) (1982) *The Place of Attachment in Human Behaviour*, Basic Books.

Prosser, H. (1978a) *Perspectives on Residential Care*, NFER.

Prosser, H. (1978b) *Perspectives on Foster Care*, NFER.

Protestos, C. D., Carpenter, R. G., McWeeny, P. M. and Emery, J. L. (1973) 'Obstetric and perinatal histories of children who died unexpectedly (cot death)', *Archives of Diseases in Childhood*, Vol. 49, p 486.

Rutter, M. (1980) *Maternal Deprivation Reassessed* (2nd ed), Penguin.

Rutter, M., Quinton, D. and Liddle, C. (1983) 'Parenting in two generations: looking backwards and looking forwards', in Madge, N. (ed) *Families at Risk*, Heinemann.

Schaffer, H. R. and Emerson, P. E. (1964) 'The development of social attachments in infancy', *Monographs of Social Research in Child Development*, Vol. 29, pp. 1–77.

Tizard, B., Cooperman, O., Joseph, A. and Tizard, J. (1972) 'Environmental effects on language development; a study of young children in long-stay residential nurseries', *Child Development*, Vol. 43, pp. 337–58.

Wolins, M. (1974) *Successful Group Care*, Aldine.

Wolkind, S. N. (1974) 'The components of affectionless psychopathy in institutionalized children', *Journal of Child Psychology and Psychiatry*, Vol. 15, pp. 215–20.

Wolkind, S. N. (1977a) 'Women who have been "in care": psychological and social status in pregnancy', *Journal of Child Psychology and Psychiatry*, Vol. 18, pp. 179–82.

Wolkind, S. N. (1977b) 'A child's relationship after admission to residential care', *Child Care, Health and Development*, Vol. 3, pp. 357–62.

Wolkind, S. N. (1983) *The Adoption of Children with Medical Handicap*, Report to the DHSS.

Wolkind, S. N. and Kruk, S. (1983) *Women Who Have Been in Care*, Report to the DHSS.

Wolkind, S. N. and Kruk, S. (1985) 'From child to parent', in Nicol, A. R. (ed) *Longitudinal Studies in Child Psychology and Psychiatry*, John Wiley.

Wolkind, S. N. and Rutter, M. (1973) 'Children who have been "in care": an epidemiological study', *Journal of Child Psychology and Psychiatry*, Vol. 14, pp. 95–101.

Yule, W. and Raynes, N. V. (1972) 'Behavioural characteristics of children in residential care in relation to indices of separation', *Journal of Child Psychology and Psychiatry*, Vol. 13, pp. 249–58.

8 Education of children in care

Sonia Jackson

Two out of every three children in care are of compulsory school age. In common with every other child in the country they are expected to attend school five days a week for 40 weeks a year. Yet we know very little of what happens to them there and no official statistics are published on the educational performance of children in care. An extensive computerized literature search (Jackson, 1988) exposed a surprising absence of research knowledge on this aspect of children's life in care. There is no book on the subject in the English language. Among the many thousands of publications on children in foster families or residential units only a handful of articles are concerned with their education. Until very recently both research reports and books about child care practice largely ignored the subject.

Almost the only exception is Barbara Kahan's book, *Growing Up in Care* (1979), which most unusually includes a whole chapter on 'Education and Teachers'. This probably reflects the high priority that she gave to the educational needs of children in care when she was Children's Officer of Oxfordshire. Another name which recurs is that of Mia Kellmer Pringle, who early recognized children in care as an especially disadvantaged group in the education system (Pringle, 1965), and built this perception into the National Children's Bureau longitudinal National Child Development Study. Most of the small number of articles concerned with the school experience of children in care are to be found in the NCB journal, *Concern*. This gap in the literature is no accident. It reflects the deep split between our education and child care systems at all levels. Research which originates from concern about services which care for children does not seem to recognize education as a particularly interesting or important aspect of the life of separated children. On the other side, educationists and psychologists rarely identify children in care as a disadvantaged category with special needs, even though the numbers involved are relatively large. Of the 72 800 children in care in March 1985, 62 per cent were of compulsory school age. Of these, 73 per cent were aged 10–15 and the rest under 10. Special boarding schools accommodated 1800 and 2300 were in Community Homes with Education. An unknown number attended day special schools, but it is clear that the vast majority attended ordinary neighbourhood schools.

The available evidence, limited as it is, leaves no doubt that coming into care carries a high risk of educational failure. Allowing for the fact that most children in care come from families which are educationally disadvantaged anyway, Essen *et al.* (1976) found that eleven-year-olds who first came into care before the age of seven scored 14 months below the norm in reading and 12 months behind in mathematics compared with children who had never been in care. The longer children spent in care, the lower their attainment and the more likely they were to display behaviour problems in school. Akhurst (1975) used Rutter's 'Children's Behaviour Questionnaire' to assess the level of behaviour disorders reported by houseparents and teachers in a group of 182 children in long-term residential care. All had been in their current homes for more than six months and had no formally recognized handicap. Akhurst found a much higher prevalence of severe behaviour disorder than in the general population, particularly among boys. In describing them their teachers used such words as anti-social, restless, disobedient, destructive. More recently a longitudinal study by Osborn and St Claire (1987) confirmed the finding that coming into care does nothing to improve the educational prospects of disadvantaged children. Not only is this a waste of human resources but it carries a high cost in terms of the quality of the children's future lives as adults.

Education and life chances

Roy Parker (1988) has reviewed the evidence on the employment experience of young people brought up in care and found a very bleak picture. They were far more likely to be unemployed than people of the same age living with their own families. For example, Stein and Carey (1986) carried out five successive interviews with 45 young people who had left care and found that the largest number to have a job at any one time was five (11 per cent) and even these were mostly in casual or temporary work.

Parker comments that one of the reasons why children in care secure such a poor foothold in the labour market is their lack of educational achievement. We know that in present employment conditions young people who are not integrated into a family network stand little chance of getting work unless they have formal educational qualifications or marketable skills. For them education may be the only means to avoid repeating the patterns of family disadvantage which caused them to come into care in the first place. Rutter, Quinton and Liddle (1983), in a study of people in their 20s who had spent time in care as children, found that whatever their early experience, final achievement at school was the most important factor in their behaviour as adults. Pilling (1986) followed up the most severely disadvantaged sector of the National Child Development Study cohort (11 000 children born in the same week). She found a close link between educational achievement and wellbeing measured on many different criteria. By the time they reached the age of 27, the educational achievers were better off in every way than the comparison group. They were much more likely to be employed, to earn good wages, own their homes, have strong leisure interests and feel satisfied with their lives.

Educational attainment was defined in this study as having five GCE passes at 'O' level or their equivalent, and it seemed to be the crucial factor in 'escape from disadvantage', especially for girls. Very few children in care achieve anything like this level unless they are adopted.

It is interesting to note that this was clearly perceived in earlier times. What seems to have happened is that since 1948 we have switched from a future to a present orientation, being more concerned with the child's immediate physical and emotional care and less with long-term outcome. This contrasts strongly with prevailing attitudes before the setting up of children's departments in 1948. Reading accounts of discussions about child care in the last century or the early part of this century, the difference is striking. The expressive needs of children were completely ignored and certainly did not count then as a factor to be considered when making decisions about them.

Voluntary societies, on the other hand, prided themselves on giving their children a better start in life.

Organizations like Dr Stephenson's (later the National Children's Home) aimed to equip every child for a trade, a fact on which their publicity material laid great emphasis (The Children's Home, 1898) and some were picked out to become teachers or clerks. After 1948, the role of the voluntary societies in providing substitute care for children declined relative to the local authorities and their educational orientation seems to have been largely lost. It persisted longest in penal institutions, such as borstals and approved schools where, as Parker points out, the trade training elements were among the activities most positively regarded by the inmates.

When the approved schools became community homes with education (CHEs) there was a shift of emphasis from training to containment, and sometimes therapy, similar to the one which had occurred earlier in children's homes. The result, although they were staffed predominantly by teachers, was an unfortunate loss of educational purpose, documented by a highly critical HMI's report (described in the *Guardian* as 'the most damning of the decade'). Almost all the children were found to be achieving below their potential and standards were generally low (DES, 1980). A later report (DHSS, 1981) on observation and assessment centres, through which at least 8000 children passed each year, also singled out education as an area where provision was particularly poor. It is sometimes said that the Centres were staffed by teachers who had turned to them as a last resort, having failed to find jobs in mainstream schools. Whether this was so or not, they were faced with an impossible task by the transient population of assorted ages and abilities.

Causes of educational problems

Why should children in care do badly in the education system? On the face of it coming into care should be helpful to them. Many of them move from impoverished, disorganized households with multiple problems to settings where at least all their basic physical needs are met and they are removed from the disturbing effects of family conflict. One explanation which many people would like to believe is that the effects of the pre-care background persist and frustrate the best efforts of carers to help children learn and do well at school. It is argued that the poor performance of children in care is to be expected and is probably no worse than it would have been if they had remained with their own families.

There is certainly some truth in the view that very poor pre-care experiences make it hard for children to function well in school, either socially or cognitively. An educational psychologist, Eva Holmes, has shown in a number of articles how severely deprived children develop coping responses which inhibit their ability to learn. They will already have discovered before they go to school that 'finding out is discouraged, that adults will rarely listen or answer questions, that adult behaviour is often quite inconsistent and unhelpful, that no one notices or cares about trying something new or difficult, that toys invariably get lost or broken' (Holmes, 1977). Even if they do not come into care before school, these children have often experienced several years of day care and seem to find it particularly hard to adjust to the classroom. They may be restless children who cannot settle down or concentrate; their attention span and ability to listen seem limited; they often behave aggressively and impulsively and their language development is delayed. Others are withdrawn and unresponsive. A research study carried out in an inner-city day nursery (Holmes, 1980) showed that most of the children had learned to be prematurely independent, to expect little of adults since the reactions they had experienced from their mothers were unpredictably demanding, punitive and erratic. Holmes describes the characteristic behaviour of these children as 'pseudo-self-reliance' and believes it often leads them to block off what the teacher in school is saying to them, preventing them from learning.

Older children, even if not from homes as disadvantaged as these, may come into care with a history of poor school performance or as a result of non-attendance with the obvious effects on attainment.

However, I shall argue in this chapter that attempts to explain away the poor educational achievement of children in care by reference to their families of origin rest on a shaky theoretical base and a value position which needs to be challenged.

Theory and practice

Expectations about what children in care might achieve in education appear to be coloured by lingering notions about the genetic base of intelligence going back to the now-discredited research of Sir Cyril Burt.

This is well illustrated by a Home Office *Guide to Adoption Practice* published in 1970. It advises that information should be obtained not only about the facts of the prospective adoptive parents' education, training and present occupation, but also about their feelings and attitudes to their own education and that of any child they might bring up:

> Agencies should try to select adoptive parents who will not put undue pressure on their children to achieve educational or work standards beyond their real ability, or develop interests in line with adopters' personalities rather than their own.

This was written at a time when adoption was still confined to babies and very young children. Nevertheless there is surely an implication that the children's 'real' ability is more likely to correspond to that of their probably working-class natural parents than that of their middle-class adopters. And not only their intelligence but their interests are likely to be inherited. 'A' levels and Mozart are not for the lower orders!

Another outdated notion which underlies the attempt to pin the reason for failure on the child's family background is that early experience is irreversible, especially if it includes the absence of a stable mother-figure during the first years of life. John Bowlby, with whose name this view is particularly associated, has in fact considerably modified his position over the years, and there is a large body of evidence, reviewed by Clarke and Clarke (1976) and Rutter (1972) that even children who have been very severely deprived can respond to skilled therapeutic and remedial help. But the best evidence comes from numerous adoption studies which show consistently that adopted children's educational achievement matches that of their adopters much more closely than that of their natural parents (Seglow *et al.*, 1972). This is true even when children are adopted relatively late after spending several years in residential care (Tizard, 1977) or when there are other factors which might seem likely to cause problems, as for black children growing up in white adoptive families (Gill and Jackson, 1983).

Expectations

Accepting that, given the right kind of help, there is no reason why children in care should not do well at school, there is a further problem. What level of achievement should the local authority in its role as parent be aiming for? This vital question is seldom asked. There is no doubt that the authority is responsible, as parents are, for ensuring that children receive efficient full-time education up to the age of 16, but how far does it extend beyond this? In the past, most child care textbooks and official guidelines have tended to adopt a minimalist position, emphasizing attendance and adjustment rather than achievement. Provided the child keeps going to school and does not cause too much trouble, what he or she does there does not matter too much.

Some people even take the view that it would be wrong for a public authority to be ambitious for the children in its care, and this is clearly implicit in the reluctance of social services departments to make grants for further and higher education, as they are empowered so to do under Section 27 of the 1980 Child Care Act. One senior government official summed it up by saying to a former children's officer: 'It is no part of your job to try to provide for a child better than his own parents would have done.' The Poor Law principle of less eligibility, which laid down that life in the workhouse must be even more disagreeable than the life of the poor outside it, still survives.

The question which needs to be asked is, should it be the aim of a social services department to provide a standard of care and education superior in quality but similar in kind to what the child might have expected to experience in an adequately functioning family of the same social class as his or her family of origin? Or should the department attempt to compensate through education for the handicaps, inadequacies and problems which caused this child to be taken into care? Is it right to aspire for this child to a degree of educational success which is rarely achieved by those of similar family backgrounds, and thereby perhaps become an agent of social mobility? Should social workers have the same or different standards for their own children and those for whom they carry professional responsibility? These are questions which need to be addressed if we are seriously interested in identifying the causes of low achievement and doing something about them.

There is, in fact, a good deal of evidence that social workers usually have low expectations of children in care and that education does not come high on their agenda. Melotte (1979) studies placement decisions over a two-month period in one local authority. During that time 56 children aged three months to 16 years were admitted to care. All the social workers (including seniors and area officers) were asked 'What factors influenced you when you decided to place this child?' Twenty different factors were mentioned by at least one social worker. None included school or education.

Martin Knapp has pointed out that social workers play a vitally important role in deciding which of a child's many needs to treat as important and which to overlook. A large-scale study carried out in Suffolk (Knapp *et al.*, 1985) found that although half the children were assessed as having school-related difficulties, educational improvement was considered to be a specific objective for only six. Of 285 objectives listed by social workers, no more than 16 related to education.

These attitudes are mirrored at all levels of the child care system. If we examine practice manuals, job specifications for care staff, criteria for the selection of foster parents and literature addressed to them, the invisibility of school is striking. If mentioned at all it is only in relation to the importance of regular attendance. Yet this is to ignore the centrality of school in children's lives, and the way in which school and home experience interact. I have suggested elsewhere that we need to look much more closely at the way in which school difficulties relate to breakdown of foster placements in early adolescence (Jackson, 1988a).

Changes of placement

Some factors which contribute to the disadvantage of children in care in the school system are common to all forms of care. The most significant is disruption. Numerous studies (e.g. Millham *et al.*, 1986; Berridge, 1985; Berridge and Cleaver, 1987) have shown how common is the experience of multiple placements. The situation may be worsening with current pressure for family placement of as many children as possible, and with residential care regarded as a short-term staging post (Parker, 1988). Since the rate of foster home breakdown remains obstinately around 40 per cent in most areas, movements between placements as well as between care and home are very common. More often than not each move involves a change of school. I interviewed a girl of 14 who had moved once for every year of her age and attended 10 different schools. Berridge (1985) reports that several children in his study were unable to remember how many schools they had attended, and 'a girl living in one home proudly opened her wardrobe to reveal the splendid mauves, greens, blues and greys of four brand new uniforms of schools she had fleetingly attended during the previous year'.

Social workers, unless they have school-age children of their own, are seldom geared to the rhythms of the education system, and so may give little thought to timing moves to minimize stress and disruption of the child's schooling. In any case, however carefully a move is handled, it inevitably involves a setback to learning while the child finds out about rules and customs and has to build a new set of social relationships. It is hardly surprising that children who are asked to adjust over and over again to new schools simply switch off or become extremely disturbed. Parker (1988) comments that, at social levels in which educational success is expected, employers, such as the armed forces or the foreign service, recognize the harmful effects of frequent changes of school by subsidizing boarding education for the children of their employees.

Along with placement moves also goes disruption of relationships. Not only carers but social workers change quite frequently, partly as a result of the development of the profession, with a better career structure and more emphasis on training. The result is that there is rarely a long-term adult in the child's life who can take an active and informed interest in his or her educational progress. It may be that this is the most important factor in the high achievement of adopted children. Adoption differs from other forms of substitute care in that it involves a lifelong commitment to the child and a predisposition therefore to take a long-term view of his or her wellbeing, to have at least an implicit educational career plan. Unless persuaded otherwise by social workers, adoptive parents tend to hold expectations about the child's school performance similar to those they would have had for their natural children.

The importance of continuity and the potentially disastrous effects of disruption are both well illustrated by the experience of Dr Michael Lindsay, Children's Rights Officer of Leicestershire, described in a photo-story in *Who Cares?* (1988). He came into care with his brother and sister at 15 months and stayed, with one unsuccessful period home on trial, at the same children's home until he was 14, looked after by the same officer-in-charge. She was 'a great motivator and supporter, bolstering you up when you began to believe people who said you were no good'. Michael showed academic promise at an early age, learning to play chess when he was only four, and had been entered for nine 'O' levels when the local authority decided that he was too old to be in a mixed-sex home and transferred him to a home for teenage boys 20 miles away. His new school assessed him as needing remedial teaching in mathematics and reading, and thought he might be suitable to take four CSEs in practical subjects. No one at the school would listen to his protests. As a black child in care it was simply assumed he must be of low ability. The professionals took up entrenched positions and only after a tremendous battle involving the directors of education and social services was he admitted to classes at his appropriate ability level. Without the support, both practical and emotional, of the officer-in-charge of his previous children's home and his social worker (who, most unusually, had remained the same for eight years), he thinks he would have given up and dropped out of school at the first opportunity. He went on to take four 'A' levels, a first class degree in English and Education at Stirling University and a PhD in Applied Social Linguistics at Aberdeen. It is interesting to note that his social worker made great efforts to maintain links with his parents throughout his time in care, and that his father, though unable to provide him with a home, nevertheless played a significant role in sustaining his motivation and belief in himself.

Different care settings

Seen from the child's viewpoint, the distinction between foster and residential care may be rather unreal – they are often sequential episodes in a string of different placements. Both the Dartington cohort study (Millham *et al.*, 1986) and the Sheffield study of the experiences of children, parents and social workers (Fisher *et al.*, 1986) found that between 70 and 80 per cent of the children they studied had spent some part of their time in residential homes though many had also experienced other forms of care. The problems that arise in relation to education may, however, be rather different in foster and residential homes.

We shall know much more about the experience of foster children in the middle years of school when research, at present being carried out by Jane Aldgate and her colleagues at Oxford, is completed. Until then we have almost no direct evidence on the subject, though there is some indication from a Scottish study that stable, long-term foster families may play an important part in encouraging young people to go on to further education (Tresiliotis and Russell, 1984). There is also anecdotal evidence that foster parents can and often do act as effective advocates for children in relation to schools and social workers. For example Sheila Easson, writing about her upbringing in what she descibes as a 'loveless and hostile' foster home, nevertheless goes on to acknowledge the contribution made by her elderly foster parents to her present satisfying life. Although they were bitterly disappointed that she failed the eleven plus, 'When my teachers felt I would not cope with the demands of 'O' levels they fought to influence them and secured a place for me in the fifth form. I passed my four subjects and was transferred to the grammar school to take my three 'A' levels . . . I believe that my removal from institutional care into a materially and educationally richer environment effected an emotional and academic reversal' (Easson, 1988).

Unfortunately foster parents are not always in a position to give children the support and stimulation they need. 'Traditional' foster parents have usually had rather limited education themselves. Prosser (1978) reviewed a large number of studies which showed that foster families are generally recruited from a narrow social band, and the most recent research shows that this is still true of mainstream fostering today. Summarizing her findings, Prosser concluded that most foster fathers were skilled manual or routine clerical workers. The family life style was characterized by orderliness and regularity rather than adventurousness or wide interests. Typically the parents were home-centred people in traditional marriages with a male breadwinner and a female houseworker. Foster mothers had usually left school at the minimum age with no further training and had few interests outside the family. It might be difficult for them to offer much intellectual stimulation, especially to older children or to deal effectively with schools and teachers. As role models they would tend to reinforce gender stereotypes and low aspirations among girls.

The picture may be changing with the growth of specialist fostering schemes, which often lay emphasis on school adjustment and performance. Enhanced allowances and status seem to attract a different group of carers, and it is much more common for both foster parents to have higher educational or other qualifications. Although the young people concerned have often had particularly difficult experiences, they seem to do better than expected in the school system and are more likely to continue their education after 16, perhaps as a result of having confident and knowledgeable foster parents (Hazel, 1981). The numbers of these compared with the total number of children and young people in foster homes is very small.

In residential units the quality of support and stimulation offered to children is even more closely related to the educational background of the carers, especially that of the person in charge. Berridge (1985) suggests that this may be why children tend to get more encouragement to do well at school in private children's homes which often have middle-class proprietors.

There is a constellation of problems which particularly limit educational opportunities for children living in residential homes and attending ordinary schools. The evidence is comprehensively reviewed by Parker (1988) in a literature survey carried out for the Wagner Report. He identifies difficulties arising from three sources: the character of the staff group, already mentioned, conditions and style of life in children's homes, and failures of liaison between homes and schools.

The low proportion of social-work trained staff in residential care is well known – fewer than a quarter have had any relevant training, a fact which the Gatsby Project in conjuction with the Open University through jointly constructed child care courses is aiming to change. But in the past, even those who did undertake training may have had attitudes to school and education which could be unhelpful to the young people in their care. Millham, Bullock and Hosie (1980) found in their study that only 32 per cent of residential staff had enjoyed their own school days; 62 per cent of those who had taken the eleven plus failed; 59 per cent had left school by the age of 16 with 'mediocre' attainments. And these were mostly people with management responsibilities who had been seconded to a training course. The educational background of junior care staff may be even less promising. A small enquiry recently undertaken into the experience of staff in nine voluntary children's homes revealed that a third had no qualifications of any kind, not even one CSE. At the other end of the scale a few had university degrees, but they were a tiny minority.

In these circumstances it is hardly surprising that staff may have difficulty in relating to school teachers or in asserting their own judgement of a child's ability and needs against the opinion of a presumed expert. In addition, they may be inclined to play down the importance of school attendance and gloss over difficulties, not expecting that the children in their charge will do better than they did themselves.

It is an occupational hazard for residential care staff to become over-preoccupied with what goes on within the institution, regarding the outside world, and still more the school, as foreign territory. Young people who have been in children's homes report this lack of interest in what goes on at school as one of the most discouraging aspects of life in care. One boy remarked that 'it's like those fairy stories where you go off on a magic carpet and when you come back it's still the same time as when you left. No one talks about it so nothing that happens at school seems real.'

Group living has the potential to offer enriching experiences to children and young people, as Clough (1988) has argued, but this is often not realized in practice. A survey of 21 Manchester children's homes revealed a depressing picture (Brown and Solomon, 1974). None made any attempt to engage the children in interesting or stimulating leisure activities. Watching television, listening to pop music and just 'hanging around' occupied most out of school time. Ten years later Berridge (1985) found little change, describing many of the children's homes he studied as 'frankly dull places in which to live'. He confirms the impression that residential staff give priority to caregiving and domestic tasks, painting a graphic picture of the child coming home from school, bursting to recount the day's events, 'only to find adult attention firmly focused on the chip pan and the frozen fishfingers'. Educational activities tend to come a long way down the list. Bald (1982), for example, describes how hard it was to persuade care staff to devote 10 minutes a day to helping children with their reading, though with the help of volunteers he got there in the end.

When children reach secondary school lack of time and facilities to do homework is a frequent complaint. One girl told a conference of teachers and social workers in Dundee (SCAFA, 1986) that the only time she could find space and quiet to work for her 'O' levels was between one and three in the morning. There are exceptions, particularly, as already mentioned, among some voluntary and privately run homes, and I came across a local authority children's home which provided every child with a worktable, desk lamp and individual bookshelf, but it was not common.

Children in care for education-related problems

More then 500 children are admitted to care each year under Section 1(2)e of the 1969 Children and Young Persons Act, usually for persistent failure to attend school. Over 90 per cent of these are of secondary school age. There is very little research on what happens to them afterwards but a small study by a principal education welfare officer came to the sobering conclusion that their admission to care had produced no educational benefit at all, while the court action (which he had often initiated in the past under the impression that it was in the children's best interests) and subsequent upheaval had usually caused their lives to deteriorate markedly in every other way (Bowen, 1985).

We also know little about how school disciplinary procedures affect children in care though the high incidence of behaviour problems among them has already been noted. A small study of secondary school children referred to a Barnardo's intermediate treatment centre suggested that those in residential care might be at higher risk of suspension, since it was assumed that there would be someone available during the day to supervise them (Miller, 1988). If they continued to come into conflict with teachers they might more quickly reach the point where the 1981 Education Act was invoked and they would be referred for a statement of special needs on grounds of having emotional and behavioural difficulties (EBD). There was a danger then that they would be left without schooling, sometimes for very long periods, waiting for the 'statementing committee' to meet or for a special school place to be found. This, in turn, might lead to a breakdown in their current care placement since few foster parents and not all children's homes can tolerate an adolescent around the house all day.

This study also raises the question of whether local authorities are more willing to acquiesce in the withdrawal or exclusion of children from mainstream schooling than parents are likely to be. Sending a child to a boarding special school may seem to solve the care and education problems simultaneously, and with the decline in social services residential provision this could be an increasingly attractive option. It can have the advantage of providing greater stability and some schools provide a good standard of education and make a real effort to help children overcome previous gaps in their learning. However, the quality of care and teaching is often very variable and the child may bitterly resent what he or she sees as an inappropriate placement, as retrospective accounts illustrate. Andrew Demetri (1982) describes, for example, how he was sent to a special school:

> No one should be able to label a child maladjusted. I have borne that mark like a stigma on my body since I was nine . . . I am intelligent enough to have profited from a normal education but because of the label I was sent to a school where there were so many disturbed boys that it was quite impossible to give those of us who were at all interested a reasonable education.

Alex Saddington describes a similar experience. At his first special school he suffered 'a severe overdose of painting and drawing'. At a later one 'all we did was muck around for a couple of hours and go home. There were no proper lessons.' Even when he managed to get into an ordinary secondary school and enter for exams, the social services department moved him 20 miles away two weeks before he was due to take them, with the result that he left school aged 16 with no qualifications. (Saddington, 1988.)

Improving children's chances

Is educational failure inevitable for children in care, or could their prospects be altered for the better? Research suggests that changes in attitudes and practice could do a great deal to help. For maximum impact the change needs to come at national and higher management levels in particular, but there is nothing to prevent individual social workers and carers from reviewing their own practice and beginning at once to move in a new direction.

Some people who grow up in care already manage to succeed despite the obstacles. An article in the *Sunday Times* (Revill and Smith, 1988) produced a large number of letters from men and women who had fought their way through to good qualifications and satisfying jobs. But all had found it necessary to fight. To make success the norm rather than the exception will need much effort. At least we are now beginning to reach the point of identifying what changes are needed. Although there is such a long way to go, there are some encouraging signs.

The House of Commons Social Services Committee inquiry on children in care singled out education as an area which gave cause for concern and where more research was needed, and soon afterwards the Economic and Social Research Council made it the subject of a research initiative. In 1988 the Association of Directors of Social Services chose it as the main topic for the annual meeting of their child care policy group. This is important because real change will only occur if policy makers at the top who have the power to determine priorities and allocate resources are convinced it is necessary.

A strong lead has also been given by one of the major voluntary children's societies, National Children's Home (Jackson, 1989), which has adopted a policy statement and guidelines designed to overcome many of the problems identified in this chapter.

It is important to recognize that change needs to occur within all the systems which affect children in care, not just in social services. Because of their life experiences they have special needs just as much as children born with disabilities. This might be better acknowledged if, for example, each local authority had a named educational psychologist with special responsibility for children in care. Primary school teachers and pastoral care teachers in secondary schools need better information about social services and what it means to come into care as well as about the particular problems which are likely to face children in care at school. As more education welfare officers receive professional training and increasingly see themselves as education social workers (a name already used in many places), this could become an important part of their job.

However, it is social workers who will continue to carry the main responsibility for promoting and supporting the education of children in care. Clearly they need to put this much higher on their list of priorities and become far more aware of the impact on children's education of decisions made for other reasons. Team leaders and managers have a key supervisory role here. At each stage they should be asking 'What is the long-term educational/career plan for this child? How will the course of action you are proposing contribute to it?' As Alex Saddington says in the article quoted above, 'Social services should be a good parent and all good parents want their children to have success in education.'

It is also important for social workers to give the lead in refusing to make judgements about children's 'ability' and discouraging others from doing so. Research by Feuerstein in Israel (Sharron, 1987) shows that children from very disadvantaged backgrounds can make startling educational progress given the right environment. But it may take several years to recover from a bad start, and chronological age can be very misleading when, because of disruptive and damaging early experiences, a child may be functioning at the level of one many years younger. Social workers and carers need to understand the crucial importance of building up a child's self-concept, so often undermined by rejection and psychological abuse. Retrospective accounts by people who have been in care often look back with gratitude to the one individual who made them feel they mattered and gave them the confidence to succeed (Kahan, 1979).

Foster parents often find this an uphill task, and one reason is that their efforts to enhance a child's self-esteem are negated by lack of success at school. The educational function of foster parents should be given much more attention, both at the selection stage and in later training and support. This does not mean ruling out people without formal qualifications; other things may be equally important such as, for example, a love of reading or music, or a keen interest in current affairs. It does imply, however, that social workers should spend more time finding out about applicants' own school experience, their attitudes to education, leisure pursuits, and expectations for their own and foster children and discussing with them how they would support a foster child's education.

Foster parent induction and training programmes could also lay more stress on helping children to make up for lost schooling and improve their basic skills. The latest boarding out regulations lay no responsibility on foster parents to pay attention to a child's education, yet research in Britain and America indicates that, where foster parents are given clear directives, the educational expectations of boarded out children can be improved. The point also needs to be made that for these vulnerable children there has to be much closer liaison with schools than might normally be necessary. Foster parent groups have an important function in enabling carers to share ideas on how to motivate and encourage children.

In caring for younger children the vital contribution of foster parents is obvious. It is they who talk and play with children, read to them and listen to them reading, choose books and toys, take them to the library or on outings to places of interest, and create a family environment which may do more or less to contribute to the child's cognitive development. They also, implicitly or explicitly, provide health and social education and have the opportunity to teach the child skills which are not included in the school curriculum but may be very important in adult life. Much of this happens without conscious thought in natural families, but in foster care it has to be more systematically planned and monitored.

Another important job for foster parents is to involve and interest natural parents in their children's school progress. Even parents who cannot provide a home or day-to-day care can be enormously effective in motivating children by showing pride and pleasure in their achievements.

Recent changes in the education system make it more important than ever that the division of responsibility between fieldworker and foster parent should be clear and that both should be well-informed. For example, the replacement of 'O' levels and CSEs by the GCSE puts a premium on continuity, close parental monitoring, planning work over considerable periods and high expectations. All this is likely to make it even more difficult than before for children in care to obtain educational qualifications unless attitudes and practice change significantly (Jackson, 1988a).

Increased demands on foster parents require a higher level of support from social workers and managers. Social services departments will have to budget more generously for educational expenses, including books, outings, private and other coaching, lessons in non-school subjects, equipment for special interests, further and higher education. At present fewer than 100 young people over 18 are receiving financial support from social services to help them stay in education. This should surely be a statutory right for those who continue in the care of the local authority up to the age of 16 and beyond.

For children of school age it could be helpful to pay foster parents an allowance for educational expenses and leave it to their discretion how they use it. Foster parents who are less comfortable with their educational role could be linked up with a teacher or educational consultant specifically to provide advice, information and ideas on this aspect of the work.

However, it is probably in the field of residential care that there is most scope for improvement. Perhaps we have something to learn from Israel or the many countries of Eastern Europe where the task of residential child care is unequivocally seen as a social/educational service and is not subject to the fashion swings characteristic of Britain (Sharron, 1987; Jackson, 1988b). If group living were seen to have something valuable to offer there might be less pressure on social workers to make repeated attempts to place children and young people in foster homes, with all the disruption that may entail.

What can residential units do to improve children's experience of school? I was able, at the invitation of NCH, to undertake a case study of one children's home which had made a determined effort to put education at the top of its agenda and seemed to have achieved considerable success (Jackson, 1989).

The original impetus came from the appointment of an officer-in-charge whose own background as a graduate teacher and educational psychologist led him to see education as a matter of central importance. Over the next few years he developed an educational strategy in collaboration with his staff in which a number of different elements can be identified. First there was the question of staff training, attitudes and expectations; then tackling the way children saw themselves and were seen by others. Another line of work was on relationships with schools, teachers and other professionals. There were direct measures to improve the children's school performance, and finally there was an attempt to create an educational ambience in the home.

My conclusion was that the work at the home had succeeded in changing attitudes of staff and children. It had gone some way to reduce the many disadvantages from which the children suffered in the school system. For the majority it created a shift in the direction of educational success and a significant improvement in their self-image. The chief elements in this achievement were a clear lead from the head of the home, supported by the regional and national management of the organization and the availability of funds to buy in outside resources.

Probably the most significant innovation was the appointment of an educational liaison officer, a former teacher with intimate knowledge of local schools. As a member of the staff group she played an important role in keeping school and education to the fore in decision making in the home. She arranged home-tutoring (paid for by the LEA), helped to recruit outside teachers and volunteers to help with homework and hobbies, ordered stationery and books, kept track of letters from schools and made sure these reached the appropriate care staff and were acted on. Her main task, however, was to act as an intermediary and interpreter between care staff, children and teachers. In this her activities were similar to those which any concerned parents would take in support of their own children, with the difference that for children in residential care from disturbed backgrounds the monitoring and intervention required are almost continuous. A large part of her work consisted of calming troubled waters and defusing conflicts at an early stage. One measure of her success was the fact that no child had been suspended from school since her appointment, something which had previously been an almost weekly occurrence.

As a teacher herself she was equally concerned with matters of academic achievement and constantly alert for opportunities to help children from the home to make up lost ground. For those at secondary school great emphasis was placed on regular completion of homework, with an hour set aside each evening for this purpose during which two teachers were available to help any child in difficulty. This transformed the children's feelings about going to school, knowing that they could hand in acceptable pieces of work, and also changed the teachers' perceptions of the children's ability and potential.

The conception of education at the home went far beyond schoolwork. Children were encouraged to participate in the life of the local community, to join clubs and take up hobbies and to acquire out-of-school skills such as riding, driving and playing musical instruments. There was an attempt to make education fun and to associate it with pleasure and enjoyment.

Education was woven into the fabric of daily life, using the fact of residential care as an asset. The community meeting, for example, had as one of its aims to help children to become well-informed about the world and confident in expressing their opinions on current events. After the home news, which gave an opportunity to draw attention to and praise school achievement, the leader would introduce a topic for discussion, usually some recently reported national or world event, or sometimes a moral or philosophical issue presented in a way the children could understand.

Although there were inevitably gaps and weaknesses, overall the achievement of this home was impressive and might serve as a useful model for other residential units. It is an encouraging example of what can be done by recognizing the importance of education and allocating additional, though still quite modest, resources to it.

Conclusion

In this chapter I have argued that the educational experience of children in care is a seriously neglected topic, reflecting a division between the care and education professions which has become deeply embedded, to the detriment of children separated from their families.

Evidence on the attainment of children in the care system points to the damaging effect of removal from home, even taking account of adverse family circumstances. Outcomes in terms of formal educational qualifications are far worse than would be predicted. Social, personal, health and practical skills education also appear to be neglected, with serious consequences for future life chances.

The disadvantages suffered by children in care compound those which already exist in society, for example those experienced by girls and by children from ethnic minorities, especially those of mixed race who are greatly over-represented in the care population. Research has shown that there is a case for arguing that the child care system should no longer reinforce these inequities but be used as a means of redressing them. This would mean rethinking the whole purpose of care and finally abandoning the doctrine of less eligibility handed down to us by the Poor Law.

References

Akhurst, B. A. (1975) 'The prevalence of behaviour problems among children in care', *Education Research*, pp. 137–42.

Bald, J. (1982) 'Children in care need books', *Concern*, No. 44, pp. 18–21.

Berridge, D. (1985) *Children's Homes*, Basil Blackwell.

Berridge, D. and Cleaver, H. (1987) *Foster Home Breakdown*, Basil Blackwell.

Bowen, D. (1985) unpublished MSc dissertation, Cranfield Institute of Technology.

Brown J. and Solomon, D. (1974) 'Leisure time interests of children in residential homes', *Residential Social Work*, Vol. 14, No. 8, pp. 246–9.

Children's Home (1898) *Musical Pictures of Life in the Children's Home*: a songbook produced for the fundraising tour of the choir and gymnastic squad.

Clarke, A. M. and Clarke, A. D. B. (1976) *Early Experience: Myth and Evidence*, Open Books.

Clough, R. (1988) *Living Away from Home*, Bristol Papers No. 4, University of Bristol, School of Applied Social Studies.

Demetri, A. (1982) *The Demetri Papers*, Voice for the Child in Care Papers, No. 2, London VCC.

Department of Education and Science (1980) *Community Homes with Education*, HMI Series: Matters for Discussion 10, HMSO.

Department of Health and Social Security (1981) *Observation and Assessment: Report of a DHSS Working Party*, DHSS.

Easson, S. (1988) 'Surviving a harsh and loveless childhood', *Social Work Today*, 4 August 1988.

Essen, J., Lambert, L. and Head, J. (1976) 'School attainment of children who have been in care', *Child Care, Health and Development*, Vol. 2, pp. 339–51.

Fisher, M., Marsh, P., Phillips, D. and Sainsbury, E. (1986) *In and Out of Care*, Batsford/BAAF..

Gill, O. and Jackson, B. (1983) *Adoption and Race: Black, Asian and Mixed Race Children in White Families*, Batsford/BAAF.

Hazel, N. (1981) *A Bridge to Independence: The Kent Family Placement Project*, Basil Blackwell.

Holmes, E. (1977) 'The education needs of children in care', *Concern*, No. 26, pp. 22–5.

Holmes, E. (1980) 'Educational intervention for pre-school children in day or residential care', *Therapeutic Education*, Vol. 8, No. 2.

Home Office (1970) *A Guide to Adoption Practice*, HMSO.

Jackson, S. (1988a) 'Education and children in care', *Adoption and Fostering*, Vol. 12, No. 4, pp. 6–14.

Jackson, S. (1988b) *The Education of Children in Care*, Bristol Papers No. 1, University of Bristol, School of Applied Social Studies.

Jackson, S. (1989) 'Residential care and education', *Children and Society*, Vol. 2, No. 4. pp. 335–50.

Kahan, B. (1979) *Growing Up in Care*, Basil Blackwell.

Knapp, M., Bryson, D. and Lewis, J. (1985) *The Objectives of Child Care and their Attainment*, Discussion Paper 373, PSSRU, University of Kent.

Melotte, C. J. (1979) 'The placement decision', *Adoption and Fostering*, Vol. 95, No. 1, pp. 55–62.

Millham, S., Bullock, R. and Hosie, K. (1980) *Learning to Care: The Training of Staff for Residential Social Work with Young People*, Gower.

Millham, S., Bullock, R., Hosie, K. and Haak, M. (1986) *Lost in Care*, Gower.

Miller, R. (1988) *Statementing and Suspending Emotionally and Behaviourally Disturbed Children*, Fellowship dissertation, University of Bristol, School of Applied Social Studies.

Osborn, A. and St Claire, L. (1987) 'The ability and behaviour of children who have been in care', *Early Child Development and Care*, Vol. 28, No. 3, pp. 187–355.

Parker, R. A. (1988) 'Residential care for children', in Sinclair, I. (ed) *Residential Care: The Research Reviewed*, Literature Surveys Commissioned by the Independent Review of Residential Care (Wagner Report), NISW/HMSO.

Pilling, D. (1986) 'Escape from disadvantage', National Children's Bureau, unpublished report.

Pringle, M. L. K. (ed) (1965) *Investment in Children. A Symposium on Positive Child Care and Constructive Education*, Longman.

Prosser, H. (1978) *Perspectives on Foster Care*, NFER.

Revill, J. and Smith, I. 'A helping hand for our children in need', *The Sunday Times* (New Society: Education Forum), 13 November 1988.

Rutter, M. (1972) *Maternal Deprivation Reassessed*, Penguin.

Rutter, M., Quinton, D. and Liddle, C. (1983) 'Parenting in two generations: looking backwards and looking forwards', in Madge, N. (ed) *Families at Risk*, DHSS.

Saddington, A. (1988) 'In my experience', *Who Cares*, No. 5.

Scottish Child and Family Alliance (SCAFA) (1986) Report of a Conference held in Dundee, April 1986.

Seglow, J., Pringle, M. and Wedge, P. (1972) *Growing Up Adopted*, NFER.

Sharron, H. (1987) *Changing Children's Minds; Feuerstein's Revolution in the Teaching of Intelligence*, Souvenir Press.

Tizard, B. (1977) *Adoption: A Second Chance*, Routledge and Kegan Paul.

Tresiliotis, J. and Russell, J. (1984) *Hard to Place: The Outcomes of Adoption and Residential Care*, Gower.

Stein, M. and Carey, K. (1986) *Leaving Care*, Basil Blackwell.

Who Cares? (1988) Autumn, No. 5.

9 Child care and ethnic minorities

Bandana Ahmad

It is often argued that lack of research on black children and young people in Britain has been the root cause of their needs remaining unidentified and unmet. Against the sustained criticism of unequal and inadequate services for black children and young people, the social work profession in general has remained static, with counter-allegations of lack of information and knowledge of 'black culture'.

Research knowledge and information are vital to any profession. However, there is ample evidence to suggest that it is not necessarily the lack of research that is restricting the acquisition of ethnically sensitive social work skills. Rather it is the methodology and interpretation of research that is mystifying the social work profession to the detriment of black children, young people and their families. Unless both researchers and practitioners make significant shifts towards the demythologization of black child care research, black children and young people will remain the victims of racism, whether by design or by default.

In Britain nearly all research work on black children and young people has certain common characteristics. Researchers are predominantly white and their approaches eurocentric. Even when 'black specialists/advisers' are involved, their involvement and status are too tokenistic to avoid stereotypical views, subjective terms of reference, pejorative approaches and methodological weaknesses in research. Furthermore, when black families, communities and children are studied, the focus of the research is often 'problem' populations, such as single-parent families, emotionally disturbed, mentally retarded, academically non-achieving or delinquent young people, or runaway girls. More often than not, the research is linked with the cultural backgrounds of the ethnic minority children and young people, rather than with their material circumstances, so that their ethnicity in itself may be perceived as a problem and the model of cultural deficit established. The majority of black people in Britain are ordinary citizens who do not have special problems, but they are seldom included in research studies. Consequently the interpretation of research may make no distinction between ethnic minority people in general and the problems of some in particular. It is hardly surprising then that the whole black or ethnic community is lumped together and labelled as a problem group in a white society.

The above points raise some fundamental issues and basic weaknesses in relation to the methods and approaches of the traditional research undertaken in Britain. The most prevalent shortcomings are:

(a) Many studies ignore ethnic diversity and differences. The use of the term 'Asian' is an example. Apart from the geographical error of describing people from India, Pakistan, Bangladesh, Sri Lanka and East Africa as having Indian origin only, to the exclusion of many other ethnic groups originating from the Asian continent, the term 'Asian' is bound to create more confusion for people whose worldwide view has yet to be developed and whose understanding of the world population has yet to mature.

(b) Research is often unidirectional, e.g. while carrying out a study on black children, the focus is likely to be on parental or cultural influences on the child and not the child's influence on his/her parents and family.

(c) Unidirectional research is open to another significant pitfall. It often makes oversimplistic correlations and excludes possible influences of other external forces, environmental or societal. It may assume, for example, that a black child's intellectual and emotional development is impaired due to lack of identity with a warm and caring parent (especially a mother), and may not examine the role of the school (particularly the teacher's warmth and care) or relationships with other significant adults in the family or community. As a result the research may arrive at incomplete or distorted conclusions.

I suggested earlier that most research studies on ethnic minority children and young people in Britain have been problem centred and that black communities are likely to be viewed as problematic *because* they are black. This homogeneous categorisation may take yet another form in some research studies, perhaps best defined as the 'monolithic' view of black families, For example, few studies incorporate both working class and middle class, both poor and rich ethnic minority children and young people in the study population. Consequently the predominance in welfare agencies and inner-city schools of poor working class black families and children, and the absence from them of rural and affluent groups, leads researchers to use the all-inclusive category of (for example) 'ethnic minorities' as a single undifferentiated variable.

It is significant that this kind of monolithic research design differs from that used to study white population groups. It would be uncommon for studies of white children and young people not to make any distinction between rich and poor, between middle class and working class. In addition most research focused on white children and their families is concerned with investigating how environmental, economic, sociological and political factors and processes affect the subjects of the study – though, in spite of this, white working class families are also 'pathologized' in some studies.

Manifestations of these differences, however subtle, cannot be overlooked, particularly when the same investigators shift from an investigatory to an interventionist approach in their research on black child care. Within this approach it is seen as desirable for black children to display abilities and behaviour that are consonant with white norms, so that, as young people, they will be truly assimilated into British society. If there is a preconception that black families are culturally inferior and deprived, then it follows that their children and young people should change their behaviours and attitudes. So, when an Afro-Caribbean or Asian adolescent experiences the rebellious phase (common to all adolescents) and runs away from home (frequent among white adolescents), research may be blinkered by negative images of their parents, and the runaway youth may even be applauded for liberating him- or herself from parental oppression or over-protectiveness.

There are other factors that merit research consideration. Leanor Boulin Johnson (1982) and many others, e.g. Mills (1959), Van den Berghe (1967), Gouldner (1970), cautioned researchers against a possible 'culprit' frame of reference. For example, if the frame of reference takes black pathology for granted, then no matter how scientific the data, the analysis may not only be subjective, but may also not relate to the needs and reality of black experience. Marie F. Peters (1982) expressed her concern about the rarity of 'ethnomethodological and descriptive' research on black families, i.e. research that compares black families with other black families, instead of with white families. She also pointed out that studies of black children and their families are often conducted in an unfamiliar and intimidating environment, where the researchers' values are in conflict with the philosophy and accepted ideals of black families. When this is the case, the researchers may be unable to obtain meaningful information which can be used in responding to the real situation.

Against this background, the black perspective in black child care research has recently emerged and been established as an alternative to research with a eurocentric bias. Much of this alternative research was initiated in the USA by black sociologists, academics and professionals, who felt that it was necessary to rewrite the history of black families and analyse their reality within the context of the legacy of the past (slavery) and the present predicament (racial discrimination), (Nobles, 1978; DuBois, 1908; Frazier, 1939; Scanzoni, 1971; Billingsley, 1968; Hill, 1972, and many others). In Britain the emergence and establishment of a black perspective has been punctuated by periods of intensity and quiescence. This has been due partly to the fact that it is only a decade ago that a handful of black scholars began to challenge the eurocentric theoretical and practical framework of the social work profession. It is also due partly to the fact that, even now, most resources and sabbatical opportunities for research and writing on black children, young people and families are directed towards white individuals and organizations. The British social work field in general has consequently neither wholeheartedly accepted the credibility of the black perspective, nor fully realized the benefit of alternative black expertise, without which black child care research has little chance to flourish.

If present and future researchers and workers are to accept and realize the valuable contribution of a black perspective, they will need to acknowledge that to disregard the emergence of a black perspective in Britain is tantamount to disregarding the American black expertise as well, mainly because it is often argued that there are more similarities than differences between black American and black British experience. For this reason the black perspective in Britain has continuously referred to the knowledge base of black American research and made necessary adaptations to fit in with British experience.

The current marginalization of the black perspective can only be overcome if white society is able and willing to challenge orthodox research assumptions. This cannot be achieved by calling upon black expertise, and merely endorsing it. It is not enough to expect the adoption of a black perspective to result in the shedding of the negative connotations associated with black children and their families. Rather, what is needed is a sustained effort to examine and challenge all negative associations – particularly those held by policy makers and by workers whose contacts with black children have a direct impact on their lives.

The black perspective can illuminate research findings in black child care in terms of reality; the white perspective can help by recognition and avoidance of the effects of stereotyping, and by mobilizing challenging and caring attitudes to eliminate the patronizing and debilitating consequences that ensue when a white value system is imposed on black children and young people. Most importantly, it can dismantle the obstacles that distort or misinform white research and analysis, and which produce arrogance in some professionals whilst leaving others in a state of helplessness and paranoia.

It is not impossible to achieve these objectives. The tools researchers can use include developing a fresh outlook, breaking new ground, trying out innovative approaches and reaching out to black experience. What could be more encouraging for potential researchers, mystified by research in general and hesitating to use their research capability? With these tools they might redesign and reshape research methodologies and approaches, and by so doing provide a springboard for other research work, not just for black child care research.

Most studies of black children and young people have focused on under-fives, black children in care, adoption and fostering and young offenders. (There are many studies, and the references in this chapter are only a selection of the available material.)

Under-fives

Although it has long been accepted that a child's first five years are extremely important, it has yet to be fully acknowledged that race and racism have direct implications, in these formative years, for both black and white children. It is still held by some that children are children and, as such, black and white children are just the same. Several studies have refuted this notion (e.g. Clark and Clark, 1947; Ammons, 1950; Goodman, 1964; Morland, 1962; Ritchie, 1963; Brown and Johnson, 1971; Katz, 1976). One of the most significant studies in Britain was undertaken by David Milner in 1975 and updated in 1983. Milner stressed that 'far from showing an inability to discriminate racial differences, if anything the evidence suggests that black children are more, rather than less, aware of racial differences and their significance than white children'. He further pointed out that, 'while the messages about race which black and white children receive are the same, the implications are radically different. Whereas white children are encouraged by these images to value and identify with their own ethnic group, and indeed to deem it superior, black children are confronted with an image of their group which is, at worst, derogatory and, at best, ambivalent.' Preference for whiteness rather than blackness, portrayal of black negative images as opposed to white positive images, the association of blackness with evil, and hostile attitudes towards black people are not new phenomena in Britain. The history of racial prejudice can be traced back as far as the sixteenth century. However, research on racial prejudice only dates from the first two decades of the twentieth century. As various studies have highlighted the effects of racial prejudice on very young black children and their families, it has become increasingly apparent that, without a shift of emphasis by researchers and professionals from perceiving black children as objects of racial prejudice to addressing racial equality for black children and acting accordingly, the full development of black under-fives will continue to be restricted.

In *Catching Them Young* Bob Dixon (1977) suggests that whether in residential or day care settings, at home or playschool, a child under five is constantly exposed to images, attitudes and opinions through stories, pictures, rhymes, songs, games and toys. In his study on children's books he found that, 'a particularly strong aspect of the indoctrination carried on in children's literature is that of racism'.

He substantiated his findings by giving examples of how the word 'black' has 'overwhelmingly pejorative associations' and how children's literature and its everyday language have embodied prejudice and racist beliefs and attitudes both at symbolic and emotional levels. For under-fives, most of whom are highly impressionable, symbolic forms are forceful influences. So, when racism, however covertly or subtly, finds expression through symbolic illustrations, it becomes explicit enough to damage both black and white children psychologically – though the effects on black children are likely to be more distinctive and harmful.

No research study suggests that white children aspire to be black or to be known as Sumitra or Alahuddin instead of Susan or Alan. It is likely to be a black child who would want an anglicized name and to be accepted as white, sometimes even to the extent of trying to scrub away the colour from their skin. Some child care workers and some research studies take the view that the adoption of a white identity by a black child is desirable because it paves the way for cultural assimilation and racial harmony – but if social work practice is concerned with caring and protecting, it cannot take a 'colourblind' approach and overlook the different needs of black children whose social and emotional development may be endangered by insensitive pressure towards assimilation.

During the past decade greater recognition has been given to the needs of black under-fives and the services required to respond adequately to them. For example, in 1977, the Commission for Racial Equality took the view that in 'a significant number of cities and boroughs in Britain, a very large proportion of children are black . . . Caring for under-fives in a multi-racial society requires attention to be directed to two major conditions of the minority communities in Britain; first, their heavy over-representation among the disadvantaged, urban deprived population, and second, their special and distinct needs which arise because of their minority racial and cultural status.' The Home Affairs Select Committee Report in 1981 urged that 'local authorities should take a joint initiative with Government to ensure that provision of facilities for the under-fives comes closer to meeting the demand for it among ethnic minorities in particular . . .' Lord Scarman (1981) endorsed this recommendation and stressed that 'the need for adequate pre-school provision is particularly marked among ethnic minority children'.

A Department of Health and Social Security committee set up 'to consider what practical action might be taken in the statutory and voluntary sectors in response to this recommendation' reported in 1984 and made further detailed recommendations, urging availability of multi-cultural resources in pre-school services, training in racial awareness as part of the continuing education programme for staff, and review of ethnic content in the Nursery Nurse Examination Board syllabus. Many more reports and recommendations (e.g. VOLCUF, 1984, 1986; NCVCCO, 1986) have taken a similar approach. As we look through them the words of Dr Kenneth Clark (a witness to the Kerner Commission in 1968, USA) concerning a number of reports of racial disorders, seem appropriate: 'I must . . . in candour say to you members of the commission – it is a kind of Alice in Wonderland – with the same moving picture reshown over and over again, the same analysis, the same recommendations, and the same inaction.'

In order to break away from the Alice in Wonderland syndrome more black child care research is needed to examine residential and field work practice, and their outcomes at both personal and institutional levels. Black child care researchers should, in future, have enough information to assess what is lacking and what needs to be done. Programmes need to be based on knowledge. Individuals within them can plan and carry out research in their work places. If they do the gains could be great. Instead of shying away from research, individual workers could acquire research skills. In addition they could open up possibilities of change, so that black under-fives in future may not suffer in the ways identified by previous investigations and research. The resulting innovations and examples of good practice could in turn influence national black child care practice and research.

Black children in care

The issue of the over-representation of black children in care is one which arouses strong feelings but about which, regrettably, there is still too little hard research evidence. In the 1970s a good deal of information available to local authorities and voluntary organizations suggested that over-representation was a major issue, for example:

(a) Out of the first 117 referrals to the Adoption Resource Exchange 72 were black children aged one to five years.
(b) Out of 129 children placed through the Exchange 94 were of mixed parentage (one parent white, one black).
(c) Twenty-one per cent of children received into the care of the London Borough of Tower Hamlets in 1974 were black (The Soul Kids Campaign, 1977).

Children Who Wait (Rowe and Lambert, 1976) estimated that 25 per cent of their sample of children likely to remain in care all their childhood were black.

The House of Commons Social Services Committee, in their report *Children in Care* (1983–84), discussed the evidence presented to them and recognized that there were serious issues and strong feelings. Their conclusion was that 'there are a number of problems specific to ethnic minority children in care which will not go away. They have to be articulated but not exaggerated. That is a major challenge facing those charged with providing care for children.' (Vol. 1, paras. 308–18).

During the 1980s a major piece of research undertaken by Jane Rowe and colleagues (awaiting publication) focusing on child care placement outcomes suggests that the issues are much more complex than had previously appeared – e.g. the firmly held view that there is over-representation of black boys in care in adolescence is questioned, and the group most over-represented in care is seen to be children of mixed parentage. It is evident that more research is needed in this important and sensitive area.

The kinds of services needed also require examination. In 1983, the Association of Black Social Workers and Allied Professionals strongly advocated protecting the interests of black children in care. In its report (1983) it called for recognition of the strengths of black families and the return to them of their children wherever possible. It also put forward the views of the black community organizations who perceived social services as 'enforcement agencies' – 'black people have a right and responsibility to help to resolve the problems of the community and they should be given the opportunity to do so'. From 1982 to 1984 the *Caribbean Times* published a series of articles by David Devine criticizing services provided by local authorities as irrelevant and inappropriate, in particular their child care services.

Within this context, Black and in Care, a consumer organization with exclusive membership of young black people in care or formerly in care, was founded in 1984. They expressed their views in various forms – conferences, workshops, reports, videos – and put forward a set of resolutions in relation to physical and emotional care, racism in the social work profession and care system, fostering, leaving care, and terminologies used to describe black children in care.

Black perception of social services as 'enforcement agencies' is important because it has implications for research. The perception has arisen from both statistical and empirical evidence which embraces not only children but other client groups, as well as welfare services which black people in general wish to use. Just as there is some evidence of over-representation of black children in care, so there is some evidence of under-representation of older black people receiving social services. Studies of black people and mental health raise concern that black people may be less likely than white people to receive counselling and support services. Other services such as marriage guidance, conciliation, bereavement counselling and client support groups appear often to cater mainly for the white community. So, when black communities examine these anomalies, questions arise such as 'why when we ask for services for older people do providers claim resources are scarce? Are there no resource implications when children are received into care in greater numbers than their white counterparts? Do agencies wish to indoctrinate our children with white values and identity? Is it because older black people have less time left for conforming to white values and norms that agencies tend to ignore their welfare needs?' There are no answers as yet to such questions, though the fact that they are asked suggests the need for inquiry. The Race Equality Unit and the Research Unit at the National Institute for Social Work are to undertake research which aims to address some of these questions and the implied anomalies.

Adoption and fostering

Adoption and fostering of black children is an area of child care which has been well researched. The shortage of black substitute care both in fostering and adoption has raised serious concern. 'Black carers for black children' has been a continuing theme in the forefront of debates on the placement needs of children in care, whether these are for transracial, cross-cultural or same race placements.

A major work in Britain edited by Juliet Cheetham (1982) contained contributions from black writers. Describing American recruitment of black substitute parents for black children, Cheetham described similar attempts in Britain as 'rarer enterprises'. She also referred to a DHSS study which showed that 'British social workers are either largely unaware of the significance of racial or ethnic matching in child placement or confused about its ends and means . . .' and 'how important it is for social workers to disentangle the arguments about ethnic "matching" and "mixing", particularly because ethnic matching preserves a child's heritage; white parents are unable . . . to teach black foster and adoptive children to cope with discrimination . . . a black child cannot develop a proper sense of identity in a white home.'

Perhaps the most useful documentation of black fostering and adoption in Britain in the 1980s has been Part Two ('Black children in care') of the book *Social Work with Black Children and their Families* edited by Ahmed, Cheetham and Small (1986). In this section, John Small critically examined the work of Gill and Jackson (1983), particularly in relation to the 'melting pot' approach and the definition of success in terms of material gain at the cost of underplaying or ignoring ethnic identity. He also analysed some of their findings along the lines followed by Mandell (1973) and Holman (1978). Small believes that, 'if a healthy personality is to be formed the psychic image of the child must merge with the reality of what the child actually is. That is to say, if the child is black (reality), he or she must first recognize and accept that he or she has a black psychic image.' In promoting the interests of black children Small listed the essential ingredients' of substitute black child care, and proposed guidelines for pre-adoptive and foster care selection and preparation. In the same book, Jocelyn Maxime (1986) examined the racial aspects of 'black self-concept' through various psychological models and reinstated the importance of 'a positive black identity'. She also outlined some effective techniques she had used in working with black children.

Concerning recruitment of black foster and adoptive parents and black residential staff, it is important that researchers actively counter certain myths attributed to black families. These myths, generally, are that the concept of fostering and adoption is alien to black culture, or that some black families, e.g. West Africans, volunteer their children into care. In contrast with this belief the New Black Families Unit, set up in 1986, within its first four months received 50 offers from black families who wished to be adoptive or foster parents. The study by Payne (1983) of long-term placement for the black child in care associated the failure to increase black fostering and adoption resources with the white and middle-class value base for selecting applicants, which – even if not by conscious intent – set criteria which eliminated most black applicants.

Cross-cultural misunderstanding is another factor that perpetuates the myth of black families' non-acceptance of fostering and adoption. As Ellis (1981) explains, 'Although the same term, fostering, is used in Britain and West Africa, the meanings ascribed to it are very different. In our society, fostering is resorted to reluctantly when there is some kind of breakdown in the normal family arrangements – it is definitely second best. In West Africa, it is a normal part of extended family life; relationships with wider family members are very important and children may move around a great deal during childhood. Fostering is usually kin fostering but children also go to stay with friends . . .' The same situation applies to families of South Asian origin, where children are adopted by aunts and uncles – however removed they may be in terms of kinship. The criteria for the arrangements are love and care and the only legal involvement is concerned with matters of inheritance.

The idea of black families for black children is slowly making headway in social work agencies. A leading agency in this field has been BAAF (British Association of Adoption and Fostering). In 1985 it established a Black Perspective Advisory Committee and appointed two Black Issues project workers. They have also produced a number of helpful practice publications which have been well used.

Young offenders

Most studies of black offenders have been carried out in the context of the police, courts, probation and after-care services. Those most affected are juveniles and young black people, but specific information is difficult to obtain partly because there is no systematic ethnic monitoring in the criminal justice system. Nevertheless, the CRE report in 1981 established that 'the highest proportion of black clients in contact with the probation service are juveniles and young persons' (46 per cent black compared to 25 per cent white, Commission for Racial Equality, 1986).

NACRO, in 1986, analysed the proceedings of one juvenile court and found that 30.4 per cent of black youngsters received custodial sentences as opposed to only 12.2 per cent of their white counterparts. Similar trends were identified by other research work. In 1982, for example, the Inner London probation service found that 35 per cent of West Indians received recommendations for supervision as opposed to 30 per cent of the total sample. Another study in Nottingham indicated that young black people were three times as likely as young white people to be the subject of reports with no (or inconclusive) recommendations.

Professional responses to young offenders have been patchy, and more extensively documented in the probation service than in the social services (e.g. National Association of Probation Officers, 1985; Association of Chief Probation Officers 1984; The Association of Black Probation Officers, undated; Inner London Probation and After-Care Service, 1982).

Cheetham (1982) argued that black adolescents 'hover on the periphery' of the social services and that social workers are 'often at a loss to know what to do'.

Policy and practice

Although in the past decade there has been considerable development of anti-racist child care policies and practice, the promotion and implementation of them have been inconsistent and sporadic. Concomitant with the continuing debate on the need for black child care policies and practice, lack of clarity in their implications for black children is a continuing concern.

Examples include:

(a) What measures are necessary to identify the racist effects of existing child care policies and practice?

(b) How should effective anti-racist child care policies be formulated?

(c) What strategies, short or long term, are needed to implement policies and establish a code of practice?

(d) What are the links between policy and practice issues?

This section gives an account of some of the crucial factors that need to be addressed if child care policies and practices are to benefit black children and their families.

It is commonly believed that black children are a recent phenomenon in British society. Yet British history demonstrates that black people have been a significant presence in British society since 1507. Reference to black children has, however, usually not included any record of their achievements. On the contrary, their image was seen in the not uncommon advertisements such as the following, dating from the eighteenth century:

> To be SOLD, A pretty little negro boy, about nine years old, and well limbed. If not disposed of, is to be sent to the West Indies in six days time. He is to be seen at the Dolphin Tavern in Tower Street'. (From the *Daily Advertiser*, 13 December 1744 – cited in File and Power, 1981.)

> Run away from his Master, a negro boy, under five feet in height, about 16 years old, named CHARLES. He is very ill made, being remarkably bow-legged, hollow-backed, and pot bellied. He had on, when he went away, a coarse dark brown linen frock, a thickset waistcoat, very dirty leather breeches, and on his head an old velvet jockey cap. Whoever will bring him, or give any tidings of him, to Mr Beckford in Pall-Mall, may depend upon being very handsomely rewarded. (From the *Public Advertiser*, 14 May 1768 – cited in File and Power, 1981.)

Further early and significant evidence of black children's presence in Britain is found in some major British institutions for children such as Barnardos, the National Children's Home and the Church Adoption Society.

In a climate where black children in white households were restricted to the status of slave, or at least servant, and black families were perceived as being incapable of bringing up children, opportunities for black children to be fostered or adopted were scarce. It was mainly white institutions that gave refuge to unwanted black children. If they found homes for them, more often than not '... placements were with white parents formally committed to Christian ideals (including the idea of "oneness in Christ" which seems to eschew racism, but also de-emphasizes the meaning of colour or traditional culture)' (Bagley and Young, 1982).

These examples suggest that black children in Britain carry a legacy of the past which, at worst, has not acknowledged the reality of their experience or recognized their social and welfare needs, and at best, has responded to black child care issues in a *laissez-faire* manner.

Not surprisingly, the need for policy formulation and practice codification in relation to black child care, was not fully realized till the mid-1970s in Britain. While now there is a positive incentive for progressive black child care work, this work has gone through some difficult stages that can best be understood by analysing the conceptual and practical development of anti-racist child care policies and practices.

During the 1950s and 1960s, the main feature of black child care policy and practice was the concept of 'Integration and Assimilation'. This concept was based on a firm belief that black children were part of the 'new immigrants' and in time they would be integrated into the western way of life. Implications of this belief included:

(a) The more black children were integrated into mainstream British culture the more likely it was that harmonious race relations in Britain would develop.

(b) Integration of black children would make their assimilation in service structures possible and thus benefit them and their families.

(c) Integration is in the interests of black children as it would remove obstacles to becoming civilized (anglicized) and accepting the superiority of western culture instead of following immigrant culture and tradition and maintaining separate identity.

(d) Adaptation of child care services for black children would work against assimilation and hence be discriminatory.

It is not difficult to see why the Integration/Assimilation framework manifested itself as a justification for discouraging of anti-racist child care policies; for maintaining a 'colourblind' approach which inhibited appropriate black child care practice; for perceiving anti-racist policies and practices as unnecessary in planning and resources; and, most importantly, for marginalizing or denying the child care rights of black children. The Integration/Assimilation approach now has little credibility but its impact on child care practice persists. Provision for anti-racist child care still suffers from the notion of absorption of black children into white values and norms, with a preference for 'fish and chips' and rejection of 'rice and peas'.

The 1970s and early 1980s saw a gradual shift from the Integration/ Assimilation model to a 'cultural diversity' or 'cultural pluralism' model. This shift was based on the recognition that the 'same for all' policies and practices worked against the interests of black children and their families since most policy and practice were essentially eurocentric (Cheetham, 1981). The 'cultural diversity' model advocated the acceptance of different cultural and ethnic groups in multi-racial Britain, enhancing cultural knowledge and creating an environment of mutual tolerance. The 'pluralist' model encompassed the diversity approach, with an added emphasis on eradicating racial discrimination and promoting equal opportunities (Ely and Denney, 1987).

With a view to promoting policy and practice within the framework of cultural diversity and pluralism, much was done during this era in developing 'cultural packages' to inform child care policy makers and practitioners about the cultural aspects of black families and children and to equip them with ethnically sensitive child care skills. The Association of Directors of Social Services and the Commission for Racial Equality, in their report *Multi-racial Britain* (1978) underline that 'only by recognizing cultural differences, and identifying and meeting different needs, will it be possible to provide an effective response' to ethnic minority children and families.

Nevertheless, cultural enlightenment and tolerance on their own give little impetus for developing anti-racist policy and practice. Black children and their families are frequently seen from a standpoint of great anxiety by policy makers and practitioners. This has negative consequences, in that the anxiety often results in *problem-oriented* practice; and the problem, more often than not, is assumed to be the cultural origin of black children. A study on case files undertaken by the Social Services Inspectorate, North West Region, in 1986, indicated clearly 'that white social workers found that different skin colour from their own, alone, added an additional level of anxiety in dealing with a case. Often, skin colour was not commented on in recording, though, through discussion, it was clear that the issue troubled the social worker' (SSI/DHSS, 1986).

Information packages on 'black culture' may reinforce child care workers' prejudices and reaffirm cultural stereotypes of black families. The prescriptive element, inevitable in this approach, fails to take note of diversities between and within black and ethnic minority communities, families and children. In addition, nearly all cultural descriptions and packages are defined from a white perspective, and not, therefore, always related to the realities of black experience. Even when a black perspective is involved, it may be perceived as 'political' with the related fear of losing control of intervention in black families' lives. In her recent book, *Anti-racist Social Work* (1988), Lena Dominelli emphasized 'White people have difficulty accepting their exclusion from activities which black people have redefined as theirs . . . Such exclusion is problematic because white people are not used to having their power challenged by black people in this way. They resent having discrete areas of their social order defined "out of bounds" by those whom they "rule"; whose place in society they have designated as inferior; and whose activities they have sought to control. White people experience anger because the normal power relationship between them and black people has been unilaterally ruptured.'

The consequences of all this fall heaviest on black children and their families, many of whom have little option but to '. . . forever shoulder the ultimate burdens of unfair labelling, classification and stigmatization' (Moore, 1981). The pain of carrying the burden is even more compounded when policies either, by omission, exclude the race dimension or, by commission, narrow the opportunities for black children, inadvertently dissolve black families or inappropriately intervene to 'rescue' a black child.

For too long the social work profession has tinkered with the welfare of black children and young people, and research portrayed the black family as the 'problem', allowing racist myths, assumptions and methodologies to interfere with their effectiveness. The demythologization of black child care research has much potential for promoting caring services to black children and young people and for influencing policy makers towards a more sensitive approach.

The poem which follows expresses how some young people feel about their situation:

It's bad for your child to be in care

I can't face this life alone
'cos I've always lived in a home
Thrown out at sixteen
with no friends or family
Thank-you social services
for your hospitality.
Here I am in a black community
I've grown up 'white' but they can't see.
Which do I turn to – white or black?
I daren't step forward, I can't step back,
help me someone please
to find my culture and identity,
why could I not have these when I was young?
They brought me up to think being black is wrong.
Black people out there,
you've got to be aware
for it's bad for your child to be in care.

Margaret Parr (*Black and in Care*, 1985)

References

Ammons, R. B. (1950) 'Reactions in a projective doll-play interview of white males two to six years of age to difference in skin colour and facial features', *Journal of Genetic Psychology*, Vol. 76.

Association of Black Probation Officers, *Constitution*.

Association of Black Social Workers and Allied Professionals (1983) *Black Children in Care*, Evidence to the House of Commons Social Services Committee.

Association of Chief Probation Officers (1984) *Recruitment, Training and Racial Discrimination and the Probation Service*.

Association of Directors of Social Services and the Commission for Racial Equality (1978) *Multi-racial Britain: The Social Services Response*.

Bagley, C. and Young, L. (1982) 'Policy dilemmas and the adoption of black children', in Cheetham, J. (ed) *Social Work and Ethnicity*, Allen and Unwin.

Billingsley, A. (1968) *Black Families in White America*, Prentice-Hall.

Brown, G. and Johnson, S. P. (1971) 'The attribution of behavioural connotations to shaded and white figures by caucasian children', *British Journal of Social and Clinical Psychology*, Vol. 10, pp. 306–12.

Cheetham, J. (ed.) (1981) *Social and Community Work in a Multi-racial Society*, Harper and Rowe/Open University.

Cheetham, J. (1982) *Social Work and Ethnicity*, Allen and Unwin.

Clark, K. and Clark, M. (1947) 'Racial identification and preference in Negro children', in Newcomb, T. M. and Hartley, E. L. (eds) *Readings in Social Psychology*, New York.

Commission for Racial Equality (1977) *Caring for Under-fives in a Multi-racial Society*.

Commission for Racial Equality (1981) *Probation and After-Care in a Multi-racial Society*.

Department of Health and Social Security (1984) *Services for Under-fives from Ethnic Minority Communities*.

Dixon, B. (1977) *Catching Them Young: Sex, Race and Class in Children's Fiction*, Pluto.

Dominelli, L. (1988) *Anti-racist Social Work*, BASW.

DuBois, W. E. B. (1908) *The Negro American Family*, Atlanta University Press.

Ellis, J. (1981) 'Foster kids in the cultural gap', in Cheetham, J. (ed.) *Social and Community Work in a Multi-racial Society*, Harper and Rowe/Open University.

Ely, P. and Denney, D. (1987) *Social Work in a Multi-racial Society*, Gower.

File, N. and Power, C. (1981) *Black Settlers in Britain, 1551–1958*, Heinemann.

Frazier, E. F. (1939) *The Negro Family in the United States*, University of Chicago Press.

Gill, O. and Jackson, B. (1983) *Adoption and Race: Black, Asian and Mixed Race Children in White Families*, Batsford/BAAF.

Goodman, M. E. (1964) *Race Awareness in Young Children*, Collier.

Gouldner, A. (1970) *The Coming Crisis of Western Sociology*, Avon.

Hill, R. (1972) *The Strength of Black Families*, Emerson Hall.

Holman, B. (1978) 'A class analysis of adoption reveals a disturbing picture', *Community Care*, No. 210, 23 April 1978.

Home Affairs Select Committee (1981) *Report on Racial Disadvantage*, HC 424, HMSO.

House of Commons Social Services Committee (1984) *Children in Care*, Vol. 1, HMSO.

Inner London Probation and After-Care Service (1982) *Probation and After-care Service in a Multi-racial Society*.

Johnson, L. B. (1982) 'Perspectives on black family empirical research; 1965–1978', in McAdoo, H. P. (ed) *Black Families*, Sage.

Katz, P.A. (1976) *Towards the Elimination of Racism*, Pergamon Press.

Mandell, B. R. (1973) *Where are the Children? A Class Analysis of Foster Care and Adoption*, Lexington Books.

Maxime, J. E. (1986) 'Some psychological models of black self concept', in Ahmed, S., Cheetham, J. and Small, J. (eds) *Social Work with Black Children and their Families*, Batsford/BAAF.

Mills, C. W. (1959) *The Sociological Imagination*, Grove Press.

Milner, D. (1975) *Children and Race*, Ward Lock Educational.

Milner, D. (1983) *Children and Race, Ten Years On*, Ward Lock Educational.

Moore, E. K. (1982) 'Policies affecting the status of black children and families', in McAdoo, H. P. (ed) *Black Families*, Sage.

Morland, J. K. (1962) 'Racial acceptance and preference of nursery school children in a southern city, *Merrill–Palmer Quarterly*.

National Association for the Care and Resettlement of Offenders (1986) *Black People and the Criminal Justice System*.

National Association of Probation Officers (1985) *NAPO and Racism*.

National Council of Voluntary Child Care Organizations (1986) *Anti-racist Policy and Provision for all Under-fives*.

Nobles, W. W. (1978) 'Towards an empirical and theoretical framework for defining black families', *Journal of Marriage and the Family*, Vol. 40, November.

Payne, S. (1983) *Long-term Placement for the Black Child in Care*, University of East Anglia.

Peters, M. F. (1982) 'Parenting in black families with young children: a historical perspective', in McAdoo, H. P. (ed.) *Black Families*, Sage.

Ritchie, J. E. (1963) *The Making of a Maori*, University of Victoria.

Rowe, J. and Lambert, L. (1976) *Children Who Wait*, Association of British Adoption and Fostering Agencies/Routledge and Kegan Paul.

Scanzoni, R. (1971) *The Black Family in Modern Society*, Allyn and Bacon.

Scarman, Rt. Hon., The Lord (1981) *The Brixton Disorders 10–12 April*, HMSO.

Small, J. (1986) 'Transracial placements: conflicts and contradictions', in Ahmed, S., Cheetham, J. and Small, J. (eds) *Social Work with Black Children and Their Families*, Batsford/BAAF.

Social Services Inspectorate, DHSS (1986) *Social Services for Ethnic Minorities: Policy and Practice in the North West*.

Soul Kids Campaign (1977) *Soul Kids are your Kids*.

Van Den Berghe, P. (1967) *Race and Racism*, John Wiley.

Voluntary Organisation Liaison Council for Under Fives (1984) *Unequal and Under Five, A Background Paper on Ethnic Minority Under Fives*, VOLCUF.

Voluntary Organisation Liaison Council for Under Fives (1986) *A Guide to Anti-racist Childcare Practice*, VOLCUF.

10 Handicapped children

Philippa Russell

The birth of a child can be a traumatic as well as a happy event for the parents concerned. Parenthood brings alarming new responsibilities, as well as pleasures. When a new baby has a disability, the initial diagnosis may be devastating for the parents. Recent research by Cunningham (1988), Davis *et al.* (1987) and others clearly shows us how important it is to recognize the impact of disability on parental expectations and self-image. But, as Hewett noted in 1970, 'the general tendency to characterize parents of handicapped children as guilt-ridden, anxiety-laden . . . over-protected and rejecting beings is unfair'. They are, rather, vulnerable families faced with a major challenge for which they require practical support as well as counselling and respect rather than global assumptions about 'pathological abnormality'.

Many disabled children require high levels of practical support in their day-to-day lives. A study by Glendenning (1983) found that 50.1 per cent of the 361 severely disabled children in her survey could not be left alone and unsupervised for more than ten minutes at a time, and Wilkins (1979) and Baldwin (1985) have emphasized the particular burdens placed upon mothers, with little support from neighbours or other relatives. In a study of families using the Family Fund, Cooke and Bradshaw (1986) found that disabled children were more likely than others to experience at least one spell in a one-parent family. These spells were longer than in families with non-disabled children, and the families of severely disabled children were less likely to be reconstituted by new marriages or relationships. Physical restrictions of care can severely limit families' social networks, and the Cooke and Bradshaw research indicates the importance of looking at family networks and structures and implications for care and support with the families of disabled children.

The high incidence of depression and low self-esteem amongst young parents generally in disadvantaged inner-city areas has been shown by Wolkind (1981) and others. The social context of disability is therefore of crucial importance in determining whether positive approaches to parent support outlined below will be effective for both family and child. Disabled children and their families require a range of supportive services, and if these are to be effective, fully used and sensitive to consumer needs, professionals, managers and carers need to review and update them constantly. In addition they need to be aware that research is significant in the development of good quality community services and in setting priorities for the future.

A number of studies have endeavoured to assess the levels of stress experienced by families with disabled children with a view to developing effective programmes for family support. Glendenning (1983), Brimblecombe and Russell (1987), Cunningham and Davis (1985a, b) and Pahl and Quine (1984) all identify a range of stress-related problems in such families. In general, not surprisingly, research identifies a greater than average degree of stress and psychological and physical problems amongst them. The above studies do not suggest that a 'handicapped child is a handicapped family' (Younghusband, 1974), but rather that disability, though a major and potentially damaging life event, is nevertheless amenable to intervention and compatible with good quality family life. The Honeylands assessment of stress, using the Rutter Malaise Inventory (Brimblecome and Russell, 1985), replicated other findings but also clearly indicated the need to avoid making sweeping generalizations about family experiences and life styles. Not all the families using Honeylands experienced abnormal levels of stress, but when it existed, it often appeared to be linked to severe restrictions on social and family life, poor physical health, and marital and economic difficulties, as much as to a child's disability.

The Rutter Malaise Inventory has been used in a number of other studies, including Pahl and Quine's evaluation of the stresses experienced by families with children with a severe mental handicap who were living in Kent (Pahl and Quine, 1984). This study found a high correlation between maternal malaise scores and mental health ratings. The Malaise Inventory asks the respondent if she or he has experienced any of 24 emotional, physical or psycho-social symptoms in recent weeks, as a basis of calculating stress. A score of five or six is considered to indicate stress. In the case of families with a disabled child, such stress may reflect existing social or emotional problems but can also be directly related to practical problems. Ann Gath (1978) and Robert Burden (1980), also using the Malaise Inventory, found similar results, namely that stress was frequently associated with a child's difficult behaviour but that the cumulative effects of economic and social disadvantage were significant. Quine and Pahl, for example, found that scores were less in mothers in two-parent families with adequate income. Being a single parent, having poor housing or money worries, lacking a close friend or experiencing marriage difficulties were clearly stress factors which would directly affect the parent's personal resources needed to cope with a disabled child.

Some families are so stressed that they are incapable of negotiating personal support (Pahl and Quine, 1984) and all the above studies clearly indicate that acknowledgement of stress is essential in order to ensure take-up of existing services.

The impact of initial diagnosis of disability on future family expectations of both child and professionals has been well documented. Cunningham *et al.* (1984) found that 58 per cent of parents of Down's Syndrome babies in the Manchester area were dissatisfied with the initial diagnosis. Pahl and Quine (1984) also found 60 per cent of parents of a wide range of disabled children very critical of the way the bad news had been broken to them. As a result of the Manchester study revised procedures were introduced which produced high degrees of parental satisfaction. Parents were told together, were given a 'follow-up' visit for clarification and further discussion, and were immediately offered access to community services and a developmental programme for the child. Recent research by both Cunningham (1988) and Davis *et al.* (forthcoming), shows the importance of counselling as an integral part of early intervention to enhance parental confidence, competence and use of services. Take-up of services and attitudes to young disabled children were both improved in consequence.

The concept of a 'parent adviser' (a named person) has been developed by Dr Hilton Davis (Cunningham and Davis, 1985) in a child development team working in Tower Hamlets. This worker acts as liaison with other agencies and professionals; monitors child's and family's progress and acts as communicator and counsellor, providing personal and emotional support to families of disabled children. Like the Honeylands study, Dr Davis emphasizes the importance of demonstrating respect for families, developing trusting relationships with them and recognizing their real difficulties.

Another role for the 'named person' may be to resolve differing views and the interests of the child and wider family network. A report on the Carraigfoyle Paediatric Support Unit in Northern Ireland (Barnardos Irish Division, 1984) observes that:

> The importance of family networks was important in the course of our work. The extended family often shared in the care of the child and provided emotional support. But sometimes this also brought emotional complications. While giving that emotional support, all parties were under strain as they (the extended family) lacked the necessary information to be able to help adequately.

Other networks may also be important. Hatch and Hinton (1986), evaluating the parent self-help group 'Contact a Family', found that membership of a voluntary or community group had direct benefits. Families were more likely to make good use of existing professional services, had higher expectations for their disabled children and felt less isolated and better supported.

Since the 1970s parents have increasingly been recognized as 'partners' with services, having not only a voice but direct skills to utilize in meeting their child's special needs. Such partnerships cannot be assumed to be present, however, simply because professionals are working with parents. The increasing popularity of the Portage home teaching scheme for parents of pre-school disabled children has demonstrated the importance of a known, trained and supported home visitor making regular visits to a family in order to monitor the child's progress and to identify goals and structure simple teaching programmes.

Portage is an important example of involving all consumers in a programme which teaches success, is sensitive to social, personal and cultural variables, and can be used in a wide range of care settings. Such a partnership is not, however, a cheap resource nor an alternative to the full range of other support services such as respite care, aids and equipment and appropriate housing.

As Cameron (1986) has indicated, a considerable amount of service evaluation has been carried out on the existing Portage model. But there are still important questions to be addressed, such as what characteristics of home-based interventions are more effective in facilitating which areas of confidence in parents and cognitive development in children. Additionally, the Portage model appears to have important wider applications, for example in teaching early language skills or in working with children with multiple handicaps or severe behaviour difficulties.

Cunningham and Davis (1985b) note the need to put any family support in the context of available and accessible resources, accurate and comprehensive information and continuity of service rather than 'one-off' interventions. The House of Commons Select Committee on Special Educational Needs (1987) has shown that the assessment procedures for the 1981 Education Act, designed to give parents much improved access to information and participation in decision making, have still not achieved their goal. Many parents continue to feel marginalized by procedures which they do not fully understand and in which they are uncertain how to express their views.

In the different ethnic communities in Britain, there have so far been few substantive studies of differing needs, perceptions and aspirations concerning disability.

The Fish Committee (1985) commissioned research which showed that many families from ethnic minority groups felt alienated and rejected. Parents who were dissatisfied with the amount and type of information on their child's disability and education difficulties numbered 42 per cent, compared with 13 per cent of other parents. Of these parents 33 per cent felt unhappy about the amount and quality of teacher contact as compared with 8 per cent of the indigenous population. Many parents were not receiving the same support, e.g. aids and equipment, access to pre-school programmes and respite care, as their UK counterparts. Dissatisfaction appeared to arise primarily because of misconceptions about families from ethnic minority groups. Translation and interpreter services were often inadequate. There were frequent misunderstandings arising from very different attitudes to disability in different cultural groups (and even within particular groups in the Asian community) with a corresponding belief that because there are large extended families parents do not need outside support and advice. Parents wanted culturally acceptable and appropriate information on procedures and services and awareness of special social or medical problems which might inhibit effective utilization of disability services.

The same committee found marked differences of attitude between Asian and Afro-Caribbean communities with regard to education of children with special needs. Afro-Caribbean families felt less satisfied with the attitude of schools towards their children, particularly concerning educational standards and over-representation of their children in schools for emotional, behavioural and moderate learning difficulties (including residential special schools). Children of other ethnic groups were under-represented in the same provision. A later study of another London Borough by Berridge and Russell (1987) found that whilst Asian families were usually satisfied (sometimes perhaps over-satisfied because language inhibited them from actually asking for better services), Afro-Caribbean families were concerned about educational standards and lack of expectations for their children. In Haringey many Afro-Caribbean children attended 'supplementary schools' run by the local community on Saturdays and holidays. In the same authority 'in order to help our children achieve' parents had opened a private school primarily for Afro-Caribbean children, with a traditional curriculum and high standards of expected behaviour. Conversely Haringey Afro-Caribbean parents, unlike inner London parents, did not complain that their children were over-represented in special education, but rather that special help was slow in being provided. Both the Fish and Haringey studies emphasized the importance of ensuring that schools reflect the needs of a multi-cultural society, that communication problems are acknowledged, and that vigorous attempts should be made to provide representation and advocacy for ethnic minority parents with disabled children to enable them to use services actively and more effectively.

There is still little substantive research or published criteria for the evaluation of early support services for families with disabled children. Important lessons can already be learned from the evaluation of the Honeylands Family Support Unit (Brimblecombe and Russell) and from Cunningham (1988) and Davis *et al.* (1988) in their evaluations of early support for families with young children in Manchester and London. The Honeylands evaluation shows the importance of involving consumers, not only in the initial development, but also in maintaining changes and developments in response to new emerging needs. All three studies confirm the importance of recognizing whole-family needs and in integrating services into a coherent 'package' to avoid duplication and overload. The value of a 'key worker' or 'named person' to ensure a seamless delivery of services and to encourage take-up is underlined as a critical factor in parental satisfaction and overall health and development of the child. Many parents (particularly those from families with under-fives who have disabilities or special needs) are concerned to integrate their children into mainstream children's services (with major consequences for more flexible deployment of professional services across a variety of children's settings). All the limited available research suggests that 'case management' will become increasingly important not only in ensuring the most appropriate mixture of provision for individual children, but in utilizing more effectively all the resources of mainstream and special children's provision.

Although there has been careful evaluation of a number of home-based programmes such as Portage, there remains little detailed information from research about the 'hard to manage' children. In particular we need to know more about the lives of children who have successfully benefited from good quality early intervention, respite care, improved educational opportunities, home-based learning programmes and to see if and how positive outcomes of early intervention are translated into school and post-school lives. We also need greater dissemination of successful outcome of services. Developments like Honeylands (where effective implementation of a team approach often blurred professional boundaries and perceived intervention as part of continuing care and listening to users) offer lessons for wider relocation if other planners and managers can have access to the research data.

'Partnership' has been a major theme throughout recent government reports on services for families and children. The evaluation of the Honeylands service and of early intervention and support strategies by Cunningham and Davis (1985a and b) clearly demonstrate that early and flexible intervention can produce more positive attitudes in parents; improve take-up of services; offer models for replication in a wide range of agencies and, most importantly, build on the resources of individual families in the best interests of the children. As Cunningham has noted, the level of theorizing about early intervention and support is still inadequate. Most studies have focused upon children rather than on wider family benefits. We still need research to identify what child, family and intervention variables predict outcomes. But the first steps have been taken in moving away from '*ad hoc*' crisis intervention towards longer-term flexible family support and towards a fundamental philosophy of always ascertaining what the consumers say. Perhaps the last major challenge will be asking the children.

Families with one or more handicapped child inevitably experience heavy stress and at times need respite to enable them to carry on caring for their child in the future. Historically this short-term care has developed as an emergency service, frequently within a long-stay hospital or other institution. Traditionally it has been offered in 'block' bookings, e.g. for summer holidays or similar periods and has often been distant from the family's own home and from local services. In the last decade, however, there has been a general commitment to flexible family support services, which include respite care as one of a range of options for individual families and children. The shift towards seeing respite care as part of an integrated service owes much to Maureen Oswin's principle (1984) that 'short-term care should be regarded as a very specialist service needing clearly defined aims based on principles of child care practice and requiring continuous monitoring of standards with an emphasis on how it might be affecting individual children'. Oswin's research (1984) stressed the need to think of children first and identified an inherent tension in the fact that respite care is frequently directed to parent relief and not seen as part of a coherent local authority child care policy for all handicapped children.

Growing concern to provide flexible short-term care now stressed the importance of:

(a) a local service, where the child can continue to attend his or her own school
(b) good quality child care which ensures that the child is not treated as a sick patient, but as a child who happens to have a disability
(c) availability on demand; research into different models of respite care has clearly indicated the importance of parents' choice of service provision and flexibility of use. There is now good evidence that many families prefer to use respite care services for short periods of time (sometimes during the day only) rather than in longer-term block bookings
(d) a service which meets the needs of all handicapped children; concern has been expressed about the lack of respite care for children with emotional and behaviour difficulties or complex medical problems
(e) age-appropriate care so that young children and adolescents receive relevant care and occupation appropriate to their age and stage of development
(f) an integrated programme of family support which includes respite care as part of a wider range of professional services. Maureen Oswin's research study of different models of respite care (1984) indicated a need for preventive services to avoid some children slipping into long-term care through escalating use of respite care.

Respite or short-term care is available in a number of forms. The most recent DHSS statistics show that over 11 000 annual short-stay admissions of children are to long-stay mental handicap hospitals. Many of the children have multiple and severe behaviour difficulties which local authorities are currently unable to accommodate. Some respite care is provided in local authority children's homes, small residential units or staffed holiday homes provided by voluntary organizations. A particular problem in some schemes has been under-use, despite parents knowing of their availability. The Honeylands evaluation (Brimblecombe and Russell, 1987) and the DHSS Social Work Inspectorate study of respite fostering in Norfolk and Oxfordshire (1984) both identified a number of families who emphasized the importance of guaranteed availability of respite care in enabling them to maintain severely handicapped children at home. The need to book short-term care as much as a year in advance discourages parents from requesting help and a vicious circle develops of cutting places because demand appears low.

Studies of short-term care in the Preston Skreens Family Support Unit in Kent (Pahl, 1981), Honeylands (Brimblecombe and Russell, 1987) and Avon (Robinson, 1987) have all found very varied patterns of use among families if the use of services is dictated by the ways and times most appropriate to individual family needs. The majority of families using both Preston Skreens and Honeylands were light users, with respite care complementing a range of other services. The Avon research (Robinson, 1987) emphasizes the fallacy of assuming that respite care is a universal panacea for all family problems. This study found that 'many of the user families had unmet needs as did many of the non-user families . . . in both groups there was a call for more home-based services such as sitters, helpers to assist mothers etc. It is evident that the respite care service alone cannot meet the needs of all families with a handicapped child . . . it is important to provide a range of services for these families.'

Although there has been no comparative research into parental satisfaction with different models of respite care, it seems that parents are more likely to be satisfied if a service is clearly linked to a voluntary organization, school or a wider service like Honeylands or Preston Skreens in order to put the service in context and to ensure that respite care is a rewarding experience for the child.

Concern has been expressed since the Curtis Committee first reported in 1948 about 'hard to place' disabled children with additional handicaps or severe behavioural problems who cannot live with their natural families. A DHSS sponsored study of 30 centrally funded schemes designed to help move children out of hospital (Leonnard, 1988) gives some encouraging pointers for future developments. Initial funding had been provided specifically for health authorities to 'set up small homely units in the community for those children who will continue to need health care and who had largely been living in long-stay hospitals'. The project offered a unique opportunity to follow through the processes by which a policy of 'normalization' and 'dignity' for a very disadvantaged group of children could be translated into practice. But, as Ann Leonnard commented, 'in a society as complex as this one . . . there are no standardized households or lives against which the households and lives of residents in these schemes can truly be measured'. Concepts of personal autonomy, dignity and risk, and ordinary home life may all be interpreted differently with different communities. However, *Out of Hospital* provides some valuable insights into the process of achieving strategic change. It is also a rare study of the everyday lives of children and young people with severe disabilities.

The Leonnard research identified certain key factors in providing good residential services for this group of children who have generally failed to find support within mainstream children's services. Firstly, attitudes were crucial, in particular support for staff by like-minded management. Secondly, planning and involvement of everybody concerned at an early stage was essential for later success. Thirdly, the actual housing was 'unexceptionally homely, comfortable, without being ostentatious, ordinary family houses in ordinary streets'. In effect severely disabled children can live well in non-purpose-built accommodation like the rest of us.

There has been little substantive research into the lives of disabled children living in residential houses, whether those of local authorities or voluntary organizations (although Barnardos has evaluated and published findings on a number of its residential projects). There is, however, growing concern at the possible consequences of wider changes in provision for all children living away from home. A number of local authorities have closed residential homes for children and young people in a shift to fostering as the method of substitute care.

At the same time more disabled children appear to be attending residential schools primarily for residential care. A number of schools in the independent sector are providing 52-weeks-a-year facilities and whilst an educational focus in care is important, there are concerns about the quality of child care practice and the 'ordinary life' philosophy practised in schools which extend their terms to cover the whole year. There has been no recent research into the lives of disabled children living at their school (or perhaps going from school to a succession of short-stay placements when on holiday). Many children living away from home for educational reasons are not also in care and in consequence the transition back to their place of origin when leaving school will not be cushioned by any pre-planning or support from local services. An important area for future research would, therefore, be some evaluation of the quality of life and personal experiences of pupils at residential special schools, in particular where there is no regular home contact, and an exploration of the reasons why such children do not remain in their own local communities at day schools and in the care of social services departments if they cannot be at home. There are no national statistics of children and young people with disabilities who are living in voluntary or private residential homes or schools. Where the latter provide education on the premises there are again doubts (but as yet no firm data) about the quality of provision offered to the children and the alternatives in the local community.

There has also been little research into the relative merits of different approaches to providing residential care for children with disabilities. However, growing concern in the 1960s and 70s (highlighted in Maureen Oswin's graphic and poignant picture of the disadvantaged lives of severely handicapped children living in long-stay mental handicap hospitals) focused the attention of health and local authorities upon more appropriate forms of care. It is now government policy that children should not be admitted to long-term hospital care as a residential service, although DHSS statistics for 1987 reveal that there were no fewer than 11 000 admissions to mental handicap hospitals for 'respite care' for children with mental handicap.

The work of Albert Kishlick for the Wessex Health Authority (1977 and 1980) demonstrated the improvement in development and behaviour of mentally handicapped children formerly living in hospital who were transferred to smaller units. The 'Wessex Units' for 30 residents were large by current standards, but they introduced individualized living environments, good quality child care and an emphasis on personal growth and development. By the early 1980s a body of opinion considered that children should, wherever possible, be the responsibility of the local authority, not the health service, and be protected by child care legislation in the same way as if they were not disabled. The Court Report on Child Health, 1978, had affirmed that all children should live in their local communities with appropriate medical and educational support. The White Paper on the Review of Child Care Law and a report by the Law Commission on Family Law (1987) similarly affirmed that current anomalies by which children with mental handicap may be placed in residential care under NHS legislation and without the protection of being in care and regular reviews, should be amended. However, 'community care' is often held to be a euphemism for ineffective support and there is at present a dearth of research material on how separated disabled children may best be cared for.

The Jay Committee had hoped that fostering would be the way forward for young mentally handicapped children unable to live with their natural families. A number of special long-term fostering and adoption schemes have been established in the UK and the USA. An evaluation of Parents for Children (Fruin, 1987) confirms a similar evaluation of a scheme in Nebraska, USA (Thomas, 1983) which shows that specialist adoption and fostering schemes can be highly successful provided that:

(a) families and children are given a sufficiently long and supportive introduction period
(b) the possibility of 'atypical' substitute families be considered (special families often being older or having more unusual backgrounds than conventional carers)
(c) there is ongoing support for the family, which takes account of changing needs as the child grows
(d) although some placements will break down, the majority can be successful and there are families in the community who are happy to accept a disabled child.

Local authorities have varied greatly in their provision for disabled children in their own residential homes. Some have successfully integrated children with disabilities, but the majority have run small specialist residential units, funded placements in residential units run by the voluntary or private sector or used provision made by the health authority.

The Leonnard research demonstrates the feasibility of providing individualized and good quality care for children with the most complex disabilities. All the children and young people studied improved in terms of personal health and wellbeing, although complex health problems were said to be the reasons which took them to hospital in the first place. In some cases, despite the profundity of their mental and physical handicaps, considerable and sometimes dramatic developments in mobility, communication and basic social skills were observed. Parents became involved and the schemes demonstrated that planning for individual needs within a small team could be effective. The schemes did not minimize the problems of managing what is often called 'challenging behaviour'.

General improvements in services for young disabled children have led to increasing optimism about the feasibility of their experiencing ordinary adult life and independent living and employment. However, as the Warnock Report noted (DES, 1978), 'We are aware that greater independence, particularly for those with severe disabilities, will not be achieved simply by administrative measures or the injection of more resources . . . in the end changes in the nature of education, training and supporting services will depend upon changes in attitude.' Attitudes, particularly following the implementation of the 1981 Education Act, have become generally more positive and optimistic for children. But recent research clearly indicates that the lessons from children's services have not necessarily been successfully applied to adult services and that the transition period is still poorly managed and often nullifies earlier progress.

The Prince of Wales Advisory Group (1985), the Royal College of Physicians (1986), Brimblecombe *et al.* (1985) and Kuh *et al.* (1987) all examined current research and practice with regard to the management of transition for disabled adolescents and young adults and raised important areas of concern for future work and development. The most substantive (Brimblecombe *et al.*, 1985) arose from earlier research within the Exeter Health Authority, which had established the need for a family support centre and parent-orientated services for young disabled children. Honeylands is still the best developed (and the most completely evaluated) of all the centre-based services for disabled children and families. But this evaluation in turn indicated that many children who were well supported until 16 met a lack of opportunities and sometimes positively harmful absence of treatment when they moved to adult services. A research study was, therefore, established in order to examine the needs of all the disabled school leavers in Exeter in one year and to compare their expectations, life styles and personal satisfaction with a control group of able-bodied peers. The study is unique not only in asking parents and relevant professionals for their opinions, but also in talking directly to the 365 young people themselves. The research indicated important and alarming gaps in services in a relatively well-resourced health authority, with a particularly good children's service. Less than half the young people (48 per cent) had seen a medical specialist in the previous year, although they had all received regular health care until they moved from paediatric services; 68 per cent felt that they had insufficient information about the actual medical implications of their disability (including the genetic implications if they wished subsequently to have children). A similar 68 per cent lacked physiotherapy, speech therapy and other specialist medical inputs; 70 per cent of the young physically disabled people and 63 per cent of those with a mental handicap lacked any daytime occupation – apart from being at home, and 62 per cent felt that they had limited opportunities for any social life once they had left school. The carers indicated a general lack of short-term care, help and advice, and generally felt unsupported.

When compared with their peers, the young disabled people revealed major and worrying differences. Loneliness was a serious problem for 35 per cent as against 12 per cent of their peers. Lack of social confidence and poor self-esteem were conspicuous and a number felt their problems sprang from being at home, where their needs were not sympathetically met. It should be noted that there has been almost no significant research anywhere (and none in this country) into the changing role of parents as carers of young adults. Maintaining an adult-child/parent relationship whilst providing for major care needs presents significant challenges. A number of services for young adults (like MENCAP's Home Foundation residential homes) are initiating training for staff working with parents and adult children. The new provisions of the 1986 Disabled Persons Act enable the needs of carer and disabled persons to be assessed separately. But the recognition of their different needs, and the most effective way of renegotiating parent/adult-child relationships requires further investigation.

Young people's depression indicated in the Brimblecombe and Kuh research was also clearly demonstrated by Julie Bargh (1987) in evaluating the National Children's Bureau's self-advocacy project for young people with learning difficulties. This project, the first self-advocacy programme to work with young people between 16 and 19 years, found a high incidence of depression, lack of self-esteem and a feeling of stigma and rejection because of the disability. As in the Brimblecombe research, the young women from Inner London also felt marginalized. They had never been able to discuss their difficulties, which they found painful to articulate. They frequently perceived themselves as being less valued than their siblings and longed for 'real lives' without knowing how to develop the social and vocational skills necessary to achieve them. Both studies clearly demonstrated that, even when mentally handicapped, young people can articulate their anxieties and their needs. Both studies also showed the sharp fall off of services on leaving school and the lack of transitional arrangements to ensure appropriate provision in adult life.

The Bargh project had been designed to provide parallel group work experiences for parents but had found it almost impossible to persuade parents of the value of group and shared activities. Other attempts to attach parent groups to young adult services have also met with varying success. The Organization for Economic Co-operation and Development has monitored a parents' group attached to a special needs course at a college of further education in Oxfordshire. Although parental take-up was better than in the National Children's Bureau project, it was clear that parents of older children were leading different lives from younger parents (who tend naturally to group together) and that activities designed to support and educate parents of young adults need further investigation.

Although voluntary organizations provide a high level of mutual support for many parents, evaluation of parental satisfaction tends to focus upon parents of younger children (Hatch and Hinton, 1986) and daytime activities and group work are less appropriate for older families with different lifestyles and obligations.

There are encouraging developments in independent living schemes, vocational training programmes and in community support for even very severely disabled young people. However, access to special projects and schemes will largely depend upon a continuum of education and care from children's services into adult life. The use of district handicap and community mental handicap teams may be an effective way of maintaining a network of services. But whereas the community mental handicap team can adopt a life-cycle approach, district handicap teams operate only in the children's field.

There is clearly a need for research and development into the provision of co-ordinated team approaches for young adults with physical and sensory disabilities and more broad-based special needs approaches (the majority of young disabled people having more than one disability and needing holistic approaches to their problems).

This chapter has attempted to show some of the problems which parents and their handicapped children face from birth into adult life. Some families, for a variety of reasons, are unable to cope for periods of time, sometimes for years. The children's and young people's needs are still very inadequately provided for and much more must be known and done before the community can be satisfied that either they or their parents have available the help they require. Research needs to be increased, and policy and practice regularly reviewed in the light of what is learned. It is possible that the proposals of the Children Bill 1988, concerning handicapped children and young people, if they become part of legislation for a more unified child care system, may give a much needed impetus to development in this area of child care.

References

Audit Commission (1986) *Making of Community Care*, HMSO.

Baldwin, S. (1985) *The Costs of Caring*, Routledge and Kegan Paul.

Barnardos (1984) *Carraigfoyle Paediatric Support Unit: The First Two Years*, Barnardos, Irish Division.

Bargh, J. (1987) *Play Back the Thinking Memories*, National Children's Bureau.

Berridge, D. and Russell, P. (1987) *A Red Bus Next Year?*, a review of consumer views of special education, London Borough of Haringey.

Bicknell, J. (1981) *Right from the Start*, Royal Society for Mentally Handicapped Children and Adults.

Bradshaw, J. and Lawton, D. (1978) *Tracing the Causes of Stress in Families with Handicapped Children*, Social Policy Research Unit, University of York.

Brimblecombe, F. S. W. (1979) 'Handicapped children and their families', in *Problems and Priorities in Medical Care*, Series 12, Nuffield Provincial Hospitals Trust, Oxford University Press.

Brimblecombe, F. S. W. (1983) *Honeylands Progress Report*, Paediatric Research Unit, Royal Devon and Exeter Hospital.

Brimblecombe, F. S. W., Kuh, D., Tripp, J., Smith, D. and Wadsworth, J. (1985) *The Needs of Handicapped Young Adults*, Department of Child Health, University of Exeter.

Burden, R. L. (1980) 'Measuring the effects of stress on mothers of handicapped infants', *Child: Care, Health and Development*, Vol. 6, pp. 111–23.

Cameron, R. J. (1983) 'A problem centred approach to family problems', in Daly, B. (ed), *Portage; The Importance of Parents*, NFER-Nelson.

Cameron, R. J. (1985) 'Parents as educators; learning from portage', in Pugh, G. (ed), *Partnership Papers III, Working Together with Special Educational Needs: Implications for Pre-School Service*, National Children's Bureau.

Chaplais, J. (1986) 'Parents as health record keepers', in *Partnership Papers VIII, Developing a Partnership in the Child Health Services*, National Children's Bureau.

Cooke, K. and Bradshaw, J. (1986) 'Child disablement, family dissolution and reconstitution', *Developmental Medicine and Child Neurology*, Vol. 28, pp. 610–16.

Cunningham, C. (1988) *Early Intervention: Some Results from the Manchester Cohort Study*, Department of Mental Handicaps, University of Nottingham.

Cunningham, C. and Davis, H. (1985a) 'Early parent counselling', in Craft, M., Bicknell, J. and Hollins, S. (eds) *Mental Handicap: A Multidisciplinary Approach*, Balliere Tindall.

Cunningham, C. and Davis, H. (1985b) *Working with Parents; Frameworks for Collaboration*, Open University Press.

Cunningham, C., Morgan, P. and McGucken, R. (1984) 'Down's Syndrome: is dissatisfaction with disclosure of diagnosis inevitable?', *Developmental Medicine and Child Neurology*, Vol. 26, No. 1, pp. 33–9.

Daly, B. (1985) (ed) *Portage; the Importance of Parents*, NFER-Nelson.

Davis, H., Booth, A. and Rushton, R. (forthcoming) 'Parent counselling and support', Report on Seminar on Early Intervention, September 1988, National Children's Bureau.

Davis, H., Buchan, L. and Clermerson, J. (1987) *The Parent Adviser Scheme: Manual for Training Counsellors to Work with Families of Children with Special Needs*, London Hospital Medical College.

Department of Education and Science (1978) *Special Educational Needs: Report of the Committee of Enquiry into the Education of Handicapped Children and Young People* (Warnock Committee), Cmnd 7212, HMSO.

Department of Education and Science (1985) *Education For All, Report of the Committee of Inquiry into the Education of Children from Minority Groups* (Swann Committee), Department of Education and Science, HMSO.

Department of Health and Social Security (1976) *Fit for the Future: Report of the Committee on Child Health Services*, Cmnd 6684, HMSO.

Department of Health and Social Security (1979) *Report of the Committee of Enquiry into Mental Handicap Nursing and Care* (Jay Report), Cmnd 74681 and 11, HMSO.

Department of Health and Social Security (1985) *National Development Team for Mentally Handicapped People 1981/4*, HMSO.

Department of Health and Social Security (1987) *The Law on Child Care and Family Services*, HMSO.

Department of Health and Social Security Social Work Inspectorate (1984) *Local Authority Social Services for Handicapped Children in England*, DHSS.

Department of Health and Social Security Social Work Inspectorate (1984) *Services for Handicapped Children: Schemes and Development in England*, DHSS.

Department of Health and Social Security Social Work Inspectorate, Banks, S. and Grizzel, R. (1984) *A Study of Family Placement Schemes for the Shared Care of Handicapped Children in Norfolk and Oxfordshire*, DHSS.

Department of Health and Social Security Social Work Inspectorate (NW Division) (1988) *Care for a Change?*, DHSS.

Dessent, T. (1985) 'Parentology: a critique', in *Working with Parents, Educational and Child Psychology*, Vol. 2, No. 1, British Psychological Society.

Fruin, D. (1987) unpublished report, National Children's Bureau.

Garth, A. (1978) *Down's Syndrome in the Family*, Academic Press.

Glendenning, C. (1983) *Unshared Care – Parents and their Disabled Children*, Routledge and Kegan Paul.

Hatch, S. and Hinton, T. (1986) 'Self help in practice: a study of Contact a Family', *Community Care*.

Hewett, S. (1970) *Handicapped Children and their Families; A Survey*, Nottingham University Child Development Research Unit.

Hirst, S. (1983) 'Young people with disabilities, what happens after 16', *Child: Care, Health and Development*, 9, pp.273–84.

Inner London Education Authority (1985) *Educational Opportunities for All?* Report of Committee appointed to review provision for special educational needs in the ILEA (Fish Committee), ILEA.

Kuh, D., Tripp, J. and Lawrence, C. (1987) 'Disabled young people – making choices for future living options', *Social Services Research Journal*, 4.

The Law Commission (1986) *Family Law: Review of Child Care Law and Custody*, Working Paper 96, HMSO.

Leonnard, A. (1988) *Out of Hospital: A Survey of 30 Centrally-funded Schemes Providing Alternative Care for Children with Mental Handicaps*, University of York.

McConachie, H. (1983) 'Fathers, mothers, siblings: how do they see themselves?', in Mittler and McConachie (eds) *Parents, Professionals and Mentally Handicapped People: Approaches to Partnership*, Croom Helm.

McFarlane, A. (1986) 'Parents' rights and children's rights', *Concern*, Vol. 58, Spring 1986, pp. 6–7, National Children's Bureau.

Mittler, P. and Mittler, H. (1982) *Partnership with Parents*, NCSE.

Oakley, A. (1974) *The Sociology of Housework*, Martin Robertson.

Organization for Economic Co-operation and Development, *Active Life for Young People with Disabilities*, report of an international conference reviewing policies and practices for young people with disabilities during their transition to adult life, OECD.

Oswin, M. (1971) *The Empty Hours*, Penguin.

Oswin, M. (1984) *They Keep Going Away*, Basil Blackwell/King's Fund Centre.

Pahl, J. (1981) *Preston Skreens: A Family Support Unit for Mentally Handicapped Children*, Canterbury Health Services Research Unit, University of Kent.

Pahl, J. and Quine, E. (1984) *Families with Mentally Handicapped Children: A Study of Stress and a Service Response*, Canterbury Health Services Research Unit, University of Kent.

Prince of Wales Advisory Group (1985) *Independent Living Options*, Prince of Wales Advisory Group.

Robinson, C. (1987) *Avon Short-term Respite Care Scheme: Evaluation Study*, Department of Mental Health, University of Bristol.

Royal College of Physicians (1986) *Report on Services for Young Disabled People*, RCP.

Russell, P. (1986) 'Portage – pre-schoolers, parents and professionals', in Cameron, R. J. (ed), *Portage: Ten Years of Achievement*, NFER-Nelson.

Russell, P. and Griffiths, M. (1984) *Working Together with Handicapped Children*, Souvenir Press.

Shearer, A. (1980) *Handicapped Children in Residential Care: A Study of Policy Failure*, Bedford Square Press.

Thomas, D., Firth, H. and Kendall, A. (1978) *ENCOR – A Way Ahead*, CMU.

Toogood, A. (1983) 'Goal setting in a locally-based hospital unit', in Cameron, R. J. (ed), *Portage: Ten Years of Achievement*, NFER-Nelson.

Wilkins, D. (1979) *Caring for the Mentally Handicapped Child*, Croom Helm.

Wolkind, S. (1981) 'Depression in mothers of young children', *Archives of Diseases in Childhood*, Vol. 56, No. 1, pp. 1–3.

Younghusband, E. (1974) *Living with Handicap*, Report of Working Party, National Children's Bureau.

11 Young offenders

Henri Giller

The policy-making process

Policy making in criminal justice generally and juvenile justice policy in particular, is a complex and complicated process (see Walker and Giller, 1977; Croft, 1978). Legislation – one output of the policy-making process – is the result of a variety of influences and sources. Among these may be some or all of the following – views of ministers, their parties, civil servants and administrators within their department, and allied departments, special advisers, academics, royal commissions, advisory bodies, voluntary organizations, professional organizations, local government and local government organizations, lobby groups, pressure groups, the media and, often vitally important in this area, public opinion. Moreover, in the penal sphere, co-ordinated policy making may be problematic given that the principal nature of the task may be to deal with pressing practical problems of the daily running of component parts of the criminal justice system. As Moriarty (1977) notes:

> Much of the resources and energies devoted to penal matters, from the Home Secretary downwards, are necessarily devoted to the inexorable day-to-day task of running a system whose tasks include the maintenance of public order and the prevention of as much crime as possible (and so sustaining public confidence in the criminal justice system) and the handling of detected offenders, especially those who present a real threat to society. Policy-making grows out of these preoccupations and needs to be addressed to making the task easier and more effectively performed. (p. 143)

Legislation, however, is not the only output of the policy-making process. Given the problems associated with legislative timetabling, priority setting, the need for consultation and the overall balance of a parliamentary programme, other strategies may be used to promulgate policy objectives. Elements of criminal justice policy, therefore, are to be found in ministerial circulars, notes of guidance, rules and other documents produced by ministers or their advisers. While, unlike legislation, those documents are not statutory law, their influence on day-to-day practice cannot be ignored.

In the sphere of juvenile justice, the policy-making process is further complicated by divided ministerial responsibility for different aspects of the system. While the Home Office and the Home Secretary are responsible for issues relating to policing and the penal system, the Department of Health has responsibility for services which are provided by local authority social services departments and for offenders under 17 years old sentenced to be detained for more serious offences under Section 53 of the Children and Young Persons Act 1933 (see note 1). These two major ministries, however, are in turn obliged to consult with other ministries on policy-making issues where children's services are involved. Among these can be the Lord Chancellor's Department, the Department of Education and Science and the Welsh Office. It cannot be assumed that the views of ministers, although part of the same government, necessarily coincide. Each has advisers and 'constituencies' (e.g. for the Home Office, the police, magistrates and judges, for the Department of Health, the local government associations, directors of social services and social work bodies) which, in turn, have their own agendas of concerns and remedies for the problems they perceive.

Ministerial control and direction of policy are similarly variable. Within the Home Office, for example, there is direct control of day-to-day running and provision of the prison system, but the probation service lines of accountability and influence must be shared with local authorities and the Council of Probation Committees; in addition the Association of Chief Officers of Probation and the National Association of Probation Officers also have a significant voice. The willingness and/or ability of the Home Office to influence judicial decision makers, be they judges or magistrates, is problematic. They are answerable to the Lord Chancellor's Department and considerable distaste is expressed by judicial decision makers when Home Office ministers seek to influence their practices or restrict their powers. At the very least, such strategies may be seen as attempts to alter the constitutional balance between executive and judicial functions of the state.

Within the Department of Health there is a less direct line of accountability for children's services which are the responsibility of local authority social services departments. Failure either in achieving policy objectives overall or in individual cases, must, in the first instance, be the responsibility of local rather than central government. However, central government may seek directly to influence the implementation of policy or assume a greater degree of control, although this may affect the balance between local and central governmental responsibility (see note 2).

Finally, while a central government may talk of developing a juvenile justice policy to apply to the entire country, research demonstrates the great variability of practice within local juvenile justice systems (Parker and Giller, 1981; Richardson, 1988). The influence of local variables, including the power of local individuals, groups or professionals cannot be underestimated in contributing to the development of, or subversion of, policy makers' intentions.

These complicated structures might be easier in operational terms if they were politically (and professionally) bi-partisan. To a certain extent this is the case with elements of overall criminal justice policy. However, in the field of juvenile justice the policy debate since the 1960s has taken on a distinctly partisan tone. Debate has centred on the question of whether the offending child should be seen as an unsocialized individual in need of help and assistance or as a calculating transgressor in need of a formal sanction (see Morris and Giller, 1987).

Policy statements stressing juveniles' lack of responsibility for their deviant actions and their need for extended social services were consistently presented by socialist intellectuals and the Labour Party throughout the 1960s and early 1970s (Bottoms, 1974). Presented as policies for dealing with juvenile delinquency (e.g. the policy proposals behind the Children and Young Persons Act 1969), they were part of a legislative programme to develop a more socially just society in which socialist values of equality of opportunity and outcome would be advanced. Expansion of the Welfare State to meet the needs of those unable to participate in a programme of social reconstruction because of some disability was a key issue.

> Delinquency was viewed as only one of many expressions of 'secondary poverty' and as a symptom of underlying social need. Intervention was justified only where the child's offence was due to causes for which the child had no personal responsibility; 'naughtiness' was to be tolerated by the community as a natural part of the child's growing up process. The appropriate remedy for delinquency lay in the reconstruction of the family unit. (Morris and Giller, 1978, pp. 17–18)

The main objective, therefore, was to enhance family responsibility by expansion of supports to families. By shifting the debate from the nature of the juvenile offence to the nature of the juvenile offender the intention was to shift legitimate intervention from the penal system to the social welfare system (see note 3).

For those on the right a very different conception of juvenile social disorder predominates. The stereotype of the delinquent is not a social casualty but a conscious perpetrator of social disruption. While juvenile delinquency is viewed primarily as a personal problem, its source is personal iniquity rather than social inequality. The causes of crime are seen as wide ranging: effects of the media, lack of power of the courts, absence of discipline in schools and families, decline in respect for law. However, this propensity to iniquity can be exacerbated by the influence of socialist conceptions of Welfare Stateism. The appropriate response to juvenile delinquency, therefore, is not provision of social help but correction of the offender by discipline and punishment. The basis of this conception is individual freedom in return for responsibility for that freedom. Maintenance of order is through the law, the courts and through the symbolic impact of criminal justice procedures (see note 4).

To a substantial extent the debates surrounding the future of juvenile justice in England and Wales in the 1970s were fought on this terrain. Aspects of research and practice were selectively used to substantiate or refute core political assumptions about the nature of youth, their crimes and the appropriate remedies. Although, however, the policy rhetoric is about the format of the juvenile justice system and effective control of crime this often signifies wider concerns of civil society. A particular model or combination of models of juvenile justice are unlikely to have more than a marginal impact on crime *per se* (Rutter and Giller, 1983). Proposals that a particular change will have this effect are often proposals to increase the overall power of the state or to increase the powers of one part of the system. The debate about crime, law and order and the involvement of juveniles may, in fact, blind us to addressing squarely the more fundamental issues that they embody. As Pearson (1983) notes:

> Too often matters of vital public importance – jobs, homes, schools – are swallowed up in the maw of 'law-and-order' discourse, and publicly addressed as if the only important consideration was whether these social deficiencies might lead to crime, vandalism and hooliganism. Certainly these matters bear upon the reproduction of consent. But if we reinstate these problems in their own terms, and in all their enormity in contemporary Britain, then the preoccupation with 'hooliganism' must begin to pale in significance. (p. 239)

Trends in research

> When I became Home Secretary early in 1957 . . . I was determined that there should be a long-term plan: a course of action that would lay a path for enlightened penal policy. In particular I believed that changes should not be based on swings in emotion and opinion, but upon reliable information about the phenomenon of crime, its social and personal roots and the effectiveness of the preventive and penal measures available. (Butler, 1974, p. 1)

> It is impossible to escape the conclusion that our current policy makers do not regard social research as a major influence on their decisions. For the most part, they want the answers to simple questions – what are the causes of crime? How can we reduce the prison population? Do broken homes cause delinquency? Research workers are apt to render these simple questions into complicated ones, to demand more rather than less expenditure, and to end with a request for 'more research'. (Jones, 1982, p. 9)

In the years that separate these two statements a fundamental change took place in the relationship between researchers and policy makers in England and Wales in criminal justice matters (Parker and Giller, 1981; Hood, 1987). In the post-war period the government's desire for a 'scientific' understanding of crime was undoubtedly rooted in 'public guilt over the breaking up of the family in a national crisis and the bewilderment at the continuance of crime and delinquency during a period of peace, prosperity and the Welfare State . . .' (Brake, 1980). A considerable body of researchers responded to the challenge to provide a 'scientific' understanding as outlined by Lord Butler and sought 'to survey with an academic impartiality . . . the general problem of crime in society; its causes and its solution' (Home Office, 1959).

The sociologists of the period, for example, armed with the analytic tools of alienation, anomie and subculture, addressed the problem by entering the world of the delinquent. Unfortunately, the delinquent solution favoured by working-class inner-city youth revealed by this sociological endeavour did not readily suggest a solution to delinquency as the policy makers had intended. Faced with the conclusion that 'Delinquency was not so much a symptom of maladjustment as adjustment to a subculture which was in conflict with the culture of the city as a whole' (Mays, 1954), it was difficult to see what the policy-maker was to do. Not only were sociologists suggesting that delinquency was not the 'real problem' but the solution to troublesome youth seemed to question the very social reconstruction consensus upon which policy makers were actively relying. For the sociologist, the ubiquity and permanence of the delinquent solution and the inappropriateness of many existing tools of theoretical analysis, as much as the sedimentation of crime within wider structures, not only made a 'solution' to delinquency remote but (ironically) indicated that, as a distinct discipline, criminology needed to relocate its frame of reference within other disciplines investigating social life. In other words, the subcultural tradition demanded that sociologists concerned with the delinquents address broader issues of 'youth', 'teenage culture', 'schools' and 'employment'.

Initially, these broader constructs were used merely to locate criminality and not to replace crime as the focus of sociological inquiry. Latterly, however, both theoretical and empirical analysts saw the appropriate questions within the issues of class, culture, the economic position of working-class youth and the means by which the state reproduced inequality. While diversification of theoretical and empirical study was born of a genuine desire to develop new paradigms and widen the whole analysis, particularly in relation to Marxist theory, the delinquent got lost in the process (see Rutter and Giller, 1983, pp. 242–66). Indeed, only recently have sociologists come to look again at the issues of crime and crime control and begun to develop perspectives on a policy-related agenda in the movement called the 'new left realists' (see Matthews and Young, 1986).

More consistent, at least in focusing on the delinquent, have been researchers applying social-psychological perspectives to the issues of crime causation. A number of post-war epidemiological studies (often using cohorts of children followed-up through adolescence and into adulthood) have produced an impressive body of literature on the nature of youthful 'disorder' (West and Farrington, 1971, 1973, 1977; Douglas *et al.*, 1968; Wilson and Herbert, 1978; Stott, 1975; Gath *et al.*, 1975; Rutter *et al.*, 1979; Wadsworth, 1979). The recurrent finding from these studies that 'delinquency arises from a complex interaction between the individual home atmosphere, the personal qualities of the [child] and the circumstances in which the family live' (West and Farrington, 1973), clearly poses problems for policy makers seeking instant solutions. For example, of the five factors identified as most strongly associated with delinquency in the Cambridge Study of Delinquent Development – low intelligence, large family size, low family income, poor parental supervision, criminality in the family – only one is a direct attribute of the child. The 'appropriate' response to the four factors surrounding the child depends entirely upon one's political orientation to the role of the state – along with economic considerations on the visibility and format of service delivery. (See West and Farrington, 1973, pp. 201–8 for what they call some 'after-thoughts' on delinquency prevention, and more recently Farrington *et al.*, 1986).

Significantly, a school of thought has developed within the social-psychological perspective which has moved away from dispositional crime causation theory towards an appreciation of the situational production of crime. This body of work, largely emanating from the Home Office Research and Planning Unit and primarily directed towards crime prevention, has had a radical impact upon the research orientation of psychologists. Clarke (1977a) summarizes the stance as follows: 'A "willingness" to offend can therefore be more helpfully seen as a decision reached in a particular set of circumstances rather than as a generalized behavioural disposition. While the decision reached will to some extent depend on the individual's capacity for rational thought at the time . . . it will also be affected by certain motivational states . . . These motivational states may reflect generalized dispositions . . . but more influential may be events that have recently occurred in the life of the individual or crises that he may have been through' (original emphasis).

This reorientation has led to several studies of the situational production of juvenile delinquency and its prevention, most notably in the area of vandalism (see Clark, 1978 and 1980, for a review). Likewise it has investigated influences which may shape motivation and opportunities, like the quality of parental supervision (Riley and Shaw, 1985) and the role of local communities in the prevention of crime (Hope and Shaw, 1988). While, like their sociologist counterparts, psychologists have moved from the individual as the principal focus of attention, unlike them they have continued to concentrate upon crime and the criminal. In this way they have retained a role in providing apparently relevant information for the policy maker (see note 5).

Finally there has been a growing and influential body of research which has sought to investigate the operation of the juvenile justice process. Stemming directly from the period of the partial implementation of the 1969 Act, these studies have looked at the sifting practices of the police (Priestley *et al.*, 1977; Farrington and Bennett, 1981; Ditchfield, 1976; Landau, 1981); the courts (Priestley *et al.*, 1977; Parker, *et al.*, 1981; Asquith, 1983; Anderson, 1978; Burney, 1985); social workers (Giller and Morris, 1981; Thorpe *et al.*, 1980); and probation officers (Harris and Webb, 1987; Millichamp *et al.*, 1985; Raynor, 1985). While informed by the sociological perspectives of 'symbolic interactionism', 'labelling' and 'phenomenology' these 'social policy' studies have proved influential with policy makers and practitioners alike. To some extent, however, such researchers have been restricted in their access to the 'soft' targets of the criminal justice process – such as social services departments (Pitts, 1988) – and have only occasionally been able to investigate the practices of more experienced image makers – such as judges and magistrates. To the extent that those with real power in the juvenile justice system remain immune to scientific investigation, research has had but a limited impact in opening up a debate on their appropriate role and functioning.

Thus far we have not considered the funding background of research. There are three main funding bodies for criminological research in England: the Economic and Social Research Council, the Home Office Research and Planning Unit and the Department of Health. These bodies have all experienced substantial financial cut-backs over the past decade and all have to meet a range of demands other than research into juvenile offending. All have been asked to incorporate criteria for more policy-oriented research when considering funding, i.e. the Rothschild's 'customer contractor' basis of funding. This principle was intended to create a more focused and realistic relationship between administrators and scientists placing 'the responsibility upon administrators to articulate their requirements for research more precisely, and has brought home to researchers the need to justify their efforts in solving the problems facing governments' (Clarke, 1977b).

But this principle has *per force* changed the nature of the relationship between researchers and policy makers. Research is unlikely to be funded now unless the policy makers' considerations are positive, leading some academics to question the wisdom of the approach. As Hood (1987) notes:

> Are there not problems in leaving them to set their own research agendas? Research programmes become truncated to meet administrative schedules. For receipt of the 'answers', two years is now the 'norm' whereas proper monitoring and evaluation often needs to be conducted over a longer time scale. As for the community researchers, their product, and their future hopes of contracts run the risk of being assessed by the criterion of how useful – and perhaps how palatable – their findings and recommendations are to the authorities. (p. 537)

In practice, administrators have found it increasingly difficult to 'articulate their requests' and researchers have been hard-pressed to 'justify their efforts'. It is significant, therefore, but unsurprising that at the end of the 1980s centrally funded research into crime and the juvenile justice system is particularly weak.

Research, policy and practice – recent interactions

These general considerations take us to an evaluation of the current state of juvenile justice with particular reference to the interrelationship between policy, practice and research. I wish to examine four principles which underpin the current policy for juvenile offenders in England and Wales and the influence of our three key factors upon them. This policy is seen in the White Paper 'Young Offenders' (Home Office *et al.*, 1980) and the implementation of two subsequent pieces of legislation, the Criminal Justice Acts of 1982 and 1988 (see Tutt, 1981; Morris and Giller, 1987).

1 Diversion from court

Since the early 1980s a greater proportion of juveniles have been formally cautioned on referral to the police rather than being prosecuted (Tutt and Giller, 1983). For example, by 1987 69 per cent (95 700) of 10- to 16-year-olds charged with an indictable offence were cautioned by the police compared with 31 per cent (42 000) who were prosecuted. While the concept of diversion was not new to the 1980s, it was clearly restated as a priority for the government in 'Young Offenders':

> All the available evidence suggests that juvenile offenders who can be diverted from the criminal justice system at an early stage in their offending are less likely to reoffend than those who become involved in judicial proceedings. (Home Office *et al.*, 1980, para. 38)

Since that time a Home Office circular (14/1985) has been published and provides a new set of guidelines for the development of diversion for all offender groups. The circular attempts to achieve three major developments: a greater use of diversion from court for a wider range of offenders (both formal and informal decision making); expansion of diversion by use of such decisions on more than one occasion; and greater consistency between police forces in the way they apply the criteria (Giller, 1985).

This policy principle can be clearly related to developments in research and practice which emerged in the 1970s. Diversion was a policy principle which underpinned the partially implemented Children and Young Persons Act of 1969. Without doubt the 1970s saw a substantial increase in the number of children and young persons cautioned by the police. In 1970, 53 000 children and young persons received a formal caution; by 1979 the figure had increased to 82 000. Put another way, while 35 per cent of known juvenile offenders were cautioned at the beginning of the decade, by the end of the decade the proportion had reached 50 per cent. However, the growth in police cautioning during the 1970s was not accompanied by an immediate reduction in the overall number of juveniles who were dealt with in the courts. In 1970, 74 300 juveniles were referred to the juvenile courts; in 1979 the figure was 82 000. It soon became acknowledged that a paradox had developed in this area of practice: an increase in the use of a measure intended to divert juvenile offenders from courts was not having the effect of reducing the numbers of juveniles entering that system. Rather than operating as a diversion, cautioning practice was said to be 'widening the net' of labelled delinquents.

Research intially emanating from the Home Office Research Unit (Ditchfield, 1976) but subsequently replicated in other settings (see Morris and Giller, 1987), clearly established the dynamics of this process. This research in turn gave rise to a questioning of the consistency of police decision making practices, the biases and selection procedures employed by police officers dealing with juveniles and the variation in organizational procedures where decision making took place. These research findings were taken up by two influential bodies. First was the Royal Commission on Criminal Procedure that was reviewing the whole of the prosecution system at the time. In its report the Royal Commission (1981) drew attention to the inconsistencies of prosecution practices across the country and urged the government to place cautioning on a statutory basis and develop more consistent practice. Second was the report of the Parliamentary All-Party Penal Affairs Group (1981) which reached the same conclusions.

Here we see an example of how research may contribute to policy change. Whether the reformulated policy in this area will achieve all the desired changes in practice remains to be seen. While the proportion of juveniles cautioned compared with those brought to the notice of the police and prosecuted has risen since the implementation of the circular there is little evidence of greater consistency in decision making between police forces (Giller and Tutt, 1987). This is despite the fact that since the 1985 circular the Crown Prosecution Service has taken responsibility for prosecution from the police and has a remit to enhance the diversion of juveniles in local systems and seek greater consistency (Crown Prosecution Service, 1986). Moreover, despite the circular's clear intention to enable diversion to be used on more than one occasion there is little evidence that this has become a widespread phenomenon (Richardson, 1988). There is some evidence to suggest that it will only do so if the diversion decision becomes linked with some additional component – such as reparation, mediation or a social work programme (Morris and Giller, 1987). In these circumstances there is a real danger that a diversion initiative may become more incursive than an order which the juvenile would have received if referred to a court. This in turn brings forth criticisms (increasingly from magistrates and justices' clerks) on issues relating to civil liberties, accountability and the 'appropriate' role of courts. It remains to be seen therefore whether further developments in diversion can be sustained in the face of these influential critics.

2 The appropriateness of adversarial proceedings in the juvenile court

For those who eventually appear in the juvenile court, the policy embodied in the 1982 Criminal Justice Act unequivocally states that the adversarial nature of the proceedings is the most appropriate method whereby to adjudicate and sentence the case. This adversarial principle is clearly illustrated in Sections 3 and 24 of the 1982 Act under which the young person has enhanced rights to legal representation when faced by removal from the community into custody or care. Moreover, by Section 25 the discretionary powers of local authorities to lock up children in secure accommodation have been considerably curtailed and only the court is empowered to sanction the loss of liberty of young people.

It is important to remember that the appropriateness of the adversarial nature of juvenile court proceedings is not a principle of great longevity. Only 20 years ago proposals were advanced which, if implemented, would have abolished the juvenile court in favour of a family council or tribunal (see Morris and Giller, 1987; Clarke, 1980). Only just over 10 years ago the Home Office and associated government departments (under a Labour administration) were seeking to curtail any expansion of a juvenile court's powers, especially in relation to welfare decision making, stating:

> A juvenile court is not, and cannot be a child welfare department, and it is of great importance that local authorities should accept and shoulder undivided responsibility for looking after difficult and dangerous young people who have become their charge. (Home Office *et al.*, 1976, para. 25) (see note 6)

The return to centralized court decision making marks an end to the debates of the 1970s in which magistrates (and justices' clerks) sought to 'regain' (in their view) decision-making power over those who entered the court system. Such a shift in policy makers' views seems more related to political considerations than any others. Research evidence would question whether such control was lost by them in the first place. The symbolic role of social services departments in the administration of sentencing in the 1970s was consistently outweighed by the practical power of courts to award other non-custodial and (increasingly frequently) custodial measures (see Morris and Giller, 1987).

In one detail, however, the re-emphasis of legality and court decision making did reflect the research evidence, namely with respect to the use of secure accommodation. The provision of such accommodation increased dramatically throughout the 1970s at a time when its use was entirely an administrative act at the discretion of local authority social services departments. Research repeatedly demonstrated that the children in security were not in any identifiable way 'worse' or 'more disturbed' than their counterparts in open conditions (see Millham *et al.*, 1978; Cawson and Martell, 1979). Whether or not a child entered security seemed to relate to the ability or otherwise of other forms of intervention to continue to work with him or her when difficulties arose. The careers of children in care who found themselves in secure accommodation were characterized by rapid movement, frequently ending up in the penal system. Since the introduction of legal criteria to regulate the use of security a dramatic slowing down in the numbers of available placements and the numbers entering them has taken place (Stewart and Tutt, 1987).

3 The appropriateness of determinate sentencing

The 1982 Act marked a substantial break in the courts' traditional powers with respect to young offenders. Hitherto elements of indeterminancy in the sentencing structure were considered integral to the aims of reform and rehabilitation. Reformation was a continuing process, and assessment of the duration of intervention appropriately determined, not by the sentencing tribunal, but by those administering the intervention. Growing criticism of the inequity of this indeterminancy, especially in relation to the young (e.g. care orders for offending) and decline of the rehabilitative ethic made indeterminancy increasingly unpopular. The new sentences introduced by the 1982 Act, therefore, were all determinate. In addition, elements of determinancy may also be clearly seen in welfare measures such as the conditions attached to supervision orders and the charge and control conditions available with care orders.

In the introduction of this policy, principle research again has had considerable influence. Detailed investigations in the 1970s into the use of care orders for offenders began to expose the unintended consequences of benign welfare legislation. The use of care orders by social workers early in offending careers could expose their clients on reoffending to being moved into the custodial sector, the court believing that welfare intervention had failed. This was so even though social workers saw offending behaviour low on the list of priority issues to be tackled by their intervention (see Giller and Morris, 1981; Thorpe *et al.*, 1980). Such findings in turn led to the formation of a body of (liberal left) opinion (both academic and practitioner) which increasingly questioned the 'justice' of such interventions (see Morris *et al.*, 1980). The recommendations of this lobby clearly sought less intervention in the lives of juveniles and saw legality and procedural rules as one of several ways to achieve this. The current policy of incorporating the principle of determinancy into the juvenile justice system represents a partial implementation of the logic which stemmed from research findings. Critics argue, however, that the radical potential of the justice movement has been co-opted by those of the right and the more fundamental reforms they pressed for have been lost (Pitts, 1988; Clarke, 1985).

Of equal importance is the impact that this research has had on practice. Professional opinion since the early 1980s has sought to avoid the use of care orders for offending where possible. In this way the volume of such orders has declined dramatically in the past decade, illustrating that concerted practice on an issue can be as, if not more, influential than policy in determining outcomes in this area (see note 7).

4 The appropriateness of proportionality to sentencing young people

Throughout the 1982 Act there were a number of attempts to ensure that sentences imposed by juvenile courts should be proportionate to offences. Criteria restricting the use of both custody and care were intended to reinforce the more general notion that there should be a graduation of intervention practised by courts, related to offence-oriented considerations. The incorporation of a tariff concept into juvenile courts, often disparaged by magistrates (Moxon *et al.*, 1985), clearly relates to the body of research and lobby opinion which emerged in the 1970s.

An additional component to this debate was the growing body of research which questioned the effectiveness of our interventions, particularly those which removed juvenile offenders from their communities, whether to the child care or penal systems (see Rutter and Giller, 1983, for a review). Evidence questioning the efficacy of residential treatment for delinquents emerged from work originating in the Home Office Research Unit studies of the approved school system (Cornish and Clarke, 1976). Despite their change of designation in the 1970s to community homes with education on the premises, the message was quickly taken up by their new local authority masters, particularly when faced with a need to make economies in the early 1980s. In the penal sphere, however, comparable research evidence on the ineffectiveness of a variety of regimes has not had the effect of abolishing custody (see, for example, Home Office, 1984). They have nevertheless enabled ministers more openly to emphasize community-based 'alternatives' and legitimately to introduce restrictions on magistrates' decision-making discretion. Such a compromise position clearly indicates an arena in which political considerations outweigh researchers' 'evidence' (see note 8).

Initial attempts to curb magistrates' discretion in the use of custody, by criteria introduced in the 1982 Act, were only partially successful. While custodial sentences have declined since the implementation of the Act, research evidence suggests this has not necessarily been due to the power of the statutory criteria (see Burney, 1985; Reynolds, 1985; Morris and Giller, 1987). For this reason the statutory criteria have been strengthened by the 1988 Criminal Justice Act. That custody has been in decline since 1983, therefore, is more likely to be a reflection of enhanced professional practice which has been developing in this area of social work in the past decade. Responding to local research findings, practitioners have begun to consolidate their approach and operate more strategically in all elements of the juvenile justice system. This strategic thinking can be discerned in a number of areas.

First, in the presentation and use of social inquiry reports, research findings on the unintended consequences of loosely argued, poorly focused reports have been assimilated (Tutt and Giller, 1984). Practitioners now construct more tightly argued, offence-focused documents which omit irrelevant social history, contain positive recommendations and vigorously present details of programmes of alternatives for offenders facing removal from the community. Central government has recently endorsed these revised strategies for both juvenile and adult offenders (DHSS, 1987; Home Office, 1986).

The second area of strategic thinking is in the provision of alternatives to custody. Muddled thinking which characterized the role of intermediate treatment in the 1970s as both a preventive measure and an alternative to custody has now been addressed by practitioners. Schemes of alternatives using a range of orders – intermediate treatment, community service and supervised activities – are now clearly distinguished from broader preventive programmes and more effectively communicated to magistrates contemplating their use in appropriate cases (Rutherford, 1986). In part this process was aided by central government injecting financial assistance for the provision of programmes of alternatives on the implementation of the 1982 Act. Another factor, however, has been the willingness of practitioners themselves to debate openly their role and function in the light of research findings which demonstrated the failure of practice in earlier times. Such clarity of function is likely to be tested in the future as the 1988 Act introduces, for the first time, the power to sanction juveniles to custody for breach of a supervised activity order when specifically used as an alternative. Nevertheless, central government has acknowledged the impact of this clarity of thought and determination of action demonstrated by juvenile justice practitioners, particularly in the way in which it has succeeded in bringing down the juvenile custody rate, and currently seeks to do the same for young adults (Home Office, 1988a).

A third area of strategic development can be seen in the issue of monitoring. It is now increasingly commonplace for practitioners routinely to generate and use live data on how their local juvenile justice system is functioning. Using this data practitioners can evaluate trends, provide information both within their own agency and to others and pivotally bring together different interest groups around shared facts. In this way strategic objectives for the operation of the local juvenile justice system can be developed, practices modified and dysfunctioning avoided or rapidly remedied. The importance of monitoring is increasingly recognized by government and is likely to be an integral component of future policy planning in a range of services for offenders (see, for example, Home Office, 1988b).

Conclusion

The foregoing has sought to demonstrate that the relationship between research, policy and practice in relation to offenders is by no means always an equal or easy one. The precise dynamics of the relationship vary over time and in relation to aspects of issues under review. Consistency is no characteristic of the relationship.

Of the three elements of the relationship it is practice which has the greatest potential to influence change – both positively and negatively. Policy makers are dependent upon practitioners – be they social worker, judge, magistrate or police officer – to administer and shape policy and in so doing to develop, sustain or subvert it. While the policy makers may endorse good practice it is difficult for them to create it or to stop bad practice. This is because practice is an 'on the ground' activity and as such rarely visible to the outside – especially if the policy makers are culturally and geographically removed from the context of practice. Likewise the researcher is dependent upon the practitioner, even where the policy maker defines the research brief. Practitioners may welcome or exclude the researcher, grant access and participation or close ranks and claim immunity from scrutiny.

In the past the joint participation of all three parties in the triangular relationship has been rare. There are often misconceptions about role and purpose and misunderstandings of the messages each is giving or is willing to receive. Ideally each should be able to offer something to the others but this is dependent upon clarifying the agenda and making values explicit. In the arena of juvenile offending the debate is still too often characterized by lack of a shared agenda and a myriad of value systems.

Notes

1 On which see NACRO (1988).

2 The response to the Cleveland child abuse problem is a good example of the delicate balance of central and local government relationships.

3 This was successfully achieved in Scotland with the development of the Children's Hearing System (see Martin *et al.*, 1981).

4 The symbolic impact of criminal procedures enables the right to promulgate a policy of diversion from courts for minor offenders while urging formal court intervention for those who continue to participate in disorder.

5 Illustrative of this is the role of the Home Office Crime Prevention Unit which emerged from the Research and Planning Unit to provide practical guidance to central and local government policy makers.

6 The inappropriateness of adversarial proceedings continues to be the emphasis given by policy makers when considering decision making in civil disputes. Proposals for a family court would fundamentally change this aspect of the existing juvenile court. Interestingly, juvenile crime seems to be likely to be omitted from any reformulated jurisdiction for a family court. On whether a role for a distinctive juvenile criminal court can be sustained in the light of these developments see Giller (1986).

7 Indeed, so influential has been this practice development that the government is now considering abolishing the power of the courts to award care orders in criminal proceedings.

8 For one of the most detailed expositions of how this political compromise sustains custody see Land (1975).

References

Anderson, R. (1978) *Representation in Juvenile Court*, Routledge and Kegan Paul.

Asquith, S. (1983) *Children and Justice: Decision-Making in Children's Hearings and Juvenile Courts*, Edinburgh University Press.

Bottoms, A. E. (1974) 'On the decriminalisation of the English Juvenile Courts', in Hood, R. (ed) *Crime, Criminology and Public Policy*, Heinemann, pp. 319–46.

Brake, M. (1980) *The Sociology of Youth Culture and Youth Subcultures*, Routledge and Kegan Paul.

Burney, E. (1985) *Sentencing Young People*, Gower.

Butler, Lord (1974) 'The foundation of the Institute of Criminology in Cambridge', in Hood, R. (ed) *Crime, Criminology and Public Policy*, Heinemann.

Cawson, P. and Martell, M. (1979) *Children Referred to Closed Units*, DHSS Research Report No. 5, HMSO.

Clarke, J. (1980) 'Social democratic delinquents and Fabian families', in National Deviancy Conference (eds) *Permissiveness and Control*, Macmillan, pp. 72–95.

Clarke, J. (1985) 'Whose justice? The politics of juvenile control', *International Journal of the Sociology of Law*, Vol. 13, pp. 407–21.

Clarke, R. (1977a) 'Psychology and crime', *Bulletin of the British Psychological Society*, Vol. 30, pp. 280–3.

Clarke, R. (1977b) 'Penal policy-making and research in the Home Office', in Walker, N. and Giller, H. (eds) *Penal Policy-Making in England*, Institute of Criminology, Cambridge.

Clarke, R. (ed) (1978) *Tackling Vandalism*, Home Office Research Study No. 47, HMSO.

Clarke, R. (1980) 'Situational crime prevention: theory and practice', *British Journal of Criminology*, Vol. 20, No. 2, pp. 136–47.

Cornish, D. and Clarke, R. (1976) *Residential Treatment and its Effect on Delinquency*, Home Office Research Study No. 32, HMSO.

Croft, J. (1978) *Research in Criminal Justice*, Home Office Research Study No. 44, HMSO.

Crown Prosecution Service (1986) *Code of Practice*, Crown Prosecution Service.

Department of Health and Social Security (1987) *Reports to Courts – Practice Guidance for Social Workers*, HMSO.

Ditchfield, J. (1976) *Police Cautioning in England and Wales*, Home Office Research Study No. 37, HMSO.

Douglas, J. *et al.* (1968) *All Our Future*, Peter Davies.

Farrington, D. and Bennett, T. (1981) 'Police cautioning of juveniles in London', *British Journal of Criminology*, Vol. 21, No. 2, pp. 123–35.

Farrington, D. *et al.* (1986) *Understanding and Controlling Crime: Towards a New Research Strategy*, Springer.

Gath, D. *et al.* (1975) *Child Guidance and Delinquency in a London Borough*, Oxford University Press.

Giller, H. (1985) 'Proceeding with caution', *Community Care*, 11 April, pp. 18–20.

Giller, H. (1986) 'Is there a role for a juvenile court?', *Howard Journal*, Vol. 25, No. 3, pp. 161–71.

Giller, H. and Morris, A. (1978) 'Supervision orders: the routinization of treatment', *Howard Journal, 17(3)*, pp. 149–59.

Giller, H. and Morris, A. (1981) *Care and Discretion: Social Work Decisions with Delinquents*, Burnett Books.

Giller, H. and Tutt, N. (1987) 'Police cautioning of juveniles: the continuing practice of diversity', *Criminal Law Review*, pp. 367–74.

Harris, R. and Webb, D. (1987) *Welfare, Power and Juvenile Justice*, Tavistock.

Heal, K. and Laycock, G. (eds) (1986) *Situational Crime Prevention: From Theory into Practice*, HMSO.

Home Office (1959) *Penal Practice in a Changing Society*, Cmnd 645, HMSO.

Home Office (1984) *Tougher Regimes in Detention Centres*, Report of and evaluation by the Young Offender Psychology Unit, HMSO.

Home Office (1986) 'Social Inquiry Reports', *Home Office Circular 92/1986*, Home Office.

Home Office (1988a) *Punishment, Custody and The Community*, C.M. 424, HMSO.

Home Office (1988b) 'Tackling offending: an action plan', Home Office.

Home Office *et al.* (1976) *Children and Young Persons Act 1969: Observations on the Eleventh Report from the Expenditure Committee*, HMSO.

Home Office *et al.* (1980) *Young Offenders*, HMSO.

Hood, R. (1987) 'Some reflections on the role of criminology in public policy', *Criminal Law Review*, pp. 525–92.

Hope, T. and Shaw, M. (eds) (1988) *Communities and Crime Reduction*, HMSO.

Jones, K. (1982) 'Reformulating social research', *Home Office Research and Planning Unit Bulletin*, No. 14, pp. 7–9.

Land, H. (1975) 'Detention centres: the experiment which could not fail', in Hall, P. *et al.* (eds) *Change, Choice and Conflict in Social Policy*, Heinemann, pp. 311–70.

Landau, S. F. (1981) 'Juveniles and the police', *British Journal of Criminology*, Vol. 21, No. 1, pp. 27–46.

Martin, F. *et al.* (1981) *Children Out of Court*, Scottish Academic Press.

Matthews, R. and Young, J. (eds) (1986) *Confronting Crime*, Sage.

Mays, J. (1954) *Growing Up in the City*, Liverpool University Press.

Millham, S., Bullock, R. and Hosie, R. (1978) *Locking up Children: Secure Provision within the Child-Care System*, Saxon House.

Millichamp, D. *et al.* (1985) 'A matter of natural justice', *Community Care*, No. 13, June, pp. 25–7.

Moriarity, M. (1977) 'The policy-making process: how it is seen from the Home Office', in Walker, N. and Giller, H. (eds) *Penal Policy-Making in England*, Institute of Criminology.

Morris, A. and Giller, H. (1987) 'Juvenile justice and social work in Great Britain', in Parker, H. (ed) *Social Work and the Courts*, Edward Arnold.

Morris, A. and Giller, H. (1987) *Understanding Juvenile Justice*, Croom Helm.

Morris, A., Giller, H., Szwed, E. and Geach, H. (1980) *Justice for Children*, Macmillan.

Moxon, D. *et al.* (1985) *Juvenile Sentencing: Is there a tariff?*, Research and Planning Unit Paper No. 32, Home Office.

NACRO (1988) *Grave Crimes, Grave Doubts*, NACRO.

Parker, H. *et al.* (1981) *Receiving Juvenile Justice*, Basil Blackwell.

Parker, H. and Giller, H. (1981) 'More and less the same: British delinquency research since the sixties', *British Journal of Criminology*, Vol. 21, No. 3, pp. 230–45.

Parliamentary All-Party Penal Affairs Group (1981) *Young Offenders: A Strategy for the Future*, Barry Rose.

Pearson, G. (1983) *Hooligan: A History of Respectable Fears*, Macmillan.

Pitts, J. (1988) *The Politics of Juvenile Crime*, Sage.

Priestley, P. *et al.* (1977) *Justice for Juveniles*, Routledge and Kegan Paul.

Raynor, P. (1985) *Social Work, Justice and Control*, Basil Blackwell.

Reynolds, F. (1985) 'Magistrates' justifications for making custodial orders on juvenile offenders', *Criminal Law Review*, May, pp. 244–98.

Richardson, N. (1988) *Justice by Geography II*, Social Information Systems, Manchester.

Riley, D. and Shaw, M. (1985) *Parental Supervision and Juvenile Delinquency*, Home Office Research Study No. 83, HMSO.

Royal Commission on Criminal Procedure (1981) *Report*, Cmnd 8092, HMSO.

Rutherford, A. (1986) *Growing Out of Crime*, Penguin.

Rutter, M. *et al.* (1979) *Fifteen Thousand Hours*, Open Books.

Rutter, M. and Giller, H. (1983) *Juvenile Delinquency: Trends and Perspectives*, Penguin.

Stewart, G. and Tutt, N. (1987) *Children in Custody*, Avebury Press.

Stott, D. *et al.* (1975) *Taxonomy of Deviant Behaviour Disturbance*, London University Press.

Thorpe, D. *et al.* (1980) *Out of Care*, George Allen and Unwin.

Tutt, N. (1981) 'A decade of policy', *British Journal of Criminology*, Vol. 21, No. 4, pp. 246–56.

Tutt, N. and Giller, H. (1983) *Diversion*, Information Systems, Lancaster.

Tutt, N. and Giller, H. (1984) *Social Inquiry Reports*, Information Systems, Lancaster.

Wadsworth, M. (1979) *Roots of Delinquency*, Martin Robertson.

Walker, N. and Giller, H. (eds) (1977) *Penal Policy-Making in England*, Institute of Criminology.

West, D. and Farrington, D. (1971) *Present Conduct and Future Delinquency*, Heinemann.

West, D. and Farrington, D. (1973) *Who Becomes Delinquent?*, Heinemann.

West, D. and Farrington, D. (1977) *The Delinquent Way of Life*, Heinemann.

Wilson, H. and Herbert, G. (1978) *Parents and Children in the Inner City*, Routledge and Kegan Paul.

12 Leaving care

Mike Stein

In recent years, and particularly since the mid-1970s, the problems faced by young people leaving care have received increasing publicity and recognition. The 'Who Cares?' project initiated by the National Children's Bureau did much to increase the awareness of young people and social services about leaving care. Between 1977 and 1979 local in-care groups were set up in different parts of the country, the booklet *Who Cares? Young People in Care Speak Out* (Page and Clark, 1977) was published and widely read, and a national magazine for young people in care *Who Cares? News* was started. The major theme emerging from the voices of the young people was their lack of power over their lives in relation to their use of money, attendance at their own reviews, their limited opportunities to shop, cook and more generally to take risks and participate while in care. The dependency created by care was linked to their fears about reaching 18 and leaving care:

> In my home you don't have to do anything. Your cooking's done, your washing's done, everything is done . . . that's what I mean. I'm not prepared for it. I don't know how I will manage, I can't even boil an egg.
> (Page and Clark, 1977, p. 53)

This initial interest and publicity surrounding the problems faced by young people leaving care has been maintained during the 1980s. The campaigning work of the National Association of Young People in Care (1983 and 1986) (the successor to the 'Who Cares?' project), the setting up of Home Base (now First Key) by Shelter, the media take-up of both Gaskin's life story (MacVeigh, 1982) and Christian Wolmar's exposé (1980) of ex-care homeless young people, as well as the completion of a number of research studies, have elevated the issue of leaving care in the political and professional consciousness. It is very much on the agenda of local authority and voluntary social services and there are examples of innovative practice which will be discussed later.

At parliamentary level the Second Report of the Social Services Committee on *Children in Care* recommended:

> That the Department consider the imposition on local authorities of a general statutory obligation both to prepare those in care for leaving and to support them thereafter, in the manner of a good parent. (House of Commons, 1984, Rec. 90)

Following this the government, in its White Paper *The Law on Child Care and Family Services* (1987) proposed strengthening existing legislation. Local authorities:

> will be required to advise and assist children and young people for whom they are caring so as to promote their welfare when that care ends. (para. 33, 8)

In addition:

> the previous duty to advise and befriend all those who leave care after leaving school provided that their welfare requires it and they request it, which lasts up to 18, will be extended to cover those up to 21 as well. (para. 33, 9)

At the time of writing, the plight of care leavers, as well as other vulnerable young people, is again a major concern of the social services in the light of government changes in young people's entitlement to benefit. The main direction of these reforms is to encourage families to take greater responsibility for their young adults but as Peter Smith (1988) suggests:

> Government emphasis on family and parental responsibility and discouragement of state dependency becomes a paradox when the State is the parent for children in its care.

This, then, provides a brief introduction to the substantive concern of the chapter – research findings and their links with policy and practice. Let us begin with a consideration of government data.

Government information

During the most recent year for which information is available (the year ending 31 March 1985), 7770 young people left care at the age of 18 in England and Wales (DHSS, 1988). This total was at a similar level to 1975 but lower by 1000 than in 1979, reflecting in part demographic changes. Surprisingly this is nearly all we do know about care leavers from published government information, which is far less detailed than official data on younger children in care. We do not know how many 16- or 17-year-olds leave care to set up on their own and we do not know, either, the type of placement from which young people 'legally' leave care (e.g. community home, foster care, lodgings), or their placement on leaving care. Similarly, central government requests no information from local authorities on how they meet their responsibilities under Sections 27–9 of the Child Care Act 1980, which empowers them to provide support and financial assistance for young people leaving care. The state – as substitute parent – seems not to want to know some very basic information about its 'own' young people leaving care.

Research studies

As well as limited government information (and perhaps partly as a result of it) there has been no large-scale empirical follow-up study of care leavers gathering quantitative and qualitative information from a wide representative sample (in terms of geography, gender, ethnic grouping, (dis)ability), and having a comparative group of non-care young people. Indeed, prior to the mid-1970s there was very little research interest in this group at all (see Chapter 2 in Stein and Carey, 1986). Since that time, leaving care has generated more research interest and this has included: small-scale descriptive studies based upon selected samples (Kahan, 1979; Godek, 1976); follow-up studies of care leavers in different geographical areas (Lupton, 1985); similar small-scale descriptive follow-up studies from abroad (Raychuba, 1987); evaluations of projects designed to assist young people leaving care (Stein, 1987 and 1988); and some preliminary comparative work into European law and policy (Slade, 1988). It is from these studies, then, that we must piece together our jigsaw.

At the outset recent research findings lead us to abandon the crude stereotype of care leavers being seen exclusively as 18-year-olds without families who have spent all their lives in large 'institutions'. Stein and Carey (1986) found in their study of young people leaving the care of a social services department that 40 per cent legally left from foster care, 31 per cent from their own 'home on trial', 13 per cent from children's homes, and 11 per cent from their own flat, bedsitter or lodgings. In the same study a quarter of the total sample left care at 16 or 17 years of age and the largest percentage of care leavers were first-time admissions to care at the age of 14. A quarter of the group had been in care for less than three years, a half more than five years and just under three per cent more than 10 years. Even from this snapshot it is clear that care leavers are not a homogeneous group and we therefore have to guard against simplistic and uniform policy and practice responses (more of which later).

Those research studies that are based upon interviews with young people most usually begin with young people's reflections upon their past care experiences. What do those studies tell us about the young people's experiences of care?

The experience of care

Firstly, and consistent with the findings of a number of research studies, we know that care leavers experience a lot of movement and disruption whilst in care (Packman *et al.*, 1986; Fisher *et al.*, 1986). In a recent study, Stein (1988) found that over half of the young people had between seven and 12 placements by the time they were 16 years of age and the average for the sample was six per young person. The DHSS in summarizing findings from a number of studies concludes:

> The instability of 'in care' placements is hammered home to the reader of these research studies by the depressing similarity of their fundings. (DHSS, 1985, p. 10)

Many young people leaving care will have had experience of both children's homes and foster care – often on more than one occasion – as well as having been in assessment centres or 'home on trial'. The reasons for breakdown are less well researched but may include the use of preliminary assessment placements, breakdowns due to disruptive behaviour and failures of placements to meet social workers' expectations (DHSS, 1985).

Stein and Carey (1986) found that for the young person a change of placement usually meant an abrupt end to 'care' relationships and a sense of failure, such as a fostering breakdown or a trial period at home not working out. This is followed by a changing social world, that is, an adjustment to new substitute parents or care staff as well as a strange neighbourhood, different friends and a new school. From the young person's point of view the situation may be made worse by changes of residential care or fieldwork staff. The extent of this type of change is, then, a very distinguishing feature of care compared with the experiences of 'non-care' young people, and is very different from social, geographical or 'itinerant' mobility where there is a constant family group.

Secondly, we know that those young people who have been in care a long time, as well as those in ethnic minorities leaving care, may be confronting important issues of identity at the time (First Key, 1987). This includes the lack of knowledge by long-term care leavers about their past, their family, the reasons for coming into care, why they were moved in care and why they were separated from their brothers and sisters. Some of the most disturbing comments come from the young people themselves:

> It was bad not knowing my past. I didn't know until five years ago – I didn't know my parents' names, I knew their surname but not their Christian names or anything like that. I didn't know my parents at all. That's one thing – that I didn't have a past that I could remember.
>
> My social worker used to tell me that I'd got a brother and sister but they never used to say where they were because I don't think they wanted us to get in touch at that time.
> (Stein and Carey, 1986, pp. 31 and 35)

A study by First Key has highlighted the cultural identity problems faced by black young people brought up in a predominantly white care system. One young woman quoted in the study expresses her confusion:

> Am I black or am I white? I used to ask that question every day and every night. It's plain to see you are black but being in care in a white community, it's hard to decide. (p. 7)

Other findings from the First Key study included the uncovering of racism and isolation in predominantly white neighbourhoods and the 'colour-blindness' of care:

> It wasn't the case of treating all children equally but wanting the black child to be a white child (p. 6)

Thirdly, research based upon interviews with young people has drawn our attention to both negative and positive evaluations of care. The former includes the stigma of being in care, the dependency created by care and the poor practical preparation for leaving. In a recent study most of the young people (80 per cent) said that they had learned some practical skills whilst in care (shopping, washing, ironing) but far less (50 per cent) felt adequately prepared to use money – budgeting, shopping and paying bills (Stein, 1988). Positive evaluations of care most often referred to getting away from problems at home or gaining some benefit from the care experience or perhaps both these things linked together:

> I was beaten up by my dad so I was able to get away from him and given a chance to find myself, to develop my own life in care. I enjoyed my children's home as I was helped to find my own values and self . . .(Stein, 1987, p. 3)

The briefest but most telling endorsement from a young person in the same study was 'some treat you like theirs' (p. 3).

Finally, we also know that the educational attainment of care leavers is very low and very few stay on at school beyond 16 years of age (Jackson, 1983; Stein, 1988; Stein and Carey, 1986). The House of Commons Social Services Committee Report on Children in Care (1984) described being in care as an 'educational hazard' and perhaps this is not surprising given the disruption experienced by many young people in care (see Chapter 6).

In summary, then, our research studies inform us that care leavers are not a uniform group. They may come into care at different ages following problems or difficulties at home or having been in trouble themselves. Their care histories will be varied in length but are likely to include movement and disruption as well as uncertainty about their past. Care may have been valued by them and helped them but it may also have contributed other problems: of stigma, of dependency, of ethnic identity, of poor educational attainment, and of poor practical preparation for adulthood. And it is these young people at just 16 to 18 years of age who are 'legally' leaving care. Moving away, then, from their past lives, what does research tell us about the experiences of young people who have already left care?

Out of care where?

'Legally' leaving care does not necessarily involve a young person moving immediately from their final placement in care – for example, they may be 'home on trial' or in a long-term foster care placement. However, in most local authorities there is an expectation that young people leaving residential care at between 16 and 18 years of age will have to move on to some other kind of accommodation or living arrangement. It is perhaps not surprising that these young people's feelings about leaving care are very mixed:

> Excited, frightened and sad. I couldn't wait to get away but I didn't want to go . . .
>
> It's still a blow. You can't go into care and be taken up in an institution without it having some effect on you . . . I want to get out but then I don't want to because I don't have anybody outside.
> (Page and Clark, 1977)

Stein and Carey (1986) recorded the experiences of a sample of care leavers for up to two and a half years after leaving care and this included those leaving from children's homes, foster care and home on trial placements. The research showed firstly that the majority of young people moved from their last placement in care and 40 per cent moved three or more times. Secondly, those young people who legally left care while residing at home (home on trial) moved most frequently after leaving care, with the fewest remaining in the same accommodation at the end as at the beginning of the project, i.e. 20 per cent. (One-third of this group moved to relatives and moved again, 40 per cent of the group to their own accommodation or their partner's house.) Thirdly, there was also a high degree of movement from those who initially moved into their own accommodation – to live on their own. Nearly 70 per cent had moved by the end of the research and this rose to nearly 90 per cent just after the end of the research. In another survey 60 per cent of young people moved from single-person flats within two years. Finally, about half of the young people in ordinary foster care placements also moved.

Young people moving, in itself, should not be regarded as a problem. Indeed, most young people in our society choose to move on from their families to live with a partner, friends, or occasionally by themselves. And we quite rightly regard it as a problem when young people in their early to mid-20s are denied the opportunity to move on from their families because of factors such as unemployment, low income and lack of housing choice. Indeed, opportunities for young people to move on from their families may vary considerably by geographical area, by social class (including employment grouping), by marital status, by ethnic grouping, by gender and by disability.

In asking why care leavers move and what are their experiences and perceptions of moving, we find that many who move from children's homes to live by themselves, in their own flats, experience loneliness, isolation and sometimes fear:

> Flat's nice but I'm lonely, very lonely . . . it's not nice being in a flat all day.
>
> I'm scared and I have to sleep with the light on. I hate sleeping on my own, it's lonely . . . it's right lonely though, really lonely.
> (Stein and Carey, 1986)

In another study (Stein and Maynard, 1985) young people contrasted the 'community' of care with living alone:

> I found it hard to live by myself . . . being brought up in care, living with many people in a household without ever being by yourself, it was very difficult to live on my own and learn to like my own company.

Another young woman spoke of being 'depressed' and said:

> I could have been dead and no one would have known or bothered.

In Stein and Carey's (1986) study, not one of the young people who moved into single-person accommodation wished to remain after 12 months and the results of other surveys highlight similar problems (Lupton, 1976; Morgan Klein, 1985; Stein and Maynard, 1985).

The most frequent movers – those home on trial – mainly moved because they had returned (or been discharged) to similar relationship problems that had resulted in them coming into care in the first place. For those young people who moved from families to other relatives similar problems would crop up again and they would move again. Young people also moved from living with partners or foster parents following the breakdown of relationships or the making of new relationships, or because of the birth of a child.

Thus the pattern emerging from research studies following up young people after leaving care is:

- Frequent and many moves.
- A very high degree of movement and expressed dissatisfaction from single-person accommodation and home on trial placements (both of which were planned placements by social services).
- A move towards shared living either in new families or with a relative (either their own or their partner's) or in lodgings or with friends.
- Main reasons for movements include loneliness, isolation, returning to past family difficulties and the breakdown of planned relationships.

The movement by young people after leaving care is generally not a planned or smooth change in their lives but frequently one of both physical and emotional turmoil, perhaps reawakening some of the painful memories associated with past movements into and within care. There is also, not surprisingly, research evidence that their experience of moving will include inadequate accommodation, e.g. hard to let council flats, expensive bedsits in poor condition, bed and breakfast and periods of homelessness.

Surveys and research studies have consistently revealed that young people who have been in care are over-represented amongst the single homeless. The Department of Environment 1981 Report *Single and Homeless* found that a third of the homeless under 20 had spent some time in care and this proportion has been confirmed by Centrepoint's 1988 study (Randall, 1988). When we consider that care leavers represent such a small percentage of the total youth population (around one per cent), then it is clear that they are greatly over-represented among the young homeless. A substantial minority, if not a majority, are likely to experience homelessness in a three-year period after leaving care. If this pattern continues into later life it means that the care leaver's own children are more likely to be received into care, for homelessness is closely linked with reception into care. A depressing and costly cycle – for both the young people and the state.

It could be argued that homelessness and housing problems amongst care leavers are only to be expected given the present state of the housing market and what we know about young people's care experiences. Housing finance has borne the brunt of cut-backs in public expenditure in recent years, resulting in a major decline in council house building and, within this highly rationed resource, priority and points allocation systems favour families. The situation is made worse by the decline in the private rental sector. The only growth area – owner occupation – is beyond the means of care leavers.

Research studies have also reported high levels of unemployment amongst care leavers, the pattern being for young people to become unemployed after completing a government training scheme. In the most recent research (Stein, 1988) only one young person had a 'proper' job, the others being either on YTS (38 per cent) or unemployed (54 per cent) and, as has already been suggested, the former is likely to lead to the latter. Stein and Carey (1986) found that 80 per cent of their sample were unemployed after two and a half years. As Smith (1988) has suggested:

> Bearing in mind the present high levels of youth unemployment and the consequent demand by employers for higher educational qualifications, it is predictable that care leavers will have difficulty competing for jobs because their education has been frequently disrupted.

This means that most care leavers are already, or are likely in a short time, to be subsisting on income support. However, benefits have recently been restructured to encourage families to take greater responsibility for their young people. During 1988 rates and benefits have become age-related, the distinctions between householders and non-householders have been abolished and income support has been abolished, except in grave hardship, for 16- and 17-year-olds. Further reductions in the levels of benefits are planned by the transfer of board and lodging payment to housing benefit in April 1989. The impact of these changes for young people whose family links are broken, missing, or fragile are self-evident – they will be condemned to poverty, social deprivation and desperation

> as suffered by many of their parents – conditions which contributed to their own admission to care. (Smith, 1988)

Although it is too early to assess the impact of these changes there is evidence that whereas young people in care are being financially assisted by local authorities to overcome hardship, non-care young people are suffering following family crises. Some of these young people with no previous history of care are being received into care to enable them to be given financial help (Pilkington, 1988; Stein, 1988; Randall, 1988).

Concerning agency support, studies prior to the setting up of leaving care projects (discussed below) showed that only a small percentage of care leavers (20 per cent) maintained a social worker link and this declined the longer young people were out of care. Also, there, was no clear policy of children's homes keeping in touch with young people, although care leavers often wanted to go back for support on occasions (Stein and Carey, 1986).

> When you come up against problems you haven't got anyone to turn to. You're frightened to go back . . . you don't feel you're wanted. You're not under their care anymore . . . (Page and Clark, 1977)

These, then, are some of the main themes arising out of the research studies completed between 1975 and 1985. The overall picture from these studies is a depressing one but they have contributed to an increased awareness of the problems faced by young people leaving care, as well as pointing to implications for policy and practice. It is these latter issues which can now be addressed.

Implications for policy and practice, management and care

Research focused on young people leaving care will inevitably generate questions not only about leaving care policy but also the management of care itself. The research findings discussed in the first part of this chapter clearly suggest the need for far greater stability in the care experience, with less movement and disruption. This would be assisted by more continuity of relationships. Stein and Carey (1986) suggest:

> This requires more recognition of both family relationships, including brothers and sisters, and friendship, neighbourhood or community links. Maybe we need, now more than ever, to face up to the contradictions that exist in viewing 'professional caring' as *the* compensatory model and to think more imaginatively about alternative relationships.

The research findings also point to the importance of young people having far more knowledge and understanding about, and involvement in, what is happening to them and to their families. To be able to leave care with some confidence young people need to be assisted to develop a stronger sense of personal identity. They may be helped by the use of life story books, more 'open' record systems and attendance at reviews, but these specific changes need to be developed as part of an overall philosophy and commitment to greater participation – so that young people leaving care not only have essential knowledge but are also prepared to take greater responsibility for their lives. This may be facilitated by decentralization of resources to provide opportunities for learning and risk-taking and an ending of financial and administrative systems which encourage dependency, e.g. bulk-buying, central purchasing and order book systems (see Stein, 1983). In addition, the research suggests there should be greater recognition of the problems faced by black young people in a predominantly white care system, both in terms of the employment of black workers and carers and the development of more sensitive practice in relation to ethnic minorities (see Chapter 9).

Leaving care

Most of the young people in the research studies discussed in this chapter left care at between 16 and 18 years of age, and for many of these young people this meant a physical move either at the time of 'legally' leaving care or within a relatively short period afterwards. Not surprisingly, training young people to be independent, to survive on their own, has become an important issue in contemporary leaving care policy. Yet research findings should make us seriously question this – particularly the evidence of loneliness, isolation and the eventual breakdown of so many young people living alone. Firstly, we know that most young people aged 16 to 18 in our society live with their families until their early 20s. Information from the National Child Development Study reveals that only 16 per cent of young people were living away from home before the age of 18 and, more significantly, fewer than 0.5 per cent were living alone (Central Statistical Office, 1988). As Stein and Carey (1986) have commented:

> A group of young people regarded as being in need of care and control up to the age of 16, 17 and 18, are catapulted into a position of greater vulnerability than that of other people their age.

We should question the rigidity of policies which lead to the eviction of young people from care at between 16 and 18 years of age, and seek to learn more from the existing patterns of 'good' parenthood in our society. Secondly, this would lead us to question the qualitative dimensions of independence training with its emphasis upon practical survival and emotional detachment at the expense of personal development and interpersonal skills. What is suggested by a critical examination of the concept of independence is a more flexible approach to leaving care, including a less arbitrary leaving age, such as the policy which exists in France (Slade and Smith, forthcoming). There young people have opportunities to return to care when things do not work out, an improved quality of care which recognizes the need for post-care support and the gradual psycho-social development of young people and does not swing them sharply from dependence to independence. It is this latter area which can now be considered.

Partly in response to the problems identified in this chapter, a number of local authorities and voluntary organizations have set up specialist after-care teams (Helmsley, 1985). Areas of work undertaken by these projects include group work and individual counselling, supporting young people in 'trainer' accommodation, work with local authority housing, housing associations and private landlords in order to make available permanent accommodation, setting up supported 'landlady' schemes, training residential and field workers and advising the department on current leaving care issues and problems. An evaluation of one such project (Stein, 1988) has provided us with more optimistic findings than those from the studies discussed earlier. In its first two and a quarter years, about half of the 54 young people who joined the scheme were able to manage their lives with varying degrees of project support. These included young people living in their own tenancies, with partners or friends, and in supported lodgings. A key factor, and one identified as lacking in most of the earlier research studies, has been support. As one young person put it:

> I've learnt to live out of care – with a back-up team. (Stein, 1988)

Finally, to return to the political arena, it is to be hoped that child care legislation in the 1988/9 parliamentary session will both strengthen and clarify the law to assist care leavers, and that the government will recognize the urgent need to review and reform its social security provisions for young people. For local authorities the most important issues raised by research are those which identify their failure to behave as a caring parent and the possibilities open to them to do so.

References

Central Statistical Office, *Social Trends*, No. 18, 1988 edition, HMSO.

Department of Health and Social Security (1985) *Social Work Decisions in Child Care*, HMSO.

Department of Health and Social Security (1988) *Children in Care in England and Wales*, HMSO.

Department of Environment (1981) *Single and Homeless*, HMSO.

First Key (1987) *A Study of Black Young People Leaving Care*, First Key.

Fisher, M., Marsh, P., Phillips, D. and Sainsbury, E. (1986) *In and Out of Care*, Batsford/BAAF.

Godek, S. (1976) *Leaving Care*, Barnardos.

Helmsley, J. (1985) 'Stepping out into unknown territory', *Community Care*, 21 November.

House of Commons (1984) Second Report from the Social Services Committee, Session 1983–84, *Children in Care*, HMSO.

House of Commons (1987) *The Law on Child Care and Family Services*, Cmnd 69, HMSO.

Jackson, S. (1983) *The Education of Children in Care*, University of Bristol.

Kahan, B. (1979) *Growing Up in Care*, Basil Blackwell.

Lupton, C. (1985) *Moving Out*, Portsmouth Polytechnic, SSR and I Group.

MacVeigh, I. (1982) *Gaskin*, Jonathan Cape.

Morgan Klein, B. (1985) *Where Am I Going to Stay?*, SCSH.

National Association of Young People In Care (1983) *Sharing Care*. NAYPIC.

National Association of Young People In Care (1986) *Evidence to Wagner Working Group*, NAYPIC.

Packman, J. *et al.* (1986) *Who Needs Care?*, Basil Blackwell.

Page, R. and Clark, G. (eds) (1977) *Who Cares? Young People in Care Speak Out*, National Children's Bureau.

Pilkington, E. (1988) 'Caught in a teenage trap', *The Guardian*, 23 November.

Randall, G. (1988) *No Way Home*, Centrepoint.

Raychuba, B. (1987) *Report on the Special Needs of Youth in/from the Care of the Child Welfare System*, National Youth in Care Network, Ontario.

Slade, M. (1988) Unpublished paper presented at Young People Leaving Care Conference, Views on Leaving Care from France and Holland, July 1988, see Slade and Smith (forthcoming).

Slade, M. and Smith, P. (forthcoming) *A Comparative Study of Young People Leaving Care in England, France and the Netherlands*, National Children's Bureau.

Smith, P. M. (1988) 'Leaving care', *Highlight*, No. 84, National Children's Bureau.

Stein, M. (1983) 'Protest in care', in Jordan, B. and Parton, W. (eds) *The Political Dimensions of Social Work*, Basil Blackwell.

Stein, M. (1987) *Leeds Leaving Care Project*, Research Fellow Report.

Stein, M. (1988) *Leeds Leaving Care Project*, Research Fellow Report. (Unpublished reports for Barnardos, to be published as a book by Barnardos in 1989.)

Stein, M. and Carey, K. (1986) *Leaving Care*, Basil Blackwell.

Stein, M. and Maynard, C. (1985) *I've Never Been So Lonely*, NAYPIC.

Woolmar, C. (1980) 'Out of care', *Roof*, March/April.

13 Consumer views

Ruth Gardner

The fact that 'consumer views' have been included in this book is in itself a measure of the growing significance of what receivers of services have to say. It is still much more common to find a passing reference to 'client involvement' in child care policy documents rather than a well thought out brief for its achievement; and research studies still tend to give reasons why clients' views were not sought (too lengthy a process, too difficult to measure, possible breach of confidentiality etc.). Nevertheless, the reading list and some of the references at the end of this chapter show that in recent years a good number of large-scale, as well as local, studies have included the views of service receivers as well as service providers, and that more is now being written about the philosophy and practice of client participation. Equally important, these studies have all endorsed the value of this perspective on the child care task.

A survey of the literature shows three main arguments for the inclusion of service users' views: moral rights, legal obligations and practical advantages (e.g. more relevant services, improved decision making).

The moral case for the rights of children in care is put strongly by Freeman (1983):

> Are children in care cases or persons? Are they objects of the decision-making process? There is no way in which one can equate flesh and blood parents with legal parents in a care setting. Policies are taken high up in bureaucracies by people who may never see the children . . . continuity in caring is absent . . . decisions are taken by social workers . . . that no parent can take: for example, to put a child in a 'lock-up unit'. The case for children sharing in decisions that affect their lives is thus greater than in the context of a natural family.

It can be argued that parents of children in care deserve support and involvement in the plans for their children's future, because of these very circumstances. Also, recent research shows that while most parents are not initially too concerned about their legal rights, they very often feel a continuing moral responsibility for their child's welfare and conduct; that they have a duty, as well as a right, to voice their opinion on these matters:

> Essentially parents seemed to be taking the view that rights flowed from responsibility. This responsibility flowed from the biological link of parent and child on the one hand, and on the other hand from the general responsibilities of being an adult . . . in this context parents also expected their children to receive in care the discipline they could not give. (Marsh, Fisher and Phillips, 1985)

The writers point out that social workers ignore this area of parents' rights at their peril.

The legal obligations of social services departments towards children and parents are dealt with later in the chapter, but it is worth noting that recent reports (e.g. London Borough of Brent, 1985, and London Borough of Greenwich, 1987) are (rightly in our view) critical of social workers' lack of knowledge and training in the law. This directly and obviously harms the rights of children and parents because social workers are simply not in a position to inform them correctly, which in turn can lead to mutual confusion and bitterness.

Ignoring consumers' rights to be heard and to have a say is so obviously wasteful of time and energy that it is surprising so much of it still goes on. It is clearly not just a matter of boldly laying all the cards on the table. In child care we are dealing with families in crisis, where everyone is likely to be suffering some shock; hence workers may try to soften the blow, or simply forget some important facts; family members may have different versions of what has gone wrong, as may the worker, and these differences are submerged, perhaps to appear again when a decision has to be reached. Hence the essential skills of workers and managers are in organizing the information which each person needs and making sure they understand it; in being aware of legal rights and independent sources of support, and not being threatened by these; in accepting that differences of opinion and outright conflict are often inevitable but do not necessarily mean that those involved either 'win' or 'lose'.

It is important to bear in mind that 'views and involvement' can mean very different things to different people. Service users and service providers need, from the outset, to be clear what they mean by these terms. What degree of partnership is possible, and what do individuals actually want? There is a great difference between a worker assisting young people to put their own case, accompanying them and putting the case alongside them or representing them. To imply that the young person or parent will influence a decision when this is not the case creates understandable anger and frustration. Professionals may need to be willing to justify *exclusion* from decision making, with inclusion as the norm.

Stein (1983) argues that unless consumers have real power within organizations, listening and involvement may mean little real action and change on the part of those with status and authority. He quotes a typology of participation:

8 Citizen control 7 Delegated power 6 Partnership	Degrees of citizen power
5 Placation 4 Consultation 3 Informing	Degrees of tokenism
2 Therapy 1 Manipulation	Non-participation

and invites debate as to what exactly we convey when we use words such as 'partnership', 'consultation' and 'involvement'.

The form this chapter will take is as follows: first we will survey recent national and local research studies that reflect consumer views; we then look at legal changes and decisions which affect children's and parents' rights, and at concurrent policy developments. Finally, examples of practitioners successfully involving children and parents in key decisions are reviewed.

Views of children and young people: research

Two of the nine DHSS-funded, large-scale research studies of child care give an extensive account of the views of children themselves. Jane Rowe and her colleagues (1984) interviewed 100 children who had been in their foster homes for at least three years (of whom 31 were under 12 years old); Mike Fisher and his team (1986) spoke to 79 children aged eight years and over, and 14 of their brothers and sisters, about their experience of entering care.

The views of children in long-term foster care, as expressed in Rowe's work, give rise to concern. The majority were settled 'but there were disturbing pockets of unhappiness, fears and worries'. This often referred to children's lack of full understanding of the past or of future plans. 'Very few children had any understanding of being in care or the role of the social services department', 'unless they were still in touch or had clear recollections of contact, most children knew very little about their parents. Even fewer had a good understanding of the reasons for their admission to care . . . the thing children most often wanted to know was what their parents looked like.'

Although these were, for the most part, apparently stable placements, over half the children felt some stigma about being in care and nearly a quarter worried about having to leave their foster parents. The implications of these views are underlined by the fact that 'foster parents and social workers (interviewed separately) were often unaware of the children's anxieties and painful feelings'.

Berridge and Cleaver (1987), quoting young people who have suffered foster home breakdowns, say that while it is impossible to know what the impact of such an event is on the young person, different adults have very different assessments. Aldgate (1989), reviewing this study with others, concludes that despite greater understanding, sheer pressure of demand for placements means that 'foster care, however professionalized, will remain a high risk care option because of the very interpersonal dynamics involved in the closeness of living in a family'.

The study by Fisher *et al.* of children entering care, found that 'on the face of it . . . [they] viewed care fairly positively', experiencing, like their parents, relief from family relationships which had become highly stressful. But while regimes in care were often more flexible than at home, for children this varied enormously and daily rules were often perceived to be arbitrary. From the very beginning, with the adults' decision that family problems mean the removal of a child or children (with or without their consent), to a strange environment, it is young people who have to 'adapt to the rules invented by adults'. Often this means meeting a succession of adults in new settings – residential and foster homes, assessments of various kinds, reviews and other meetings, together with changes of schools and friends. Regulations could be seen as petty and inconsistent; one young person is quoted as saying 'There's a new rule come out every time somebody goes in, always. My mate, he could smoke when he were 15, just got to his fifteenth birthday, then they changed the rule again saying you had to be 16.'

Views of children and young people: pressure groups, studies and surveys

Although children's views have only recently been collected systematically in the name of research, there is a series of accounts of care from the inside which collectively represent the 'Who Cares?' movement. Meetings at the National Children's Bureau in the mid-1970s of young people in care were written up as *Who Cares? Young People in Care Speak Out*. This gave young people's views publicity by reproducing their words, unsoftened by adult interpretation. For instance:

> A social worker's there to help you understand and to tell you the truth. If we're in care – and it's our lives – we have a right to know what's going on in our lives and why our parents can't have us home . . . For all you know they might be dead. Like (X) said, all the time he was growing up in care he thought his parents were dead, but when he got out he found that they were both alive. (Page and Clark, 1977)

The foreword to *Who Cares?* emphasized that 'the co-operative way of working with children described here had extremely wide implications . . . Reciprocal courtesy and honest discussion would seem to be the grounds of future development.'

The Children's Society went on to hold similar group sessions for young people in their care, using the views collected to influence local policies (Nelson and Seddon, 1979). 'Who Cares?' groups, where young people in care can meet to discuss and challenge some of the idiosyncracies of the care system, now exist in several local authorities and in other countries such as Japan and Canada. Detailed retrospective studies of care (Kahan, 1979; Mann, 1984; Loveday, 1985) have given greater understanding of the 'insider's view'.

Eventually the National Association of Young People in Care

(NAYPIC) evolved from the original 'Who Cares?' group, a process described by Mike Stein (1983). NAYPIC has been extremely active in collecting and crystallizing young people's views into a 'campaigning voice'. Particularly influential was their evidence to the Social Services Committee on Children in Care (House of Commons, 1984). In 1983 they received responses from 465 young people to a questionnaire on child care reviews. (Reviews are meetings held by the responsible social services department to satisfy a legal requirement that the 'health, welfare and progress' of children in care be regularly monitored at not less than six-monthly intervals.) The NAYPIC survey (Stein and Ellis, 1983) indicated, as have other studies (e.g. Gardner, 1985) that most young people wanted to be present at their reviews and two-thirds of these also wished to remain in the meeting throughout, instead of being required to leave while adults discussed them. One-third of young people in children's homes and one-quarter of those in foster homes had not attended a review. We imagine that these proportions have not altered much since 1983.

Answers to the question 'what is a review?' clearly demonstrate children's lack of a clear understanding of the care system: 'where they discover your private life'; 'a test'; 'a general survey or examination'; 'where people discuss your future and come to no definite conclusion'.

There is no doubt that young people can find reviews very confusing unless they are carefully prepared. The purpose of the particular meeting needs to be made clear, numbers attending kept as low as possible and new information shared with the young person in advance, rather than in the middle of the meeting. Skilled chairing and good review forms can overcome many of the difficulties (Gardner, 1985).

A subsequent NAYPIC document (Denton, 1984) considers another subject of great importance, access by young people to their case records. Four hundred and fifty-five questionnaires were returned from 40 local authorities and 176 were analysed. Only just over one-quarter of these respondents had seen any part of their file and less than 20 had viewed all the contents. Of those who had seen the file, less than one-fifth thought that it was entirely accurate: 'I should have a right to check the file because I sometimes wonder if people write the truth about me'; 'They don't need half the information they've got, especially personal details. Some of what is written is only done because it gives them something to do.'

The report produced practical recommendations. The great majority of respondents, aged between 13 and 19, wanted:

- to check files regularly with the social worker or on their own
- limits on the amount and type of information held
- to assume ownership of their records on leaving care.

Family Service Units and some other agencies have now developed recording methods that take into account most of these points, which we will describe later.

Concerns about the quality of social work recording have repeatedly been voiced by researchers and others, for example: 'Officers [of the Department of Health and Social Security] had much difficulty in ascertaining from the files basic data about children, their families and contacts. This led them to question whether social workers and seniors were always fully aware of the facts of the case' (DHSS Social Work Service, 1981). Once recording is clear and precise it is likely that communication of information will be more straightforward, but fundamental questions have to be answered: Who is the record for? Which information has to be recorded? Is its status (corroborated fact, opinion, hearsay) indicated? If someone has asked for that information to be withheld, what are the reasons for this? Should their request be negotiated, or overridden if the information is of importance to others?

Increasingly, young people are prepared to air their views about the child care system in public. Many more young people in care now are teenagers and as the care population changes, so the appropriateness of policies and practice has to be reviewed. Restrictions appear often to be created by adults through a wish, which may be misplaced, to protect young people from the complex reality of care, or by acceptance that the stigma of being in care is something better not recognized. In a study published in 1987 (Gardner) we talked with young people across the country about a broad range of personal and structural aspects of care – for example, going out for the evening, medical examinations and social worker visits. The ostensibly routine issue of medicals revealed some of the unintended misery of care:

> Overall, 10 of the 11 young people who 'disliked' or 'hated' medicals were female and frequently mentioned that they would have preferred a female doctor. One commented 'I was sexually abused when I was little and I don't like the idea of a man touching me'.

We also found that the majority of young people, black and white, had friends from different ethnic backgrounds – but this was not commonly true of adult carers. Some authorities have produced ethnically sensitive policies (London Borough of Lambeth, 1981), but we found in this study that nearly all authority figures were white people and there were many examples of institutional racism, 'no commitment to meeting black children's dietary needs, anxiety that black children in a large group may "provoke" racism, etc.'

The organization 'Black and in Care', like NAYPIC, run by and for young people, has emphasized the particular difficulties faced by black children without the support and security of their own cultural network, in a white care system. Their booklet and video *Black and in Care* (1984 and 1985) puts the message over forcefully, from young people with first-hand experience:

> There is definitely racism in the care system. They treat them all the same regardless of need, and they cut your hair because they don't know how to

look after it; you all eat the same food and if you don't like it or you're not used to it, it's too bad. There were other black children where I was brought up, but all the staff were white.

In 1972 Gwen James and other interested professionals set up the organization now known as 'Voice for the Child in Care'. The group has tried to shift opinion towards children's rights, with considerable success, for instance in pressing for complaints procedures for young people (James and Wadcock, 1985). A current campaign is for independent representation for young people in closed accommodation (Voice for the Child in Care, 1985).

Views of parents: the research

Four of the recent large-scale research studies include parents' views; two of these, by Jane Rowe and Mike Fisher *et al.*, have already been quoted. The third study is by Jean Packman *et al.* (1986) – *Who Needs Care?* Here, 270 parents of children who had either been in care or had been considered for care, were interviewed. Their views shed light on the process by which decisions are taken about delivering social services to families, so that the investment of time and effort by the researchers in securing these interviews has evidently paid off. It is interesting to note that only five per cent of those chosen for interviews refused to participate.

When asked about the problems families had been facing, parents and social workers often agreed that children's behaviour presented major difficulties; but their views tended to diverge on what was to be done about this. Parents could give fuller information about the extended family (often an important source of support in crisis) than could social workers, whose 'knowledge was rather shaky' in this area. Although parents' separations during their childhood did not appear to relate to their own children entering care, their experiences of intense unhappiness in childhood 'did seem to correlate with an admission to care of their own children . . . parents (mothers and fathers) of the admitted children described their own childhood in unhappy terms'. For instance, one mother is quoted as saying 'I can always remember our Dad hitting me . . . my Dad tried to interfere with me when my Mum was in hospital . . . I had a dreadful childhood'.

This kind of evidence, people's own accounts of their experience rather than just the bald facts of their case history, offers a more rounded view of child care. In the study described above, one-quarter of the parents were unhappy with their accommodation, yet this was seen as a problem by only one in seven of the social workers. 'More than a third of the mothers (35 per cent) reckoned they were in poor health at the time the children were being considered for care (the social workers had thought this applied to one in 10).'

In an investigation of the problems of maintaining links between children in care and their families (Millham *et al.*, 1986) the authors describe the reactions of family members in a small number of detailed case studies. They conclude that 'all parents remained very confused about their rights and obligations under specific legislation . . . one local authority imposed a ban on all contact between parent and child during the first 10 days to facilitate the child's settling-in. This accorded ill with mothers' considerable anxiety at the outset of the children's care experience, distress greatly increased by their inability to picture the child's actual situation [and] . . . also ignores the fact that most parental visiting patterns are set very early in the child's absence.' They also found (as have other studies and enquiries) (London Borough of Brent, 1985) that social workers usually make little or no contact with the extended family.

Because of lack of advice and encouragement, and the great social skills required, visiting children in care is often an obstacle race for parents, one of whom described supervised access as 'a bit like trying to do some shopping while there's a store detective watching you. You can't enjoy it – it sort of worries you and you feel guilty although you haven't done anything wrong' (Packman, 1986).

Social workers are sometimes not clear about their powers and duties in the first instance. This means that parents who thought they were receiving unconditional help and advice but subsequently find their family life under surveillance, may well become resentful: 'Certainly it was not uncommon to find parents describing their social workers as "wolves in sheep's clothing" in spite of the workers' valiant attempts to appear as sheep in sheep's clothing' (Packman, 1986).

The Sheffield study (Fisher *et al.*, 1986) also indicates a lack of congruence between the views of parents and social workers about what purpose care is to serve. Parents often wanted a break from behaviour which had contributed to their stress over many years, and to see this behaviour controlled: '"It's for control that they're in care" (Mother); "It's to get them on the right track. I'd rather them go into care now than wait while they're 18 and end up in prison" (Father).' Social workers often tried to make the problems seem ordinary by saying they were 'part of growing up', and wanted parents to recognize their own contribution to the family's difficulties; 'they did not realize that parents would take this to imply parental incompetence. However correct it might have been, it led parents to feel that they had to prove their worth and justify their level of concern, and so the discussions became even more fraught and tense' (Fisher, *et al.*, 1986).

This research again shows that a comparison of the views of parents, children and social workers can show clear discrepancies. Understanding these different perceptions is an important basis for 'a genuinely negotiated approach to care'.

Parents whose children have entered care often feel they have failed and, particularly where there has been a court hearing, there may be antagonism between the parents and social workers. We have suggested that more open and honest discussions at an early stage could avoid some of this bitterness, but parents often need independent advice and support. The Family Rights Group was set up in 1977 'to offer advice to families with children in public care and to plug some of the gaps in professional training on child care law and good practice' (The Family Rights Group, 6–9 Manor Gardens, London N7 6LA). The Group is currently working to promote greater involvement of parents in child abuse procedures and to set up a support network for grandparents. Another organization, Parents Against Injustice, supports parents involved in child abuse investigations (Parents Against Injustice, 'Conifers', 2 Pledgdon Green, Nr Herham, Bishop's Stortford, Herts CM22 6BN). Recent local research and enquiries have indicated ways in which families could be involved in a more honest and yet sensitive way in the process of investigation (McGloin and Turnbull, 1986; Brown, 1986; Cleveland Inquiry, 1988). Parents Aid (1983) has produced a useful general guide for parents, an example which has been followed by some social services departments.

Legal framework for the involvement of children and young people

The statute most often referred to in recent years as justification for involvement of young people in plans for their care is Section 18 of the Child Care Act 1980:

> *General duty of the local authority in relation to children in their care*; in reaching any decision relating to a child in their care; a local authority shall give first consideration to the need to safeguard and promote the welfare of the child throughout his childhood; and shall so far as is practicable ascertain the wishes and feelings of the child regarding the decision and give due consideration to them, having regard to his age and understanding.

Clarke Hall and Morrison (White *et al.*, 1988) give two judgements concerning closure of children's homes, where the decisions involved are seen as falling within Section 18 and 'related' to the children living in those particular homes. In these and similar cases, children's wishes and feelings are, at times, ignored for reasons of policy (e.g. the promotion of fostering instead of residential care). Freeman (1987/88) argues that someone independent of the local authority, such as a children's ombudsman or special advocate, is needed in such cases, since legal aid is difficult to obtain and 'it is all too easy . . . to consult the children or their representatives and then to ignore the views expressed'. Clarke Hall and Morrison also interpret Section 18 as a duty 'to ascertain the wishes and feelings of a child old enough to make them known and the *feelings of any child in spite of young age and limited understanding*' (our emphasis). Section 18 has raised much debate about how far certain decisions 'relate' to children in care, how far the child's 'welfare' can be decided in isolation from his or her 'wishes and feelings' and exactly what is 'due consideration'. Nevertheless, despite – or perhaps because of – the questions raised, there is no doubt that this section together with the duty 'to review the case of each child' (Section 20, Child Care Act 1980), has set a marker for social services; they have a duty to plan, not just from day to day but to 'promote the welfare of the child throughout his childhood'; and, fundamentally, they must plan not only for children, but with them. Social workers thus carry considerable responsibility towards each child on their caseloads. Experience has shown that the skills and personal qualities required seem to have been insufficiently recognized in generic training.

The House of Lords' decision in Gillick vs. W. Norfolk and Wisbech Area Health Authority and the DHSS was an important test ('Law Report', 1985). It referred to the need for a doctor to be able to judge whether a young woman aged 16 or under is able to take an informed decision independently of her parent or parent substitute. The Law Lords said that young people could take such decisions. Lord Fraser's view was that 'parental rights to control the child existed not for the benefit of the parent but for the child' and that 'in practice most wise parents relaxed their control gradually as the child developed and encouraged him to become increasingly independent. Moreover, the degree of parental control actually exercised over a particular child did in practice vary considerably according to his age and intelligence.' In the course of the judgement, Lord Denning was quoted as saying (in Hewer vs. Bryant, 1970) that parents had a 'dwindling right which the courts will hesitate to enforce against the wishes of the child and the more so the older he is. It starts with the right of control and ends with little more than advice.'

This judgement reflects the tenor of Section 18 of the Child Care Act 1980 in recommending consideration of the particular child's 'age and understanding'. Denise Annett of the Children's Legal Centre concluded from it that 'adults caring for children will have to justify their exclusion from participation in decision making by demonstrating that the individual child lacks the understanding to make a valid judgement about the issue in question' (Annett, 1985).

The case of Graham Gaskin may well encourage greater openness with records about the lives of children in care. Mr Gaskin was refused access to part of his file by Liverpool Social Services and he approached the European Commission of Human Rights on the basis that 'the file represents the only coherent record of his childhood and adolescence'.

The Commission agreed (on a casting vote) that denial of access was a breach of Mr Gaskin's right to 'respect for his private life'; their decision as to whether he should be given full access to the file will be given in 1989. During the hearing, comparisons were drawn with other European countries; five nations give children a legal right to see files ('Gaskin's Fight', 1988).

In 1984, a right of appeal was introduced for parents, guardians or custodians against any decision to terminate access to see their child (Section 12 G(3), Child Care Act 1980). This allows some parents a way back into their child's life, or at least may prevent their involvement ceasing without an independent examination of the case. The Code of Access produced by the DHSS (1983), while not as widely applied as it should be, sets a standard for involving those on the receiving end of social work decisions.

The setting up of panels of guardians *ad litem* has been another important step in ensuring that the courts are thoroughly aware of a child's situation and views. Despite local problems of organization and pressure of work, the central idea has attracted support, namely that the court appoint an officer to report on the child's circumstances and future welfare independently of the other parties (usually the local authority and the parent). The Magistrate's Court's Rules echo Section 18 of the Child Care Act: 'the guardian *ad litem* . . . with a view to safeguarding the interests of the relevant infant before the court shall . . . take into account the wishes and feelings of the child, having regard to his age and understanding, and shall ensure that those wishes and feelings are made known to the Court' (DHSS, 1984). Needless to say, training for this heavy responsibility is not consistently available and children receive an erratic service in some areas. Court procedures vary, but many juvenile courts will help young people to speak for themselves if they wish to do so, even where there is a solicitor for the child and a guardian in court.

Changes in child care law likely to take place in 1989 include a presumption of reasonable access; the court's power to determine disputes on access; and party status for anyone whose legal position could be affected by the proceedings, or who is seeking legal responsibility – whether parent, step-parent or grandparent. Courts may also be able to direct others, e.g. a friend of the child, to take part in the proceedings as a witness or to question witnesses, and social services departments may be required to introduce complaints procedures for users of their services. The Law Commission has proposed significant extensions of children's rights, including the obligation of courts to consider children's wishes and feelings, to allow children to make applications for themselves, and to be able to make children parties to legal proceedings. Sixteen- and seventeen-year-olds would in general be able to make decisions for themselves on where they live, access arrangements and other matters of personal importance (The Law Commission).

Policy in social work agencies

The research expressed views of young people and legal requirements have influenced policy and practice to some extent and there are now more frequent references in policy documents to 'consumer involvement' and 'rights'; for example:

> Parents and children of an appropriate age have a right to be involved in planning and decision making. They should be given written information explaining the legal implications of care, their rights within law and within departmental policy. (Newcastle, 1988)

> Children and families at the point of placement should have their rights and responsibilities explained to them verbally and in writing with information on complaints procedures and how to pursue them. (Waltham Forest, 1986)

Occasionally more detailed statements are made, for example:

> Working in partnership with parent(s) and children implies harmony but this cannot always be achieved. Real participation in the total work process will require honest examination of facts and feelings, and this may result in hostility and anxiety. Confrontation and conflict may well be an essential part of the partnership process, particularly in cases of child abuse or neglect. (Hammersmith, 1983)

Policy concerning children's involvement in their own reviews has been changing. Reviewing this, the Children's Legal Centre analysed answers from 57 local authorities, some of which showed such variation of practice even within a given authority 'that it was impossible to receive them as a corporate response'.

Specifying the purposes of reviews, 'monitoring' and 'taking decisions' were closely followed by 'collaboration with others'; yet only six authorities specified involvement by young people in care, with Wakefield standing out as wanting 'to give the child/young person a real voice in decisions about his present and future'. The Children's Legal Centre survey also pointed out that the decision-making powers of those present at reviews was not always made explicit, and we have seen that this can cause confusion and anger. Their conclusion could as well apply to all decisions in care, not just reviews:

> A negative assessment by adults of young people's ability to handle a review which they wish to attend is profoundly subjective and paternalistic . . . young people may need sympathetic and careful preparation for hearing disturbing facts . . . and indeed they sometimes back off . . . obviously social workers should respect young people's judgement in such matters. (Children's Legal Centre, 1985)

The ability of chairpersons and the design of review forms appeared to be significant in facilitating reviews. Ultimately, however, the aptitude and skills of social workers or carers are clearly of crucial importance. The last part of this chapter will, therefore, contain descriptions of open practice, which allows children and parents an active say in what is going to happen and, in particular, opportunity to communicate their views to those with influence, and to gain a response which takes account of these views. The case for such an approach has been set out fully elsewhere (Gardner, 1987; Gardner and Tonkin, 1988). These and other such examples were gathered in the course of the National Children's Bureau's recent research on participation in decision making by young people in care. In its present phase, which has been funded from 1984 to 1990, this has included collecting views of young people who are not in touch with any support group or organization; organizing workshops for young people to exchange information; intensive local development work including training for workers and managers; and preparing guides to good practice.

Our first example of open practice is of child care records that are both lucid and accessible. For most workers, notes are a tedious afterthought. This is demonstrated by piles of cardboard binders stuffed with assorted letters, reports and children's keepsakes, such as photographs. For the children, as we have seen, the file may be the only remaining source of continuity – it literally represents their lives.

At Woodcross, a Barnardo's Adolescent Unit now closed, George Coyle and his colleagues reconstructed the files used by workers and children so that they were attractive, durable and easy to use. They also arranged for the detail and complexity of life in care to be clearly identifiable in colour-coded sections. These began with a full fact sheet and notes on using the file, and were followed by separate sections on correspondence; records written by residential staff (e.g. weekly summaries taken from log sheets, with monthly evaluations of these); court reports, family charts and summaries of the home situation; school reports; histories of placements; reports from earlier placements and Court Orders; clothing accounts; and medical information. Plastic wallets in some sections secured photographs, receipts or medical cards. This approach reduced the amount of irrelevant recording and meant that each kind of information was equally and readily accessible.

If these details seem prosaic, it has to be remembered that they constitute perhaps the most important tool the worker has in making sense and coherence of a young person's life. This life, however short, has often been crammed with moves, each punctuated with accounts of adults' feelings and opinions about the child but from which the child's own voice is conspicuously absent. The Woodcross approach insisted by notes in each section of the file that these records were designed to include the child's own perspective, for example:

> Ensure this [the family chart] is updated when a major shift in the patterns [is] noticed. Draw up the changed chart only after discussion with the young person in order to check accuracy. Use colours, crayons, felts; in other words try to make the exercise fun with the young person. Always conclude with a summary of the chart and date it.

Coyle notes 'over the years, the young people have developed a degree of confidence which allowed them to make their own entries in the log/files [but] no system will stand on its own – it has to be 'plugged in' to a supporting philosophy that the consumers and staff can identify as genuine'. This was precisely the finding of a study on social work recording carried out by Brunel University and the British Association of Social Workers (Ovretveit, 1985).

Our second example of good practice is involvement of young people in care in 'teenage preparation groups'. These are usually organized by specialized fostering workers but sometimes by generic social workers or a combination of the two. They are intended to give young people a choice about whether fostering is right for them or not. Such groups are now incorporated into some fostering schemes around the country, for example in Bradford (Fraser and O'Hara, 1985). The idea deserves to be tried out much more widely with monitoring of its effect on the stability and happiness of placements, in so far as this is possible.

The Bradford scheme has focused on teenagers who had formerly been in CHEs or places of custody, or who persistently absconded or did not attend school. The reason given for setting the groups up was that while foster parents were carefully prepared to receive young people workers 'were not doing the same for the teenagers . . . It seemed we were expecting these teenagers, who have usually experienced a wide variety of parenting, to magically move in and settle in to a new family.'

In the Bradford scheme, each group has a five-day programme, in which a small number of adolescents use games, video and discussion to explore with two workers what it would be like to live in someone else's family. The kinds of decisions they may face in a foster family are explored in a comic-strip format with various options for the teenager to consider, e.g. an argument in the foster home – do you run away? sulk? try to find a way to discuss what went wrong? The various choices and possible consequences are depicted and then discussed. Teenagers can also make a short video about themselves for their potential foster parents. Their expectations of families and their past experiences (some of them traumatic and brought into the open for the first time in this setting) are examined against information about available foster families, some of whom are also introduced via photos and stories.

Of course in order to make any choice a genuine one, there have to be options, and some young people decide against being fostered. David Berridge looked at consumer studies on residential care and spent a week living in each of 20 children's homes. He concluded that residential care still has a lot to offer:

> Many young people in care who maintain contact with their families claim to prefer to live in a residential setting, particularly where it is locally based . . . as children's homes now cater largely for adolescents, the majority of residents will have clear preferences regarding their placements and these should be considered. (Berridge, 1985)

Many young people enjoy group living, work hard and go on to foster placements:

> It has been a time when they have found they are not alone, other teenagers have been through similar experiences . . . whatever a teenager decides, we recognize what they are saying and listen to it, we do not try to force them to change their minds. This is not always easy for us or their social worker because we might feel a teenager would do really well in a family . . . we acknowledge the risk involved and offer no guarantees that it will work . . . The teenagers often say to us: 'It's me who is going to live with them, not you, not my social worker.'

This is really the crux of a relationship between child and responsible adult; how quickly and how far to let that 'dwindling control' go. The ability to amass information, to sift it and to take decisions for better or worse is one basis for 'adulthood', if that word is to mean anything at all. Yet no such faculty will develop if decisions are always taken 'in children's best interests' by another. Sooner or later that 'other' parent, guardian or carer has to take a risk (and usually needs some help to take it) in letting the young person 'go it alone', perhaps misguidedly or perhaps even disastrously. Risk has to be accepted as a factor in this as in other areas of social work, and management's job is to ensure that advice and support is regularly available to everyone involved, particularly the child. The most important message of all, as the Cleveland Inquiry confirmed, is that the child or young person is 'entitled to be taken seriously' (Secretary of State for Social Services, 1988).

References

Aldgate, J. (1989) 'The interpersonal dynamics of the family and of residential care', in *Children and Society*, forthcoming.

Annett, D. (1985) 'How Victoria Gillick increased the rights of young people', *Social Work Today*, 25 November 1985.

Berridge, D. (1985) *Children's Homes*, Basil Blackwell.

Berridge, D. and Cleaver, H. (1987) *Foster Home Breakdown*, Basil Blackwell.

Black and in Care (1984) *Report of a Conference organized by the Black and in Care Steering Group; Black and in Care* video (1985); report and video available from 20 Compton Terrace, London N1 2UN (see also *Speakout*, the NAYPIC Video, available from the same address).

Brown, C. (1986) *Child Abuse Parents Speaking: Parents' Impressions of Social Workers and the Social Work Process*, University of Bristol, SAUS, Working Paper 63.

Children's Legal Centre (1985) *It's My Life Not Theirs.*

Denton, G. (1984) *For Whose Eyes Only? Files and Young People in Care*, NAYPIC.

Department of Health and Social Security, Social Work Service (1981) *Children in Care in London*, DHSS.

Department of Health and Social Security (1983) *Code of Practice, Access to Children in Care*, HMSO.

Department of Health and Social Security (1984) *Guide for Guardians* Ad Litem *in the Juvenile Court*, HMSO.

Fisher, M., Marsh, P. and Phillips, D. with Sainsbury, E. (1986) *In and Out of Care: The Experiences of Children, Parents and Social Workers*, Batsford/BAAF.

Fraser, S. and O'Hara, P. (1985) *Community Parents' Scheme: The Groupwork Preparation of Teenagers for Family Placement*, Bradford Social Services.

Freeman, M. D. A. (1983) *The Rights and Wrongs of Children*. Frances Pinter.

Freeman, M. D. A. (1987/88) 'Taking children's rights seriously', *Children and Society*, Vol. 1, No. 4.

Gardner, R. (1985) *Child Care Reviews*, National Children's Bureau.

Gardner, R. (1987) *Who Says? Choice and Control in Care*, National Children's Bureau.

Gardner, R. and Tonkin, B. (eds) (1988) 'In care and involved', Inside Supplement, *Community Care*, 31 March 1988.

'Gaskin's Fight to File Goes to European Court' (1988), *Childright*, No. 48, June.

House of Commons (1984) *Second Report from the Social Services Committee*, Vols I–IV, *Children in Care*, March 1984, HMSO.

James, G. and Wadcock, D. (1985) *Signposts – A Guide to Setting Up Complaints Procedures for Children in Care*, NCB.

Kahan, B. (1979) *Growing Up in Care*, Basil Blackwell.

'Law Report' (1985) *The Times*, 18 October 1985.

Law Commission, No. 172.

London Borough of Brent (1985) *A Child in Trust: The Report of the Panel of Inquiry into the Circumstances Surrounding the Death of Jasmine Beckford*, London Borough of Brent.

London Borough of Greenwich (1987) *A Child in Mind: Protection of Children in a Responsible Society. Report of the Commission of Inquiry into the Circumstances Surrounding the Death of Kimberley Carlile*, London Borough of Greenwich.

London Borough of Lambeth (1981) *Good Practice Guide for Working with Black Families and Black Children in Care.*

Loveday, S. (1985) *Reflections on Care*, The Children's Society.

Mann, P. (1984) *Children in Care Revisited*, Batsford.

Marsh, P., Fisher, M. and Phillips, D. (1985) 'Negotiating child care', *Adoption and Fostering*, Vol. 9, No. 3.

McGloin, P. and Turnbull, A. (1986) *Parent Participation in Child Abuse Review Conferences*, Directorate of Social Services, London Borough of Greenwich.

Millham, S., Bullock, R., Hosie, K. and Haak, M. (1986) *Lost in Care: The Family Contacts of Children in Care*, Gower.

Nelson, J. and Seddon, J. (1979) *Children in Homes*, The Children's Society.

Ovretveit, J. (1985) *Social Work Recording and Practice, Action Research Project*, Brunel University and BASW.

Packman, J. with Randall, J. and Jacques, N. (1986) *Who Needs Care? Social Work Decisions About Children*, Basil Blackwell.

Page, R. and Clark, G. (eds) (1977) *Who Cares?, Young People in Care Speak Out*, National Children's Bureau.

Parents Aid (1983) *Guide for Parents with Children in Care*, available from 66 Chippingfield, Harlow, Essex, CM17 ODJ.

Rowe, J., Cain, H., Hundleby, M. and Keane, A. (1984) *Long-term Foster Care*, Batsford/BAAF.

Secretary of State for Social Services (1988) *Report of the Inquiry into Child Abuse in Cleveland 1987*, HMSO.

Stein, M. (1983) 'Protest in care', in Jordon, B. and Parton, N. (eds), *The Political Dimension of Social Work*, Basil Blackwell.

Stein, M. and Ellis, S. (1983) *Gizza Say? Reviews and Young People in Care*, NAYPIC.

Voice for the Child in Care (1985) *The Case for Independent Representation*, available from Voice for The Child in Care, 60 Carysfort Road, London N8 8RB.

White, R. and Carr, A. P. with Hoggett, B. (1988) *Clarke, Hall and Morrison on Children*, Butterworth.

Other Reading

BASW (1980) *Clients are Fellow Citizens*.

Croft, S. and Beresford, P. (1988) 'Power to the people: an exercise in propaganda?', *Social Work Today*, 28 July 1988.

Hardingham, S. (1988) 'Consumers' Association', *Insight*, No. 12, 26 July 1988.

Jones, L., Pringle, K. and Zaccheo, M., (1988) 'Can young people change the care system?', *Social Work Today*, 25 August 1988.

Stein, M. and Carey, K. (1986) *Leaving Care*, Basil Blackwell.

14 The cost of services

Martin Knapp and Eileen Robertson

There is a strong and growing demand for costs information to feed into the planning of child care servies. Yet the supply of costs data is still inadequate: today's routinely available cost statistics are incomplete, too highly aggregated, encourage inappropriate comparisons and are too often employed without regard for the outcomes of different care options. This chapter charts the sources of demand for costs and introduces the inadequacies of extant data collections. It then addresses three important child care debates, examining the influences of cost assumptions and illustrating how the improved costs evidence that comes from appropriate research can offer powerful policy insights. The three areas covered are residential and foster care for children who cannot live with their birth families, intermediate treatment and its alternatives, and the 'contracting-out' of residential child care to the voluntary and private sectors.

1 The narrowing divide

In the early 1970s there could have been few more heinous professional offences than to utter the words care and cost in the same breath. The social work profession was coming to grips with the new Seebohm departments and annual growth rates in social services spending were reaching double figures. There was little reason to search for the budget constraint. Cost-influenced planning, much less cost-dominated planning, was anathema to the child care worker. In those halcyon days, it was not that child care goals such as child development or rehabilitation were to be pursued at any cost; rather that financial decisions were not really the concern of the fieldworker or the head of a residential home. Budgeting was done by 'someone in accounts' and the decisions handed down without much quarrelling. For a period in the late 1960s and early 1970s, budgetary growth was more than incremental; resources flowed freely. Child care researchers and commentators expressed little interest in cost.

At the same time, there was no great push from local authority accountants and treasurers to get involved in social work matters. The treasurers had for a long time been guided by their own codes of professional excellence. The Chartered Institute of Public Finance and Accountancy (CIPFA) published abstracts of local authority accounts which were standardized across the country and which were annually pored over by treasurers and annually ignored by all but the most senior or diligent of social services employees. There was no 'value for money auditing', little performance review. Auditing in the 1970s, as one special projects' officer in today's Audit Commission describes it, was what people did when they found accountancy too exciting. The links between child care decision making and financial management were few.

As we move into the final decade of the millennium, however, we see that the twain have met. Child care policy documents in local authorities often lead with a cost or expenditure review. Social policy degrees and many social work training courses now include economics somewhere on the curriculum. And, of course, the auditor – armed with a pristine copy of the *Value for Money Handbook* and barely able to contain the excitement at having left straight accounting – is a regular and not always welcome visitor to the social services department. The Social Services Inspectorate, like the Audit Commission an organizational child of the 1980s, includes costs in some of its special studies, something which its predecessor, the Social Work Service, did not contemplate. The research and policy literatures in the last few years have also been much more likely to include at least a brief cost commentary. For example, the Residential Care Review Committee, chaired by Lady Gillian Wagner, commissioned six consultants' reports, one for each of five client groups and one on costs (Wagner, 1988; Sinclair, 1988). Even this chapter is evidence of the narrowing divide between care practice and resource management.

On the whole, and as we shall illustrate in this chapter, this trend must be applauded. But as cost issues and child care practice considerations meet each other under the same policy umbrella, so a number of worrying inadequacies and misconceptions come to light. For example, the integration of cost and effectiveness insights within 'value for money', 'performance' or 'efficiency' reviews has revealed how poor are the costs data lovingly tended by local authority accountants over many years and how limiting are the so-called effectiveness data. Rightly, though belatedly, most people are highly critical of our extant information systems. Many local authorities have therefore set about improving their information collections with enthusiasm and imagination. Others have been prodded into action by their auditors or inspectors. Nevertheless, we are still in the position in which overworked child care professionals with no economic training are grappling with policy and practice decisions which have huge financial ramifications, and we have accountants and auditors with no child care training trying to incorporate perspectives on child care practice so as to adjudge value for money and efficiency.

This chapter is written with these issues and constraints in mind. The primary aims are:

- to ask why we need cost information about child care services
- to reveal some of the inadequacies of the available cost information used to meet that need
- to offer some research evidence on the costs of child care services

which go some way toward meeting these inadequacies and so contribute to child care policy.

2 The demand for cost information

As fiscal belts were tightening during the 1970s, costs appeared with growing frequency in policy debates. They even occasionally entered discussions of social work and child care practice. What particularly prompted interest in the cost implications of child care policies and what particularly helped to articulate concern about the cost constraints which appeared to hamper care practice were, first, the publication of an Audit Inspectorate report in 1981 and second, the commencement of the House of Commons Select Committee on Social Services' investigation of child care in 1982. Indeed, a series of interrelated events between October 1981 and April 1983 had a great impact. In that short period we had the publication of the very interesting – though flawed – study of child care services in eight English and Welsh local authorities by the District Audit Service of the former Audit Inspectorate (1981), the launch of the government's Financial Management Initiative (FMI), the careful interrogation of DHSS witnesses by members of the Select Committee, and the arrival of both the Audit Commission and the Social Services Inspectorate. Each of these events had a tremendous influence on the information demands placed upon social services departments and the planning expectations and constraints of those departments. Indirectly, they had their impacts on non-statutory child care organizations.

The FMI and Audit Commission heralded the arrival of what immediately became known as the 'three Es': Economy, Efficiency and Effectiveness in the provision of public services. The FMI brought these three Es to central government and the Audit Commission employed them in local authority contexts. But of course, there is also a need to include a fourth E – equity or distributive justice – as a policy criterion.

Economy is simply the saving of resources; it is frugality. The pursuit of economy need pay no heed to the impact of a lower level of spending upon children, families or communities. One feature of social services management in the 1980s has been a trend towards centralization of decision making about costly placement decisions. Some authorities have decreed, without careful consideration by senior management, that no child should be placed in a community home with education, or observation and assessment centre, both of these residential resources being perceived as far too expensive. The most recent estimates would suggest that the cost of a week's placement in a CHE runs to about £500, and the cost of a week in an observation and assessment centre to about £450 (CIPFA, 1988). The Audit Inspectorate study (1981) argued that close control over the admission of children to these high-cost, specialist facilities and careful monitoring of periods of residence within them, were essential if value for money was to be achieved. In the pursuit of economy a number of local authorities also tightly control decisions about the placement of children in private and voluntary establishments, particularly 'out county' placements. Low ceilings have been imposed on 'agency budgets'. The pursuit of economy obviously requires detailed and accurate cost information.

The second E, the promotion of effectiveness, does not in principle require any particular regard to be paid to costs. Improving effectiveness is to enhance the wellbeing of children, or to take the service of an agency closer to whatever its agreed objectives may be. But effectiveness is particularly hard to gauge. How does one measure the comparative or differential effectiveness of two alternative services when the dimensions of effectiveness are far from clear, when the scaling of positions along each of those dimensions is complex, when the time lags between a care intervention and the eventual impact can be huge, and when the current populations of the two service options are far from similar? It is very difficult to prove that one service is more effective than another. It is difficult, even when the weight of professional opinion is behind it, to alter the balance of care speedily so as to place more children in foster homes or for adoption or in IT programmes. In these circumstances, child care professionals and managers have often resorted to cost arguments to support their effectiveness preferences. The best example of this is the use of cost data to support and encourage a growth in the proportion of children fostered with families as an alternative to residential provision. Fostering looks very cheap and is preferred on child welfare grounds for many of the children in the care of local authorities. Quite wrongly, the cost imperative may have more impact on the balance of care than the nebulous concept of child welfare. As Parker noted, there was 'the happy coincidence that the most desirable provision was for once the most economical' (1966, p. 19), although the danger is always lurking that children's interests are sacrificed for the sake of economy. There is also a tendency to polarize the policy choices: residential versus foster care. One can see the same difficulties of 'proving' an effectiveness difference, leading to greater reliance on cost arguments than is either appropriate or advisable in present debates about the development of peripatetic assessment as an alternative to residential assessment and the substition of intermediate treatment for community homes with education. There is, then, a demand for cost information to support an effectiveness position which cannot be directly tested with available data. This seems a dubious and ultimately dangerous basis for planning.

The third E in the Financial Management Initiative's list of desiderata is efficiency, which combines the resource and outcome sides of the care process. It seeks to minimize the cost of producing a stated level of outcome or effectiveness, or to maximize the effectiveness that can be achieved from fixed budgets. 'Efficiency' is one of those controversial terms of the 'new managerialist' approach to public service management. But the pursuit of efficiency, properly understood and properly located within a multiple objective policy framework, is beyond criticism. And because few efficiency investigations can proceed without cost data, cost-based planning is also beyond criticism. Disagreements and disputes arise, of course, in the interpretation of evidence, centred around the credibility and validity of the data itself. Furthermore, it is rarely appreciated that efficiency can often be best promoted by spending more and not less. An efficiency saving is too often a euphemism for a draconian cut. It is too narrowly specified as a policy criterion. For example, a penny of prevention today could save a pound of care later, and probably dramatically improve the lives of many children at one and the same time. This emphasis on prevention as both economical and effective is one of the central planks of auditors' discussions with local authorities. The problem is that preventive services can be very difficult to target on families in need, and the 'efficiency' of prevention is not self-evident. The same applies to arguments for expanding foster care as an alternative to residential provision. The Audit Commission assumes, and advises local authority auditors to assume, that increasing fostering rates as an alternative to residential care, and increasing adoption as an alternative to fostering, will both save money and promote the wellbeing of children. We will need to confront these assumptions about 'efficiency' with evidence.

Finally, we come to the fourth E, which is so easily overlooked in the headlong pursuit of value for money. The equity or distributive justice of social policy, whether that objective seeks to increase or decrease the equality with which services are offered and outcomes achieved, will often require cost information. The annual rate support grant from central government to local authorities is based on grant-related expenditure assessments. These GREAs, as they are known, take into account differences in the circumstances and characteristics of local authorities. Needs will vary considerably between authorities, as will the level and balance of services available to meet them. Those service differences will reflect both local traditions and policy preferences over a number of years, but will also be influenced by variations in the prices with which resources and services can be purchased. Central government cannot equitably allocate resources between local authorities without cognizance of variations in the costs of provision.

Thus we can see how each of the four Es – today's dominant policy criteria – generates a demand for cost data. Cost information is also employed, rightly or wrongly, in pursuit of other objectives: perhaps to constrain the over-zealous transformation of systems of care or to maintain the status quo. Vested interests can often be best protected by pointing out how expensive a proposed change will be. Cost data are also used for defensive accountability. Local authorities might simply collect and present cost information to demonstrate to their auditors that cost statistics are collected! Such posturing is unhelpful but rare. Infinitely more worthy of applause is the integration and employment of cost information in the long-term planning of complex policies. Child care packages are not the sole responsibility of social services departments or local authorities. Many such packages will include a significant input from the local education or housing department, the National Health Service, national and local voluntary organizations, the church, and so on. This fragmentation of service delivery responsibilities, and thus the fragmentation of lines of accountability, can generate practice and organizational confusion, and may result in the inappropriate deployment of scarce resources. Providing key workers and case managers with cost data is essential if they are to co-ordinate effectively and efficiently the services required to meet a child's or family's needs.

The demand for cost information, therefore, stems from the need to aid or complement the policy process. As Seebohm (1970) argued 'social planning is an illusion without adequate facts and the adequacy of services mere speculation without evaluation . . . The personal social services are large-scale experiments in ways of helping those in need. It is both wasteful and irresponsible to set experiments in motion and omit to record and analyse what happens.' Policies are not to be pursued without regard for the resource constraints. That is as unrealistic and as myopic now as it always has been. At the bottom line, reducing the cost with which services are provided without sacrificing quality means that more services can be provided out of the same budget. (This does not preclude the possibility that the money saved on child care might be syphoned away and spent on defence or education, but the potential for increased spending remains.) Equally, cost insights should not unreasonably hinder the policy process, nor dominate beyond their bounds.

3 Supplying cost data: the inadequacies

The new cost awareness that runs through most child care organizations has created problems, the major one being the uncritical nature of this cost acuity. Fundamental flaws in the costs data, obvious to anyone who cares to take more than a cursory glance, are too often overlooked, presumably on the assumption either that they do not matter or that nobody else, including elected members and auditors, will notice. Unfortunately, the latter assumption has some validity, which makes the inappropriateness of the former assumption all the more dangerous. The cost information which underpins today's policy and practice decisions is of poor quality – though an improvement on the situation 10 years ago – and it is employed in ways which can easily produce the wrong conclusions and encourage inappropriate action. Cost statistics which have been designed for the purposes of line management (and often, it must be said, for patterns of line management which were abondoned three reorganizations ago) are aggregated to a high level, erroneously compared from one setting or one authority to another and then squeezed into the new straitjackets demanded by either creative accounting or performance indicators, or both. Square cost pegs are rammed unceremoniously into round policy holes.

It is probably not far from the truth to say that each social care agency has its own particular cost information needs. It would be wrong then to make blanket condemnations of present information systems, and it would be foolishly optimistic to assume that a few research studies, however well-intentioned, could kill every methodological blight or bring every policy flower into bloom. Nevertheless, there are flaws common to most extant cost data employed in today's policy processes which the well-placed research study can certainly highlight and probably help to overcome. In this chapter we seek to bring some of these flaws into focus and we show how they have been addressed in some research studies. We discuss the flaws under four heads:

- completeness
- disaggregation
- like-with-like comparisons
- outcomes.

Completeness

Given the many and various services that could be received by children and families, and the likely complexity of care 'packages' offered in response to what are commonly multiple deprivations, it is not surprising that a major weakness of available costs data is their incompleteness. This is not so much a criticism of the data themselves, but of the limited, if not to say naive, way in which they have been employed. Only very rarely, for example, is foster care costed in a way which includes the potentially large time inputs from social work staff and specialist fostering officers, and hardly ever does the recruitment and selection of foster parents figure in the calculations. IT, similarly, is costed as if it is a stand-alone service, devoid of field social work, educational, probation or other inputs. Administrative and other overhead costs, notoriously difficult to apportion, get very short shrift. Often the 'hidden' costs of a care package – that is, the costs above and beyond the budget of the directly involved service (the residential home, the boarding out payment, the IT centre) – exceed the direct costs, and often they will fall to agencies other than the social services department. We will get some idea of these hidden elements in the section on outcomes where we shall see, for example, that there are grave dangers of propelling the growth of foster care proportions forward at too fast a rate on the basis of misleadingly low cost calculations. The completeness requirements of an adequate costing of child care options has a number of corollaries. First we should note that some resources appear to have a zero price – volunteers, for example, or the support provided by informal carers – yet they have a non-zero social value. It is the latter, linked to what the economists call opportunity cost, which we seek to measure. A policy which sought to shift more of the burden of care onto volunteer helpers could well fall foul of a severe supply constraint, or might succeed only by pulling volunteers away from other work of social value. The opportunity cost of employing the volunteers in these circumstances is certainly not zero. (See Knapp, 1984, pp. 125–9, for an account of the sources of divergence between market prices and opportunity costs.) In most cases we can accept the observed costs that appear in child care agency accounts (which are, effectively, the market prices) as reasonable approximations to opportunity costs.

A second corollary concerns the treatment of durable resources. Buildings, vehicles, furnishings and other durable goods purchased some years ago must not be treated as 'free'. Depreciation allowances in an agency's accounts aim to deal with this problem, although for costing purposes it is generally more appropriate to calculate an opportunity cost for the use of the durable resource based either on its sale value (for a resource to be run down or closed, such as a redundant children's home) or its replacement value (for a service or resource type which is to continue to expand, such as family centre provision). When these costs are calculated they need to be spread over the expected life span of usage, conventionally achieved by calculating an appropriate annuity value. We shall see later that the one-off costs of finding a permanent placement for a 'hard to place' child can amount to £10 000, yet the placement will last on average only four years. These not inconsiderable initial costs need to be spread over the full placement period.

This leads to a third consideration. Many child care interventions have long-term consequences. Just because budgets tend to be prepared on an annual basis is no reason for confining cost descriptions to the financial year. Ideally we would be in a position to calculate costs over the full length of a care period, even if that period lasted 18 years, and ideally cost indicators would be obtained and presented in a way which maximizes the likelihood of their being employed in such a manner. But we must then recognize that costs will not be static over time, and that future costs have less importance attached to them today than present costs. We must discount future costs (and effects) back to today's values, for we do not value a pound tomorrow as highly as we value a pound today. Inflation will obviously require an additional revaluation.

Some costs are not readily reduced to quantitative magnitudes. For example, some of the costs borne by families may include the psychological burden of care as well as forgone employment and leisure opportunities. Some of the broad societal costs of custody for young offenders may include concern over the incarceration of young people in prison establishments.

It is difficult or perhaps impossible to attach a monetary tag to these 'costs'. This does not necessarily make them any less important than the quantified costs. They need to be remembered.

Finally, when charting the costs of child care packages we will sometimes need to record who bears the costs. Decisions by one agency can have their greatest cost effects on another. If an education department excludes a child from school it could well be the social services department which bears the heaviest cost. Yet the distribution of the cost burden need bear no resemblance to the distribution of responsibilities for taking decisions. Indeed, in some instances no single public agency – indeed, no single tier of government – has the power to shift the balance of provision on its own. The fragmentation of responsibilities between social services, education and housing departments, the NHS, the Home Office and social security budgets may encourage practices and placements which are a long way from the best interests of clients and their carers. We will see in Section 5 how the fragmentation of funding responsibilities with regard to young offenders can potentially strangle the supply of non-custodial alternatives to detention centres and youth custody centres.

Disaggregation

Most cost statistics are available only at a highly aggregated level. The annual Department of Health statistics aggregate the costs up to just four national figures – local authority residential care, voluntary sector residential care, foster placements and others – and the annual CIPFA figures aggregate across all facilities of a given type within each authority. Even a local authority's accounts for a single residential home aggregate the resources provided on behalf of a dozen or so residents. Where possible we need to break these aggregated costs down to a disaggregated reporting to obtain individual level cost statistics. For the purposes of efficient policy and effective child care practice we need to ask: for whom and in what circumstances is one care plan or service more cost-effective than another? If we can move away from the grand generalization and the reliance on broad averages, we can properly focus attention on individual children, their needs and those of their families, and on the consequences for carers. Proper recognition is accorded the diversity of individual circumstances and their implications for service systems in general, and for costs and outcomes in particular.

However, individual level data is costly to collect, and consequently few studies have analysed or presented their findings at a disaggregated level. Aggregated figures are certainly relevant and interesting, but it would be more informative to collect and present evidence in such a way as to be able to make statements of the kind: placement option A is superior (more cost-effective or more beneficial) to option B for children with characteristic X and in familial or social circumstances Y. Social work training is based on the individuality of circumstances and needs. Evaluative information, whether cost-based or otherwise, which rides roughshod over this individuality is less likely to influence practice for the better than it might otherwise do.

Like-with-like comparison

Most cost comparisons between care alternatives, between local authorities or across the different production sectors fall into the trap of assuming like is being compared with like. They ignore the many potential cost-raising factors which really must be identical in incidence if the cost comparisons are to have meaning. Foremost among these factors will be those child characteristics and circumstances which influence the need for care, including handicapping conditions, special difficulties, delinquency and so on. Decisions about the most appropriate placements for children are based on these client characteristics, so that we would not expect to find identical groups of children in different care settings.

Client characteristics and circumstances are not the only determinants of cost. There are many factors, some well beyond the control or influence of service managers, which will raise or reduce the costs of care. Residential home size, local labour market pressures, the quality and coverage of paediatric facilities and others are likely to be relevant. As we shall see below, these factors go some way to explaining the very marked variations in average cost that are observed both between and within local authority areas. Some of these inter-authority variations in cost reflect or are influenced by differences in their inheritances of relatively unadjustable capital stocks, or by the supplies of substitute and complementary services such as special education or a voluntary organization's IT service, or by the actions of certain third-party agents such as magistrates, general practitioners or social security officers. We need to understand their influences if we are to understand costs. For example, we shall later see how differences in child characteristics between foster and residential placements can exaggerate the true savings to be achieved by shifting the balance of care towards fostering.

Outcomes

The final limitation of today's cost data concerns the ways in which they are commonly employed. Only very rarely are cost figures quoted alongside information on outcome, output or effectiveness. The connections between resources and outputs are many and complex, and very often indirect, and it is rare to find clear evidence from British research which describes those connections. The analysis of child care outcomes justifies a volume of its own and it is not our intention to grapple with the conceptual or practical issues of measurement here. Nonetheless, outcomes do constitute one side of the cost-effectiveness equation and information on cost is of limited utility without data on outcomes. In presenting and discussing the research evidence below we will need to take the effectiveness dimensions on board.

We will now turn to three particular areas of child care to highlight some of the policy issues requiring a cost perspective and to illustrate the ways in which research can specifically deal with the inadequacies noted above.

4 The costs of foster and residential placements

We can readily illustrate these data inadequacies by looking at the long-standing debate about substituting foster placements for residential care. We can see, for example, some very early claims that the cost of fostering is a lot less than the costs of running residential homes. The seventh Annual Report of the Church of England Central Home for Waifs and Strays, 1887, included an appeal:

> The cost of maintaining a child under seven years of age, who would be boarded out, is calculated at £13 per annum; a child over that age who would be placed in one of the Homes, at £15 per annum.

Two generations later the claims were similar but now the appeal was for economy rather than donations:

> Expansion of boarding-out should relieve pressure on accommodation in children's homes and residential nurseries, at a time when restrictions on capital investment limit severely the improvement of existing premises. . . . Boarding-out is the least expensive method of child care both in money and manpower, and in the present financial condition of the country it is imperative to exercise the strictest economy consistent with a proper regard for the interests of the children. (Home Office, 1952, para. 2)

The same arguments run through policy statements today. The problem is that the costs relied upon then, as now, are no more than the boarding out payments made to foster parents and the revenue accounts of residential homes. Just about the worst style of foster care practice would be to make a hasty placement and then simply ensure that boarding out payments were made regularly. Equivalently, just about the worst costing of foster care would be to rely solely on the boarding out payments, perhaps making some notional adjustment for recruitment. *Inter alia*, these costs miss the costs of recruiting, assessing, selecting and matching foster families; field social worker and 'fostering officer' support costs; other services received by children in foster placements and by their birth and foster families; administrative overhead costs; and the hidden costs of foster care borne by foster families but not met by boarding out payments. There is a long list of omissions. If foster care costs are to be compared with the costs of residential home placements – and a lot of people want to make such a comparison, and with justification – then it is clearly not enough to be missing so much. And at the same time we must be careful not to miss important cost elements for residential care. What do these costs look like in practice? (A fuller account of these costs is provided in Knapp and Fenyo, 1989.)

It is not easy to 'complete' the costs of foster home or residential placements. No routine information exists which records the number of contacts between a foster family and social worker, or the duration of each contact, nor do we have statistics on the usage of specialist child care services, involvement in specific cases by senior management, recruitment inputs or any of the other services which combine to define foster or residential care. Unfortunately there have been few (non-routine) studies which have attempted to fill this yawning information gap, but it is possible to piece together an almost complete jigsaw of costs.

Recruitment costs

The task of recruiting, selecting, training and 'matching' foster families with foster children will always be time-consuming, and particularly so when seeking placements for children with special or 'difficult' needs. The Audit Commission's Child Care Report (1985, Appendix 13) included a hypothetical costing of these overhead and associated costs based on assumptions about what they call the 'man-days' required for publicity, field enquiries, assessment, visiting and placement. At today's prices (1989) the Audit Commission's illustrative costs amount to £14 per child week, averaged across all fostered children. Other evidence has concentrated on the costs of finding placements for identified children, that is estimating the 'lump sum' costs of placement. The London Borough of Wandsworth (1977) costed the placement of eight adolescents with foster parents at £2400 (1989 prices), rather smaller than the estimated £8500 for finding permanent placements for 'special needs' children in The Child Wants a Home project run by the Children's Society (Thoburn, Murdoch and O'Brien, 1986) and the £10 000 for Essex County Council's three home-finding units, again making permanent placements (Wedge, 1986). If we take these last two figures and assume the average duration of placement to be four years, these lump sum costs are equivalent to about £50 per child per week. This is over and above the boarding out payments and other costs. This figure refers to the 'harder-to-place' children, and a cost closer to £20 per week will be more accurate for the 'typical' foster child.

If we are to include these recruitment costs in a comparison of foster and residential care placements then we must also take into the reckoning some appropriate estimates of the costs of recruiting residential care staff and matching children in care to the available residential vacancies. We are not aware of any figures for such costs, beyond the anecdotal, though we would be surprised if they exceeded the costs of recruiting and matching foster parents. This must remain an hypothesis for subsequent study.

Social worker and other service costs

Each fostered child should be on the caseload of a social worker, and many foster families will have their 'own' social worker providing support and supervision. Obviously practices vary from authority to authority and from one voluntary organization to another, but social work support is always going to be an important component of a foster care programme. Evidence of the size of this component comes from two studies conducted in

1982–83: a one-year longitudinal study of children admitted into the care of Suffolk County Council and a cross-sectional study (with one-year follow-up) of all children in family placements in the care of a London borough. The Suffolk study took a cohort of admissions to care and followed them until the end of their care period or for one year, whichever was the shorter. Costs were calculated from information gathered during interviews with case holders at four points during the year. The London study was based on a one-day census of all children in family placements, following each of them until their placement changed (including discharge from care) or for one year, again whichever was the shorter.

For those Suffolk children entering care and spending the whole of their care periods (or the whole of the first year) in foster placements, the 'hidden costs' ranged from a very small proportion of the boarding out payments to a large multiple. Hidden costs averaged 176 per cent of the directly recorded boarding out rates, but could be as much as 360 per cent for those children in care for only a few days. These costs are averaged over the full care period or full first year. The London study does not focus specifically on admissions to care, and some children in the sample had been in the care of the authority, and often also in the same placement, for six years. The costs are based on services received over a four-month period. Except in a few cases this did not include the start of a care period or placement, so the results are not strictly comparable with those for Suffolk. But the London Borough results demonstrate that the hidden costs can be substantial when compared with the boarding out payments even after many years of placement. It is well known from other studies that social worker inputs to all placement types decline over time (Millham, Bullock, Hosie and Haak, 1986). This was also found to be the case in these two single-authority studies, but the directly provided 'support' costs – field social worker and fostering officer time, other social care services, health and education inputs where associated with child care needs and so on – can cost far more than the boarding out payments themselves for short care periods, and certainly remain high for the longest periods. A conservative estimate would put these particular 'hidden' costs at more than 50 per cent of the average boarding out payment for a typical cross-section of children in foster placements, to which must be added the recruitment costs and others. The lion's share of these costs is claimed by social worker and fostering officer time and proponents of an expanded foster care proportion should not overlook these 'burdens', nor their implications for placement supervision and quality assurance, particularly in the early days of a new placement.

Equivalent 'hidden' costs may be computed for residential care. Again, almost every child in a residential home – whether local authority, voluntary or private – should, and mostly will, be on the caseload of a field social worker, and many will receive special health and education services not provided within the budget of the residential facility. Thus, the currently reported costs of residential care must be supplemented with data on the non-residential elements of care packages if we are to take a consistent line with foster care. Evidence on these hidden costs comes from two sources: the Suffolk cohort study cited earlier and a special collection in Mid Glamorgan in 1983 (Knapp, 1986a; Knapp and Baines, 1987). The costs of residential care packages fluctuated in response to a number of factors, especially residential home and duration of placement. For example, the Mid Glamorgan findings revealed that children resident in a 'non-specialist' community home received services not funded from the home's own budget which were equivalent to 30 per cent of the direct costs of a community home (revenue costs plus an imputed capital cost element) for children in the home for less than three months, and 13 per cent for children resident for three months or more. The hidden costs for 'specialist' residential homes were proportionately smaller. In observation and assessment centres, for example, the proportions were 12 per cent for children resident for less than three months, and 7 per cent for longer-term residents.

If we pull these figures together – and we should do so only with caution given our earlier advice only to compare like with like – we find that in absolute terms the hidden costs of foster and residential care are not greatly different for placements lasting more than three months. The biggest difference comes in short-term placements. Here the average hidden costs of foster care were approximately £60 per week in Suffolk in 1982–83 – roughly £82 at 1989 prices – considerably larger than the equivalent figures for the Mid Glamorgan residential sample. The major element of hidden cost, field social worker time (including fostering officer time if authorities have separately designated posts), also differs significantly between foster and residential care. This finding is at variance with Hazel's (1981) assumption of equivalence of the field social work inputs into these two care varieties and with the Audit Commission's (1985, Appendix 13) conclusion from data collected in three areas. Notice that these indirect costs of foster and residential care do not include the administrative and senior management overheads for which no data currently exist but which are unlikely to be of such a magnitude or distribution as to influence greatly the differences between services.

Foster family costs

Many London and Metropolitan boroughs find they cannot recruit enough foster families within the authority boundaries. Boarding out is often possible only some distance from a child's home area, and the boroughs find themselves competing with other authorities in order to recruit families, usually by offering higher rates. In these circumstances, simplistic criticisms of local authorities for not boarding out enough children ('bad child care') or for paying excessive boarding out rates ('bad economics') are dangerous. There is a supply constraint. The expansion of foster care as an alternative to (some) residential care is crucially dependent on an adequate supply of foster families. As local authorities try to raise their foster care proportions they have to find placements for children with special and demanding needs, and higher boarding out rates will have to be paid. These higher payments are intended to compensate for what the DHSS called the 'wear and tear' of fostering but they raise the question of whether 'rewards' should be paid (they were abhorred by the Curtis Committee) and still stimulate fears of baby-farming and criticisms of inequity (Hill, 1987).

The problem is that foster families bear costs which require adequate compensation. A little-known US study by Culley, Settles and Van Name (1976) suggested that these foster family costs were of three kinds. There are direct costs, which are the out-of-pocket expenses incurred in raising a foster child. These are likely to be higher than the costs of raising a child in their 'birth' family because of the felt need to compensate for deprivation or to continue a material standard of living enjoyed in a residential home. These direct costs are calculated annually for Britain by the National Foster Care Association. Second, there are indirect costs, the opportunity costs to families of forgoing work (and its income) or leisure (and its implicit value). Of course, indirect costs of this kind arise for all children, fostered or not, although different children will make different demands on parents. Low wage rates in many labour markets, particularly for women, reduce the opportunity cost of paid work outside the home. Third, there are what Culley *et al.* call the non-economic costs, which include the time and effort the family members put into raising children that does not compete with the family's money making activities (1976, p. 3). The psychic costs of fostering would be included here. These non-economic costs are likely to be higher for children with special needs or characteristics (hyperactivity, delinquency, enuresis and so on) and for 'inclusive fostering', which encourages the involvement of the foster child's birth parents to the full.

There are direct, indirect and non-economic costs associated with each and every foster placement, but the important policy datum is the amount needed to compensate a family for such costs. We would generally expect the latter to be rather smaller than the former because of the joy associated with bringing up children. The benefits will be greater for some families than for others and may be related to the characteristics of the children fostered. This is one reason why some families currently foster and the majority do not. What we have, in effect, is a supply of foster families dependent upon a number of factors, one of which is the boarding out rate. That some foster families are prepared to accept boarding out payments which are below full costs should not be an excuse for complacency nor a reason to maintain boarding out rates at their present level. There can be few local authorities which have a more than sufficient supply of potential foster families and/or which would not benefit from having a wider choice of families to match with the needs of children in care. A number of studies have identified foster child and foster family characteristics correlated with a high breakdown propensity – recently Berridge and Cleaver (1987) and Fenyo, Knapp and Baines (1989), and of course Parker (1966) in his seminal study – which local authorities and voluntary agencies would do well to note when matching children with families. Might it be the case, perhaps, that a marginally higher boarding out payment would have reduced the breakdown rate among certain families? And surely a higher payment level would encourage a larger supply from which to make more effective matches?

Child characteristics

If we were to aggregate each of the costs identified above we would find that, on average, foster care is still a less expensive care option than residential care, although the difference between the two is somewhat narrower than the routinely available statistics would have us believe. But there remains at least one major problem. Comparisons made 'on average' are simply not appropriate. Children accommodated in residential homes are different in many ways from children boarded out. They are likely to be regarded as 'more difficult' or demanding: they are more likely to have physical or mental handicaps, delinquent tendencies or backgrounds, emotional or behavioural characteristics such as aggression, hyperactivity or propensity to self-mutilation, and to be older. But these characteristics are associated with higher costs in both residential care (see Knapp and Smith, 1985; Knapp, 1986b) and foster placements (Knapp and Fenyo, 1989). At least some of today's cost difference between residential and foster care can therefore be laid at the door of different clienteles. If today's residential care population were to be transplanted overnight into foster placements, the boarding out payments, social worker and other support needed per child would have to be a lot higher than the average needed for today's foster care population.

In other words, the average costs of residential and foster care presently available do not compare like with like. The implications for policy should be clear. In projecting the savings to be reaped from a switch from residential to foster care, the Audit Commission (1985, Appendix 18) assumed that the costs of the latter do not vary with respect to numbers of children fostered and their characteristics. This would not appear to be the case, so their model exaggerates the savings to local authorities. The need for like-with-like comparisons of costs is paramount. If, as research has shown, the costs of both foster and residential placements increase with 'difficulty', and if, as most people believe, today's foster care population is less difficult on average than the residential population (Millham *et al.*, 1986; Parker, 1988; Vernon and Fruin, 1986), then comparisons of today's cost averages will exaggerate the difference between the two services. The extent of the exaggeration is not possible to quantify precisely but the proven sensitivity of costs to the characteristics of children suggests it could be considerable.

This does not mean that it is necessarily wrong on financial grounds to plan the expansion of foster care and the gradual contraction of the residential child care sector. What it means is that the commonly employed cost argument for this expansion seriously underestimates the future costs of foster care and dangerously exaggerates the savings that will flow from changes in the balance of care. If the funding base for social care services is fragile, these *real* future costs could have unfortunate implications for the development of child care and for its effectiveness, particularly in the provision of adequate resources, human and other, to achieve reasonable success.

5 Intermediate treatment and its alternatives

In the case of residential and foster care services – the two principal options for children who cannot be accommodated with their parents – most of the key decisions are taken by local authority social services departments and most of the resource consequences will be felt by those same agencies. Certainly the NHS, local education departments, voluntary organizations, and children and families themselves will bear some of the costs of the different care packages, but the largest share falls to statutory social services. Even in these circumstances – with one agency responsible for most decisions and (in principle) the same agency able to monitor the resource effects – we have seen how easy it is for agencies to fall back on only very poor costs data, and we have also seen the dangers of doing so. The same problems arise in the second area of child care we have chosen to illustrate here, but with added complications. Services for juvenile offenders and their families are by no means predominantly provided by local authority social services departments, and a great many of the crucial decisions are taken by magistrates. The overlapping child care and juvenile justice systems are therefore both complex and subject to additional influences and constraints (see Chapter 10). The pursuit of efficiency in the utilization of available resources and services becomes much more difficult. Indeed, the very criterion of efficiency becomes less important in many circumstances. Paradoxically, perhaps, this heightens the need for good quality cost information and for its sensible employment.

In the Personal Social Services Research Unit we have been undertaking research for some years on the costs and cost-effectiveness of intermediate treatment, custodial sentences, community service orders, youth treatment centre provision and other placements for juvenile offenders. Some of that work is as yet incomplete – the Department-of-Health-funded longitudinal study of intermediate treatment (IT) and its alternatives continues until 1990 – and some of our work remains confidential, but a number of valuable cost insights can be reported. In every one of these research activities we have found poor financial information which can easily mislead, yet we have also found a strong and growing demand for cost perspectives on policy and practice decisions. We can discuss these cost and cost-effectiveness issues under three headings. First we describe the disaggregation of the costs of IT, and then we report the comparative costs of alternative placements. Finally we reflect on the fragmentation of responsibilities and the influence of costs on policy.

Disaggregating the costs of IT

The way in which average costs are calculated is by simply taking a particular cost head and dividing it by some indicator of the amount of 'care activity', which usually means the number of clients. This tends to be unsatisfactory for two reasons. First, the initial cost head may wrongly include or exclude certain items. Capital or maintenance costs may be excluded, or some cost components which are included may actually benefit clients or activities other than the one in question. For example an IT centre may have facilities which are used by a nursery group, or may house an area team. Second, within a particular service such as IT different groups of clients will place differential burdens on the service. Many IT centres offer services as an alternative to custody as well as 'preventive' work for youngsters 'at risk' of offending or of a custodial sentence. An 'average' becomes fairly meaningless in this context. It is essential to disaggregate costs by breaking down expenditure into activities or client groups.

We can illustrate this disaggregation by reporting a small research study which examined the cost of IT in Tameside metropolitan borough (Knapp and Robertson, 1986). There is a single IT centre within Tameside. We were interested in the costs of different programmes provided within the centre and with the costs of the alternative care services that IT youngsters would otherwise have received. It was not possible to include an effectiveness component in this particular study, although this is needed to inform policy properly. The juvenile justice system is managed and serviced by different agencies. In recent years, IT work – particularly within social services departments – has come to include servicing of the system. IT work in Tameside, for example, includes courtwork, writing reports and representing the social services departments in court, dealing with remand cases, diversionary work (which involves monitoring referrals and recommendations to prevent the problem of 'net widening'), juvenile panel attendance, and case-holding (carrying with it statutory responsibilities as well as direct work with young people). IT workers carrying out these functions relieve other parts of the authority and other agencies from these tasks. In the examination of the resources going into IT it was therefore important to take account of these intricate system effects. For example, a young person who receives a custodial sentence will also have had the 'benefit' of services from the IT team, such as the preparation of a social inquiry report or supervision, without necessarily receiving any IT as such. In other words, the clients of the IT services in Tameside include at least all those young people who come into contact with the police, and not just those who subsequently received an IT requirement.

The method we developed in this study distinguished four main areas of work by the IT team: courtwork, groupwork, individual one-to-one work, and casework.

As we move from courtwork to casework, so the size of the relevant client population diminishes. To the available accounting costs we added the hidden costs and indirect agency costs. The total cost of running the IT centre was then divided between these four activities according to the staff time and resources devoted to them. It was then possible, having obtained the number of cases held by IT officers, the number of court cases in the borough, and the number of groupwork and individual sessions run in the IT centre to calculate four constituent average costs: the cost per court case, the cost per young person receiving IT groupwork, the cost per individual session and the cost per case held by IT staff.

This allows the total cost of a package of services to be calculated, picking up individual variations in service given to the different groups of youngsters served by the Tameside IT centre. Extending the length of an IT requirement or moving from groupwork to more one-to-one work with youngsters referred by the courts could be costed quite easily. It was also possible to cost the transfer of caseholding responsibilities from fieldwork staff to IT staff, and to calculate the implications of IT social workers acting as court liaisons for the whole authority. The cost implications in each case will be small but can still represent large proportions of available discretionary resources within, say, social work teams. Thus the disaggregation of costs is helpful for a number of purposes.

Comparative costs

We next looked at each IT client over a one-year period and in discussions with IT staff assigned him or her to a category representing the alternative disposal which would have been made in the absence of IT. These alternatives were: community home with education, community home, supervision order, or detention centre, and for each we attempted to calculate the costs that would most likely have been incurred. Costing these alternatives presented some difficulties. For residential care we were able to make use of the local average operating costs for community homes with education and other community homes, to which we added a proportion to represent 'hidden costs' such as visits by social workers, assessment, administrative support and so on (see Section 4 above). A similar exercise was possible to calculate supervision order costs having already obtained information about contact time between supervisor and young person. Average weekly operating costs in custodial establishments are published annually by the Home Office. The figures for detention centres and youth custody centres demonstrate considerable variation in average cost (as do other prison establishments), but for the purposes of this study we made use of the average detention centre figure.

Total cost per sentence for IT and the alternatives are given in Table 1 below. IT is cheaper than all its alternatives with the exception of the straight supervision order. In some cases, the cost difference between IT and the ordinary supervision order could be argued to be the 'price' of ineffective gatekeeping or net widening. Compared with custody, IT is cheaper even though the sentence is longer. On a weekly basis the results are unchanged although the magnitudes are affected. These weekly costs are also given in Table 1.

In order to calculate the global average cost of IT across all client groups served it is necessary to weight these costs by the numbers of clients in each category. This gives an average cost per 'IT sentence' which is roughly £3230 at 1988–89 prices compared to the weighted average cost for the alternatives at the substantially larger figure of £5930. There are shortcomings in this research. Post-sentence (licence and supervision) costs were not included. Simplifications were necessary as well as 'guestimates'. The study covered only a single local authority area, and the individual packages were based on 'typical' or 'representative' clients. Nevertheless the method does attempt to deal with some of the complexities of costing a service which sits in the centre of a complex system.

On the strength of this evidence it seems that IT is cheaper than either residential care or custody, but that a cost premium is attached to providing IT services to those young people who have been pulled 'up-tariff' or who would otherwise have received a less intensive form of intervention.

Does relative cost influence policy?

The long-held assumption of a cost advantage for IT has been shown to be supported by the available evidence, although – as ever – the cost difference is not as simple as some arguments suggest. There is, however, virtually no comprehensive, valid evidence of the relative effectiveness of custodial, residential and community-based treatment or care programmes for youngsters with offending histories (see Rutter and Giller, 1983). A research team at the Institute of Criminology, University of Cambridge, is currently researching the question of relative effectiveness. Until their results are available, we must work with the common notion that IT is at least as effective as the available alternatives for the majority of youngsters. Under this assumption, IT looks particularly cost-effective, and we might have expected this to have influenced sentencing or placement patterns.

Whilst the residential child care populations in most areas in the country have been declining, the custodial population has followed a different trend. It is difficult with available statistics to examine anything other than national sentencing patterns but these seem to indicate that whilst the level of juvenile crime has remained fairly constant, the rate of custodial

Table 1 The costs of intermediate treatment and its alternatives (Tameside Study, 1984–85)

	Alternatives to IT specified for Tameside clients			
Service and cost base	Supervision Order	Community Home	Comm. Home with Education	Detention Centre
Total cost per 'sentence':				
Intermediate treatment	1894	3640	7487	3727
Alternative service	986	12124	19718	5878
Weekly cost:				
Intermediate treatment	36	70	144	77
Alternative service	19	357	379	587

Weighted average cost per 'sentence': intermediate treatment £3230
alternative services £5930

All prices are inflated from 1984–85 levels (as used in the original study) to 1988–89 prices using the public administration earnings index (Department of Employment) sentencing has been increasing. Many people hoped that the development of IT would have had more of an impact. There will, of course, be areas where IT has had a marked impact on the use of custody, but the overall level of influence still appears to be slight. If anything, IT may have been more successful in reducing the number of care orders. There are obviously constraints which prevent local authorities and other agencies from providing sufficient IT for all those young people who might conceivably benefit from this type of provision. But problems can also arise in the contrary situation, where 'too much' provision is available (Robertson and Knapp, 1988).

Insufficient IT provision is not a surprise. Most social services of which child care is part, it might be argued, are supplied in sufficient quantities to meet basic demands upon them. Even if savings are realized, however, by the closure of, say, residential child care establishments, hard pressed social services departments are quite likely to bow to the pressures of a growing elderly population or the need for preventive work with child sexual abuse problems rather than use the resources to create community alternatives to custody. In the competition for resources young offenders come low on the list of popular causes. In addition, IT is as much an alternative to custody as it is to residential child care, and the savings generated by reducing the custodial population will not fall to the social services department but to the prison department. Thus the financial incentives which might persuade local authorities to sink funds into IT are few. This applies particularly to services for young people at the 'heavy end', where the alternative is custody. The development of IT of this kind has been *in spite* of the financial pressures and incentives rather than because of them.

Surprisingly, perhaps, 'too much' provision may be as problematic as too little. Most of the relevant decisions rest with magistrates, whether under care proceedings or criminal proceedings. IT projects can only be successful if they are seen as such by the judiciary. It may take some time to establish the credibility of IT schemes, especially at the heavy end. Until that credibility is established, projects may run with vacant places. The obvious corollary is that the average cost per client rises and IT then begins to look rather more expensive than expected. This may develop the incentive to fill vacant places. If magistrates cannot be persuaded to change their sentencing patterns quickly there is the danger of 'net widening': young people being drawn into a level of intervention which is inappropriate given the level of offending and the service beginning to provide for a group of clients to whom it was never intended to offer IT. There could be two consequences. First, 'net widening' may lead to what has been inelegantly labelled 'up-tariffing' where young people who have been through an IT programme and commit further offences may face a more severe sentence because they have already received IT, even though it was not necessarily appropriate. They effectively jump a step on the sentencing ladder. Second, the services which the young people would have received had they not been on an IT programme could well have been cheaper. For example, the Tameside results indicate that a straight supervision order is cheaper than one accompanied by IT.

The IT projects with low numbers of clients relative to capacity are left with a dilemma: if they stick to their criteria for accepting young people on to an IT programme they stand accused of running a very costly programme. If they allow lower-end offenders on to the programme they can accelerate young people through the sentencing ladder and can again stand accused of being costly in comparison with the service alternatives. This dilemma shows clearly how financial incentives and limited cost information can influence practice in a way which hinders the development of the service and may be detrimental to young people. Nothing can be done except for IT practitioners to continue to work toward influencing and persuading magistrates to change sentencing patterns over time. The temptation for management will be to cut back IT provision, but managers must be prepared to bear the high average costs of IT in the short run in order to reap the client and resource benefits in the long run.

The problems that arise with too much or too little provision follow from the fragmentation of responsibility and funding. Although magistrates make the final decisions, the availability of effective and credible alternatives to custody can influence them. One way to help during the slow and expensive build-up of a credible IT project would be for central government to provide bridging funds. This policy was adopted in 1983 with the launch of the so-called DHSS LAC 83(3) initiative, which provided £15 million to finance local alternatives to custody. As well as helping to develop and adapt services to meet the demands of magistrates and young people the initiative also raised the general profile of IT. The initiative was less successful in that it did not recognize the 'start-up' period in which take-up may be below expectations and costs somewhat above them. The start-up period in fact extended for some years, generating difficulties when local authorities were asked to pick up the tab.

Nevertheless, if local authorities are expected to provide IT at all, whether through central government initiative or in the normal course of provision, they must be given some incentive other than that they are offering a generally preferred option to custody and residential care for young people within their areas, and quite substantial savings for the Home Office Prison Department. One such incentive might be to make local authorities responsible for meeting the cost of young people in custody (see, for example, the discussion in House of Commons Social Services Committee, 1984). There would need to be an appropriate adjustment to the rate support grant and these extra grant payments could be made according to some definition of need. In these circumstances local authorities would be much more likely to respond to the relative cost-effectiveness of IT and invest more in the development of alternatives to custody. Another route to achieve the same financial incentives would be to transfer the ownership or management of young offender custodial establishments to local authorities. What such a policy would do for the blood pressure of some backbench Tory MPs is beyond comprehension, but in the politically charged atmosphere surrounding the oft-proposed 'privatization' of Britain's prisons such transfers – were they desired by local authorities – might not seem quite as absurd as they may once have appeared. In either case, however, increasing the financial incentives to local authorities to provide more IT will only take us some way towards the balance of provision desired by many people. Decisions still rest with magistrates and sentencing patterns tend to change only slowly in the absence of legislative reforms.

The available evidence suggests that IT is cheaper than both custody and residential care, and may well be a cost-effective way of dealing with many young offenders who currently receive custodial sentences. Public resources could be more efficiently employed. Somehow these resources need to be transferred, but the political and organizational barriers are daunting. Efficiency cannot be achieved simply by pushing resources into the community without an accompanying diversionary pull of young people away from custody.

6 Voluntary and private residential homes

One interesting feature of the search for value for money or efficiency in public policy has been a more focused consideration of the contributions to be made by the private and voluntary sectors. In fact, there is little evidence as to the relative efficiency of the different sectors, even though many central and local policies are predicated on the belief that 'privatization' of public services is a good thing. Of course, cost differences between the public and non-public sectors can only be part of any debate as to the advisability of changing the balance of provision or funding. The justifications for a greater reliance on the voluntary ('non-profit') and private ('for profit') sectors include the assumptions of greater flexibility and innovative potential, the promotion of consumer choice and opportunities for participation, the encouragement of the specialization, and the development of citizen and policy advocacy (Knapp *et al.*, 1989, Chapter 10). For the purposes of this chapter, however, we will concentrate on the cost dimension. We will also be concentrating on just one form of 'privatization': the contracting-out of residential child care, whereby the legal responsibility (and most, if not all, of the financial burden) rests with local authorities, but the child care services are actually provided and managed on a day-to-day basis by voluntary and private agencies.

We must stress again that cost is only one of a number of relevant considerations in policy design and practice response, but it is relevant. Even if other criteria are far more important, there are still three questions to be answered. Are the costs of residential child care identical in the public, voluntary and private sectors? If not, why are they different? If there are identifiable reasons for the cost differences, what implications do they have for a policy which encourages contracting-out?

Inter-sectoral cost differences

The short answer to the first of these questions is that the costs of residential child care are certainly not identical across the sectors. A survey conducted by one of the authors in 1983, covering nearly 800 residential establishments for children, revealed marked inter-sectoral differences. At 1988–89 prices, for example, 'non-specialist' community homes in the local authority sector within the survey sample cost an average of £245 per resident week to run. (Capital costs are excluded for the moment.) This compares with average costs of £181 in the voluntary sector and average fees of £170 in the private sector. (Note that these are 1982–83 costs inflated to 1988–89 prices; the actual costs and fees today could well be very different for a variety of reasons which we cannot discuss here.) These figures conceal wide variations, within the sectors: for these same 'non-specialist' community homes in the local authority sector the highest cost home was more than three times as expensive as the lowest cost home.

It is these *within* sector cost variations which provide us with a route to the explanation of *between* sector differences. It is possible to 'explain' statistically the cost variations between, say, different local authority homes in terms of differences in scale (larger homes may be cheaper, other things being equal), occupancy, location (salaries are higher in London), the range of services offered, the characteristics of residents and one or two other factors (see Knapp and Smith, 1985; Knapp, 1986b, 1987). These cost-influencing characteristics of homes, areas and residents do not account for all the observed variation, but they take us a long way towards the qualification of the kind of bare statistics published annually by CIPFA and move us towards like-with-like comparisons. But once we have admitted that cost variations within each of the three sectors are partly attributable to these various factors, might they not also be relevant to the discussion of between-sector variations?

The sources of inter-sectoral cost differences

This is precisely the approach taken in some earlier PSSRU research (described in more detail in Knapp, *et al.*, 1989, Chapter 9). Having made the necessary adjustments for accounting and definitional differences between the sectors it was possible to identify the following sources of the observed inter-sectoral cost differences: home size; proportion of available places occupied; child characteristics; service diversification (i.e. provision of day care, day education, base for area social work team, etc.); location (more local authority homes are located in London); staff motivations (voluntary and private organizations are able to employ staff at lower salaries without any discernible short-term impact on quality of care or child outcomes); child care outcomes themselves; and 'competition' among the non-public sectors for local authority placements. Some of these factors were of only limited relevance – size, occupancy, child characteristics and service range variations made little difference – and the residual difference begins to look like an efficiency difference.

Implications for contracting-out

Contracting-out of residential child care is certainly not new – the voluntary organizations predate the public in the provision of child care services *per se* – and the local authority children's departments established in 1948 were intially heavily reliant on the voluntary sector to provide residential services. Since those early post-war days the proportion of children in residential care who are accommodated in voluntary (or private) homes has fallen steadily. What our cost research suggests is that at today's relatively small scale of operation, the voluntary and private sectors offer efficiency alternatives to the public. That is, they appear to provide good quality services at lower cost.

Local authorities respond to this cost difference. We have, for example, been looking at the numbers of children placed in voluntary homes by different local authorities across England. We found that a 10 per cent increase of voluntary home fees relative to local authority costs will generate a six per cent fall in the proportion of a local authority's residential child care population placed in voluntary sector establishments (Knapp, *et al.*, 1989, Chapter 10). There is, it would appear, a price-responsiveness among local authorities.

These findings are, we believe, robust. But they reflect *today's* circumstances: at the scale of operation to be found in the 1980s, suitably regulated contracting-out, probably on a fee-for-service basis, can enhance efficiency. But contracting-out is not the simple answer to a *purportedly* over-bureaucratic, trade-union dominated, inflexible and unresponsive public sector. At its present scale it is likely to offer some long-term efficiency gains, without upsetting other policy objectives. Whilst they can be exaggerated, these efficiency gains undoubtedly exist and have implications for all three formal sectors, in so far as there are efficiency-generating features of private and voluntary agencies which could, with advantage, be adopted by the public sector. But there must be doubts about the durability of this efficiency difference should there be moves substantially to increase the relative scale of the non-statutory contribution of residential care.

For a start, voluntary organizations, and to a lesser extent private sector agencies, rely quite heavily on the services of highly motivated staff who accept salaries which are lower than in the public sector. But they do so to a lesser extent than used to be the case, and there would certainly be difficulties recruiting a large number of additional staff with similar motivations in order to take over a greater proportion of the residential child care sector. Second, many voluntary organizations subsidise local authority placements by charging fees which are well below the full costs of provision, and many private children's homes charge low fees because proprietors take only a low salary (in return for capital gains) and rely heavily on the support of family members in running establishments. To a degree these are short-term responses to the contracting residential child care sector and the falling numbers of children placed in non-statutory homes by local authorities. That is, they are 'competitive responses' to recent changes, and we would not expect them to be sustainable over long periods. Third, the costs of contracting, regulation and support are borne by the public sector placing agency. Large-scale contracting-out – as we have recently seen for residential and nursing home care for elderly people – can impose high public sector costs because of both the scale of the monitoring and contracting task and the greater risk of divergent objectives and scandals. Finally, and a direct consequence of this greater regulation, it has been observed in many service contexts that the greater the proportion of services contracted-out by government agencies, the tighter the restrictions on non-public service providers and the greater the degree of 'institutional isomorphism' or conceptual similarity. Contracting-out tends to *reduce* rather than increase the organizational, quality and outcome differences between sectors (see DiMaggio and Powell, 1983; Knapp, Robertson and Thomason, 1989).

7 Costs and the child care process

Child care is demonstrably complex. It is governed by a bewildering body of ancient and modern legislation. It is organized mainly from a local authority social services department base, but is heavily influenced by decisions taken by education departments, the NHS, the judiciary and various non-statutory agencies. It must take on board the often conflicting expectations of children, their birth families, staff or informal carers, and the general public. It must not simply respond to expressed needs or demands, but must also prevent unnecessary suffering or deprivation, and in performing each of these tasks it must always bear the criticisms of those who believe, often vociferously, that doing nothing would have been a better option. In this chapter we have argued that it is because of this complexity that costs information is needed – even if the demands of a costs perspective seem at first to increase the complexity further. We have illustrated how sensibly defined and appropriately measured costs can help to cut through parts of this complex system to point the way to the efficient utilization of available resources.

The evaluation of cost in the provision of any kind of social service has always rested uncomfortably among the rather grander and more appealing evaluations of effectiveness, service delivery and quality of care. Cost evaluations are often seen, sometimes rightly but usually not, as somehow subordinate to other concerns. An attitude often expressed in the austere economic climate of the last few years is that cost considerations should not override welfare matters; no price should be attached to improving the lives of children and families. Laudable and desirable as that may be as an ideology; in practice it is unworkable and, to be sure, unethical. There will never be enough money in any agency's budget to enable it to carry out all the programmes of activity or care that it wants to provide. The economic reality is that resources are limited and there is competition for what is available. The ability and potential for developing services depends a great deal on the ability to command resources. For social services departments to make best use of the resources at their disposal they need to be cognizant not merely of the effectiveness of service options (the impact on the welfare of children and families) but also the cost-effectiveness. In this chapter we have shown how cost information and cost research, properly coupled to effectiveness and other relevant criteria, can feed into child care policy and service development processes. We have suggested how it is possible to procure cost information which is both reliable and accurate to ensure that only correct signals are transmitted to policy makers and managers.

It is not necessary for every child care professional to be able to plan and conduct a comprehensive cost or cost-effectiveness analysis for every policy or practice option. But it is necessary for every child care professional to be aware of the meaning and validity of the costs evidence and associated arguments which today have such an influence on child care policies and practices.

References

Audit Commission (1985) *Child Care Report*, Audit Commission.

Audit Inspectorate (1981) *The Provision of Child Care: A Study of Eight Local Authorities in England and Wales*, Department of the Environment.

Berridge, D. and Cleaver, H. (1987) *Foster Home Breakdown*, Basil Blackwell.

Chartered Institute of Public Finance and Accountancy (1988) *Personal Social Services Statistics 1988–89, Estimates*, CIPFA.

Culley, J. D., Settles, B. H. and Van Name, J. B. (1976) *Understanding and Measuring the Costs of Foster Family Care*, Bureau of Economic and Business Research, University of Delaware.

DiMaggio, P. and Powell, W. W. (1983) 'Institutional isomorphism', *American Sociological Review*, Vol. 48, pp. 147–60.

Fenyo, A. J., Knapp, M. R. J. and Baines, B. (1989) 'Foster care breakdown', Discussion Paper 616, Personal Social Services Research Unit, University of Kent at Canterbury.

Hazel, N. (1981) *A Bridge to Independence*, Basil Blackwell.

Hill, M. (1987) 'Payments for adopted children – right or wrong?', *Journal of Social Policy*, Vol. 16, No. 4, pp. 461–88.

Home Office (1952) Circular 258/52, November.

House of Commons Social Services Committee (1984) *Children in Care*, HCP 360, HMSO.

Knapp, M. R. J. (1984) *The Economics of Social Care*, Macmillan.

Knapp, M. R. J. (1986a) 'The field social work implications of residential child care', *British Journal of Social Work*, Vol. 16, No. 1, pp. 25–48.

Knapp, M. R. J. (1986b) 'The relative cost-effectiveness of public, voluntary and private providers of residential child care', in Culyer, A. J. and Jonsson, B. (eds) *Public and Private Health Services*, Basil Blackwell.

Knapp, M. R. J. (1987) 'Private children's homes: an analysis of fee variations and a comparison with public sector costs', *Policy and Politics*, Vol. 16, No. 1, pp. 221–34.

Knapp, M. R. J. and Baines, B. (1987) 'Hidden cost multipliers for residential child care', *Local Government Studies*, Vol. 13, No. 4, pp. 53–73.

Knapp, M. R. J. with Baines, B., Fenyo, A. J. and Robertson, E. (1989) *The Costs of Child Care*, Gower.

Knapp, M. R. J. and Fenyo, A. F. (1989) 'Economic perspectives on foster care', in Carter, P., Jeffs, T. and Smith, M. (eds) *Social Work and Social Welfare Yearbook 1989*, Open University Press.

Knapp, M. R. J. and Robertson, E. (1986) 'Has intermediate treatment proved cost-effective?', in Harrison, A. and Gretton, J. (eds) *Crime UK 1986*, Policy Journals.

Knapp, M. R. J., Robertson, E. and Thomason, C. (1989) 'Public money, voluntary action: whose welfare?', in Anheier, H. and Seibel, W. (eds) *The Nonprofit Sector: International and Comparative Perspectives*, de Gruyter.

Knapp, M. R. J. and Smith, J. (1985) 'The costs of residential child care: explaining variations in the public sector', *Policy and Politics*, Vol. 13, No. 2, pp. 127–54.

London Borough of Wandsworth (1977) 'Adolescent boarding-out project: an evaluation report', Mimeograph.

Millham, S., Bullock, R., Hosie, K. and Haak, M. (1986) *Lost in Care*, Gower.

Parker, R. A. (1966) *Decisions in Child Care*, George Allen and Unwin.

Parker, R. A. (1988) 'Residential care for children', in Sinclair, I. (ed) *Residential Care: The Research Reviewed* (Volume 2 of the Wagner Committee Report), HMSO.

Robertson, E. and Knapp, M. R. J. (1988) 'Promoting intermediate treatment: a problem of excess demand or excess supply?', *British Journal of Social Work*, Vol. 18, Supplement, pp. 131–47.

Rutter, M. and Giller, H. (1983) *Juvenile Delinquency: Trends and Perspectives*, Penguin.

Seebohm Committee (1970) *Report of the Committee on Local Authority and Allied Social Services*, Cmnd 3703, HMSO.

Sinclair, I. (ed) (1988) *Residential Care: The Research Reviewed*, HMSO.

Thoburn, J., Murdoch, A. and O'Brien, A. (1986) *Permanence in Child Care*, Basil Blackwell.

Vernon, J. and Fruin, D. (1986) *In Care: A Study of Social Work Decision Making*, National Children's Bureau.

Wagner, G. (chair) (1988) *Residential Care: A Positive Choice*, HMSO.

Wedge, P. (1986) 'Family finding in Essex', in Wedge, P. and Thoburn, J. (eds) *The Hard to Place Experience*, British Agencies for Adoption and Fostering.

15 Theme and variations

Roy Parker

The theme of this book has been the need to ensure that the findings of research are applied to the development of policy and practice in child care. In this final chapter that objective is reiterated and four further variations explored in order to explain some of the structural obstacles that stand in the way of its attainment. However, suggestions are also made about how these difficulties might be overcome.

Policy and practice

In discussions about the contribution that research can make, policy and practice are often treated as if they were one and the same. This is misleading because it is plain that the connection between research and policy and that between research and practice are markedly different. Indeed, if we are to understand the difficulties that surround the application of research results to practical affairs the nature of this difference is of the utmost importance.

The recent history of child care research is a history of its closer association with the policy process. Several factors have combined to lead in this direction. At the central government level the adoption of the customer-contractor principle (first enunciated by the Rothschild committee in 1971) together with the reform of the management of research contracts and the setting up of research liaison groups have created a better organized demand for research. Although some of the research that has been commissioned through this machinery has been concerned with the improvement of practice the emphasis has remained on the evaluation and monitoring of policy or on the provision of the information about those matters that are uppermost on the political agenda. Even where the subjects of the sponsored research have dealt with practice issues the moving force behind their selection has been, in the broadest sense, political. That seems to be inevitable as long as the research funded by central government conforms to the customer-contractor principle.

There are other developments that have also served to tie research more closely to the political and policy processes. Most notably there has been the emergence of the efficiency audit which has entailed studies of the performance of various social services departments. In the child care field, for example, the first steps were taken with the publication in 1981 of the report drawn up by staff of the Chief Inspector of Audit in association with the management consultants Arthur Andersen (Audit Inspectorate, 1981). This was an enquiry into the methods and costs of child care in eight local authorities. Since then there have been other examples, both nationally and locally, of the employment of management consultants or the use of their approach.

The influence of policy considerations upon child care research has also been reflected in the changes that have occurred in the work of the Economic and Social Research Council. In the early days of the Social Science Research Council (as it was called when it was established in 1965) little control was exercised over the kinds of research that were supported except through peer assessment of the proposals submitted. This system lasted until the 1970s when, faced with a reduced budget and under the influence of the Rothschild report, the Council began to take the initiative in setting research priorities. Political pressure mounted for the 'usefulness' of the research that it funded to be clearly demonstrated and this certainly assisted the development of work in fields such as child care. Indeed, an important programme of child care research was launched in 1980 and although the intention was that it should help both policy makers and practitioners the studies that emerged were more readily applicable to the policy field than they were to practice. They highlighted deficiencies and wide variations in practice which, rather than showing how practitioners might improve their work with individual children and families, pointed to the need for the better regulation of practice by management. A good deal of translation and interpretation had to go on in order to make the material accessible to social workers and, even then, its impact remained limited.

Research sections began to be formed in the reorganized social services departments that were established in 1971 in the wake of the deliberations of the Seebohm Committee (Seebohm, 1968). Although progress was uneven a new and important research resource was created. Yet the studies undertaken by these local researchers frequently reflected the concerns of management rather than those of practitioners. Many research units were (and still are) firmly located within management sections and are described as 'providing a service to management'. Certainly, their usefulness in this role has been increasingly recognized. Management has organized and shaped the internal demand for social services research and, to a large extent, determined the level of expenditure and set the priorities. None of this is to be decried. Indeed, it would be hard to see how improved management through better information systems, quality control or the evaluation of policy could be accomplished without some such development. The point is, however, that the demand for research has not come from practitioners and that, in any case, it has been difficult for them to secure a foothold in the commissioning process. The same, of course, can be said of the consumers of the child care services.

It is not that policy makers or managers, whether at the central or the local level, are indifferent to the needs of practitioners, but that they have different priorities. They wrestle with different kinds of problems to those that confront social workers; and it is this difference that creates the initial incompatibility between research for policy and research for practice. Managers are mainly concerned with categories (or at least with how individual cases relate to categories) as well as with decisions that establish patterns of practice and that commit the organization to doing things in certain ways or operating according to certain principles. Their orientation provides the basis for a natural alliance with researchers, for researchers are primarily concerned with the discovery and explanation of patterns of events; with the determination of regularities and irregularities; with the creation and recreation of classifications and, above all, with generalization.

By contrast there is a strong commitment in social work practice to declassification, to individualization and, associated with these things, to a particular view of the way in which decisions are and should be made. There is a long history of according pride of place to the exercise of judgement, to the application of experience and to the use of the insights that are believed to be derived from the close and sympathetic acquaintance with individuals and their problems. In social work, especially where children are involved, cases and decisions tend to be regarded as unique: in the eyes of many practitioners this is as it should be and stands as one of the characteristics of their profession. The idea of a practice judgement still reflects much of what Halmos (1965) called 'the faith of the counsellors'. Indeed, there were long periods during which social work training was mainly aimed at sharpening students' sensitivities to individual predicaments.

Viewed against such a background it is not surprising that research and practice have experienced an uneasy and often mutually unsympathetic relationship. Researchers accuse social workers of not being interested in research whilst practitioners counter that many of the researchers' results are unhelpful, obscure, negative and dispiriting. Unlike local managers or civil servants social workers do not see much value in obtaining general and generalized information. Such information seems to offer them little assistance in their work with individual clients. Even when it does suggest what should be done in difficult circumstances it rarely indicates how it is to be accomplished. Only when social workers enter the arenas of community action or pressure group politics are they more likely to be able to use the kind of generalized information that research has traditionally provided, for in these contexts such information can be deployed to advantage as a source of influence.

If research is to make a greater contribution to practice as well as to policy then the demand for research from practitioners will have to be better organized. This might be done through representative bodies such as the British Association of Social Workers. It might also be achieved by the closer alliance of social workers with researchers, with clients, with other professionals or through their more frequent involvement as researchers. However, the obstacles that stand in the way are formidable. First, social workers have to be convinced that research can be helpful. Secondly, and closely associated with that, they have to develop a clearly articulated agenda of questions that are susceptible to exploration by research. Thirdly, even when these things are achieved practitioners need to command some degree of research purchasing power. Finally, the researchers have got to respond in appropriate ways to practice demands. That will demand changes in the way that questions are conceptualized as well as in matters of design.

However, several things could help to reduce the severity of these obstacles. The willingness of practitioners to ask for the kind of child care research that they want will be encouraged by its demystification. That might be achieved by greater emphasis being placed upon the essential simplicity of research. After all, re-search is, as the word implies, a process of looking again, of being curious, of being interested in surprising patterns, of being able to reflect upon what happens in a systematic fashion and, above all, of having the confidence to adopt a critical attitude towards conventional wisdom, accepted practice or current fashion. Good research does not have to be complicated or necessarily expensive; but making it simple calls for considerable thought about how to pose pertinent yet uncomplicated questions. Indeed, there is much simple research that could (and should) be carried out by social workers alongside their daily practice.

The balance of child care research might be shifted towards practice interests were funding less often controlled by policy and management interests. There are various ways in which their dominance might be reduced, from the participation of practitioners and consumers in the processes that determine what kinds of research are undertaken to the creation of special funds for child care practice research. A trust might be persuaded to support such an initiative.

Nonetheless, a substantial part of child care research is going to remain oriented towards policy; but that does not mean to say that it will be irrelevant to practice. What it does mean is that the material may have to be re-worked and re-presented in ways that make it relevant to issues of practice. This requires the application of the kind of imaginative and interpretative skills that were demonstrated in the 'pink book' *Social Work Decisions in Child Care* (DHSS, 1985).

Paradoxically, perhaps, the failure of policy-oriented research to be of much help to practitioners may be because it has not been directed towards the development of theory. Theories of one kind or another have played an important part in social work education (too much and too uncritically some would say); but where theories – especially theories about behaviour – help to make sense of the otherwise inexplicable, social workers do seem to apply them. We may need more research that is specifically aimed at the development of theory; that is, more basic research that has no immediately obvious benefit to either child care policy or practice and which may, in any case, be developed in disciplines other than social work or social policy.

Finally, the problem of relating research to practice is partly the problem of exceptions. Generalizations accommodate exceptions because they are statements of likelihoods. This is the stock-in-trade of researchers as it is of managers and policy makers; but for the social worker confronted with individual cases, statements about the probabilities of the situation seem to provide no help. This is sometimes because they expect research to supply answers that are universally applicable. That is wishful thinking. The results of research can inform and help to focus judgement, they cannot dispense with the need for it. However, in the quite proper desire to promote the development and use of research we may sometimes over-sell it and in doing so encourage expectations that will almost certainly be disappointed. Both the scale and the sophistication of child care studies are still relatively modest: we must be realistic about what they can contribute.

None of these changes will be achieved easily, for child care research, like so much other social research, is seriously under-funded and under-supported. As a result work is rarely sustained for long enough on any one topic and indeed on any one study. Quick results are at a premium. Research (and especially good research) is a scarce commodity and that being so it is an unfortunate fact that the equally legitimate claims of policy and practice are unlikely to be equally met whilst the demand for research is so much better organized and controlled on the policy side than it is among practitioners.

Categories and comparisons

The 'child care' system is a social construction. A particular group of children is identified as being different in certain respects from other children and, indeed, from adults. They are classified. Yet the categories that we employ for such purposes are typically derived from legal enactments or from the administrative requirements of organizations. They tell their own story of the assumptions, beliefs, values and expediencies that lie behind them. They serve a variety of purposes from helping to resolve the problem of how scarce resources are to be allocated to circumscribing and defining the jobs that people do. They may make little sense to those who are classified and they may be experienced as demeaning or stigmatizing.

There are innumerable ways in which children and their parents are classified. What is of the utmost importance therefore is to recognize the power that a particular classification exercises over the manner in which problems are perceived and solutions sought, as well as the power that it has over the way in which identities, opportunities and handicaps are shaped and consolidated. Of course, we cannot manage without systems of classification but they do tend to narrow our vision. This would not be so bad were it not that categories have a habit of becoming petrified. It is no accident that advocates of change frequently concern themselves with questions of reclassification and with the invention of new terminologies. Knowledge also advances as a result of new ways of seeing things. It does this in large part by reclassification and by the re-examination of the connection between categories that were not previously considered in relationship to each other. In reality, however, researchers are always in danger of accepting or having to work with prevailing categories and definitions because these are frequently the terms in which questions are couched and because much of thc available basic data that they have to build upon have been organized and produced within similar frameworks.

The narrowness and artificiality of confining child care research to the conventionally defined child care system and its problems is clear. Despite the difficulties research must endeavour to shake itself free from this straitjacket. Yet to do so creates something of a dilemma because both managers and social workers are part of the very administrative divisions which research is then liable to transcend. The more that research breaks free from the prevailing operational boundaries in child care the more difficult it becomes for its results to be easily applied, since the action indicated may well fall outside the particular authority of either social workers or policy makers.

Thus, the tendency for good research to seek new categories and to contrive new definitions in the quest for better understanding may well be viewed as complicating problems that are already complicated enough. However, the practical value of not confining the definition of a problem to a particular administrative or service context is at least twofold. First, it is more likely to correspond with the way in which children and parents actually experience their problems and secondly, it may reflect more realistically the case management approach in social work in which the most relevant package of assistance is assembled from diverse sources. For reasons like these child care research that pursues a problem or an issue along lines that lead to destinations outside the currently defined child care system not only advances understanding but can also play a part in ensuring that child care is encouraged to take a less narrow view of its problems and solutions. Let us take a few examples.

One way forward is through the conduct of more comparative studies. With some notable exceptions (Packman, 1986; Colton, 1988) these have been rather scarce in child care. For example, there is an almost complete separation of child care research from education. This is remarkable when one bears in mind that much of the time of 5- to 15-year-old children in care is spent at school. What relation does school have to care and care to school? One could ask the same question – and have as little chance of getting much of an answer – about children at risk who attend day nurseries. Yet the day nursery is regarded as an important factor in the protection of vulnerable children. Is it enough simply to know that they are subject to observation? What do they do in the nurseries? How do they relate to other children? What do the nursery officers think about their progress or about how their parents behave towards them? How does the experience at day nursery or at school impinge upon what happens at home? In a study of children returned home 'on trial' we found an interesting association between the success of the placement and the fact that children attended special schooling; but this was an incidental finding, we did not set out to examine the relation between these two systems and hence could do no more than speculate on what it was about special education that seemed to be beneficial. Was it the smaller classes, the style of teaching or more individual attention? Was it improved attendance? Was it that the children had a better chance of experiencing a sense of achievement? Or was it something about the greater involvement of parents with such schools?

There is a tendency to regard children in care or at risk as different from other children; certainly their families are liable to be considered to be different from other families. The fact is that we do not know how correct or incorrect these assumptions are because very few studies have been mounted that compare the problems and experiences of the 'care group' with other groups. It is indeed strange, for example, that no comparative studies have been made of groups of children in residential care and in boarding schools or, say, between teenage unmarried mothers who are in care and those who are not. Child care research, unlike epidemiologically oriented research has employed few control groups or tried to see the child in care as a reflection of issues and problems that might extend more widely in society but yet be dealt with in a different manner when encountered outside the context of care.

Another way in which a less narrow approach to child care problems and solutions might be encouraged by research is if greater emphasis were placed on longitudinal studies. These are unpopular with those who commission reseach for, by definition, they take a long time to mature and traditionally they have involved the use of large costly cohorts. Although there is nothing much to be done about the duration, longitudinal research can be undertaken on quite a modest scale. The important thing about such studies, however, is that they focus (almost of necessity) upon the evolving careers of children and their families and since these careers inevitably thread their ways through, in and out of and around different administrative systems, such research is not so closely constrained by conventional definitions or short time perspectives. The research follows where the careers lead.

Some of the benefits of such an approach can be seen in the results of a recent study of parental breakdown carried out by Quinton and Rutter (1988). When they looked at the childhood experiences of a group of parents whose children had been in care on at least two occasions they found that the parents themselves had suffered extensive disruption and deprivation. The inter-generational continuity was virtually complete. In contrast, when they looked at the parenting ability of a group of women who had been in care as children, the majority were found to be providing adequate or good care for their toddlers. So here the continuity of deprivation was far from complete; indeed, the general tendency was for it to have been broken. So although it is true to say that virtually all of the parents of the children in care in this study had suffered deprivation it did not follow (and we should not fall into the trap of assuming) that most children in care will subsequently prove to be inadequate parents. The experience of care is not a sufficient indicator (looked at over a long enough period) of irreversible damage to parenting capacity. This is an important conclusion for it draws attention to (a) the value of looking at careers over time; (b) the fact that having done so, being in care is found not to be an inevitable prelude to another round of parenting breakdown; and (c) the need to ask the next crucial question, which is 'what is it that serves to break the cycle?' The researchers did explore this question and suggest that it is a combination of experiences that is of crucial importance, most notably what happens to children at school and what kind of partner or partners they find as they approach adulthood. This is where the implications for practice begin to emerge. Taking the issue of the selection of partners, it is plain, for example that this emphasizes the importance of the environment in which young people find themselves when they leave care. If they live in circumstances where they associate with people who have problems and inadequacies they are unlikely to acquire a supportive and stable partner. Social workers could plan ahead to try to ensure that discharge from care does not precipitate a lonely, ill-equipped and unsupported youngster into situations of marginal existence. In this sense it may well be not only what happens to children whilst they are in care that matters but also how they are prepared for *not* being in care and what happens to them thereafter.

Comparative research is therefore important across different fields and over time. This section began by drawing attention to the constraints imposed by the dead weight of child care categories. It suggested that revision and replacement had to be the order of the day. But some categories are so familiar and so dominant that we can fail to see them: they are just too big. These need to be looked at again too. Take, for example, the distinction between adults and children. It is not only that children themselves have not often been the direct subjects of research but that the questions we ask are typically framed from an adult point of view. This tends to place adults at the centre of children's worlds. Yet a good deal of evidence now exists that suggests that much more attention should be paid to the relationships between children. For example, over 20 years ago I was able to show that the presence of own children of about the same age as a foster child was prejudicial to the success of a foster home placement (Parker, 1966) and this has been broadly confirmed by other studies, most recently by Berridge and Cleaver (1987). Our present (and as yet unpublished) study of children who return home 'on trial' also suggests that problems are likely to arise more often when a child goes back to a household where there are new children than when they arrive to find a new adult. On the other hand, rehabilitation seems to be more smoothly accomplished when children return together with brothers and sisters as a group than when they do so singly. It is surely time for studies to look specifically at child–child relationships, at when these are competitive and detrimental, at when they are supportive and defensive and at how, in any case, they affect and are affected by the behaviour of the adults around them.

Research advances in many ways but the crafting of new categories or the reinterpretation of old ones are prominent features of its vitality. Although this presents some difficulties for the potential uses of its findings it is not incompatible with their needs. Indeed, it may do much to assist the child care services to operate in ways that are not circumscribed by the particular organizational demarcations of the moment.

Quantity and quality

Although there is significantly more child care research now than there was 20 or even 10 years ago it is still in short supply. The problem of its modest volume is exacerbated by the fitful manner in which important themes have been pursued and also by the uneven attention that different issues have been accorded. For example, the first systematic enquiry into foster care in Britain was published by the government's Social Survey in 1957 (Gray and Parr). Nothing followed it until Trasler's study in 1960 and then there was a gap of six years until my work was available. Four more years passed until George's research appeared (1970). The erratic and uncoordinated pattern has continued with studies like Holman's into private foster care (1973), Rowe's on long-term foster care (1984), Shaw and Hipgrave's on special fostering (1983) and Berridge and Cleaver's (1987) general enquiry, making their appearances at odd intervals throughout the 1970s and 80s. Researchers often wish to continue to investigate a subject that they have embarked upon and, in particular, to exploit laboriously collected data more fully; but because of the shortage of funds and the unpredictability of support this has rarely been possible. Typically, new subjects rise to the top of the agenda and, in any case, there is a tendency for one good study to be considered sufficient to cover this or that field.

The fact that the Department of Health has now commissioned a series of studies into child abuse may mark a new pattern in which there is a concentration of support on a limited number of specific areas of research. However, that creates other problems in the development and utilization of research; namely, the likelihood that some topics will be considerably better covered than others. When this happens (and it has been a significant feature of child care research in the past) the choices between different courses of action may be distorted because more is known about one option (usually more about its negative aspects) than about another. For example, much of the early work on the effects of maternal deprivation centred upon the institutional care of young children; little attention was paid to the ways in which similar deprivation might occur in other settings. Similarly, although at least one in five of all children who have been committed to care are allowed to be 'home on trial' without the order being discharged only one study has been published on the subject (Thoburn, 1980). Compare this with the record in the fields of residential care or fostering. The knowledge that research has provided about child care has been uneven. Those who seek to use it should also bear in mind those areas that are unexplored by research.

Because of its intermittent nature the users of research find themselves facing the question of its outdatedness. Issues, policies and practices all change and in some cases quite rapidly; furthermore, the greater the success of research in influencing action the more likely this becomes. The problem of keeping research up to date will only be eased when there are well-established, extensive and continuing programmes of research. However, the 'critical mass of evidence' theory offers a more immediate solution. Despite its history of unevenness child care research has created a number of 'critical mass' situations. It is not simply that in some fields there are now enough studies for one to build upon the other, but that the thrust of their conclusions point in the same direction. One has been mentioned already; namely, the deleterious effect of placing foster children in homes where there are own children close to them in age. We also have a considerable body of evidence that tells us that the longer children stay in care the less likely they are to return home. Other examples could be added. Their existence illustrates the urgent necessity for some broad programme of support for research in child care so that more 'critical mass' situations can be reached and more quickly.

The results of isolated pieces of research should be approached with caution. Replication studies should receive much greater encouragement. So far they are few and far between. That is a danger, for where there is an urgent wish to utilize the findings of research, isolated and unreplicated studies can exercise an unwarranted influence. Yet determining when a 'sufficient' body of evidence exists for it to be applied with reasonable confidence is not as straightforward a matter as it might seem. Somebody has to be in a position to synthesize an assortment of results; sometimes from obscure sources, sometimes from other disciplines and sometimes from other countries. It is a skilled task that should not be regarded as an optional embellishment or frill that can be attached to the fringe of other activities. Indeed, it is an indispensible part of ensuring that research findings are used in an appropriate and responsible fashion. The role of the research distiller and scrutineer must become more common.

So far we have considered some of the 'quantity' problems that arise from the relatively small investment that has been made in child care research. There are also other issues that revolve around the question of quality. Child care research has laboured under two major handicaps. First, most studies have had to be small-scale because of the paucity of funds. Secondly, research has to rely upon the availability of and access to much source material that lies outside its control. Of course, in this it is typical of most social science research; but there are additional difficulties because some data do not exist. For example, it is not always possible to identify a particular population of children from which a sample can be drawn.

Child care research has had to be designed to take account of these difficulties and, as a result, it has been obliged to work in ways that sometimes fall short of textbook methodology. How much confidence, therefore, should a possible user place in a study, and how can that be decided? One answer has already been indicated; namely, look to see how far the results have been confirmed by other studies. Another piece of advice, of course, is to note the openness with which the researcher acknowledges the limitations of the work and whether the possibility of the results being differently interpreted has been made clear. Yet such prescriptions pose a dilemma, for in order for research to be more readily understood and applied it needs to be made more clear-cut and unambiguous. It needs to be simplified. Unfortunately, the price of simplification is to increase the difficulty for the reader to decide how good a piece of research really is. It is important, therefore, that the tension between the goal of digestibility and that of the independent assessment of quality be recognized. A balance has to be struck. If the users of research do not check its quality themselves they should be sure that there is someone else who is doing it whose conclusions they trust.

There is, of course, always a danger that those who use research will lower their critical threshold when the research tells them what they want to hear. Indeed, some research is commissioned with the aim of confirming the desirability of a course of action, of disarming critics or of providing a justification for what has already been done. For these reasons there may sometimes be a vested interest in not looking too closely at the quality of the evidence as long as it accords with prevailing preferences and preconceptions. Conversely, research that is seen as 'bad news' may often be exposed to a searchingly critical examination and all manner of weaknesses detected that would pass unremarked in other circumstances. These are factors that have to be borne in mind when the question of the quality of research is considered.

Of course, there are various ways of 'using' research. The rather modest small-scale study whose results challenge some accepted idea or principle should perhaps receive more attention than a similar piece which confirms what we already believe. Even research that suffers from methodological defects can stimulate a new line of thought or enquiry, or startle us out of a comfortable reliance upon familiar assumptions. Some rather tentative or unsophisticated research may not be good enough to be absorbed into policy or practice but it should not necessarily be ignored. It may help to keep us alert to the possibility that there is a different way of seeing things or, indeed, different things to be seen. If it is remembered that research has many uses we may find that there is rather more 'useful' research than we at first thought.

Sources and statistics

Child care research depends upon its sources of information. The easier these are to tap the more ground that can be covered and explored in greater depth. Where sources are hard to locate or to utilize research has to spend a great deal of time in gaining access to and assembling data. The problem is exacerbated if basic data about, for example, the size of certain populations and their characteristics are incomplete or absent. In these situations research has to make good these deficiencies before it can embark upon the kinds of studies that both policy makers and practitioners are likely to find most useful. For example, if one wished to discover whether differences existed between the circumstances of neglectful families and those of families in which children are sexually abused, it would be exceedingly useful to be able to identify these two groups quickly and accurately. If this could not be done from routine records then the research would have to go back to square one and elicit this information for itself. Take a further example. We know from many studies of child development that various physiological, emotional and social changes can occur quite rapidly as children grow up. Research will often need to be precise about the ages of children. Yet nationally we have collected and presented child care data in such broad age bands that it has been impossible to identify any single year age group except those under one.

Thus, there are many areas of child care (both nationally and locally) where research is obliged to begin well back from the actual starting line of the project for want of appropriate basic data. Of course routine data are not collected and held for the benefit of researchers; they have to serve many other purposes. Yet the need to engage in much essentially descriptive (rather than analytic) research does arise from the lack of what might be regarded as good housekeeping information. It is not that this information is not collected, for much of it can be found on individual files, but that it is not regularly aggregated. Many social services departments produce most of their aggregated data on child care in order to complete the annual return to the Department of Health. What the Department asks for (and the form in which it is required) only goes so far. Some local departments do much more and others call for special returns or enumerations from time to time as issues erupt or when enquiries are held. Generally speaking, however, the amount of accurate and up-to-date aggregated information that is readily available is quite limited.

This has important implications for the relationship between research and its use. For example, more research is likely to be used if the potential users have a hand in formulating the questions. But how do they identify key questions? One answer is that they do so by observing patterns and trends. If no regular record is kept of, say, the number of matrimonial care or supervision orders being made by different courts it is hardly likely that anyone will ask why there are several hundred a year in one court and virtually none in another. Likewise, nobody is likely to ask why very few foster parents apply for custodianship if no record is kept (or if nobody inspects it). Good questions are likely to be produced by sharing experience and one way of doing that is by recording, counting and classifying. However, returning for a moment to our discussion about the imbalance between research for policy and research for practice, it needs to be said that if the collection and use of routine data continue to be regarded as an essentially management function then research will continue to be drawn away from practitioner issues. Practitioners too have to become aware of the value of routine data for their purposes and, after all, it is mainly they who provide it.

With the rapid computerization occurring in social services departments and in voluntary child care organizations this should become a less demanding activity. Furthermore, data sets will be created that are available for subsequent interrogation so that certain questions can be answered speedily and without the need to mount elaborate research. The research which is done could then be devoted to the exploration of more focused and more imaginative questions.

It is not only in social services departments that there is a rather limited amount of routine basic data available. It is often impossible to identify specific groups of children in a variety of regularly available sources of information such as the Family Expenditure Survey, the General Household Survey or, indeed, the Census. It would be valuable, for example, were the precise status of children in households more often indicated. For example, are they looked after by parents, grandparents, aunts or uncles, foster parents or friends? A determined effort to inform ourselves better about the basic facts of childhood in the United Kingdom would serve the children's cause in many ways, including making it easier to do the kind of child care research that could be usefully applied to the improvement of the lives of some of the most disadvantaged.

There is, of course, another way altogether of approaching the idea of 'basic data'. That is by listening to what those who have experienced the child care system tell us. There are, however, problems to be overcome. Three in particular might be noted. First, opportunities for adults and children to tell us what they think have to be created. This can be done as an integral part of the research on an interview or discussion basis. It can also be done in conjunction with membership bodies (such as Parents' Aid, NAYPIC or the National Foster Care Association) and under their auspices. Or it might be done, for example, by the creation of a number of remunerated panels to which certain questions could be referred from time to time. It is not necessarily enough, however, to include so-called consumers in these kinds of studies. Child care is a national issue and its policies and practices evolve against a backcloth of what is believed to be or is claimed to be public opinion. There is certainly a case for the views of a wider cross-section of the population to be canvassed about, for example, what forms of care they would prefer for their children had they to be looked after by someone else. Questions like these can be included in various opinion surveys on a commercial basis.

The second problem in extending the use of the basic data that the consumers of child care services can provide is one of different perspectives. The agenda of questions with which researchers approach people may bear little resemblance to the story that they wish to tell. What researchers consider to be important may be far removed from the problems that dominate their lives. However, given skill and humility one of the advantages that researchers have over social workers in this respect is that they do not have specific responsibilities for taking action. Therefore they are not constrained in the matters that they are expected to cover and, in any case, may be spoken to more freely (or differently) if they are understood not to have an official role. For reasons like these they may be able to offer people a good opportunity to explain their problems, give their opinions or express their feelings. If they are able to do this then the research reports that emerge could be of considerable value to both policy makers and practitioners since they will reflect a perspective and highlight issues that might otherwise remain unknown.

There is a third problem that needs to be noted in considering whether consumer-style research might increase the willingness of managers and practitioners to use it: it may well introduce new complexities in what already seem to be complicated situations. In principle, however, this is something that all research is liable to do: as I was told many years ago, 'the trouble with research is that it has a problem for all our solutions'. Even if that is true it is surely better to know about it than to proceed in ignorance. Nonetheless, it remains important to bear in mind that consumer research may more often than other kinds of research emerge with findings that look to practitioners as well as managers uncommonly like problems rather than solutions.

The nature of sources and statistics is therefore of considerable concern for it influences the kind of research that is done and this, in its turn, influences the ease or difficulty with which its results are likely to be translated into practice. The better the basic data that an organization produces the greater the likelihood there is that its members will be able to identify the questions that, from their point of view, need to be addressed by research. Consumer studies offer challenging perspectives and essential information. These are indispensible if the child care services are to take account of, as they should, the opinions, aspirations and experiences of the children whose welfare is their concern and of the adults who play a significant part in their lives.

Postscript

Let us return to the theme of the book: for the sake of thousands of children we must make use of the research that is available and ensure that it continues to be applied in the future. All the chapters have shown in their different ways what is possible and what still needs to be done. Two things would help immensely. First, a substantial increase in the investment in child care research and, secondly, the creation of an environment in which research would not proceed by fits and starts nor be in danger of losing sight of its primary purpose – that of helping to improve the quality of life of all children but particularly those who suffer the gravest disadvantages.

References

Audit Inspectorate (1981) *The Provision of Child Care: A Study of Eight Local Authorities in England and Wales*, Department of the Environment.

Berridge, D. and Cleaver, H. (1987) *Foster Home Breakdown*, Basil Blackwell.

Colton, M. J. (1988) *Dimensions of Substitute Care*, Avebury.

Department of Health and Social Security (1985) *Social Work Decisions in Child Care*, HMSO.

George, V. (1970) *Foster Care Theory and Practice*, Routledge and Kegan Paul.

Gray, P. G. and Parr, E. A. (1957) *Children in Care and the Recruitment of Foster Parents*, The Social Survey.

Halmos, P. (1965) *The Faith of the Counsellors*, Constable.

Holman, R. (1973) *Trading in Children*, Routledge and Kegan Paul.

Packman, J. (1986) *Who Needs Care? Social Work Decisions About Children*, Basil Blackwell.

Parker, R. A. (1966) *Decisions in Child Care*, George Allen and Unwin.

Quinton, D. and Rutter, M. (1988) *Parenting Breakdown: The Making and Breaking of Inter-generational Links*, Avebury.

Rothschild Report (1971) *The Organization and Management of Government Research and Development*, Cmnd 4814, HMSO.

Rowe, J., Cain, H., Hundleby, M. and Keane, A. (1984) *Long-term Foster Care*, Batsford/BAAF.

Seebohm (1968) *Report of the Committee on Local Authority and Allied Personal Social Services*, Cmnd 3703, HMSO.

Shaw, M. and Hipgrave, T. (1983) *Specialist Fostering*, Batsford/BAAF.

Thoburn, J. (1980) *Captive Clients*, Routledge and Kegan Paul.

Trasler, G. B. (1960) *In Place of Parents*, Routledge and Kegan Paul.

List of contributors

Ahmad, Bandana, BA

Director, Race Equality Unit, Personal Social Services, National Institute for Social Work; previously Principal of International Schools in Tehran and Peking, local government officer in London Borough of Haringey, Social Services and Personnel Department; member of CCETSW Black Perspectives Committee; Chairperson of Multi Cultural Resource Centre for under-fives.

Bullock, Roger, MA

Senior Research Fellow, Dartington Social Research Unit (University of Bristol); Open University Tutor 1970–1984.

Publications (in conjunction with other members of the Dartington Social Research Unit) include *Chance of a Lifetime?* (1975), Weidenfeld and Nicolson; *After Grace – Teeth* (1975), Human Context Books; *Locking up Children* (1978), Saxon House; *Learning to Care* (1980), Gower; *Issues of Control in Residential Child Care* (1981), HMSO; *Lost in Care* (1986), Gower; *Once too Often* now known as *Access Disputes in Child Care* (1989), Gower (all publications of the Dartington Social Research Unit).

De'Ath, Erica, BA Psychol. (Open University)

Chief Executive, Foundation for the Study of Infant Deaths; previously Children's Society, Head of Department, Social Policy Initiatives; National Children's Bureau, Senior Development Officer, Parenting Project; Open University Lecturer, Health and Social Welfare.

Publications include *The Needs of Parents; Practice and Policy in Parent Education* (with Pugh, G.) (1984), Macmillan; *Partnership in Action; Working with Parents in Pre-school Centres*, Vols 1 and 2 (with Pugh, G., Aplin, G. and Moxon, M. (1987), NCB; *Working with Parents, a Training Resource Pack* (with Pugh, G.) (1986), NCB; *Step Parenting* (1988), BMA Family Doctor Publications; Children's Society Briefing Papers (free on request): *Young People Under Pressure: Runaways and Others* (1986); *Somewhere to Live* (1987); *Focus on Families: Divorce and its Effect on Children* (1988); *The Family Centre Approach* (1988).

Gardner, Ruth

Senior Development Officer, National Children's Bureau. Previously social worker and manager in Inner London Boroughs.

Publications: *Child Care Reviews* (1985), NCB; *Who Says? Choice and Control in Care* (1987), NCB.

Giller, Henri, PhD, LLM, LLB

Managing Director of Social Information Systems Ltd.* and Fellow of the University of Keele. Previously lecturer in law at the University of Keele, and Research Associate at the Institute of Criminology, Cambridge, and at the Institute of Psychiatry, University of London.

Publications include numerous papers on juvenile justice issues and co-author of *Justice for Children* (with Morris, A., Szwed, E. and Geach, H.) (1980), Macmillan; *Care and Discretion* (with Morris, A.) (1981), Burnet Books; *Juvenile Delinquency: Trends and Perspectives* (with Rutter, M.) (1983), Penguin; *Understanding Juvenile Justice* with (Morris, A.) (1987), Croom Helm.

* Social Information Systems is an independent consultancy organization which monitors and evaluates service provision for all social services client groups. Currently details of one in 10 juveniles sentenced by courts in England and Wales are monitored by Social Information Systems.

Jackson, Sonia, MA, DSW

Lecturer in social work, University of Bristol School of Applied Social Studies. Previously primary school teacher, child psychologist, local authority social worker, Director of Educational Advice Service (Advisory Centre for Education).

Publications include *Childminder* (with Brian Jackson) (1979), Routledge and Kegan Paul; *Other People's Children* (1981), BBC; *The Education of Children in Care* (1988), Bristol Papers No. 1, University of Bristol, School of Applied Social Studies.

Kahan, Barbara, MA, Hon MUniv (Open), Dip. Soc. Sci.

Director of the Gatsby Project. Chair of the National Children's Bureau. Professional adviser to the House of Commons Social Services Committee.

Previously Deputy Chief Inspector, Home Office Children's Department; Assistant Director Social Work Service, DHSS; Adviser to the National Association of Young People in Care.

Publications include many chapters and papers on child care and training issues; a number of HMSO publications on child care, records and management of change in personal social services. *Growing Up in Care* (1979), Basil Blackwell; joint author of *Residential Task in Child Care* (with Banner, G.) (1968), Residential Child Care Association; *Staff – Finding Them, Choosing Them, Keeping Them* (with Banner, G. and Lane, D.) (1986), Social Care Association.

Knapp, Martin

Deputy Director of the Personal Social Services Research Unit, University of Kent. His research spans a number of child care issues, including intermediate treatment, the 'contracting out' of residential care and the evaluation of foster care.

Publications include *The Economics of Social Care* (1984), Macmillan; *The Costs of Child Care* (1989), Gower.

Marsh, Peter, BSc Soc. Sci. MPhil. Dip. A.S.S. CQSW

Associate Director of Social Work Studies, University of Sheffield. Currently Research Director of Social Work in Partnership, an experimental social work project which is developing and evaluating task-centred partnership practice – to improve the effectiveness of care services to children and elderly people and to increase the participation of clients in all aspects of that service.

Publications include *In and Out of Care* (1986), Batsford.

Packman, Jean, MA, PhD

Senior lecturer in charge of social work courses at Exeter University. A long-standing interest in child care originated in the years spent in Oxfordshire Children's Department, pre Seebohm, where she worked for Barbara Kahan. She has since studied and lectured on child care policy and practice and was responsible for one of a cluster of DHSS funded research projects that have been influential in the 1980s. She is joint editor with Bill

Jordan of a series of books on social work practice and related subjects published by Basil Blackwell.

Publications include *The Child's Generation* (1970 and 1981), Basil Blackwell and *Who Needs Care?* (1986), Basil Blackwell.

Parker, Roy, BSc Econ., PhD

Professor, Bristol University. Member of the Seebohm Committee.

Publications include *Decision in Child Care* (1986), Allen and Unwin; *Planning for Deprived Children* (1971), NCH; *Caring for Separated Children; Plans, Procedures and Priorities* (ed) (1980), Macmillan; 'Residential care for children', in *Residential Care; The Research Reviewed* (edited by Sinclair, I.) (1988), National Institute for Social Work, HMSO.

Parton, Nigel, BA, CQSW, MA

Principal lecturer in the Social Work Section at Huddersfield Polytechnic. Formerly worked as a social worker in a social services department. Member of the Violence Against Children Study Group whose book *Taking Child Abuse Seriously: Contemporary Issues in Child Protection Theory and Practice* (1989) is being published by Unwin Hyman.

Publications include *The Political Dimensions of Social Work* (ed, with Bill Jordan) (1983), Basil Blackwell; *The Politics of Child Abuse* (1985), Macmillan; also various articles on child care, child protection and child abuse in academic and professional journals.

Robertson, Eileen

Research Fellow in the Health Economics Consortium, University of York. Formerly a Research Fellow in the Personal Social Services Unit, University of Kent.

Russell, Philippa, BA, OBE

Principal Officer, Voluntary Council for Handicapped Children, National Children's Bureau and part-time seconded Associate Director of the National Development Team for People with a Mental Handicap. Mother of a young man with a mental handicap.

Publications include *The Wheelchair Child* (1989), Souvenir Press; *Working Together with Handicapped Children* (with Margaret Griffiths) (1985), Souvenir Press; *Honeylands; Developing a Service for Families with Handicapped Children* (with Professor F. Brimblecome) (1987), NCB; also chapters in other similar publications.

Stein, Mike, BA, MPhil.

Lecturer and Barnardo's Research Fellow in Applied Social Studies, School of Continuing Education, University of Leeds. Formerly probation officer, Leeds, and Area Social Services Officer, Bradford Social Services Department. Adviser to National Association of Young People in Care.

Publications include *Leaving Care* (with Kate Carey) (1986), Basil Blackwell; *The Politics of Child Welfare* (with Nick Frost) (1989), Wheatsheaf; currently completing a three-year study of a leaving care project.

Utting, Bill

Chief Inspector, Social Services Inspectorate, Department of Health.

Index